D1072154

USHANT

D. (Conrad Aiken). Painting by Lorelei Three (Mary
Hoover Aiken), 1937.

USHANT

An Essay by Conrad Aiken ❦❦❦❦❦❦

NEW YORK   OXFORD UNIVERSITY PRESS   1971

IN MEMORIAM: GORDON BASSETT

"This minor asset
for a major Bassett":
and for a winter at Charlestown which with
MARY HOOVER *and* EDWARD BURRA
he himself made memorable ❀ ❀ ❀ ❀

— E coelo descendit γνῶθι σεαυτόν *— Juvenal, xl. 27.*

γνῶθι σεαυτόν — and is this the prime
And heaven-sprung adage of the olden time! —
Say, canst thou make thyself? — Learn first that trade, —
Haply thou mayst know what thyself had made.
What hast thou, Man, that thou darst call thine own? —

S. T. COLERIDGE, *Self-Knowledge.*

And now, therefor, after having been long on the way, we Argonauts of the ideal, our courage perhaps greater than our prudence, often shipwrecked and bruised, but, as I say, healthier than people would like to admit, dangerously healthy, recovering health again and again — it would seem as if our troubles were to be rewarded, as if we saw before us that undiscovered country, whose frontiers no one has yet seen, a land lying beyond all other known lands and hiding-places of the ideal, a world so overflowing with beauty, strangeness, doubt, terror, and divinity, that both our curiosity and our lust for possession are wrought to a pitch of extreme excitement. Nothing on earth can satisfy us. Alas! how with such vistas before us and with our conscience and consciousness full of such burning desire, can we still be content with the *man of the present day?*

FRIEDRICH NIETZSCHE, *Ecce Homo.*

By heaven, man, we are turned round and round in this world, like yonder windlass, and Fate is the handspike. And all the time, lo! that smiling sky, and this unsounded sea! Look! see yon Albicore! who put it into him to chase and fang that flying-fish? Where do murderers go, man! Who's to doom, when the judge himself is dragged to the bar? But it is a mild, mild wind, and a mild looking sky; and the air smells now, as if it blew from a far-away meadow; they have been making hay somewhere under the slopes of the Andes, Starbuck, and the mowers are sleeping among the new-mown hay.

HERMAN MELVILLE, *Moby Dick, Chapter* CXXXII.

Key

USHANT

I

—— beginning without beginning, water without a seam, or sleep without a dream, or dream coterminous with sleep and the sleeper; flux and reflux, coil and moil; participation and concentration compounded, and then resolved again; participation and dispersal, then the subtle or violent catalysis, reorganization, the wave setting off in a new direction, the influence deflected, lapse and relapse, lapse and collapse, but out of the falling the magnificent rearising, out of the scend the pitch, out of the course of the ship the sheer, or the sheer of the ship towards stem and stern, the infinitesimal ship like a tiny luminous dream in the terrible, yes, lethal, yes murderous, sleep of the sea —— and yet not in any sense separate, ship from water, dream from sleeper, wave from wave, particle from particle, drop from drop, electron from nucleus, world from world, but all together participating and dispersing, participating and again concentrating, wave-shaped and then plane-shaped, crest-shaped and then trough-shaped, revolving or secretly still, the numbers constant for each element, limited and finite yet part of an infinite series —— :

Spout, whale! Blow your conch, lost fisherman off the dangerous shores of Ushant! lost pilot casting a soaped lead in the tempest that howls towards the coast of Tralee! Dive through your pearly rainbow, laughing dolphin! Halloo, old scavenger gull! Scream downward towards your divine wrack, cormorant! We are all true brothers in the devilish dance together, whale and Pole Star, the sunken ship and the drowned man's last dream, the last dream floating godward like a lost sigh from the sea, a lost cry from the dark whelmed cabin, where water and carved woodwork, seaweed and rivet, red carpet and the wandering plankton, now and forever dance the divine timeless dance together!

——— yes, beginning without beginning, wave out of wave, shape out of shapelessness, the remembered out of the forgotten; like stem out of thresh or stern out of thrash, or island out of sunshot mist; the roundness looms out of nothing; and the sound, the bell, the horn, tolls out of silence, wails into silence, lost, lost, lost, lost, lost: and yet not lost at all, but turning ever further through the rings within rings and rings beyond rings of the one and only beginningless and endless dream ——; yes, like the Gulf Stream lifting its leviathan snake-length through opposing and reluctant water, water flung against water, sea-thrust hurled against sea-thrust; northward and eastward bearing its long largesse of kelp and wreckage, bladder-wrack and broken crates, grapefruit and sponges, the jellyfish undulant as a transparent digestion in the Sargasso Sea of steamy, vast, fructifying and oh so deliberate rhythm of generative movement — while southward and westward, hugging bleak shores only warmer than itself, the Arctic Stream bells before it under crepitant Northern Lights the great slow flocks of the icebergs, ruminant among dazzling floes of waste and ice, those that heave slowly on the invisible wave, making visible the wave as a movement of white under blue; snow, snow, snow, under the scream of the sea-eagle and the blue-eyed seal —; water revolving swift spokes through water, current coiling through current, sleep and dream interchangeably immersed as they, the one visible and transparent in the other, the long timeless translucent flow of memory under the glass of eternity — :

4

Take now your cross-bearings, O mariner! Level your small bright sextant at the last pale folding away of the headland, the last winking of the last eye of light! This is the departure, this coast will perhaps be seen no more. Seen no more? Departure from what? Nantucket Lightship? Bishop's Rock? The Straits of Belle Isle, or the fantastic goblin-haunted fiords that lead, or mislead, to some ghostly Northwest Passage? But who ever truly departs or ever for that matter truly arrives? Does the solar system, the great fiery organon of the universe itself, ever depart or arrive? And how then shall a mere ship or a mere human make landfall, and indeed of what land? Something we fetch with ourselves, like the pilgrim bringing home with him his bright phial of dust from Bethlehem, or a tear-bottle of water from the Ganges or Jordan? Do we put down forever automatically before us like a carpet the unalterable world that we are and have? Or if not unalterable, never wholly old or wholly new?

Two bells. *Tin-tin.* And then repeated, farther off, more faintly. *Tin-tin.*

Something has been sighted off the port bow? Or it is one o'clock in the morning? One in the afternoon? The dog-watch? The middle watch? One o'clock in the dark of the sea. And into the sleep of each of the twelve sleepers who lie in the narrow bunks, longitudinal or transverse, of Cabin 144, the sad little sound interpolates itself as part of his dream, a tiny signal forward or backward. Or so, at any rate, in the mind of one who lies awake, the two sounds precipitate the thought; and raising himself on one cramped elbow and looking toward the porthole, past the double tiers of motionless figures, he thinks again of the singular determinism that rules the dreams of those who sleep, no more, no less, than it rules the ideas of those who wake. What does each of them bring to the bell-sound, whether it is the watchman's sighting of a ship or the chronometrical and astronomical measure of time? For himself, he has at once, plainly visible through and around, over and under, the small dim scene before him, a vaster and more appalling vision: the universe is a clock, the stars, suns, moons, comets, nebulae, are the burning jewels of that majestic invisible mechanism, into which, perhaps, the great horologist is this very minute gazing fixedly through his inquisitorial eye-piece. Is it going as it should? Is it gaining? Or losing? And the jewels on which this divine and dreadful mystery so marvelously pivots, restraining and directing the obscure compulsion, the *primum mobile,* are they perhaps beginning to show signs of wear? The great Gaze looks long and steadily into the dark central recesses of the Movement, the enormous spaces of the nothing in which time moves, and yet always seems to remain in the same place, as if it were somehow consumed by its own motion, motion sinking into itself; but does the Gaze observe also, as it were at the very center of all this catastrophic and instantaneous eternity, another, and very different gaze, an outward-looking gaze, the gaze of the one who lies awake in Cabin 144 on a ship, this ship, at sea? A gaze which calmly, quite calmly, and certainly without despair, turns itself upward and outward to the other, and even beyond it, to the outermost, the Question?

But the smaller gaze at this point checks itself, draws back with a motion as of inhibited vanity or pride: for it at once sees that this vision too is only an infinitesimal and fleeting particle, a dustmote, projected no doubt on the downward and inward rays of that other. The pride, if pride there may be, must be at most a participatory pride. The smaller vision, if as true, and even perhaps as necessary, is merely perhaps a coefficient of the greater; a tiny island-awareness in the ever-conscious, ever-luminous chart of the great cartographer's dream. Yes, the large and the small, simply; and if there is to be obeisance in one direction, should there not be obeisance in the other as well — ? Are they not all in one ship together? In this dim cabin together? Exactly (as D. now remembers) like the small

6

intensely vivid wood-engraving of a lantern-lit cabin interior; everything aslant in the wildness of the storm; the lamp alone perpendicular, as it hangs from the ceiling over the spread map on the table; that cabin in which the four doomed mariners of Falconer's "Shipwreck" contemplate, in the small symbols of print on a chart, the inevitability of their death by drowning on the marble rocks of a lee shore.

The relationship, then — (said D. to himself) — was that of the finder of the camera to the landscape which it "finds," and in which it is found: the two are in fact participants of one scene. And is the finder the "I" as well as the *eye?* the one who sees, the one who knows, the one who is consciousness? But here again all was divisible, all was relative. The frightened boy who slept fitfully in the bunk below, kept awake now by D.'s own snoring and now by that of the mad Swiss in the far corner, and who, when he did sleep, awoke from a repeated nightmare of bombs falling, falling at approaching terrible intervals, *crumpcrump-crumpcrump-crump-crump* up the dark Irish Sea towards Liverpool, like a man stomping with heavy steps towards a murder, towards Calder, towards Hoylake, along the sandy edge of the links, then at the last minute veering away, and down the Mersey to Paradise Street, he too had his finder, and in it drew at this very moment his own strong draught of the infinite. And yes, the mad Swiss, too; for D. saw now that the cropped head, propped on the pillow on the upper berth in the far corner, glared furiously, wide awake, at the blurred eye of the toplight above him: as last night, and the night before, lying there fully dressed, his anger still unappeased. The frightened boy (half English, half American) feared the return to Liverpool, feared the raw ruins, the dreadful changes that lay in wait for him like spectres, and that already, in his dreams, reached wraithlike fingers towards his heart; feared but was also fascinated: he must go and see. But the mad Swiss, why was he so angry, so plunged into his

7

own chaos, merely because he must return to his sister's villa on a crag perched above Airolo, with its vines, its grapes, its wines? Surely this was better than to go on painting those outlandish houses in Alberta, day after day, week after week, year after year, with no or little knowledge of its people, its language, its customs? Fifteen years, and even now his conversation in English consisted almost entirely of "*god*-damn, *god*-damn, *god*-damn!" over and over again, viciously, venomously, repeated, and interspersed with crude fragments of what might once have been a yodel. But why the anger, when, after all, this voyage, for him, was a return to home, his household gods, his own soul's landscape? Why?

Yes, each had his own, and each, like himself, must intermittently, all his life, return thither — for did one ever truly escape, ever — (after a certain point) — change it? The frightened boy even in his recurring nightmare was already again busily searching, and shaping as he searched, the half-familiar, half-strange landmarks and boundaries. The hated school on Cape Cod, where his foreignness had made him unpopular with the native children, and his diction had been derided, the remembered streets at Wallasey, ferries hooting on the yellow sunstreaked Mersey, double-decker trams trundling along the waterfront — already in these images he was prophesying his own ambiguous landscape, the landscape in which he would always be uncertain. The young face was already marked with the fear that haunted the borders of that landscape. Precisely as the mad Swiss, on the other hand, had forged for himself a mask of anger.

"*God*-damn, *god*-damn, *god*-damn! o-lay-o-lee-o-lay! I got a cough, yes! No wonder, neither — that god-damn train, *een*-out — *een*-out — *een*-out — the damned door opening and shutting all the damned night — steaming hot as hell one minute, then cold as a son-of-a-bitch the next — een-out — een-out — that's why I got a cough!"

8

"You smoke too much."

"No, I got a cough."

And Blimp, that superb rotund walrus-moustached caricature of the caricature "Colonel"; Blimp, with his malapropisms, his endless monologues as he slumped all day in the cabin's central chair, forever mouthing the inevitable cigar (against the rules, and no one dared to stop him) — he too was once more returning to the loved landscape.

"Yes, I'm going back. But I don't rightly know *why* I'm going back. Well, yes, there's only three of us left out of thirteen, two brothers and a sister, and children and grandchildren, and sixty nieces and nephews, but they won't know me. No, they won't know me. A hundred pounds of food I've got with me, but with so many to feed, they won't any of them get very much for Christmas, no sir, not very much."

Hardie, too, dying of diabetes, on his way back to Faversham to entrust his two boys to his sister before it should be too late. And Blunden, now waking and retching, in the bunk above Blimp's, dismayed by the sea, troubled by the sea. . . .

A cockroach scuttled across the wall above Hardie's motionless half-lifted arm; and dropped out of sight; and as D. gazed back at the empty sockets of the twin ventilators which looked down at him like two blind vitreous eyes from the ceiling, he thought — *Sunday*. The first day. And God said, Let there be light, and there was light. That, of course, was before he got around to such trifles as the sea, this trifle that now surrounded them, and so effortlessly bore them up, but which also at a moment's notice could so soundlessly and painlessly engulf them. The more than wine-dark, the less than gong-tormented sea! Which now again, like these others, he was once more crossing, vainly no doubt once more pursuing that *ignis fatuus* which had so often tempted him to Ariel's Island. Perhaps it was true as Jacob said — perhaps it was true that Ariel's

9

Island — this England — had all his life, for him, been a substitute for the lost mother? which in turn would so easily and
logically (there was indeed something a shade slick in it) explain
why invariably, at moments of crisis in his erotic life, he had
seemed to be under an absolute, a tyrannical, compulsion, either to
seek it again or to leave it. The pattern was obvious — the pattern
was his life. . . .

And now once more, as before: to take refuge from his defeat
(if it was exactly that) by the ruthless Faith, in a kind of faithless-
ness by series: he would avenge himself in no common fashion, but
by once again embracing an island, together, to be sure, with all its
inhabitants, and a house. But had he *really* been defeated? Not
much use in going over *that* again! — defeated, certainly, in the
sense that he had lost her — lost her, certainly, in the sense that
he had been forced by subterranean scruples (which, ah, he somewhat shrank from analyzing) concerning her highly moral immorality, to give her up — so that in perhaps the deepest sense the defeat was a defeat self-inflicted, and, in the upshot, a defeat of poor
misguided Faith as well. "Faithless and Pitiless were two pretty
tails: their clitorises harder and sharper than nails."

But no — that was to reminisce: and to reminisce, dear Faith had
said — (it had been only later that he had realized, and with an
added horror, that the words had not only constituted a clear warning, but implicitly of course a revelation of her already definite and
cold-blooded decision to betray him) — she had said, yes, that to
reminisce was weakness: it undermined one's freedom always to "go
forward." Go forward? In this connection decidedly a euphemism.
For quite apart from the monstrosity of her behavior (part of its
monstrosity being the very fact that she had embarked on it *pur
sang* at the very moment of their greatest happiness) the truth of
her all-too-convenient little slogan was more than dubious. At the
best a half-truth: perhaps in the deepest sense no truth at all. To

10

reminisce, to recall, to remember, to summon up to the sessions of sweet silent thought; whether in a letter; or over a Gibson martini, with the pearl onion delicately revolving above the whorled glass navel of the stem; or as they walked round the stately green bronze horse, and his green bronze rider, in the grass-plat so hideously parterred by red and yellow tulips; or after the most luminous and interstellar of embraces, there under the lodging-house window with the tattered shade, this was the ultimate essence of life; and it was precisely in proportion to one's ability to combine a maximum of just such awareness of the past with the nexus of the moment, and the *then* going forward, that one accomplished, with any grace, any beauty, the "precarious gait we call experience." Anything else is cowardice deliberately invoked in order that one may indulge the whim at random: one denies the good, and dishonors it, ostensibly in the name of freedom; but really because one knows that the good and beautiful are good and beautiful exactly in so far as they are *binding*. If one is immoral, therefore, to remember them is fatal.

Pitiless and Faithless.

"Let us not reminisce in our letters — !"

How heedless, heedless he had been, not to see the terrible shadow behind the words, or indeed not to have seen in a hundred previous scenes, and phrases, and actions, in the secretiveness, the violent departures and more violent returns, the measure of her nature. "We were becoming *too used* to each other" — ah, there precisely it was: she had said it in the fatal letter, but then, she had as good as admitted it before.

"This crap from the maples," she had murmured: — scuffing among the littered blossom on the path; "this crap from the maple trees — ! this discarded sex! . . . Do you know what!"

"No. What!"

"It's not so good. I detect myself every day now in the act of imitating you."

"Just as I find myself imitating you."

"Yes. I suppose we might analyze it as a part of courtship — or is it a part of marriage?"

It was true, the reciprocal imitation — the words, the phrases, the gestures — they had constantly found themselves falling into it, and been amused, and a little disconcerted; it was undoubtedly a natural part of courtship, and beautiful, too, as if they were really engaged in a kind of unconscious dance. This crap from the maples — this discarded sex! And afterwards she had repeated it in the fatal letter, too — "let us admit it, we are getting *too used* to each other; and I now recognize it as a fact that I simply *miss you too much!*" Seen in retrospect the signal was all too evident: the knife was already in her hand to be sharpened, and she would use it without mercy either to him or to herself: without mercy to herself, for she had not, as yet, quite clearly seen the consequences.

A sudden creak in the lower transverse bunk, at the angle of the bunks that led sidelong to the solitary dark eye of the porthole, and old Blimp rolled himself unsteadily to his feet, hung on for a moment to the metal edge of the upper berth, breathing hard, then toddled to the slop-bowl and began urinating intermittently and heavily into the foul water that was already there. The round white back was turned towards D., swaying, the big bottom in expensive-looking pajamas: then again he lowered himself cautiously, slowly, creakingly into his bunk, and was almost immediately gently snoring, joining the symphony with Hardie and Blunden. As the sea snored beneath the ship, the sea which they were all proposing so desperately to cross — for what? For what had this adventure been so elaborately planned? For elaborately planned, in every human instance, it obviously had been. They, like himself, had had to go through that strange pre-voyage period (in which already the ship, imagined, lay somewhere at sheer, somewhere at anchor, or somewhere sliced a red forefoot into a blue-black Atlantic wave) — that interim state of gathering oneself together, both physically and psychologically, for the effort, the sortie into the unknown. The period of tidying up, of sorting, and selecting: was there not something typical of all life in these preparations for a voyage? The anxious decisions, or hurried, as to what to take, what to leave behind; this treasure or that to be chosen; this beloved trifle abandoned, this that might or might not be useful — and in a way, not just for a journey, or *this* journey, but perhaps for life, or death. And where? and for how long? and would they, or himself, be back again?

Tout ce qu'il faut quitter!

The loved landscape, yes, to be walked into for the last time, and looked at and analyzed for memory; as well as that of the soul, for this too was at least in part inevitably to be left behind. I shall not be here again, we will not be here again, or if we come, neither it nor ourselves will be the same. Leaves, trees, will have fallen. These good men will be gone: Hardie to a grave in Kent, farewelled by the coal-mines of Pennsylvania, as his two boys, in the berths under the porthole, are now being farewelled into life. Those who are doomed to die, and those who are already dead; the uncles, the aunts, the grandmothers and grandfathers, the wild brave cousin, the friends, the children. The young poet, with the clear brow of genius, at Harvard, stopping them in the Yard and pressing one hand to his back — "Funny pain I've got here in my back — they don't seem to know what it is — I started it on the racetrack down at Soldiers Field." Playing the piano, too, the handsome face half in the yellow lamplight, the expression saturnine, grave, remote — and then in the hospital by the river bend, writing about bulrushes, — cat-tails, bedded in the brine. Paul, dead; and the two Johns dead; and Jack, the poet-revolutionist, dead; and the athletic doctor, met too at sea, on such a ship as this, with the long swift pace of the natural runner, the carriage lightly forward from the waist, the apparently immortal vitality in the eyes and voice: these lives now reappeared in turn, vivid and small in the camera-finder, particles of his soul's landscape — he was now as much these as himself, they and those others who still lived, the friends, were himself.

Yes, the men rather than the women — and why, exactly? Something odd in this — the men *were* oneself, the women, no matter how deeply loved, nor with what all-givingness or agony or ecstasy, were not; they paralleled, they accompanied, they counterpointed, but they did not, in the same sense, become intimately the alphabet of one's soul. Their importance — and supreme of course it was — lay somewhere else: supplementary, complementary, unabsorbable: oh, look at them there, the beauties, how they sing and shine, and light up all of life: and as to their unquestioned necessity and all-importance, well, their very numbers bore witness. The continuing and ever-changing woman, who "changed," to be sure, from time to time (never let it be said of us that we rest on our Loreleis) but perhaps essentially in the end hasn't changed at all. The first, the second, the third: the present one, the previous one, and perhaps as well the ones to come. But all, bless their hearts, a species of constant; a series of constants, each one in turn the x of one's y or the x^1 or x^2 or x^3; or of course even the x^4, unmet, unknown, still locked magically in the imagination.

The series extended backward in time, like the series of friends: diminishing and vanishing milestones beside the swift railroad track, lost in smoke, obscured by rain or snow, but not forgotten and even now recoverable. And on each the figure, the number, the symbol, remained distinct, on each the character still kept its own cryptic and precious meaning significant of a particular area and era: the first John, of Beacon Hill, the Frog Pond in slant spring rain, a pair of bats circling above the frozen red pond in the red sunset: in the attic bedroom the violent midnight debates, and quarrels too, over the right course for fiction, for drama, for poetry, for politics, for life: uncouth, prophetic John, with his news from the Left Bank, but more accessibly and provocatively (as it took up there his own incipient knowledge) the rumors from Ariel's Island, from which the outbreak of war had dislodged him, just as he was beginning, through Paget and the Noble Lord, and the two poets and Félice, bless her naughty heart, to extend his conquest of it! It was the "first" John who had enabled him to retain (through gossip, an armful of Henry James, small new books, pamphlets, literary direction-finders) a precarious foothold, a kind of bridgehead, in Ariel's Island: even to keeping poor dear Félice still there at her Bloomsbury window, frankly dressing or undressing for his seduction and delight, where he sat at his own window attempting to get imaginary actors on and off an imaginary stage.

Félice! It had been his first infidelity, or attempt at infidelity, for to be sure it hadn't amounted to much — an awkward embrace or two in the all-too-social darkness of a summer evening, the other voices, the other lovers, everywhere round them on the shabby lawn that sloped down to the Serpentine. The abrupt ending too, like the abrupt and abortive beginning! but just the same, it *had* been the first infidelity, and it *had* therefore its germinal importance. More and more candidly she had dressed and undressed by her window, more and more overtly he had himself leaned out to watch. A day? two? three? and then, as he leaned there on the windowsill with his hands, she had suddenly alarmed and disconcerted him by levelling a pair of opera glasses at him. Was there something perhaps a little practiced in this? He had had that feeling, certainly, but nevertheless the opera glasses gave him an idea. He seized the square of cardboard which had stiffened a shirt from the laundry, wrote on it in large letters COME OUT AND HAVE A BEER, and presented this for scrutiny. But without success: she simply made, out of the window, a downward gesture, as of derision, with her hand, and withdrew. Perhaps she was really, he thought, not addressing herself (*façon de parler*) to him, but to someone else — ? the occupant of another window, another room — ? a theory which gained in plausibility when that evening, or the next, he overheard a conversation between an Egyptian and one of the boarders, in broken French.

"*Monsieur, avez-vous peut-être une petite télescope?*"

"*Ah! Pour voir les jeunes filles, n'est-ce pas?*"

"*Non, non — pour voir les étoiles!*"

"*Mais non, monsieur, je n'ai pas une télescope, je le regrette!*"

But next day after lunch she had been more in evidence than ever, and closer to her window than ever; she was dressing to go out, that was manifest; and at last she put on the hat, and then, to his surprise, thrust a parasol forth, opened it in the sunlight, closed and withdrew it. Without loss of time, he waved his own hat out of the window, and then his ash-plant walking stick, and galloped down the stairs, and round the block to meet her.

And sure enough, there she came — but attended by Booker, the translator who had the room beneath his own. They were both still in the state of embarrassment attendant on so recent and informal an acquaintance, talking with downcast or averted eyes, and he retreated, abashed and unnoticed.

So that was it. It had been Booker all the time. He might have known it.

But to his astonishment, an hour later, there she was again! And again the same pantomime with the parasol, and a gloved hand beckoning and pointing, as if to indicate the south end of the square, that nearest to the British Museum. Should he, this time, believe it — ? He believed it, and, this time, she was alone. She had — she said — been as flabbergasted as he had, when, instead of a young man with blond hair and blue eyes and spectacles, a tall dark stranger had approached, and with every air of proprietorship. But she had dished him, she had got rid of him, she hadn't liked him. And now, what should they do — go to the White City? Or the cinema? Not pretty, not homely, dark, rather serious, slow-spoken: they got off very well together, thanks largely to their shared and comic mishap, but they went neither to the White City nor the cinema. They dined at the Brice in Wardour Street, took a bus to Hyde Park Corner, walked past the Serpentine, then sought a shadow in which they might not too conspicuously embrace. And then, his arm around her, and his hand on her breast, she said, as they walked homeward —

"Tell me — what is it you like about me?"

"This!"

"Is that all?"

"Isn't that enough?"

Too much, as it turned out. For at Appenrodt's, beginning over the beer to be confidential — too confidential! — she asked him if he had noticed something.

"Noticed something?"

"Yes."

"But what?"

She didn't simper — she was quite serious about it, a little proud.

"Well, that I'm pregnant."

"Why, no!"

Somehow he had managed to conceal his stupefaction, as she went on.

"But I mean, you know, there at the window!"

"No —"

"It doesn't show — ?"

"Not in the least!"

And so it all came out: the husband on a tanker in the Pacific, not due home for three months; the house in Surrey, for which she was in London buying the furniture; and all the rest. She had been a trained nurse in Liverpool. Would he have guessed? Would he help her select the furniture and rugs? Would he like to come down to Surrey for a visit? the week-end? the summer, all summer? —

Well, he had covered his dismay, his deep dismay, had got through the evening, even to seeing her home and kissing her good-night on the porch in Montague Street: but he had changed his room the next day, he had never seen her again.

Poor dear Félice! she had been the "second" vision, there over the beer and iced coffee, and in the Bloomsbury window. For of course it was Irene who had been the first, three years before in Leicester Square, her slippers seen for a moment (and forever) against the vivid chalk scenes, blue-and-green, of the pavement artist, who sat against the railing with his cap on the stone before him. The farouche and gentle John, full of *angst*, plagued by the nightingales, the tedious necessities of sex, tormented by music, haunted by the pure shape of a vase, had unwittingly given him back these, restored the colors to them just when they were beginning to fade. And the crowd of Germans, daylong and nightlong packed round the consulate, and addressed by the Consul from hour to hour as to how to get themselves home, if they could, to the Vaterland. This, and the unfinished play. And the illicit visit to Parliament, using Keir Hardie's name, to witness the declaration of war. In the odd boardinghouse on Beacon Hill (with Steinlen's Ballade d'Hiver looking down at him in gaslight, beside the mulberry-colored medallion of Chinese brocade) he had kept these trophies through the soft New England snow. Of the play, nothing now remained but the prologue. *"The actors will be here any minute: they have been delayed. The snowstorm was unexpected, was not their cue. But in their absence, perhaps the entrepreneur will do. An empty stage: and they were about to remember other lives, other times, other passions: different costumes, different speech, different fashions: but instead, all is silence and ourselves. I, the announcer, speaking invisibly from the wings, manager of props and lights, puller of switches and shifter of scenes; I do not pretend to know what it all means; lifeless one minute, full of furious nonsense or disaster the next: and dependent, unhappily, on a text!"*

The same theme, exactly; the character-constituents of the soul's landscape, the Pauls, the Noble Lords, the Félices and Irenes, the pavement artist with his dirty cap on the wet stone; and now Blimp, the frightened boy, the mad Swiss — as, too, the French taxi driver at Halifax, who had driven him to all those rather sinister little waterfront shops, trying to find somewhere a contraband watch, a substitute for the one dropped through the little hammock in the sleeping-car berth, and broken — they all joined in that receding *passacaglia* of symbols; and further back still, in adolescence — ah, that iridescent fever, that iridescent mirage; — and in childhood, beyond, the still brighter anagrams, ever simpler and more mythic as they receded, always adding up to the same meaning, but deeper: the soul's landscape like an infinite series of overpaintings, a palimpsest in endless sequence, which, no matter how often one removed the successive surfaces, to reveal a new hieroglyph, forever came up with the same mystic equation: YOU. A private constant, in its way comparable to the animal's primordial memory of his inescapable mother, the sea, she who wells up in him forever, precisely as the water wells up in the little holes which the child digs near the ribboned margin of an outgoing wave. Yes, behind and beneath all this, the sea, the sea, the sea.

The sea — and come to think of it, old Blimp had himself had one of his better moments on the subject.

"The Origin of Specie! By that scientist Darwin, it was, The Origin of Specie. Had us all back to the monkeys, he did, and before that, too. Evolution, that's what it is, we came out of the sea, blimey, with our bloody scales on, and crawled up on a beach and learned how to breathe. Yea, and all quite right, too. No nonsense about it, you can have your Christian twaddle and stick it up the flue. No, sir. Why, did you ever see, you know, in one of those bottles or jars they have at the medical schools, and the 'ospitals, a specimen of the human embroy — ? If you don't believe me, just take a look at the human embroy, the way it is at the very beginning! Why, it's like a crustacean. Yes, like a crustacean. . . . No, like a fish! . . . Or earlier, like a scorpion, or spider! . . ."

The origin of specie, by that greatest of counterfeiters, God.

And here, too, at the very beginning, was the principle of *uprootedness* that especially now, at the end of a great war, seemed so terribly to govern all lives. This was perhaps their common predicament, perhaps it was always the common predicament, the perpetual and inevitable disruption or disturbance: each of them, with his own poor or rich history, his simple or complex environment (how little it mattered), his long annals of adjustment, achieved, partially achieved, or achieved not at all; and then the giant footstep of interference. What was this but a shipload of ants in panic? ants in a peasepod, borne hopelessly downstream to — no doubt — the cloaca maxima? The Grey Empress, they called her; a troopship only within the fortnight, now that the war was over, converted to passenger service; filthy, rusty, rat-ridden, cockroach-riddled, the unwashed vomit still caked and shining on decks and corridor floors, the stinking urinals out of order, the crew hardened and coarsened by war and privation and fear to an almost complete indifference to human nature, or even creature comfort. And up there above, nevertheless, the teakwood deckrails, scrolled, chased, hieroglyphically carved and filigreed with the innumerable initials of heroes! The heroes who had gone this way never to return! Or, if to return at all, to return lame, halt, blind, or maimed in spirit. For that which goes forth, comes back changed or dead.

Ah, that ghostly freight of signatures which the world must now forever carry! — Jones from Memphis, Smith from Walla Walla; the dates and addresses so pathetically, nostalgically inscribed (as if already looking back to the beloved little past from the unimagined vastnesses and awful profundities, it might be, of the future) — and the humble, proud, beautiful initials which would never again mean anything to anyone! or only anonymously, at any rate, as The Heroes! It will be like that with us: we too will go that way: bequeathing not a name, or none that can hope to acquire or keep for long any significance, but at most symbolizing a tentative deed or two, a thought or two, a grace or two; a change of inflection, the partial diminution of a fear. The shedding, as Blimp might say, of one more scale.

Germinal, too, like that, in the sea, or on it, as so many times (D. thought) in his past, had been the dream, between Gibraltar and Cape St. Vincent, of the novel, *Reading a Book,* or *Ushant:* on the P. & O. ship returning to Ariel's Island, from the bullfight, the Alhambra, with Hambo, who of course was himself present in the dream, but disguised. On his way back to the House; ah, that House, which at the outset of the war he was later to abandon and in a sense betray, and to which he was now once again making his way, but guiltily and tardily! Yes, that House — to which Lorelei Three now preceded him — what would Jacob say of it? what would he make of that? What vanity, pride, ego-projection, fantasy of power and subtlety, or longing for position and security on the one hand, and for a destroyed childhood on the other, had been symbolized in the protracted struggle to acquire and to keep it, with one Lorelei after another, poor darlings (for how difficult it had been for them!)? If for the sake of a continuing intimacy with the three children, and that was unmistakably true, nevertheless the other contributory motives had been complex and various. That House — how, across an outrageous Atlantic, or bitter North Sea, or the Bay of Biscay, it had still the power to lure him! And even now, dark, windowless, shuttered from air attack, hollow and cold as it had been when first he saw it, forlorn in a forlorn and still unlighted street in Saltinge, the steep cobbled street that crumbled down to the Strand, to the muddy river, the quayside, the fishing fleet — even now the vision of it, perhaps in fact now more than ever, because it had been abused, was as compelling for him as ever the fabled gold and spices to the voyagers of the past. What was the secret within those honey-colored walls of Caen stone, ravished from the castle on the Marsh? Was it, in fact, with its Latin and zodiacal inscription, its heraldic origins in the European past, precisely the vital contact with the historical sense that such an uprooted one as himself must crave, and find, and, in the end, endow with far too much of one's own *anima*? Certainly it had existed in its own sovereign right before he had ever seen it: it already had, if the lady novelist who had first converted it into a dwelling-house was speaking the truth, its own very private ghost, who perched amiably enough on the footboard of the bed at midnight, and later was heard by Hambo (if Hambo too was speaking the truth), learning the hunt-and-peck system on the Remington portable, also at midnight. But like the alien sea-shell into which, outgrowing his other, the hermit crab inserts a possessive foot, it had now perhaps become part and parcel of the owner, had subtly blended with himself, himself and it becoming one creature. By degrees, each slowly persuading and modifying the other, they had fitted each other perfectly, the rooms, the "gardens and pleasaunces," whether of house or soul, harmonized at last into a perfect symbiosis. But why? Was it in fact simply the Savannah house repeated, transposed to another country, translated into another language, made more beautiful, but now wholly (unlike that other) his own? And if Ariel's Island was his mother, whom he must cross the sea to rediscover, would the ingenious Jacob say that the House was the veritable womb?

Ushant. You shan't!

The two houses were in many respects, allowing for the total differences of *ambiente,* quite surprisingly alike — not structurally, but physically. An antique pear-tree in one garden, an antique peach in the other. In the pink hawthorn, the saucy roulade of the chaffinch; in the chinaberry-tree the muted and mysterious self-communings of the mockingbird. And in each, the long rich drawing-room, with high windows, the long rich treasure-house of rare and beautiful things: the tip-top table in each, the hieroglyphic rugs, the Chinese vases: oh, yes, it was clear that he had, unconsciously and too naïvely, recapitulated the whole thing as nearly as memory and its right interpretation had been able to do. Every one of the precious *objets d'art* at Saltinge had been, as it were, the *Doppelgänger* of something at Savannah. And the wonderful room at Savannah, into which he had been forbidden to enter, and which only secretly, from time to time, he had managed to explore, had thus, in extension, and as in an algebraic equation, become at last his own. And the majestic frozen stillness, the silent absolute, of Hiroshige's Snow on the Kiso Mountains, which had hung on the central wall at Saltinge, between the embrasured windows, and opposite the tall green-tiled mantel, echoing the stillness of the Leach bowl which the first John had half-reluctantly (it had been very funny) given him — in this had he not really sublimated his feeling (as concerned at Savannah, the rich room) of having been left out in the cold? —

Rooms, Streets, and Houses — they would both have figured in *that* project, long since abandoned, or at any rate shelved, they had both been noted down as heroes; as of course both would also have inevitably figured in *Twenty-Thousand Days: An Analytic Biography.* And perhaps both too in *Ariel's Island* and *Ushant?*

Extraordinary, it had been, that dream on the P. & O. boat: complexly ambiguous, ambivalent and shimmering; perhaps that was the central difficulty, perhaps that was why it always so resisted pinning down, and still continually altered in conception as he resurveyed it. The sheets of P. & O. notepaper, with the P. & O. letter-head, and the three-funnelled white ship steaming past a low brown coast of palm trees, were still there, waiting for him, with the pen-cilled notes which he had missed his breakfast to put down, so afraid had he been that so elaborate and evanescent a dream might evapo-rate even as it was being remembered. How miraculously vivid it had been. At the top of the old mansard-roofed country house (such as that in which Nicholas lived, a mile outside of Saltinge), in the long room which for generations had served as a nursery school for the children, the walls broken-plastered, hung with large, faded, old-fashioned maps, the pinks faded, the blues still vivid, the four translators sat at the refectory table, the "refractory" table — an imi-tation antique, imitation Jacobean, with carved and galled legs, and footrests, but an imitation already itself so old as to be antique — and bent over the German *novella* which they were engaged in translating. The four translators, Hans, Elspeth, The Teacher, and himself, had, as usual, only just seated themselves, opened each his copy of the little book, but at once, as usual, found themselves in disagreement as to where, precisely, on the previous occasion, they had left off. They had not gone much farther, certainly; it somehow always seemed that they had made very little progress with the curi-ous little story, which was itself the account of a progress; but the really odd thing was that they could never quite agree just how *much* progress — in either sense — they had made. They could agree neither on the page, nor on the exact point in the narrative, as if in fact there were something basically ambiguous in the narrative itself; which, in turn, responded to the ambiguity in themselves, whether as individuals or as a group. No less confusing was of course the fact that the four characters in the little German story (of which the colors were as pure and clear as those of the wonder-ful "transfer papers" which one used to melt, or macerate, on to the back of one's hand as a child) were precisely the same as those of the translators. These too were Hans, Elspeth, The Teacher, and The Narrator, oneself. The Teacher (who was from the West) had once explained this, so that at the time it had seemed quite sensible; but it still remained a source of disagreement and discussion. It had all begun, to be sure, very casually, as a kind of mock lesson in German: The Teacher had simply turned to Elspeth and said —

"Well, now dear Elspeth, it's time for you to do your German!"

But then they had been for a while uncertain where to begin. The story, such as it was, involved nothing more extraordinary than a day's walk, an expedition, a kind of holiday or picnic. Hans and Elspeth, followed at a little distance by The Teacher and himself, set forth from the country house (like that in which the translators were now sitting) into the town. And it had opened with some such ordinary sentence as:

"So the two young people, who were really little more than children, Hans and Elspeth, began to walk down the toy road, past the round toy trees, towards the toy German town. Little more than children — or it was so, when it suited their convenience, that The Teacher and The Narrator referred to them!" Children, if at all, of course, in the most relative sense — it was simply that they themselves were older, more adult — or thought themselves to be. But here, too, there was a definite divergence of opinion, which was further complicated by the existence of an earlier version of the story, one which had as a matter of fact never been published, but of which they were all fully aware, even to knowing, if a little vaguely, its contents. For one thing, the time-sequence had been reversed in it; the story had begun *after* the four people had arrived at the *genius loci*, the center of the little heraldic town, the Cathedral Square: they were already there: and they were already irrevocably immersed, involved, in the complex and urgent tragedy which they knew (even Hans knew) was ultimately to overwhelm them. This version began there, at the café table: a bottle stood with glasses on the red cloth, in the Cathedral Café. It began, in fact, in the frozen silence of an admitted disaster, like a wave frozen in the act of falling, at which they sat staring; and from that point the book had then (or so they believed) worked its way back to an analysis of the successive steps through which the disaster had come about. And was there some question whether in this version the scene had been Spanish, and not German at all? — a little town in Andalusia?

— A question, among the many others, that was raised whenever the four translators sat down to work together, at the long nursery table, on which, incidentally, lay those curious little esoteric brochures concerning the worship of the phallus. The disagreements, the discussions, the quarrels, were as endless as amiable: and that was part of the fascination of the whole enterprise. They were reading a book, and they were also *in* the book; they lived in two realms, two capacities. And if one added to this the further complexity which lay in the fact that all this had been transacted by himself, D., in a broken but continuing dream, on the P. & O. ship somewhere at night west of Gibraltar, one began somewhat to understand just why the concept had for so long resisted capture. It constituted indeed, taken altogether, an admirable parable, or equation, of the complexity of "process" which is the inescapable, if also largely unanalyzable, quintessence of life. The little story was a progress; just as the reading of the book, and the translation of it, were a progress: and the four people were involved in the progress, but simultaneously, and in two dimensions. And beyond this, *any* step in *any* direction must be towards ambiguity. Seven Types — ? Child's play. No, it was a continuum of shimmer, one meaning dissolving beautifully and naturally into the next, no one of them central, but all of them primary. Just as, in turn, the four characters were inseparably bound together, inextricably parts of each other, so that each spoke for the others quite as much as for himself. And

26

if they could be said to form a kind of spiritual or psychological hierarchy, then it was a hierarchy that was in a sense reversible. All very well for The Narrator, the paternal "I" of the story (who could be pretty condescending, too, at times), when speaking to The Teacher from the West, to refer to Hans and Elspeth as "children": they were *all* children. They knew themselves, naturally, to be involved, and to belong to each other, morally, guiltily, affectionately, socially: but who could sort out in what degree of each? Who and what was each? and at what distance from each other, or exactly in what pattern, did they stand? Hans, of course, who was really the dream's rather thin disguise for dear mythopoeic Hambo, and to whom the dream had been narrated the next day, as the ship steamed north towards Ushant and the *Raz de Sein* and the *Chaussée de Pierres Noirs,* stood in the relation of "son" to The Narrator, that was understood; but there was also an element of rivalry, and this too was equivocal; for not only were they rivals for Elspeth, beautiful dark closed Elspeth, as precisely as the young bull and the old are rivals (No, my son, let us have them all!), but also they were inexhaustibly committed to a greater and deeper rivalry, that of the pride of mind: if Hans had come to The Narrator to learn from him, and had in part already himself achieved mastery, it had been a little at the expense of balance; and he had remained, it now occasionally appeared, in the hope that he might at last be sufficiently powerful (and he was) to destroy, at any rate symbolically, the one who had nurtured him. But could this be accomplished by the annexation of Elspeth, merely? The Narrator thus all simply to be deprived and humiliated and mutilated? Or must the father image be more elaborately sublimated and murdered?

Here, to be sure, arose at once the always re-emerging question of Hans's — as they all agreed — approaching madness; unless of course it was a feigning, a Hamletism, but with the murder nevertheless as its true ultimate motive. And in any case, at what critical point *would* Hans go mad — and how *much* actually foreseen was it, by all three? And was it, in the last stages, even to be hastened, and deliberately, by The Narrator — did he attempt to force a wrong turning in the little town, a dangerous direction, a sinister short-cut towards the Cathedral Square (the more quickly and surely to encompass for Hans his final and signal possession of Elspeth), but knowing to a hair the amount of excess difficulty which would prove fatal for him? Some too bizarre encounter, or anxiety, or misgiving, one of those vague circumstantial "correspondences" — those equivocations, or puns, whether of appearance or event, that were always cropping up for dear Hans, and which he so often made too much of — and which, in the end, by their very unreality or speciousness might lead to his undoing.

Here, as the progress through dank alleys, over cobbled pavements, under the far sound of the vari-voiced bells, moved towards the center, here, they all knew, was the acme, the high point, of evil. Here it was that they must all participate in what was of course their shared and conscious and inevitable crime. The Narrator's, most of all — : he, as the one presumably most conscious, should have been the one to make the most allowances, even, if necessary, to submitting to his own destruction. For the alliance, between Hans and himself, was of the deepest: they were brothers: they were son and father: they were co-conspirators in their grand, Daedalian, secret and profound, and absolutely unremitting, warfare on the unconscious, its sworn and mortal enemies: and what therefore more natural in this league than that it should envisage women, and notably Elspeth, as something decidedly suspect, perhaps even inimical.

"Even as Hans spoke" — to take a passage at random — "he exchanged, or appeared to exchange, with The Narrator, an unworded and implicit something else; their perpetual secret; their affection for each other, a sharing, a co-operation, as of man with man against

woman; himself and The Narrator against Elspeth, but nevertheless with an acknowledged affection, too, for Elspeth, who so de-
sirably stood always there between them. But if they thus at such
moments felt the deep necessity to join forces, and signalled it to
each other, they just as quickly found themselves separating again,
their league dissolved. As if Hans said, first, 'We are brothers':
next, 'We are son and father': and lastly, 'No, we are rivals!' But
even in rivalry maintaining their superiority, oh yes, their inalien-
able superiority to woman, although of course they must (even so)
admit their love for her, and for Elspeth . . . !"

And the different levels of reality, all of them related intricately
to the constitution of the soul's landscape, each series of symbols
arranged in sequence above or below another — could they be
enumerated now for further analysis? To begin with, of course, D.,
waking from a dream, in the upper berth of the P. & O. ship many
years before, a ship which was perhaps in difficulties as it turned
north towards the dangerous shoals south of Île d'Ouessant,
Ushant — he had heard the alarm signals, or something of that
nature, while still in the dream; there, by the dream mechanism,
they had been translated into bell-sounds, but bell-sounds of another
meaning: bells from one or another quarter of the little red-roofed
hill town, perhaps from the Cathedral itself, about which they were
reading. But the alarm signals ceased, as he listened; the ship again
seemed quieter; there was no longer that running and stumbling of
heavy-booted feet overhead, and instead only the regular, remote,
and now reassuring engine-beat, the strong beat of a ship's healthy
heart: they were out of danger, perhaps, and he could reimmerse
himself in the dream. And there, in the dream again, they were
reading a book, they were about to resume reading a book, four
people sitting down in a nursery schoolroom to translate a book
from the German. That was the third level. The fourth, in turn,
being that the four identical people, or at any rate people with the

same names, were then participating in the action itself, themselves actually walking down the road between toy green trees towards the toy town, where loomed before them, always, the obscure shape of a catastrophe. The fourth; but in addition to this a fifth — ? for in this the four reader-participators were now locked in endless and complex discussion as to *what it all meant.* Not only that, but a forever unresolved argument, good-natured, to be sure, but none the less Gordian-knotted for that, as to what had actually 'happened,' how far they had gone, whether in the book or into the town, and towards the *dénouement,* the foreseen disaster. Did they, in truth, know it all? That was the fifth. And just as inescapable was the sixth, the perennial question of mere 'leakage,' of what was unavoidably lost in any translation; misunderstood, it might be, or simply at bottom untranslatable: that which is not to be communicated. Well, then — which of one's planes of invention, or awareness, was one to accept as the most real? or must one finally accept them all as simply reducible to the insoluble "I"? With, alas, as a possible seventh, overshadowing everything, the fact that the basis for every symbol was rooted in the sensory phenomena of experience, phenomena thus become noumena! as Hans, in the dream, in the book in the dream, and in the story in the book in the dream, was derived unmistakably from the — how real, how actual, apart from D.'s own investment of him with his own properties and magic? — Hambo of Spain, of the bullfight, of Saltinge, of London, of Boston, and Mexico. . . . Not to mention the P. & O. boat, on which the dream had occurred, and perhaps at the very moment when Hambo was writing that immense poetic "ship's log," that mythopoeic logarithm, of a letter, that mythopoem (in imitation of D.'s own letter, and in a similar situation) to his all-too-imaginary Nita. To the Nita who in the dream became Elspeth, and who therefore, in a very real sense, had "created" Elspeth. Dark, secret, close, and as hard as nails, with steel-shod little high heels especially invented for the perforation of hearts. The tiny streamlined Nita who would go through life as murderously as a bullet. . . . Faithless and Pitiless — !

Translation — it was all translation, D. thought, the transfer pictures re-emerging on the back of one's wetted hand, but in reverse; bright, but different. And in the same way, now, poor Blimp, snoring in his bunk, on his way to England with a hundred pounds of food for his nieces and nephews, the home-town boy who had made good, and was now returning with largesse, Blimp too would eventually succumb to this digestive process of observation and imagination and, surrendering his three-dimensional existence (the genuine embroy), take on instead, for D., either the two-dimensional value of a "Hans," or the multi-dimensional value of a dream (like *Ushant*) in which, like Hans, he played an ambiguous part.

Back thus to childhood, and infancy — the first day. And God said, let there be light. And there was light. Light, a "blue" light (if R. could be believed) above one's bassinet — or could it be a memory of sky? Then the lights, of opening doors and balconies; and the difference between indoors and outdoors; the sudden assault of the *whole* light, so dangerous, but found also to be precariously acceptable. Yes, and in the south particularly: the light there that was like the spring of the tiger: the dark there that was like the swarming of cottonmouths round one's eyes. The everywhere critical division between light and shade, demarcation as definite and vivid as the striping of the tiger. And if one must begin somewhere, if somewhere there must be a beginning, nevertheless the more one thought of it the less could one discover with any assurance just where it was: — at most, it may be, possibly, just *there,* in light itself: as if in fact one had lived, to begin with, a long life of which light itself was the sole principle, and one's awareness of light one's sole awareness. To have emerged from that, very much as an exhausted swim-

31

mer from a wrecked ship — perhaps in the *Chanel de la Helle* — crawls up on a shore, was already in a sense to have begun the long and vivid process of dying which we call life. To be able to *separate* oneself from one's background, one's environment — wasn't this the most thrilling discovery of which consciousness was capable? and no doubt for the very reason that as it is a discovery of one's limits, it is therefore by implication the first and sharpest taste of death.

Natural enough, in that case, the terror that was light's invariable accompaniment — for it was inevitably the cutting edge of revelation, and of course it was oneself that was being cut. Into what shapes — ? Shapes of roundness, flat shapes, dully gleaming squares, sharp diamonds and triangles: the secrecy of the diagonal: illuminated movements of curve or angle, surfaces that glowed or sombred, and then, in altering light, the kinaesthetic and palpable textures altering also, the smooth, the flocked, the veined, the corrugated, the pocked, the pleached — granite surface and ivy surface, the cool or warm wall which found its way to shadow in a corner. But above all, the endless variability in the light itself as it shifted over outlines, or filtered, for instance, a little monstrously, through the hairs of a coarse profile, or became slippery and ophidian as it glided over something extended and smooth. The shadows leaned towards, and then away; bent down or as mysteriously departed; one existed as if at the center of a world of luminaries in orbit, and also as if membranously attached to them: as they approached or receded, one felt one's innermost vitality secretly and deliciously warmed or nurtured, or perilously abandoned. Root and stem, one was consciously a tropism of exquisite response in the very center of one's own world, coiled about the source of one's own delight.

Fascinating, that out of this so elementary and as it were abecedarian experience, these huge globed and golden monosyllables of meaning, an onomasticon in which the living particles were alternately as huge as stars or as minute as atoms, floating separately in the dark galaxies whether of ether-dust or plasma, one should so instinctively and automatically become oneself the onomastic who could organize a language for the *plenum,* and fill it: and that out of these primary simplicities should slowly emerge the complex, the increasingly complex, forms of developing consciousness and memory. The forms were in a way simply congealings of light, whether into shapes or events — ? for they seemed to be interchangeable. And upon these later would be imposed some of the "false" memories, the hearsay, which would be incorporated subtly and surreptitiously into memory, and then flung back.

Such, for example, was the drawing of D. as an infant, the drawing by his father, as the sole occupant of the floor in the boarding-house room at Savannah: that deliberately hideous, and actually very funny, drawing, of which nevertheless the many details (the Angelus of Millet on the wall, the whatnot in the corner, the wash-stand, the large bed with knobbed railing, the amateurish picture of the haystack, known all one's life as painted by father) had been in effect, but deceptively, absorbed by himself. The grotesque infant with one hair standing upright on his head, and grinning to show one tooth, dominated the scene already, in the pen-and-ink drawing which had been sent to grandmother; dominated all. Naked except for his diapers, there he squatted, the new emperor, the new inheritor of the virtues and vices of his ancestors. In this memorable drawing, D.'s father had managed to convey something quite appallingly flagrant, the feeling one has, but most of all when one has just become a father (as D. himself remembered), of life's blatant effrontery, its sheer impudence. The egoism of the ovum is only surpassed by that of the baby; and one unconsciously, or even consciously, begins at once to resent it. And in this crude caricature one could recognize all too easily the contention for mastery of the father's anger and pride. It was as good as an admission that (if the brat only knew it!) he already had the upper hand, and was destined to become a powerful, cunning, and treacherous usurper. That child's father and mother were already as good as dead.

Merrymount Nipmuk: so this somewhat deplorable character was to have been called — indeed, *was* called, in the fragment of narrative' which had been given the tentative title of "The Lives and Adventures of Merrymount Nipmuk": the name, like the title, perhaps a trifle labored, but the implications clear. The Nipmuks, had they not been one of the lesser Indian tribes of New England, poor but honest, on the whole unspectacular? but with just, especially in the later generations, a saving dash of the aboriginal naughtiness that could be symbolized by the reference to Merrymount, and to that gay phallic Maypole which Morton, the poet, had somewhat rashly and prematurely dedicated on the seaside hill south of Boston, north of Wessagussett — its "flag to April's breeze unfurl'd"? And suitably enough, D.'s father's drawing still reposed, as it always had, between the pages of grandfather's sermons, sermons which had led his church into the wilderness of comparative unbelief. There it had reposed, on the shelf in that tiny cottage on Cape Cod, which, unknown to D., had long before been lived in by Cousin Abiel, the Quaker, and from which Cousin Abiel had written the famous naughty letter to grandfather, then studying for the ministry at Harvard — it had described with much too much gusto the marital habits — or perhaps premarital — of the local Quakers. Grandfather, the far-seeing liberal; Cousin Abiel, the sly wag and iconoclast; a small faded pamphlet of grandmother's poems, capable but undistinguished; and the drawing of D., rampant in diapers, by D.'s father: here, in brief (for Abiel's letter was folded demurely in the book, too), was a not wholly accidental symposium of the family. Here they slept together more securely, more memorably, and more intimately, than in the prim Quaker graveyard at South Yarmouth, or the suburban cemetery at New Bedford, or under the moss-streamered live-oaks and telephone wires beside the Thunderbolt River at Savannah. Here, they spoke in chorus, with one voice; and said one thing: *the ancestors.*

These forms, these coagulations of light, into scenes or events, the shapes of experience, which gradually became the shape of oneself (like the telegram at Savannah, on the sunny morning after Christmas, which announced grandfather's death, and the ensuing walk to the telegraph office — but what was death? this was the first adumbration of death, and it meant a visit with grandfather to Buttonwood Park, sitting there under the trees, and bears in cages, an imaginary tea at a rustic table, and the fragment of a letter from grandfather, which lay, too, in the pages of the volume of sermons, sent from San Francisco, and all about trains) — these shapes of experience were of course to be put together later, and then, like a color of light, or a color of shade, cast back on the simpler forms which had preceded them. But now the immediate shapes were the palmetto leaves which raised dark hands before the windows of the boardinghouse room: the mosquito netting which hung dreamlike over the bed, itself a part of sleep: the bells, that reverberated for meal-times, no doubt some sort of gong which hung in the lower hall, and sent footsteps hurrying up and down on curved stairs round the wide pale stairwell (it was not dissimilar to the bell that rang an alarm on the P. & O. boat, and had been so wonderfully "translated" into fire-bells, or Cathedral bells, from the toy German town in the little story which they had been translating in a dream, his own dream, itself later to become concept of an artifact): these were undeniably there, and of their own authority. As, also, the first really identifiable "scene," or action. This involved the stairwell, too. There were ladies, there were voices downstairs, at the bottom of the echoing stairwell, and they were having tea, but this of course must have been an item of knowledge added later; and into this, down into this, between the dark banisters of the railing, he had released — now that he had himself been displaced — his brother

K.'s milk-bottle. That was all. Nothing before, and nothing after. Why did one so particularly remember this? Because there was so unmistakably an element of calculation in it, a *suppressed* beforeness? Probably. But to suppose that this was actually one's first recollection of a scene was only superficially, or in a partial sense, true. For one also remembers, but in a different and less demonstrable way, much that was inexpressible, and survived only as the feeling-tone that accompanied certain situations and actions, or even times of day: when one walked into a field, alone, through the lichened pasture-gate, in the pale early morning, or thus again past the stone wall on to the nether slope of a mountain, still in shadow against the east: or at night in spring along a pitch-dark country lane, the unseen ditches at either side, the tassels of birches against one's face: or at the moment of one's waking from a terrible or delicious dream — the execution dream, for example, of waiting in the chair for the onset of the electricity, then its profound assault on one's throat and breast and heart, fluctuatingly intrusive, but not at first intrusive enough, so that although one knew that one was dying, and tried to cry out an appeal for a deeper and more final intrusion, one succeeded only in a murmur so faint that no one heard it, and one's dying thought was "even in death I cannot be effectual, or make myself understood": in such moments, it was from the unconscious memory that the scene took its secret validity. This shapeless but conforming ever-ready validity of memory was like a cloud which had always accompanied one, and out of which one had managed, at intervals, but to an always unpredictable degree, to disengage an apparently separate awareness. It was as much part of oneself as one's body. And at first for increasingly long periods, like the fish learning to live out of the sea, one experienced a growing, if spurious, confidence that one was at last speaking for oneself, without reference to any past, one's own or another, but just the same, one had always known that this was sure to be temporary, and that at length the process would reverse itself; so that then, more and more often, and again too for periods of increasing length, one would sink back into that cryptic cloud, finally to remain there for good. And this cloud, this memory, whether ancestral, or one's own, or both, seemed to extend backward in time forever. More even than one's father and mother, this *was* father and mother.

But theirs too, theirs too.

As, among other crowding details, the Hieronymus Bosch cornucopia of pertinences and extravagances, where, among the always taller and more distant trees, and the wider aisles between them, showed now the suddenly angelic buildings, and the abnormal bell-tower, like a preposterously tall insect with red legs, from which, again, whizzed down that fatal bell-sound: among these, and against the mysterious masonry wall, a part of the daily walk, that endless secretive wall over which hung ivy and cypress vines, the gay eyes of flowers, but from behind which on the steamy southern wind rose a fetid and unwholesome smell: among and against these details was the picture of the fat pig. Yes, to think that *that* oddity should so have persisted in memory for all one's life: the fat pig, his mother's only, and very limited talent for drawing, the drawing of the fat pig — and why, indeed? how had it started? with *her* mother — ? Anyway, there it was, one of those preternaturally luminous *nuclei* of recollected feeling, the fat pig being always produced on demand, and drawn again, on any available scrap of paper: not always quite the same, which was both disconcerting and intriguing, the ambiguous head of relativity already cropping up amongst the clover: and certainly somewhat sinister. It had had a quite horrible verisimilitude and grossness, and not least of the secret attractiveness of the whole affair was one's feeling that it was mother's sole vanity, her only parlor trick, so that one was both amused and sorry. Produced first for oneself, in later years of course it came obediently up again for K. and R., just as before. Those fat pigs were legion, they were innumerable; the nursery on the top floor, with the long window which seemed to exist primarily for the magnification of rain, was littered with them. How often had one heard K. say, "Mama, draw me the fat pig, draw me the smiling pig!" "Wide" and "Handsome" they had then been nicknamed for a time, and himself "High": a joke of D.'s father. And for Handsome (how depressingly appropriate the epithet had been — O god, those photographs of Handsome, bow in hand, and gauze wings somehow gummed to his shoulders, deplorably made up as Cupid and standing naked in a wicker clothes hamper) they had begun all over again. Her book on her knee, she would trace once more the twelve-cylinder pig, with the coiled watchspring tail and the tiny smiling eyes. Years later he was to find the sole survivor of them all, tucked away between the pages of Mayne Reid's *The Young Yagers*. And yes, it was true, she *had* said that it was grandmother who had first invented this terrible creature, this family god, years before, for mother and the Beloved Uncle.

One had advanced, then, so to speak, through a constantly changing palimpsest of acts and scenes, the references working forward and backwards at the same time, so that as one proceeded through the streets of Savannah, under those nameless tall trees, beneath which one found tiny but infrequent red berries, and down towards the shopping center, where the toy shop was, and the barbershop where one had been shorn of one's curls, and at last to the telegraph office, where something, some message, was to be despatched about grandfather to the Beloved Uncle, it was both to re-enact, through one's mother as well as oneself — (for surely she was remembering precisely such situations before, just such expeditions down the steep cobbles of Union Street, in New Bedford, towards the far small vignette of ships' masts and spars, the whalers, the brass eagles of tugs) — to re-enact previous episodes, at the same time that one was anticipating other such walks to come. The walk into the toy town in *Reading a Book,* and in the projected novel, this would in turn be a repetition: and how about Mexico? And in all of them, death was the recurrent theme: someone had died, whatever that meant; messages must be broadcast, it was as if the family, scattered here, there and everywhere, had at such moments to exchange these far small signals, feeling one another at a distance, telepathically, as with affectionate antennae, in order to become, out of it all, a unit again. And of course it was *au fond* his feeling of *joining* that unit and being admitted to it that was paramount for him in the whole vivid event: grandfather, of the revolving bookcase (which D. was later to be allowed to inherit) had died, and D.'s mother had just said this, at the top of the stoop, pulling on her gloves in the sunlight, and D. had been specially dressed for the important walk to the telegraph office: it was an occasion. The fact that the other two children were too small to be taken only further emphasized that in effect a formal announcement had been made: D. was now a full-fledged member of the family. Against the background of a southern Christmas, and its spurting Roman candles, which D. and his father had set off in the Park on Christmas Eve — and, oh, the days of glorious anticipation, while the rainbow-hued fascicles waited in the corner of father's surgery, blue, vermilion, poisonous green, yellow, spangled, with the ingenious twists of colored paper at the end, for igniting with the stick of punk — against all this it was no wonder that — as D. now realized — this was the first *continuous* scene which he could remember. The obvious formality, newly introduced into his relations with his mother, was unquestionably an important element in this, and perhaps more than anything else accounted for the extraordinary clarity of his picture of her, there on the stoop; for it still remained by far the clearest picture of all; even to the sharp-winged hat, which, as it sat rather far forward on her head, gave her a little the air of flying. To be sure, D.'s father had later taken a photograph of her in this very costume,

39

gloves, hat and all, and had won a prize with it at his Camera Club; the photo still in fact existed, somewhere; but no, this had little to do with his remembering it, the thing was there, his first recollection of a continued action, and of continuity in one's private existence. It had marked the beginning of a new kind of being.

Nor could anything have been more appropriate as a setting for it than that wonderful "stoop," as they called them in the south — the stoop of the new house, to which they had moved after R. had been born, a removal, however, of which one retained no recollection — an actionless glide, timeless too; suddenly they were simply there. And the brick stoop which led to the second story, with its iron railing and brownstone steps, and the little door under it which opened into the surgery's waiting-room (ah, and all the fascinating dilapidated magazines on the table there) — this was the real essence of the house, to begin with, this and the two immense trees which grew before it, above the rich dark dirt of the street, and which, whether in sunlight or moonlight, kept forever a moving pattern of leaf-shadow turning and revolving over the serene housefront of tall windows and wrought-iron balconies, like an evanescent stencilling. Live-oaks, holm-oaks — those were one's first trees, the symbols therefore of all that was tree: they had naturally reappeared at Saltinge: in them, one found one's whole notion of greatness and rootedness, of earth-living and earth-dying. Under these had the Italians come, with their little strapped one-legged organs, the flea-faced monkeys wearing dirty green hats and suits, suits with a hole for the tail, the skinny hands holding out boat-shaped hats for pennies. And here too had come, more alarmingly, the two strange men with dancing bears, the huge animals skipping heavily in a tethered circle, their sides shaking, while the men, pretending to be frightened, kept beating the ground with long wooden staves. And it was up one of these trees, on the never-to-be-forgotten morning, and presumably because they now had as audience the entire family, the Negro servants, Selina and Clara, included, that one of the bears was encouraged to climb, while all the family clung to the railing in delighted terror. As good as a circus, or better: for the bear, having hugged his way up to the main fork of the great tree, a little above the level of the stoop, settled himself there with manifest relish and refused to come down. The bear's owner commanded, cajoled, even at last put his head against the bark of the tree and wept, but it was all no use, the bear enjoyed it hugely, and so did the family. But then the miracle happened. The two strange men conferred together (heaven alone knew in what language) and it was decided, apparently, that the best thing to do was to send the second bear up after the first. Where all else failed, example might serve: the tame oxen would lead the undefeated bull from the ring. Two bears in a single tree, their own tree! It was quite beyond belief, but it was true. And there, what was more, the bears had stayed, all that wonderful morning.

Like everything else, the stoop's importance had been transitional, temporary; but for what it was, it remained paramount. It had been like a bridge that spanned from infancy into childhood, even in fact to the end of childhood, for of course it had inevitably figured in every event, of the slightest significance, which had affected the family during the decade in which they had lived there. If its magic had naturally faded a little with familiarity and possession, it had none the less been potent, not to say protean. Most of all, at the very beginning, it had been a ship, so that as one descended the worn brown steps one of course moved closer and closer to the water, the ocean, that imaginary ocean which was so incomparably more real and fascinating than any mere Atlantic, or Bay of Biscay, was ever to be. This surrounded and washed up against the stoop on all sides, this far-extending sea: it began with the brick sidewalk, roared east and west along the block, and so out of sight; and on this one could of course set sail for New York, or Boston, or New

Bedford, or, more near at hand, the Cotton Islands. One was in direct contact with all these places; they were to be landed at in a morning's voyage. Moreover, as the adjacent stoop, next door, which backed up to theirs, was only separated from it by two or three feet, it was thus possible to step from one to the other, across a fiord of terrifying depth and darkness, out of which rose a smell of dirt and mould (it was probably too narrow to be swept): and in doing this one was achieving the highly dangerous exploit of transferring in mid-ocean from one storm-tossed vessel to another. But even better than this — and how much of one's perpetual preoccupation with the sea could be traced to it? — was simply to stand there with one's hands on the railing, on a sunny day, and sail past the world, the whole wonderful world, and all the unexpected things it unfailingly brought to light: the endless miracle of texture itself. One could never get enough of that, one never tired of it. The nearness of everything was a part of the joy, but another had been, though one had as yet no name for it, the sense of the infinite, the limitless cruelty of light: if it made one feel alive, it also made one feel crucially alone.

> *"One — two — three —*
> *Out — goes — she!"*

So had gone the ritual poem with which, every night after prayers, his mother had reached the ringed pale hand to the fish-tail of red and yellow gas-flame to turn it out: that fish-tail, with which D.'s father had demonstrated, by silhouetting their hands against it, the circulation of the blood. "Out goes she": and out into their own darkness they had then gone, as she into hers. Bewildered as they, too, she had seemed to be, by that fact of approaching darkness, as childlike in its ominous presence as they, as fearful too of that feeling of being crucially alone. Here, in these before-sleep shadows, had come the premonitions of separateness, that profound and embarrassing and enthralling problem which a little later, or even perhaps already, was to face one, as in a looking-glass (but the looking-glass was the sun) with the queer question: "How is it that I am *I?* Why was I not someone else? How did I get here in this particular time and place and guise, why is my name what it is and not another? And if it had been another, would I too then have been a different person? Or could I change? And suppose I had had a different father and mother, what then? Would I have been the same without them as *with* them? or if they had them- selves, for example, not existed at all, would there never have been the existence, the 'me,' which is so palpably and immediately the realest thing in the world?"

Explorations in human personality — how early one had em- barked on that — as on a ship, as on *this* ship, and all those other ships — forever, as now, trying to find a pattern in that so in- corporeal entity, that *animula vagula glandular!* As here, with the frightened boy, on the curve of his own Great Circle to the smoking ruins of Paradise Street, following a course which for him had become inevitable, laid down for him by dead reckoning: visible elements in it being the English father, a doctor in Liverpool, who had done his heroic duty, and stayed at his post there during the blitz, while the neurotic New Englander whom he had married (they had met when she was doing the grand tour, somewhere in the Lake District) hurried the children for safety back to her native Cape Cod and the shores of the Bass River. The boy would have lost caste? — Did he already foresee this? Or was he even now steeling himself to make up, by himself and for himself, for that admitted deficiency in his mother, that lacklustre quality in her character which was not exactly cowardice but which, except for a sheer fluke, would have made her, as she ought to have been, a typical small-town New England old maid? Yes, there in the bunk below, in Cabin 144, lying for the moment asleep, was what one might describe as the "unfinished" psychological article, of which, however, the finish was foreseeable; while above him, awake, was the one who foresaw for them both, the one whose "weird" was now, in that sense at least, pretty well "dreed." And how little was the difference, really, between two such lives! Out of the capricious alternations of good fortune and bad, fair weather and blight, agonies, injuries, and delights, did they all perhaps achieve a kind of *equivalence* of compensation, enough at any rate so that they could at least function, after a fashion? they at least "ran." And miraculous to be sure it was. Each individual was an almost incredible piece of testimony to the fact that life itself was not only innately indomitable, but also possessed powers of adaptation which were literally incalculable. Perhaps the agonies and injuries were in some sort a necessity, if the individual was to accomplish an even partial originality of shape and purpose. As the tiny pine-tree is cunningly wounded and dwarfed by the Japanese gardener, in order that it may become a masterpiece worthy to be contained in a Ming bowl — !

And was one's father perhaps almost always of necessity the Japanese gardener — ? by the injuries of repression, the calculated cruelties of discipline, the surgical invasions of his clairvoyance, so that conscience had nowhere to hide; but also by the brilliance of his example, the sheer godlikeness of that superior being, his genius for both action and speech, so that he was the genius of language, and therefore of understanding, made incarnate — did not the father, any father, play involuntarily this dual role? Hardie, there, who had already lost three toes from gangrene, and would lose more, who knew he must die but denied it, and who, as if it were the greatest lark in the world, was taking the two small boys to Kent, to deliver them over to his sister: had not his father been as obviously a hero, to have produced such a hero? As now Hardie, with an unmatched tenderness and precision, was himself producing heroes.

The ancestors, the ancestors, the unconquerable ancestors, whose tongues still spoke so clearly, whose hands still reached so unmistakably, and whose wills were so indistinguishable from one's own! One was lucky if one merely remembered, merely observed. Each bud, and then each leaf, each flower, taking up the precious pattern, repeating it; perhaps only with the most infinitesimal variation, the slightest imaginable, and probably accidental, accretion, of one's own. Or was all somewhere indicated in the dark backward, never to be otherwise varied than intended, not in the tiniest item? D.'s father, and the cameras, the pinhole camera made of a soapbox; and then the purchase of a small Kodak for D., while the ship docked for two hours at New York en route to Charlestown; the paraboloid lens, and the "portable inexpensive ophthalmoscope" — all these were an evolution of determinants farther back, and then themselves passed on, whether in the inheritance, or as breathable elements in one's environment, which one or other of the children would select. K. to select, for example, the medical and surgical, but along with it also a facet of the poetic or linguistic "set"; R. the mathematical and art-loving; D. the psychological and poetic, too, but *manqué*. Each, in his somewhat abortive way, was, and had always been, engaged in carrying out one or another of the father's uncompleted projects. But who would ever complete that boat? and where, in terms of their own mythopoeic and heuristic translation of the inherited impulse, had it gone?

Ah, that boat, which was to have been built in the back yard, in the sequined shadows of the peach and chinaberry trees! The plans had come, the fresh, crisp blueprints, and were unfolded on the dining-room table, over and over again, for absorbed analysis: father's pencil traced the ghostly outlines, demonstrating just what (out of all the cross-sections, and the dotted lines that indicated those parts which were invisible) the beautiful creature would look like. Yes, they would order the lumber for it; one day this would

45

arrive, and be put down in the yard, there to be unpacked, sorted out, each numbered section put aside in its right order for assembly; and in the end, there, in their own yard, *on dry land* among the fallen peach bloom, or delicate chinaberry blossom, but as if by its own intrinsic magic invoking the sea, would be the bright new boat of golden wood. That conception; of a boat being built *there*, trapped in a walled garden, miles from the ocean; had had for all of them a special and recondite power: the co-operative image had been one of their most sacred, it was like imprisoning a humming-bird in a crystal bowl. And what had happened — ? Nothing. Less and less often were the blueprints looked at, they were finally left untouched in a drawer of the secretary (the secretary with the secret drawer, mother's writing table, which stood in the dining-room), and then had at last disappeared entirely. Well, there was, as D. now realized, something all too typical about father in that: here again was the brilliant enthusiast, the passionate amateur, whose imagination flew in every direction, but perhaps never for long enough in any particular one. The portable inexpensive ophthalmo-scope, so long talked about, had indeed materialized, a fine little brass jewel of an instrument, and they had all had their eyes ex-amined in turn for astigmatism ("half a diopter," or whatever), which in its way (in the darkened surgery) was as much fun as the magic lantern; but for various reasons it had never been a success, never revolutionized ophthalmology as it had been thought it might — it was inexpensive, all right, but apparently beyond a point it wasn't good enough, or precise enough. And the parabo-loid lens, together with the fascinating design of the infinitely complex machinery for grinding it, explained to them, or to D., at any rate, so eagerly — nothing had ever come of that, either. But that boat, that heavenly unbuilt boat, that dream of a boat — !

Perhaps, even now, D. thought (the ship-sounds suddenly again

46

encroaching around him, a faint hum from far above — it might have been a bell, or simply water whining in one of those innumerable painted pipes that everywhere wind through a ship's steaming and obscene anatomy) — perhaps even now he was himself still occupied in building and launching and sailing that adventurous little Argonaut: that unbuilt boat was the Grey Empress, at this moment, and all the countless other ships he had sailed in, forever pointing a hopeful bow in a new direction: towards Liverpool tonight, as on the first of all occasions from Quebec, with the Scotch carpenter, and Ebo playing his fiddle on the steerage deck: towards foaming Ushant and moaning Cherbourg: towards Gibraltar and Ceuta: towards Naples, and the broken rim of Vesuvius, and Pompeii, deserted and mortuary in April rain: all these, and all the others, of course they were the unbuilt boat in the backyard, he had been building it ever since. Even, or perhaps most of all, on the two voyages when he had twice met Cynthia, and fallen in love with her, and lost her, and then tried to make it all into a bad play called *Purple Passage*. Ah, Cynthia from the regions which! Cynthia who was later to be described, by a literary innkeeper, as the most beautiful woman in England! But no — that was to do an injustice, a grave injustice to Faubion, fleshpot Faubion, dark-eyed, vulgar, wonderful, forthright Faubion, who had felt savagely for his feet under the table, the last night of the voyage, and later knocked emphatically at his stateroom door — Faubion, on her way to Hawarden, but never to be seen again, despite the suggested tryst in London. Only, instead, the letter from Cheshire, in the round, open, little-girl hand, very simple, very true, to say simply that as her aunt was sick, she could not come. Faubion — how much better would she have been for him than the stained-glass-window Cynthia, and her precious tweeds and scarves, and the photo of Rupert Brooke in her chaste little boudoir in Chelsea. If one had to desert one's wife and abandon one's children (who were truly one's life), were

47

it not better done for a Faubion, whose very name breathed an earthen vitality, the rich dirt of the street in Savannah?

Values, values, — how wrong one must be about them, to begin with, or was it that one had to go through the more precious and ultra-violet mistakes, in the course of one's misguided climb to what one considered was knowledge, sophistication, worldliness, self-assurance (and an illusion, anyway), in order to appreciate, but very likely too late, the more searchingly satisfactory virtues, or vices, of the infra-red? Well, no doubt D. had himself, for Faubion, represented some queer sort of ultra-violet (if definitely not ultra-pansy) — and the exchange would have been much the same. Perhaps it always was. Of the two partners in the dance, one must necessarily be more earthy than the other, and this was what inspired the dance to begin with: perhaps each of the dancers hoped to find in the partner that which he himself lacked, the strong seeking out the subtle, the subtle seeking out the strong, the twinned stars then moving elliptically into a new orbit, so that each learned something unknown from the other. But all of life was like that — the meeting with each new person was like that. In each new meeting was the instinct for the love-dance, and out of each, no matter how fleeting or slight, one hoped for the blossoming of that moment of semantic discovery, which at its best must be reciprocal — : the new bead of light and meaning to be added to one's ever-lengthening chain, each one an increase in the vocabulary of self. "What is there in thee Man that can be known?" Only this, this process of collection, this mysterious process by which the psychic mirror stored away its reflections of the ever-changing colors and shapes of other psyches, other things, and fashioned thus the luminous Joseph's Coat, ever more variegated and prismatic, through which it gave back to the world the brief light of the soul. Mimicry, mimicry, mimicry — one's whole life was spent in mimicry. And in the end, one's personality was nothing whatever but an anthology of these mimicries

48

and adaptations, one was oneself simply the compiler. The onomastic.

And of course the only difference between the early and the
late, in experience, was of simple and complex, single and com-
pound, the plain and the ambiguous. The pity being that of these
multiples of iridescent complexity one so seldom any longer paused,
or had the patience, to analyze back to the still wonderful — (if
only one perceived them) — primary units of sense that composed
them. If one could still, as at the beginning in Savannah, and in
that amazing house that was oneself, set out on that first divine
exploration beyond the borders of one's own private separateness!
Just as mobility had first enlarged one's experience, one's map, of
the nursery, and then of a whole floor, a story, of the house, with
all the marvelous stairs and corners, and the obscure patterns in the
carpets, the inviting shadows and caves under tables, or the fringed
and fragrant hollows under sofas — for one's earlier adventures
were quite absurdly like a dog's or cat's — so in the next phase the
sense of one's separateness as an individual (which had been signal-
ized forever, and crystallized, by the walk to the telegraph office
with mother) began its own necessary expansions and discoveries.
After Wide had been born, and after mother's mysterious illness and
seclusion, he had been removed from the nursery, which adjoined
her room, and of which the folding-doors had been provokingly kept
shut, and given a room of his own.

"Guess you gwine to be a big boy now," Clara had said. "Yes,
suh, guess you gwine to be a big boy," — thrusting her black hands
miraculously into the flames of the nursery fireplace.

Here was again that flattering overtone as of a newly found importance. A room of his own, with an inside window which looked
out into the long "black hall," a bed of white metal, and bright
brass knobs which could be unscrewed from the posts; a chair, too,
and a small low table, where had stood the red fire-engine, which

had for so long smelled of smoke, deliciously, from the fire of excelsior which D.'s father had made in it; and the set of Zouave soldiers, slotted in their box. All this meant a definite and peculiar squaring away of oneself, an acquisition of distance. It was as if one had taken on the dimensions of the new room, or had even come to resemble it. That arranged room was now one's rearranged self, and not only rearranged, but somehow secret. Ah — secret — yea! And this suddenly found secrecy was both attractive and vitalizing. Now for the first time one could do things without being watched. Light matches, for instance! Not everything one did would be known.

It had meant, too, a further expansion of separateness and independence, quite naturally and strategically, down those long back stairs which led first to the pantry, and then, by the outside stairs, to the kitchen and outhouse and yard, and so, again, to the whole outside world, the fascinatingly filthy alley beyond the outhouse, which in turn led to all of secret and subterranean Savannah. This, naturally, was a realm largely unknown to father and mother. If the stoop (and the great beautiful Room) had become a bridge to one sort of world, the official world, now the peach-tree and chinaberry-tree, framing the latticed door to the fetid alley, had become the guardians and symbols of a new birth, a new life: between them he had gone forth to take inevitable possession of his own private world.

Tin-tin: tin-tin: tin-tin.
The sleepwalking bells again, far aloft in the sonorous night, the hand of destiny, as in that wonderful movie, *The Last Moment,* reaching detachedly out of darkness to seize the frayed end of the bell-rope, strike six times, and withdraw. That was all there had been, to show that the boy had run away to sea; that, and an angle-shot of a coil of rope on a tar-seamed deck. The running away to sea, and to life, which was to lead him ultimately back again to the

dark circle of midnight water in which he had drowned himself, or was still in the act of drowning. Three o'clock in the night of the soul.

And even now at Saltinge, blessed little Saltinge, hateful little Saltinge, sleeping on its hill between the three baby rivers, while the gilded Quarter-Boys on the church clock pivoted in the dark to smite yet another flat-voiced bell, *ting-tang, ting-tang, ting-tang,* even now the House there awaited its occupant, the unlighted war-stricken house of stone and timber, showing as if hopefully or prayerfully to the night its soulless windows, expectant even now of the turning on of lights. And Lorelei Three, bless her heart! — was she not already approaching it? pausing only for a night's rest in London, at the dirty little hotel in Russell Square, before taking the nine-fifteen from Charing Cross — ? approaching it exactly as the altar-boy, taper in hand, approaches the unlighted candles on the altar?

"Only a few more nights, old House!"

"You betrayed me."

"Only a few more nights, old House!"

"Betrayed me, betrayed me. Left me alone for five years of war. Roofless and windowless, open to the rain from the Channel, the foam from Ushant, the blown sleet from the Weald of Kent. Betrayed me!"

And D. could hear, in the folded interval between past and future, and therefore as if timeless, someone running down that cobbled street, the Strand, at half-past four in the morning: walking fast, then beginning to run again, running no doubt down towards the telephone kiosk at the foot of the hill, by the wet weighbridge. For a doctor? Someone was dying at this inconvenient hour? After all this gale, too? No, more likely it was the fisherman's apprentice, late for his duty at Strand Quay, where he must report for duty on the Girl Vine, of Newhaven, to catch the half-tide for a Sunday's fishing in the bay. Plaice, robin huss, skate, sand-dabs, and a conger eel brought home perhaps for his own dinner. And the night's gale, now spent, had dropped a starling's nest from a cornice of the Dolphin Inn, the evicted starlings whizzing off in the dark towards the castle on the marsh, or to be lost at sea beyond the salt shingle of Dungeness, where once the footsteps of John Keats had crunched. Those Quarter-Boys again, with their everlasting imitation of a ship's bells, now striking the eight, the hour — *ting-tang, ting-tang, ting-tang, ting-tang* — in their dark porch, facing towards the dark sundial on the opposite wall, facing also the inscription which it was their duty to annotate: *Tempus edax rerum.* For our life is a very shadow that passeth away. At this minute, just beyond the edge of the churchyard and its yew, bow-legged hatchet-faced Mrs. Ffykes perhaps turned over in the soft bed, and dreamed again of a buzz-bomb. The millionaire American in St. Eustace's, on the next corner, turned over also, and dreamed of a Wall Street crash, and the inevitable repercussions in Lombard Street. And the little wry-necked Vicar — what did *he* dream of? Incense and holy water invading the sacred precincts?

Down the stoop at Savannah D. had stepped towards this, was again stepping towards this, leaving the funeral wreaths and purple ribbons on the door behind him, a copy of *Jackanapes* in his hand, and the epigraph from *Tom Brown's School Days* in his head. "I'm the poet of White Horse Vale, sir, with Liberal notions under my cap!" The White Horse was galloping over the moonless downs towards the Long Man of Wilmington, all night was galloping, and the Long Man awaited him on his own chalk hillside, silent, motionless, staff in hand — but would they ever join, as they should? would they ever join? — or had the White Horse really moved at all? did anything move at all — ?

I I

———— up from his cabin, his sea-gown scarfed
about him, sea-wind in his hair and eyes and
ears, the sea-roll under his feet, as now these
many years, this lifetime; for the seal's wide spindrift gaze at
eternity, or the lesser gaze of consciousness into the tumultu-
ous past of one's own Gulf Stream, pouring its eastward way
through the confusion of one's own sea, the everlasting thesis and
antithesis — for yet another view, outward as well as inward, the
two forever harmoniously or discordantly working as coefficients of
each other, the rim of the one enclosed geometrically and lucently
within the other — up from Cabin 144 again, where the locked
porthole sang mutely against the sea, and the stale ribbons fluttered
in stale air from the twinned blank eyeballs of the ventilators; while
Hardie slept, exhausted, the spots of his blood still staining the
porcelain edge of the wash-basin, and, in the bunk below him,
Cavan, with patient hands, fanned away the flies from the sleeping
face of his infant granddaughter, to and from, slowly, to and fro,
while the child's mother had her breakfast of kippers in the dining
saloon — and Blimp intoned, Blimp monologued, Blimp smoked
and reminisced, lived his life over again for them all, set out from
Surrey to London, from London to Canada, from Canada to Cleveland, there to make his way, to make his fortune, manufacturing
trumpets, slide-trombones, bugles, French horns, oboes — his art

learned in the brass-foundry, the chandelier factory, in London —

"And now take babies," he had intoned — "take babies, this child here, lying so quiet and peaceful — you would think, yes you would, that they're not intelligent: but you'd be wrong, babies are more intelligent than dogs; that's right, that's what they say — babies are very intelligent. No, you can't get around them, no sir, you can't. Comical too, they are sometimes! There's our little Susie, at home in Cleveland, she's my grandchild; and let me try to hide behind the pages of my paper in the evening, when I'm reading, you know, why, I don't fool her for a moment, up come the little hands! Yes, and if we turn on the radio, my how she loves that — hangs on to the two dials, she does, and dances — one foot up, one foot down — and laughs! Oh, how she laughs! — "

"O aye de aye de O. . . . God-damn, god-damn, god-damn — "

"No, let 'em sleep, in the morning kids is drowsy-eyed. . . . Now get up, my honey."

"You say you lived at Faversham?"

"Sure I lived at Faversham."

"You know the Garretts?"

"The Garretts? Sure, Jack Garrett."

"That's right, Jack Garrett. He got married. He married Louise Baker. You know the Bakers there?"

"Sure I know the Bakers."

"Well, I was born in Epping Forest. At Chingford, in Chingford Forest. Yes, and our swimming pool was the Lee. . . ."

"Come on, honey — come on, darling — and if you wake your brother I'll take the whip to you. This morning, you're going to — "

"God-damn — god-damn — that little ship, she's got *twooooooo* chimneys — ! — "

"Yes, we're going to keep you on the top line — "

"Naw — "

"We're going to keep you on the top line — "

"That's right, send him to school up there — "

"Naw — "

"You're going to see Jesus Christ this morning!"

—— to and fro, the patient human hand, waving off the persistent flies, while the child slept, and Hardie slept, and Blimp, now a little beginning to lose his paralyzing hold on his audience, sat in the camp chair and traversed past and present and future with oracular solemnity —

"Yes, sir, that bloody cockroach had climbed right into the bunk with me — and when I went back to get into bed — you know, I can't go very long at night, about three hours, that's all, after my operation — there it was, flattened out where I'd been laying on it, dead as a kippered herring. They ought to teach them to dance to music, they seem to love company."

—— up from the cabin, the sea-gown scarfed about him, past the deserted Troop Reception Room (Seating Capacity 300), the battered piano standing silent on the silent and empty platform, the rows of chairs vacantly facing it — and one could have a play here — ? a minstrel show? the always-recurring dialogue between Dr. Quicksand and Mr. Tattletale, instead of Mr. Bones and Interlocutor — or Dr. Saltpetre? the two untiring disputants of the human soul, hammer and tongs, negative and positive, the silent one who hides and secretes in order that his opponent, the talebearer, should be incensed into yet wilder outbursts of orotund and confessional eloquence, to ever more exalted flights of shamelessness —

—— and then, in the glare of the deck, the sparkle of fine spray, but with that phrase, that line, brought up from sleep and dream, out of the remote but still turbulent and rebellious past, that ghost, that unappeased ghost —

Your ghost will walk, you lover of trees! —

. . . The fragment of verse, itself blown downwind from an

almost forgotten fragment of past, torn from a forgotten poem, intervened here in sunlight like a fiat from the hand of creation. And God said let there be a firmament in the midst of the waters, and let it divide the waters from the waters. That was what the yellow leaf of verse said, borne down from the wooded hillside at Troutbeck Bridge, over the stone shoulder of the little chapel above the inn. On Sundays, the naked bell was not in the least English (as D. had mentioned many times to Chapman); it was an American train setting out for a trial run through the Lake District, with pauses for observation and lunch at all points of scenic or poetic interest. Wordsworth's Seat, Dove Cottage, Rydal Mount, Greta Fall — the daffodils, dancing on the immaculate lawns beside Rydal Water — the precious golden pollen of the past — all this was to be caught up in the brash American present. But was it true, as someone has said, that Wordsworth had first written the line as "I wandered lonely as a *cow* — ?" It was entertaining to think so; and certainly not wholly out of character, if one bore in mind such a poem as Martha Raye, to take an instance. For dear William, dear as he was (and in some ways the dearest, the little red volume of verse had indeed been D.'s *vade mecum* on that bicycle trip through Ariel's Island) dear William sometimes nodded; and alas, when he nodded, he snored.

Your ghost will walk, you lover of trees —

The yellow leaf, borne downwind, blown out of its careful album in the past, was of course Lorelei's, the beautiful young Lorelei's; it was her message; and if it brought with it the sound of the little brook, the Troutbeck, from the moist English mountainside, murmuring its way politely down to Lake Windermere, it brought also the remembered playing of Lorelei at the piano, there in the rain-dark hotel room — Debussy's Arabesque, and the Golliwog's Cakewalk. And the sound of trees in autumn, both English and American, their sounds and colors, the autumnal earth-cry of the deciduous, the dying, these too now spoke again in the solitary little verse.

And it was right, that she should thus speak her reminder, or speak it with this particular symbol: they had first encountered under the scarlet maples on the little imitation "Chinese Landscape" hill that overlooked Fresh Pond, in Cambridge, Massachusetts; these had set the key, these and the pink-blue, blue-pink stars of wild chicory which grew all round the poor little house in Cambridge where later they had lived (so greatly to Aunt Sybil's distress) on the wrong side of the tracks. Yes, from the very outset their long walk together had been autumnal, an October walk, through crackling drifts of leaves, the dust of leaves, under skies which already sparkled with the ghost of frost: it was as if they had all along known that there was a premature cold to come. Bare boughs, the shadow of unsuccess, the loss of innocence, but without the acquisition of wisdom, as if youth itself had become wrinkled — it was the beginning, in fact, of things that would *never* be finished, poems, loves, lives, books — it had seemed from very early, perhaps always, to be in the very principle of things, or at any rate in himself, that nothing should ever be truly completed. It was like that first of all his books, at Savannah, the serial by Henty, which patiently, week after week, he had clipped from the Sunday paper, pasted on to small sheets, and, binding it clumsily together with glue, tried to make into a semblance of a book, in a deep sense feeling he was thus somehow *making* a book. Why had he lost all interest in it? It had simply disappeared.

The bright little symbol now linked all these disparate things together: even here at sea in the wide empty sun-dazzle, on the blown boat-deck in the early-morning light; the long light that lay low along the south, a silver sun-dazzle mottled in streaks on the far grey of the jagged-edged sea. The white-painted thermo tanks, each working solitarily and secretly by itself, chirped like birds as they

worked, twittered like birds, the song of sea-air joining in the loud
continuous chorus of the sea; while at the far end of the sloping
deck, above the rattling companionway, little Geordie appeared for
a moment, little genius Geordie, accompanied as always by the
diminutive, fur-coated, sparrow-legged English governess, Miss
Nyrie. Thin-legged, the fur coat muffled up to her chin, only the
pink nose-tip showing, she strode lightly away out of sight, — with
what thoughts of homecoming, after all these years in Vancouver?
— while beautiful little Geordie danced after and around her,
thinking with his hands, with his eyes, with his mouth (that sensitive cleft-palate mouth), with the whole electric little body: here
was genius revolving around courage. She had taken his hand in
hers, bending affectionately to say something to him, the profile
grave and sensitive (at the same time ingoing and outgoing, D.
thought), and out of what she was inaudibly saying, one could see
him in the very act of creating — imaginatively — a vast and wonderful and invisible world.

"Star-scrapers — !" he had said — "yes, I'm going to build star-
scrapers! They will be high enough to scrape the stars! They'll be
better than skyscrapers!"

The leaf-symbol of verse out of the past brought them all together, syncopated all things; leaf-symbol and tree-symbol; that
tree-symbol which Jacob had commented on before. Why this tree,
this perpetual tree? *Your ghost will walk, you lover of trees* — but
the next line was gone, nothing now was left but perhaps a faint,
far, and slightly stagey suggestion of moonlight. And of course the
magic of that particular autumn, that rain, the walks in the drifting
veils of rain, to Bowness, to Ambleside, to Grasmere, to Kirkstone
Pass.

"Who pays to ride up Kirkstone Pass, he surely is an arrant ass.
He'll find, in spite of all their talking, he'll have to walk, and pay
for walking."

58

But again, all this, even this halcyon pause with Lorelei, was itself not only a double-exposure, but a triple-exposure. For not only had he first gone there himself, with Ebo, on the first of the bicycle tours, and again returned to it alone after parting with dear Ebo in the middle of Scotland, at Persey Bridge, after the quarrel (ah, that fantastic quarrel); but also he had been there again on his way to London, the first visit to London, with Heinrich, and yet again two years later, this time bringing — all the way from Florence — Chapman, the first English friend, who was to be to D. what Squanto had been to the Pilgrims at Plymouth, that fabulous Indian who, as he had spent two years in Cornhill, and spoke a little genuine Cockney, became their guide and interpreter. And to be able thus to take an Englishman to a corner of England unknown to himself, to one's own private little discovery, the unspoilt hamlet with its unspoilt inn, where still the coaches stopped to water the six splendid horses (and for the coachman's pint of 'arf-an'-'arf) before they drove glittering away to Windermere or Keswick, this had contributed perhaps the first and most important of the psychological "joins" which were gradually to bind him, more and more deeply and secretly and securely, to that island which he had learned, as a child, was where poets and heroes came from: Ariel's Island, the island of Goose Green in *Jackanapes,* and the customs office in Hawthorne's *Our Old Home,* and the poet of White Horse Vale. The island, too, of *Bleak House, Nicholas Nickleby, Great Expectations* — above all, the island which contained, and radiated from, London, and of all the books which evoked the magic and dark wonderful mystery of unknown London, the city of cities. The Beloved Uncle had gone there; he had bicycled through the story-book country, over the high-arched stone bridges, through villages of thatched cottages and Constable trees; and, no doubt, past Goose Green itself and its duck-pond; and thus at last to the great city, and to Gray's Inn.

59

"The trouble with me" — years later D. was to say to Chapman; and in Gray's Inn, too, it had been, where they had gone for an evening of pianola music with the Noble Lord — "the trouble with ME is, that I fell in love with an island. I'm the unhappy man who fell in love with an island, when he was too young to know better. Incurably, hopelessly, and fatuously, in love."

"England?"

"England. And how neatly it explains everything. Exonerates all. Very handy, don't you think — ? All those 'love-messes,' as forthright Laura so felicitously called them: all the infidelities: the pattern of instability, restlessness, dissatisfaction: the remarkable inability to remain faithful to any of the beautiful Loreleis, or the minor Loreliebchens in between — for what chance did *they* have, poor darlings? — yes, it explains all. For if your own true love is an island, your mother, your alma, your soul, what's left with which you can attach yourself to a mere beautiful woman? Tenuous and feeble at best. Off you go again, if only to see if the precious image is still there, and still what you thought it was; and sure enough, it is; and then you resent it, for that involves an infidelity to — the father, perhaps? So back you go once more, agonized, to measure the shoreline of Long Island, or the wooden houses of Staten Island, or the skyscrapers of New York, against the pale sunshot headlands of Eastbourne, the red roofs and chimney-pots of Liverpool, the ghostly samphire-gatherer cliffs of Dover. . . ."

Insoluble, unsolvable, the chord suspended — was it never to find resolution?

It had done much, too, to explain the unsuccess, of which the practical Lorelei had justly been so critical: for if one perpetually shifted from one country to another, one job to another, one field of endeavor to another, where was the *Ding an sich* to come from, the soluble bread and jam for the sticky little mouths, and the schoolbooks for the grubby little hands, not to mention the pretty little bootees for the pink little feet? What would happen to the three little D.'s? A life of casual reporting, one minute the American correspondent for an English journal, the next the English correspondent for an American journal — it had been something unpleasantly resembling adultery. The interminable piecework, too, the ill-paid hackwork, the articles, the reviews, the bad short stories; a desperate year of teaching, at which he had been a complete failure, another desperate year engaged on the most improbable undertakings for the WPA's heroic if somewhat misguided efforts towards a grand guidebook to America — at a day's notice an essay on the architecture of Cambridge, the music and drama of New England, even an expedition to Deerfield, to savor in a few winter hours the history of three hundred years — three crystal centuries of spiritual ecstasy and heartbreak vulgarized in as many paragraphs — the record indeed looked shameful. It had been at best a series of somewhat sordid and discontinuous improvisations, with only now and then the saving grace of disinterested service to — when circumstance, alas, permitted, by which one meant one's own weakness — "truth," "beauty," and "man." Oh well, not that, in justice to oneself, one had not had one's moments, and still hadn't! Perhaps in fact one could even say that any life, in the upshot, was in measurable degree an adulterous improvisation — the precarious gait of experience. But set against this the heroic simplicity of grandfather's life, that essential goodness and singlemindedness, his devotion to the ultimate, as well to the immediate, interests of all mankind, and anything else looked compromised and cowardly. That marble bust in the church at New Bedford, which faced across at Emerson's, but appeared to disregard it, was a reminder. Since then, goodness had been sacrificed to ingenuity, simplicity to what was not even success; the family was as good as dead. Was there, among the grandchildren, or the great-grandchildren, anyone really worthy of that stature? How typical of this decay, so general in New England, that even the family woodlot at Dartmouth, the profits of which the Beloved Uncle had been in the habit of sharing with him, had been put up for sale for taxes; and that when he had travelled thither with Lorelei Three and the Beautiful Cousin, to inquire into the question of saving it, he had found there, at the Town Office, a letter — addressed to his mother, and to Savannah — and she now dead these fifty years! A dead letter indeed; and dead acreage, too. Cut over, burned over, surrounded by impassable swamps and thickets of bullbrier and poison ivy, where not even the blueberry could grow, the land was useless and inaccessible, there was no longer even a road into it, and he had let it go. For three hundred years the family of farmers and yeomen had cut their wood there, and now it was gone. Their ghosts, and their beloved trees, alike were gone.

Troutbeck Bridge.

The road to that, at the time, had seemed random and circuitous, but as a matter of fact it had been no such thing. What indeed could have been more completely logical? One could now recapitulate every step towards it, recognize every signpost and fingerpost. From Cousin Maud in New Bedford, the great lady of the family, much-travelling Cousin Maud, for whom the opera season at Heidelberg was as accessible and familiar as County Street, or Beacon Hill, or Washington Square; from rich, fabulous, mannish Cousin Maud had come as a Christmas Present for D. the copy of *Jackanapes*, and the necessity, therefore, for eventually making one's way to Goose Green. And from her, too, had come a second book, much larger, and with many more pictures, but just as unmistakably and alluringly English, which completed the influence of the first: for this wonderful book made it absolutely inevitable that if one ever wanted to see for oneself, in all its dreadfulness, the Slough of Despond, or, after doing so, climb the Delectable Mountains, then naturally one would have to go to England. After those two magical volumes, every other book that even so much as mentioned England added to the already overwhelming probability that not only would one sooner or later *go* there, but that very likely one would want to *stay* there. And if Hawthorne saw to it that one took ship for Liverpool, Wordsworth and De Quincey insisted on one's then going north to Coniston, Hawkshead, and Grasmere, and Burns that one should press on to Dumfries and Ayr. And the little rain-dark inn at Troutbeck Bridge had at once become pivotal in the adventure. In that projected *reductio ad absurdum* of one's life in terms of "rooms, streets, and houses," an analysis of life in terms of environment; this inn by the bridge, with its bowling green, and wrestling green, and the stone chapel on the hill above it, and its long plaster front, flush with the road (which always smelled of horse-stale, where the coaches stopped), this unpretentious little inn had become central. It had been a first love.

For one thing, on his return from Persey Bridge, he had been all alone there, and had been thoroughly spoiled by the whole family: this young American, from Harvard, who rode his bicycle (with a loaf of bread strapped in a hat on the carrier) by day, or climbed mountains, or swam in the lake, and read Shakspere over his pint of half-and-half in the evening, was to all intents adopted by them. After that, to go to England was simply to return to Troutbeck Bridge, to find out what had happened in the interval, and settle down. The mountains had all been climbed, the Delectable Mountains: Dollywaggon Pike, Langdale Pikes, Helvellyn, Fairfield — most wonderful of all was that long day spent in making the whole horseshoe tour of Fairfield. The waterfalls had all been visited; Shakspere had all been read. The twenty-five-cent copy of Palgrave's *Golden Treasury* was worn out. And by now he was a part of the scene there, even to partaking in its changes. The meadow, where in the first autumn he had watched the mowing contest, the long line of mowers advancing abreast into the field, the blades flashing in unison, was the next year a green for wrestling, wrestling Cumberland Style, the men locking their hands in the small of each other's backs, and working slowly and subtly and powerfully for the sudden astonishing *dénouement,* and one of them off the ground and kicking into the air. And the year after that, again, it had become a bowling green, a thing of extraordinary beauty. And similarly he had shared in the changes of the family itself. The old father had been the first to die: a year later, the mother, whose Westmoreland accent had always completely defeated him. Then the son and daughter took over, Jack and Alice, Alice, with whom, although she was considerably older than himself, he had thought himself just a little bit in love.

A little bit in love—? Well, not exactly!

No: it was simply the earliest occasion when he had experienced recognizably a definite desire, a definite lech, for a "mature" woman, but without much more than what the chemists call a "trace" of the process of falling in love. How old, exactly, had she been — ? Hard to say, but probably twenty-four or -five when he had first gone there, and was himself nineteen; and exceedingly attractive; warm dark eyes, dark hair, a rosy complexion, slight, graceful, a demure country miss; but jolly, too, and with a sly sense of humor. Her hands — yes, she had had quite beautiful hands, and a quite beautiful forehead. But he had not been in love with her, no, he had merely hoped, timidly — oh yes, that timidity — and without the least notion of attempting to do anything about it, that *she* would somehow make the overtures, whatever fantastic form they might take, and that he would at long last lose his oh so troublesome virginity. What he had really, and ardently, hoped, in fact, was that one night she would all suddenly and beautifully and naturally appear, without a word, in his room. And that there, in this room which he always took, at the back, on the lane, to the

sound of the little brook placidly chuckling its way to Lake Windermere, he would be deliciously seduced. The fantasies about this
had been endless and absorbing; they started every morning at
breakfast — the scones, the tea, the trout, the jams — which she
served him in the little fusty private dining-room, under the ugly
stained-glass windows and the aspidistras; they accompanied him
all day on his expeditions. They had been given a new violence and
vividness after his abrupt encounter with the couple copulating
under a tree, on the far side of Lake Windermere, one morning: he
had shot round the bend of the road so quickly on his bicycle that
there was no time for them to make any the slightest pretense of
being engaged in anything else: a quick movement to pull down an
edge of the skirt, but ineffectual, and that was all. Not that there
was any need for them to conceal anything, for he himself, in the
shock of discovery, the dismay, the excitement, even the horror, had
not dared to look again. He had pedaled on without so much as
glancing back, his heart hammering. And now, to those fevers of
longing which had tormented him for seven years, or eight, or nine,
and the guilt and shame which were the inevitable accompaniments
of their indulgence, was at last added an image. He now knew,
quite appallingly, quite deliriously, what it looked like. It would
be — if she did come to his room at midnight — like that, with
Alice. Like that, with Alice.

But although this enthralling fantasy travelled with him all the
way back to Harvard in the autumn, and returned with him to
Troutbeck again in the summer, nothing had ever come of it. There
had been no tremulous little midnight knocks at his door, much
less a savage battering *à la* Faubion, as on the last night of *that* voyage years later; and only, instead, the miserably and humiliating
adventure of the travelling salesman.

O dear god, that travelling salesman. And the shame of it all,
which was to keep its redness and soreness for years!

For one morning, over the breakfast things, there in what had bè-
come his private dining-room, Alice had let it be known, very
lightly, very casually, that — had he heard? — they had "another
American" staying with them; and would he care to meet him?
How wonderfully tactful and civilized the English were, about
such things! The "other" American was, of course, at this minute,
having *his* breakfast in solitude in the "other" breakfast-room, across
the tiled corridor. And what could one do but say yes? Yes, he had
said yes. And in, presently, came the auto salesman from Detroit,
with the entire equipment in those days considered *de rigueur*: the
cap, the goggles, the dust-colored coat that came to the heels, the
yellow gauntlets, everything. He was selling cars, he said, in this
god-awful country, he was a pioneer in an unenlightened land,
where they didn't even understand English; it was worse than
France; he had been as far north as Glasgow and Edinburgh, and
had sold a few cars, and seen a few things, god help him; and now
he was killing time till his boat sailed from Liverpool.

A fine, dreadful, and in its way highly instructive and fructifying day had ensued. Yes — D. considered — it was probably
true, if a little perplexing, as Dawson had said (on the Ultonia,
formerly the Polynesian or Rocking Polly), that he was "over-
civilized," and needed a little shocking: Dawson had done his best
to contribute, too, as in that unforgettable description of the flooded
Ohio as a sort of gliding galantine of dead pigs and dogs. But that
considered attempt to shock was as nothing compared to the quite
naïve frontal assault, unrehearsed and unsuspecting, of the auto
salesman from Detroit. A few years older in years, but a hard long
lifetime older in experience, vulgar, vivid, unperceptive, go-getting,
everything, but above all so happily unperceptive and assured as to
credit D. also with just such unperceptiveness and assurance and
experience, he had outpoured the tale of his erotic adventures and
conquests and defeats (if he was indeed defeatable) in Europe

66

and America with the blandest of assumptions that such things were commonplace, that D. must himself have been engaged for years in a precisely similar activity, and that it was, it went without saying, of paramount importance, in the establishment of any acquaintance between them, that they must get down to it at once. America and *France*, he had at once amended; but Christ, this England was something else again. Christ, what were these English women made of! Of course, in London, there were the whores, all round Russell Square and Leicester Square, and that was all right, if you liked whores; but what the hell were you supposed to do in the country? — in this god-forgotten *country?* This was all day the theme, as fascinating as alarming to D., who with some difficulty had managed to keep up appearances as a worthy competitor in these matters, while they drove to Carlisle for lunch, and toured east towards the Pennines, and homeward again in the evening for the usual choice of beef or lamb for dinner. It was the theme of the dinner as well. And why not, right this minute, do something about it? Yes, by Christ, they would, they would go out and *do* something about it. They would finish their beer and do something about it. If you could use a car to pick up girls in the U. S., why couldn't you do it here — ?

And so the all-too-justifiably apprehensive D. had been hauled off for a yet further drive, this time to Ambleside, just at twilight, when the girls were taking a last stroll along the road, in ones and twos and threes; and the auto salesman from Detroit, dazzlingly outlandish in that paraphernalia of his, drove past the groups at a snail's pace, or even stopped beside them, and, all unaware of international differences in such *mores,* or protocol, unabashedly addressed himself to one terrified English girl after another. None of them had replied with a single word: they had been simply speechless with astonishment and fright: they had jumped like rabbits, had all but flung themselves through the hawthorn hedgerows and into the fields. One of them, putting her handkerchief to her mouth, and staring at them over this with eyes the size of dollars, had then simply *run*.

The defeat was sufficiently convincing: it was overwhelming; but the auto salesman from Detroit, now angrier than ever, was not to be so easily downed. They would try again; and they did. The smart Packard roadster, its lights angrily combing the hedges, was turned around and headed once more for Grasmere, but to no avail. It was getting dark, the girls were fewer, and if anything more alarmed than the others had been. The salesman's discomfiture was now final; they had had to give up; and of course D.'s relief — he had been genuinely frightened, lest a complaint should be made, and they might find the police awaiting them in Ambleside on their way back — was profound. But also it was ambiguous; for a very real part of his fear had been lest they actually *succeed* in their singularly candid chase, and find themselves suddenly with a brace of young women on their hands. What would happen then — ? He had been certain that he would disgrace himself by inadvertently disclosing his complete inexperience and incompetence; not to say shyness; he would himself have been just as frightened as those poor girls had been. Just the same, the notion had its appalling attractiveness. And even if one had fumbled the event, one would have learned something, something, too, of what one so desperately *wanted* to learn: for better or worse, one would have approached the sacred mystery, never again to be quite the same.

But it was not to be. That adventure, and that discovery, were to be reserved for the later meeting in Leicester Square with dear Irene, pretty Irene, Irene in a white muslin dress, her small black patent-leather slippers vivid beside the blues and greens of the pavement artist's drawings on the flagstones, and the pavement artist's shabby cap. And the discomfited auto salesman from Detroit had driven home, now more than ever emphatic in his dislike of England. Christ, what a place! His disgust became comprehensive and mellifluous. It was almost as scathing and searching as, years later, that of John, reporting tennis at Wimbledon, when, looking down between matches from an embrasured window in the arcade, and studying the "form," as he put it, he had suddenly observed, shaking his head: "My dear D., when you look at these English women, *en masse* like this, not only those bloody dresses and shoes, but what's *in* them, the whole god-damned sexless phenomenon, you find yourself wondering how the British race manages to propagate itself! You really do."

The auto salesman from Detroit had been almost as sweeping. The French were a hell of a lot better. Yes, the French were better. But even the French — well, Christ, he had picked up a little French girl on the Channel boat, going over, and come down a week later with a damned fine dose of clap. Had to go to the doctor in Paris. Which had turned out all to the good, as a matter of fact, for that French doctor knew his business; they probably all did, they certainly ought to, but anyway he certainly had some wonderful stuff. Came in a tube. Had D. ever had a dose? No? Well, he would, sooner or later, Christ, a man wasn't a man until he's had at least half a dozen doses, that was god's truth. Yes, that stuff was wonderful. Cured him in a few days — four days, by god. And this — alas — had led in turn to his presenting D. with a spare tube of the miraculous ointment, an impressive green tube, with a French label, in an impressive green box; which, when he was leaving, a week later, after the salesman's departure, he had simply not known what to do with. Why in heaven's name had he not simply taken it out one day, on a ride to Ullswater or wherever, and skimmed it over a hedge, behind a rock, into the heather, the gorse, anywhere — ? He had not been very bright. No, instead, heaven help him — and how characteristic of his lifelong stupidity and incompetence, the panicky indecision in any crisis, no matter

how small, which had again and again precipitated just such fol-
lies (it was perhaps an aspect of the family *petit mal,* or whatever,
his own little queer share of the family inheritance) — instead, on
the last morning, he had merely dropped it in the bottom drawer
of his chest of drawers, hoping — fatuous hope — that Alice, when
she cleaned the room, would not notice it; or that it would escape
attention for long enough so that other guests would have come
and gone, and it would therefore remain unknown just which one
had left it. Folly indeed; for as he well knew, if only on the evidence of the register in the lobby — that highly poetic register,
full of encomiums of the scones, the trout, the jam, and of course
the many-times-repeated "home from home" — the number of
guests in any summer was always small, perhaps no more than half
a dozen. And the likelihood of anyone else being put into that particular room, during the remnant of the season, was practically nil.
Alice would see it, Alice would find it. But would she know what
it was? He had tried to hope that she wouldn't, but of course he
knew better. In any event, if she showed it to Jack — dear god, the
whole thing had become such a nightmare that for a long time he
thought it would be impossible ever to go to Troutbeck again.
What would they have thought of him? Of course, the tube had
been *unused* — he had pinned a sort of forlorn hope to this. But
that he should have had it at all! — And would they have been
sufficiently imaginative to guess that, after all, it must have been
given to him by that queer auto salesman, who was so very *different,*
a different *kind* of American, wasn't he? — But no, it was no good,
and he had known it. He would have to hope that they would forget
all about it, or somehow attach no importance to it. It had been a
disaster.

Your ghost will walk —

Contrapuntal with this, then — and had it been even in the same
little back room? — was the autumnal honeymoon, with Lorelei

One, the sound of the Chopin Mazurka tinkling on the bad yellow-keyed piano against the mournful soft continuum of English rain: contrapuntal with this, and of course with the somewhat raucous visit there with Chapman. Two years had elapsed after the episode of the auto salesman from Detroit. Perhaps his alarm about that egregious tube had scared him off, or was at any rate an obscure part of his motivation in deciding that summer to go instead to New York — there to live in a fine, slum boardinghouse near the Twenty-third Street Ferry, by the corner of Death Avenue. Death Avenue, and the slow freight train clanking along the waterfront, preceded by the man on a horse, with his red flag. And the bedbugs, and the free lunch across the way, and the visits from the old painter, Yeats, who invariably, when asked if he was the father of the great Yeats, replied, "*I* am the great Yeats!" Yes, perhaps the visit to New York had been truly an evasion; what on earth could one want, as an undergraduate, with a summer vacation in New York? Well, no — that was not quite to do it justice. There had been other recognizable motives, and logical enough they had been. The Shelley and Keats and Coleridge diseases had been more or less survived, he was beginning to be convalescent from them; now it was the turn of the "city" celebrants, Whitman most notably, but with some attention too to such minor and different devotees as John Davidson and Henley. The city, the city — he had had his first taste of London, the two weeks with Heinrich after his ignominious retreat from Troutbeck, and in Gray's Inn; but the summer in New York was the first real revel in it, the first saturation, and with old Walt, naturally, as guide. "Bussing my body all over with soft balsamic *omni*busses," Tinck had misquoted it. But it was true, too — there was unquestionably an element of evasion, he had really wanted to go to Troutbeck; he had a little funked it; just as in the succeeding year he had funked the prospect of being class poet, but so rightly; and making an excuse of the Dean's injustice to him over a matter of cutting lectures, and of an ethereal piece of self-deception *à propos* his broken-hearted love for hoyden-ish Anita, he had set sail for Naples.

Curious: but the more he thought of it the more he saw it to be true that it was not Harvard that was the center of his life while he was there, but the places to which he could escape from Harvard. Like the school in the country outside Concord, it was a necessity, a duty; delightful, novel, and even exciting; the four years at each were as various as enriching; but from the other point of view, that of "rooms, streets, and houses," neither had itself been spiritually central. No, from Concord, for all its Hawthorne and Emerson associations, and its undeniable small magic — the overgrown stone gates and the century-old lilacs and apple-trees — from Concord it had been to New Bedford, or Cambridge, or Watertown, or Duxbury, that he had been drawn, to the houses of the two uncles, to grandmother's at Watertown (where the only silver-rod grew), and to Cousin Maud's at New Bedford, or Cousin Lew's. Was this one of the effects of having been orphaned, and further orphaned by the adoption of R. and K. by Cousin Ted? Was it all quite simply the need of, and search for, a home? a sustaining, but above all *uninstitutional*, locus of one's own? Yes, there was no doubt about it. And for that reason there had been no room at the school to which he could now look back with anything like affection or nostalgia, it was only the birch woods that he thought of there with pleasure, and the Tarpeian Rock below the little pond, the hillside apple orchards, the cider-mill, the wild flowers and juniper beyond the haunted house, and along with these, and in its way more treasured still, the playing field, from which he even now kept, in the body's memory, the feel of baseball and football, of cleats in the stiff half-frozen turf, and the effect of northwest wind, in the spring, on a pitched ball. And the Five Friends, the five boys of genius! — Only from these did he turn away to bicycle towards

Cambridge or Duxbury, along the Concord Turnpike, or in winter take the one-horse sleigh to Concord and the train, with any regret. For in that period it was to "the houses" that he moved, as by a compulsory tropism, to the houses and the dear people who lived in them, the "family." These had become, as it were, the explorable outlying regions of his own changing person, in its experimental journey from one insecurity to another.

As now, on this sunlit boat-deck, with the immediate "ha!" of the Atlantic loud about him, the intermingled roar of wave and iron and wind, the wind slapping hard ropes against the sides of the motor-lifeboats, while the discreet little thermo-tanks kept up their chirping chorus; these explorations too had been voyages; or at any rate the beginnings of voyage. There was always the something that must be left, the something else that one set forth to find, whatever the reasons might be. Were they always, and invariably, forced moves, as in chess? Was it compulsory, for instance, for Blimp, old Blimp who was almost eighty, to start out once more to revisit England and the scenes of his childhood — to pat the nieces and nephews on the head, give them each a half pound of sugar, and try to find the foundry, in London, where he had served his apprenticeship? Was there any choice? None for Hardie, to be sure: he might deny it, but there was none. He must take his children to Faversham, and die. Or if there was any choice, ever, it was in the *how*, merely; and the elements in the *why* remained for the most part as unknown as unchallenged. The voyages from Concord to New Bedford, more clearly than any others, had been all too patently passages to the "more than India" of a lost childhood; or, to be more precise, to a social orientation *lost* in childhood.

Involved in these approaches, too, had been the apparent, the increasingly apparent, need of the family to exorcise its guilt towards him: and for himself to assist them in this. Bandied about from one relative to another, from aunt to uncle to cousin, and for a decade

73

therefore more at home in school or college than in any corner of any house, he had become for the entire family an embarrassing symbol, a reminder, the something that had been sacrificed: each of them, it now appeared, felt secretly that he or she should have done a little more about it, each now had at all times the air of wanting to apologize, to make him more than ever welcome, to make him feel that he belonged, that he was at home. As embarrassing to himself as to them; and he too in turn felt apologetic, as if his very existence was a sort of admitted, or unadmitted, nuisance, and a source of distress on all sides. He had felt the need of mitigating this, and had cultivated the art of the tentative approach, as well as that of the casual disappearance: he was both there and not there: he would not stay too long, or move too close, or presume too much, lest both he and they should feel that he was encroaching. Fugitive, therefore, had been the method, a light alternation of dropping in and dropping out, with quick alternations too of scene, so that, as with a skater on bending ice, his weight should nowhere remain too long at one point. If one could arrange for one's conduct, *vis-à-vis* the family and the family friends and circle, a "musical" technique, as of hail and farewell, the greeting followed by the affectionate exchange of news and then the not-a-moment-too-long-delayed farewell and disappearance, then the family guilt about it, and his own, would be so equally distributed and shared as perhaps eventually to vanish without comment. Unless, of course, by some miracle, at whatever point, the conspiracy of silence should at last be broken, and the whole lamentable burden, the burden for all of them — for Aunt Sibyl, for the Beloved Uncle, for the Frightened Uncle and for Aunt Deena, and of course for the New Bedford contingent as well — be looked at *en plein soleil*, and laughed at by the whole family, as by the chorus in a Greek tragedy, and so dispersed forever.

Which, to be sure, was exactly what happened. And, as perhaps no one had foreseen, it had come about through the peculiar psychological chemistry of family acting upon family, the slow, conscious, absorption of D. into them, and of them into D.; so slow, indeed, that no one of them (unless it was Aunt Sibyl) had at the time really seen it happening. Out of the fugitive arrivals and departures in that beautiful dance of rooms, streets, and houses, through the various lights and shades of the varying and recurring seasons, the holiday visits from school or college, the unannounced returns from Troutbeck Bridge or Glasgow or New York, whether to Aunt Deena's suburban Ladies' Home Journal monstrosity of a house in Cambridge (she had nevertheless provided an attic room for him, with built-in window-seats and bookshelves), or to Cousin Lew's first, second, or third houses in New Bedford (and alas, that drama, that downfall, of *hubris*), or to the earlier of Aunt Sibyl's creations in Cambridge, or the later, both of them enchanting, but the later the one that was to become supremely his own, his chair by the fire, his hearth, his heart — out of this contrapuntal succession of salutations and explorations, precisely and punctually as it had been at Cuernavaca with Hambo, watching the lightning-flash flirtation of the hummingbird and the banana blossom, the flight-and-return vigil, with its ultimate reward, when at last the great voluptuous and fleshly blossom had disclosed its secret, its hidden honey, to be probed with bliss — out of this had at last come the moment, whether with the Beloved Uncle or Aunt Sibyl it was now difficult to remember, when the admission had at last been made, the fact so long avoided at last stated.

"Of course we felt that you were never treated fairly. No, you were never fairly treated, you didn't get a square deal. But what were we to do, what could have been done — ? Where was the money to come from, who was to look after you? how take care of three orphaned children, with not a penny anywhere to be seen? You can see how it was. A decision had to be made, and quickly.

And then came Cousin Ted's offer to take Wide and Handsome, which was all very well for them, but had the effect of leaving *you* out in the cold — financially, socially, psychologically, totally. They vanished out of your life, and you out of theirs; behind those giant box hedges, they were to all intents imprisoned from you; they ascended into a world of grandeur which by its very splendor and munificence was only to increase your feeling of isolation and inferiority. Not to mention Cousin Reggie's unfortunate insistence that, adopted or not, they must be allowed to share in any inheritance from the immediate family, which, without in the least benefiting them, was in the end to leave you impoverished. Had *we* been better off, and without our own children, our own problems — ! But there it was. And you elected to choose the poor, dear, Frightened Uncle, the heroic little Frightened Uncle, as guardian, and his dreadful intellectual dragon of a wife, the unbearable and impossible Aunt Deena, and to be lost in *those* social shallows! Which, of course, you couldn't help, it was a trap; you, like everyone else, couldn't bear to hurt his feelings, on that Sunday-morning walk up Concord Avenue; and, given your choice, you couldn't bring yourself to say to him that you preferred *us*. And it's been bad for you, and hard for you, too; but now it will be better, now you must come to us as much as you wish, this is your place — in the Uncle's study, where he keeps the secret glasses, and the gin-bottle, in the right-hand drawer of his desk (as he does also at the library); in the panelled dining-room, where every Sunday evening we have the unvarying supper of scalloped oysters, and toasted brownbread (with unsalted butter) and strawberry ice cream, and coffee in the Worcester cups, under Aunt Sibyl's portraits of the family; the Wild Cousin, the Beautiful Cousin, and the Beloved Uncle, looking so young and handsome as he smoked the inevitable pipe, and read the inevitable book, probably one of his own precious collection of books about tobacco — : yes, all this will now be yours. The lawn, too, where the rhododendrons must be watered every evening, and the wistaria on the porch trellis (the porch where we take our coffee), which, as it has no sex, they say, will never bloom! . . ."

Dear creatures, even now he felt as if almost verbatim he could repeat any one of those Sunday-evening talks, hear the Uncle's laconic brevities of humor, the Aunt's light, sunlit laughter, and that slow, fascinating, wonderful, single-minded persistence and insistence with which she pursued any argument, any thesis.

"Have you written any more of your little stories? little plays? Why do you think you have to write these little stories, these little plays? It's all very interesting, of course, but what exactly do you mean? what is it that you are trying to say? They are so vague, so diaphanous! But Balzac. Now Balzac is solid, you can read Balzac over and over, it's life itself. And *Vanity Fair*, look at Becky Sharp, as alive as if she were in this drawing-room this minute! But why do you have to write these little stories, these funny little stories, which seem to have no beginning, no middle, and no end?"

"But my dear Sibyl don't you see he must write them as he *wants* to write them? He doesn't have to write like Balzac or Thackeray, and besides he's young, isn't he?"

"Well, I don't understand them; and Balzac and Thackeray are excellent models. Could we have another log on the fire, please, a birch log? and would you poke it back a little? and *I* wouldn't say no to another martini, my, those taste good tonight!" And then the Beautiful Cousin, sixteen, whom Cousin Maud had been so afraid he would fall in love with and want to marry, as they so preposterously resembled grandmother and grandfather, rushing in from the garden to say, all breathlessly, that Nancy and Jack were going to have a baby! To which Aunt Sibyl replied, amusedly, languidly, twitching the torn lace, the forever torn lace, of her dress about her slippers, "Well, isn't that *clever* of them!"

That had been, then, the moment of release, or the beginning of it; it was the point from which it had first been possible to glimpse, at least — in the far distance, but now definitely attainable — the outlines of security. Here at last, in the *gigue* of rooms, streets, and houses, was a point of rest, one to which he could return with every confidence of safety and enrichment. Here, by degrees, everything could be allowed to fall into place, as seemed to be the most natural thing in the world, if only it could be discussed.

And discussed, of course, it all had been. How patient, how kind, how wise and perceptive, they had been with him! They had recognized his need, and indulged it — his immense need, which only too often they must have found somewhat exhausting. But now that it could all be referred to, and discussed — forgotten for a moment to be discussed again — the waning guilt, theirs as well as his own, began to wane more rapidly, and between them it was as if the subtlest possible miracle of surgery were being accomplished: they were engaged, the three of them, tacitly, in the miraculous process of chipping and peeling away the coarse lumps and flaws of the mould, the matrix, from the emergent image beneath, the tender and still rather amorphous identity, which they, and D., and the invisible hands of the ancestors, were together creating. Very slowly, very gently, they had gone about it: the process was almost that of ritual, had, at times, even an air of incantation: and as D. now considered its slowness (for it had really extended over years) it occurred to him as probable that it had begun even earlier than he had suspected. Just as, on the other hand, it was destined to continue for the rest of their lives. It went back to the earlier of Aunt Sibyl's two "created" houses, the one in Kennedy Lane, and that period of D.'s two years at school in Cambridge, and the half year of school in New Bedford: the period when, as she more than once delightedly put it, he had been a holy terror, and definitely something of a monster. His influence on the Beautiful Cousin, and the

Wild Cousin, had been bad, had been considered to be bad, and
the real problem had then been to keep him away from them as
much as possible, while at the same time not too much appearing
to discourage his coming. Yes, it had begun, no doubt, back there;
and in the days at Concord; but it was after the second return from
Troutbeck Bridge, with his news of Ariel's Island, and after
the twenty-first birthday in New York, for which the Beloved
Uncle had provided twenty-five dollars, with the suggestion that
not a penny of it be left (it was spent at Keen's Chop House),
and again after the third return from Troutbeck and London, that the wonderful alliance had really, and forever, been
joined.

Nor, from this point on, was it only his own identity that was in
the process of being shaped: it was now also the shaping of something more complex, the shaping of a family, of a family "ghost."
And if prior to this the "family" had been a necessity for *him*, a sustaining pattern against which to measure himself, and out of which
as by a kind of transfusion he could absorb the rich colors which
his somewhat timid and tentative and undifferentiated character so
clearly needed (and perhaps this was an unvarying feature of adolescence?), after this, it began to appear, he was himself to become increasingly a necessity for the "family," or more particularly for Aunt
Sibyl and the Beloved Uncle. He was to become, in a sense, the
"binder": in this gradually more complex and "aware" creature of
their own and the ancestors' imagining, they could, in their own
turn, "find" themselves if only by finding themselves reflected. He
gave them back to themselves. He reminded them who they were,
what they were, what they had been, what done, what loved, what
lost, what — even — betrayed. And the more conscious, as the result of this reciprocal endeavor, he was to become, the more *they*
were to become dependent on him for the affective, and affectionate, exchange, with all its loving notations, which was the only solu-

tion in which one could live. If they had helped to save *him*, shaping him with their unselfish, or paternal, or instinctive, or certainly not selfish, love, it would now become *his* turn to save *them*: as save them, and critically, too, from themselves, he was exactly, at last, to do. Not for nothing would it then have been that his notorious infidelities, his scapegrace behavior, his deliberate living beyond, not only the wrong side of the tracks, but the "pale" as well (as Cambridge saw such things), had prepared an example of the impermanence and unimportance of all save the family ghost in such matters. Not for nothing the succession of Loreleis (he had never mentioned the Loreliebchens, or only to the Beloved Uncle) and the abandoned children, the little D.'s, and the suffering inflicted alike upon them and himself; look, he would be able to say: see what happened to me: remember, now, what excellent advice you gave *me*, when, in this very room, after the fatal interview with Lorelei Two, I announced that I had fallen in love with her, that it was irremediable, and that I would leave Saltinge and the children in order to live with her! You were the first to say, and the ones who knew best, that I loved the children too much, the three little D.'s, and they me: it would cause hideous suffering, but most of all for myself: and if I argued that as with R. and K. and myself there was much to be said for launching the young, *sans* the freezing shadow of the father, thus precociously on the world, you were not to be entirely convinced. "It may be all right for them" — Aunt Sibyl had replied — "it may be: it *has* in some ways been good for you, granted — painful, but good: it's made you self-reliant, independent, and even, by starving you for love, *affectionate*: and it might, it *might*, do the same thing for them. But what about you? You do not know yet how much you will suffer, but I can tell you that you will; you will suffer more than you ever did in your life. You will want them, and you won't have them. The distance between them and you will become greater all the time, you will lose touch with them, the shadows of prejudice and misconception will add to your difficulties; they will end by distrusting you; and you will know that for a fly-by-night *ignis fatuus,* which you dignify with the name of love, but which is really nothing but an unfortunate infatuation — everybody admits it but you — you will in the end simply have lost the most precious thing in your life. You will see! You do not know yet how much they mean to you, and least of all, at this distance from Saltinge and the House, can you *possibly* measure how it is going to affect you."

Words of profound wisdom and truth, which had proved indeed to be a singular understatement; and, when Aunt Sibyl, so perilously late in life, already indeed in the beginning of the long shadows, herself threatened just such a removal from the Beloved Uncle, he was to be able to turn them to good purpose. "I should leave him. I owe it to my self-respect to leave him. I ought not to stay here another single minute. Where does the money go to — ? Who is he spending it on? It's disgraceful. That little trollop at the library is only one of them, I know; there are probably others; and for all I know he may have — don't laugh — another *family* somewhere. I mean it. Those mysterious telephone calls — have you noticed them? tell me, haven't you noticed them? It looks to me very like blackmail. Someone is trying to get money out of him, and *is* getting it, for it's vanishing. And it's not either, I may say, that I haven't had *my* chances, too: I have: there was someone at Broadstairs whom I liked very much: there was a French painter at Auvergne — and you needn't look at me like that — who was extremely attractive, and very nice, and who asked me to 'fly' with him, or some such romantic term, but I didn't. (Perhaps I ought to have gone.) But that little hussy at the Institute, sweeping in here when he's ill, in furs that *I* can't afford, not that I'd be seen dead in them, and *bathed* in perfume, so that his room smells of it for days, and passing me on my own stairs as if she owned the house — it's more than I can bear." Over and over it they had gone, in the shadow of the sterile wistaria; and her cross-questioning of him had been acute and embarrassing. For of course he knew only too well about Daphne, and about all her predecessors. And about those extremely sinister telephone calls, when, even from the far end of the drawing-room, with the study door half closed, one could hear the crackle of the high-pitched angry voice on the receiver, and the Uncle's curt "Wrong number!" And what *had* it been all about? Daphne's father? brother? He had never known; the Beloved Uncle had never told him. Certainly it was not Daphne, gold-digger that she was; nice, plain, Daphne, who had gone away a little later, to marry an art dealer at Princeton, and there had died of heart disease, the Uncle had somehow learned. Ah, those scenes at the Institute in the morning, the ritual of the coins! For it had been arranged between them, in order that they might have the necessary privacy, that they should go early every morning, an hour before anyone else arrived: the marble corridors and offices were silent and deserted: and it was understood that each day she had the right to all of the silver and small bills that she could find in his trouser pockets. With what sly relish and mustachioed gusto the Uncle had related it! And with what naughty appreciation of the truly appalling risk that he was running! But then, his whole life had been in this sense a perpetual risk, based as it was on a free moral counterpoint, which, in the circumstances, and in the Boston and Cambridge *ambiente,* with membership in the Union Club, the Odd Volumes (not that *that* wasn't richly appropriate), and his exalted position, not to mention the distinction inherited from grandfather, and his passionate devotion to his work, was nothing less than miraculous. His whole life, in fact, had been a masterpiece of *double-entendre,* it had been a double life (and Aunt Sibyl had never tired of stressing the duplicity) of unsurpassed daring and success. And of course, as a dramatic foil to the life of grandfather, and that marble bust in the grey church at New Bedford, which as it looked across the empty pews, radiated a moral beauty as candid and fine and flamelike as it was unassuming, it was masterly; it constituted — on the part of the ancestors, whose legerdemain it was — a stroke of genius: it was irony at its tremendous best. And the perfection of comment upon it was in the Beloved Uncle's only, and recurrent, dream about New Bedford: it was invariably of returning to grandfather's house in County Street, the high-columned house under tall elms that looked like a brown Greek temple, but to find that not only was grandfather no longer living there, but that the house had become a brothel, and the neighborhood a red-light district. He could feel, at last, perfectly at home. Thesis and antithesis — the dialectic was perfect, the tragi-comic reversal complete. And yet, not quite. For the final perfection and completion had been achieved when grandfather's house, which for so many had become a shrine of goodness and humanitarianism and religious freedom, and dedicated to that pure form of fideism which was the flowering of his own brave genius, was acquired by Methodists and apotheosized into a Methodist Church. What revenge was this? and revenge for what? what random lightning? No doubt the grandfather, who had a sense of humor, would have enjoyed it, if a shade wryly. He would have seen it, as it needed to be seen, as one more instance of the inexhaustible pluralism of things, the creative dance, the song of the seven seals, or the dance of the rooms, streets, and houses: just as, two blocks away to the north, between it and the granite steeple of the Catholic Church, dear Aunt Jean's house, perhaps the most living and lived in, and loving, and loved, of all houses, had simultaneously been transmogrified and embellished to emerge as the most modern and blatant of "Funeral Homes." Progress — progress! With the accomplishment of these minor but sordid miracles, and the destruction of Cousin Maud's noble house, and the cutting down of her English hawthorns — in order that a score of cheap, imitation-tiled-roof villas might replace them — the great ironist had pulled off the hat trick.

That ghost would walk, that lover of trees! not that Cousin Maud would necessarily have been angry about it, for she was a dyed-in-the-wool realist, there was no nonsense about Cousin Maud. But those hawthorns, her father's hawthorns, the famous hawthorns from which the street itself had originally taken its name, these she would truly have mourned, these and the constellations of crocus and daffodil that danced round them in rings. And if her ghost should indeed float at night across the ghostly ferry from Fairhaven, and the family burial plot there, to which she was forever asking family consent for the removal of one more "lost" ancestor, found in some less desirable sanctuary, she would mourn her trees philosophically enough. Estates of that size were outmoded. Houses of that size were too difficult to keep up — where was one to get the servants? She had rattled about in it — on the increasingly rare occasions when she was there at all — like a pea in a mausoleum. The taxes alone were impossible — the grounds could no longer be properly cared for. A pity, though, about the carriage-house — she had always loved that carriage-house, it was an architectural treasure, a New England gem, a thing of rare beauty; and this they might, if only in the interests of New England history, have spared. But no, that practical ghost, that lover of trees, would not really have demurred even at this. Herself a practitioner of change, a pragmatist, forever up to date, forever on the go, a masculine woman if ever there was one, and yet a true "woman" (it was said that she had lost her only sweetheart in the Civil War), she would have been the first to maintain that things cannot remain as they are, and that the mansard-roofed house of stone, built by her father, and by his profits, and his father's profits, in the China trade, was no wonder house. A good house, yes, but a practical house, no. Who nowadays would want a gymnasium, with marble floor, on the top story? D.

remembered from childhood that fabulous gymnasium, the parallel bars, the flying rings, and above all its extreme implausibility there at the top of the house. And so extraordinarily out of key with everything else in it — with the Chinese *kakemonos* above all, which had all his life been his envy. What had become of them? What? On the occasion of that final visit, with Lorelei Three and Nicholas, on the eve of the journey that was to serve as the theme for yet another unfulfilled project, *A Heart for the Barronca,* they had climbed up to the stone porch of the stone house, in the quiet spring garden, where the crocuses were for a last time in bloom, and stared in through the French windows at library and drawing-room and dining-room: the chairs still stood in the stiff rows which had been arranged for the auction, and attached to them were the tags which no doubt gave the names and addresses of the heirs or purchasers: against one of them leaned a stack of pallid Egyptian water-colors by Joseph Lindon Smith; and there, on the library wall, sure enough, was the favorite *kakemono,* The Immortals in the Mountains of Eternal Youth. Itself still vivid and resonant, its blue-and-vermilion perfection of form forever falling silently there like an immortal waterfall of design, a clear phrase of the everlasting, it triumphed over the rows of empty chairs which now commemorated the end of a house, the end of a family. The rows of chairs were exactly like those arranged for a funeral: as in the long room at Savannah, the two sombre coffins parallel before them; or in the drawing-room at Aunt Jean's, so soon after, the room of the crystal clock, the carved jades and soapstones from China, and the books from grandfather's library, most notably *Twenty Thousand Leagues Under the Sea.* Change, destruction, and death — change, progress, and creation: but The Immortals in the Mountains of Eternal Youth would outlast all: and the nobility of grandfather and Cousin Maud; the gentleness of Aunt Jean; the subtlety and wit and dark grace of the Beloved Uncle, and his courage, too; and the magic and wisdom of

Aunt Sibyl — these and all the others, these had now themselves become, as in this ancient but still unfading Chinese painting (now about to be lost), The Immortals in the Mountains of Eternal Youth. For what is beautiful will endure forever.

But now, the classic grace of the old carriage house was as yet unharmed: the hawthorn trees budded for the last time, like the unpruned roses that made a hedge for the kitchen garden: a forgotten row of parsley was bright green, the green-yellow daffodils were swinging: and he told Lorelei Three and Nicholas of the famous visit here of the Beloved Uncle and Aunt Sibyl, when, after dinner, as they crossed the black-and-white marble tessellations of the hall, Cousin Maud, turning to Aunt Sibyl at the foot of the curving staircase, and patting her elbow as if she were a child, had said, and with such air of command that it could not possibly be disobeyed, even by anyone so formidable as Aunt Sibyl, "And now you run along up to bed, Sibyl! you must be tired from the train journey from Boston, and A. and I can have a nice talk!" Wonderful woman. There had never been any gainsaying her, or wheedling her either. Nor any deceiving her. Her estimates of the family had been as precise as a psychologist's, she had measured them, every one; they all knew they had been irrevocably assayed and graded by that stern keeper of the tablets, filed away as grade B or C, or dismissed altogether; and all from a viewpoint (she made no bones about it, any more than she boasted of it) which was loftier than any *they* could ever hope to command. Not that she was morally inflexible: social graces, she would have been the first to insist, may compensate: when she found that her favorite cousin, who managed her estate, had defalcated to the tune of some seventy thousand dollars (R. having been summoned to go through the books), she had simply looked up from her knitting, through the thick glasses, and said calmly, "Well, put them away, and we'll say no more about it." And then she had had the cousin down from

Boston to dinner the next night as if nothing had happened. She knew that he knew that she knew; and the only change ever made was that he was quietly dropped from her will. She thought no less of him — she loved him, in fact; but she had known, "had always known, that he was weak." And that was that. The seventy thousand dollars had long since been allowed for.

Calm: yes, she had always been invincibly calm, there had never been any the least raising of the voice, nor much change of expression, on that extraordinarily pugnacious little face (she had really been astonishingly like a Boston bull terrier, snub nose, curt and curled lip, everything): even in her carefully prepared gambits of humor, as to R. on that same occasion — or, no, it must surely have been earlier — when she had quite quietly and suddenly said to him, "Bee, dear, what would you say if I were to ask you to marry me — ?" And R., with a presence of mind which had endeared him to her forever, had replied, "I would say yes." But of D. — no, she had had her misgivings about D. Like dear Aunt Sibyl, she had been totally mystified by "the little stories, the little plays," and, as she had been much attached to the three Little D.'s, and particularly to the youngest, her namesake, she had been of course compelled to regret and deplore what she called his "manner of living." A writer, a playwright, in the family — ? A perhaps dubious, slightly dubious, enterprise. There were of course writers and writers: sermons, like those of grandfather, yes: scientific treatises, too, such as D.'s father had contributed to the Medical Journal, or written for the government after the expedition to view the total eclipse (when D. had accompanied him), with his original, but apparently inadequate, theory of the "shadow-bands": these were legitimate, and respectable, they were indeed useful. They helped to get things done, or understood. But to be all plainly a writer, and impecuniously, too, in bland disregard of the needs of one's unhappy progeny? this was a doubtful asset to any family. Not that

87

she had ever rebuked him: she had said it in overtones, as in her question whether, in addition to writing for the theatre, he intended to do anything else. As, too, when, *à propos* of nothing, and looking up over the blurred lenses from the perpetual knitting, she had suddenly volunteered the information — "You know, your father was a remarkably intelligent man. A fascinating talker. As your mother was too. I think you could say he was brilliant. . . . A great pity!"

The implication was obvious. And to make matters worse, the little stories, the little plays, had been unsuccessful; he had had to improvise and compromise, to turn his hand to hackwork and journalistic odd jobs, an admission of defeat. Better to have gone into the newspaper, there in New Bedford, with Cousin Lew, who had built that pretentious modern house next door — not that she thought too much of *him*. But the newspaper was at least solid, it had been in the family for three generations, it would have been profitable; and it would have brought the family back to New Bedford, where, after all, it belonged. Grandfather had had his opportunities — he too could have gone anywhere — Boston had called him, so had Chicago — but he had felt that his duty lay at home. For home, of course, it was.

And of course home, in the deepest sense, it would always remain. Curious that to begin with he had not seen this: in the annual voyages to and from Savannah — down the muddy river and out past the barber's-pole lighthouse to sea — New Bedford, and Boston, and Cambridge had for some time seemed to be merely a pallid counterpoint to the more violent and extravagant densenesses of Savannah — the north was cooler, was quieter, was politer: it was even, at the outset, unimpressive. What here was comparable to the stinking and feculent alleys that ran like a savage counterpoint, or commentary, immediately behind the respectable brick housefronts? the rich and rancid life of the Negro quarters, which lay only a few blocks away? He was an old *habitué* of these, had fought, and had

88

his head cut, in the gang-fights, gang-fights with rocks; he had listened through the alley shutters to the animal cries of Negro love-making; outrage and death were already his familiars. Yes, and there was also the perpetual antagonist, his sworn enemy, Butch, at the corner of Abercorn Street, and the almost daily fight for one's very right, as a Yankee, to exist: and the periods, like that during the Spanish War, when for weeks he had been virtually a prisoner in his own house. (That particular siege had been miraculously raised after a Sunday dinner for the officers of Company K, Fourth Illinois: for when Butch and his gang saw D. emerging in the company of Captain Davis, in full regalia, his sword at his side, the golden epaulets sparkling in the sun, they had at once staged a sham battle, Indian style, to impress such important people; and D.'s status had at once become so magnificent that hostilities had ceased.) No, in the north there had been no such alternations of the vivid and the sinister: one did not, as there, fully expect to see bloodshed every time one went outdoors, like the murder of the fireman, or the Negro barber with his throat cut; or such gentler pastimes as the weekly rat-hunt, when a dozen or two rats were released simultaneously on the green, and all the dogs of the neighborhood went after them. Not to mention that jungle graveyard, turned park, where one could pry loose the bricks of the ancient vaults and crawl down into the warm dust to find crumbling boards and an old brown bone or two. But this comparative tameness of the northern scene was to a considerable degree illusory, and based on the mere fact that it *was* different, and that one could not all at once really see it: based too on the fact that its rituals were subtler, and that one had not at first been ready for them. For in the end, there could be little question that of the two places New Bedford was by far, for his own purposes, the richer and more sustaining, and not merely because it was his inheritance, or because, when the Quakers "thee'd" and "thou'd" him, he was made to feel that he belonged, but because it was semantically his, his own language. Savannah, after a few years in the north, began to seem, if still magically beautiful, and of an incredible and cruel fertility, an alien place, another country. Had one truly ever had roots there — ? either one's family's or one's own? — was it enough that one had a grave there, had been born there, had shot a ricebird there, caught a catfish there? that one had stolen pencils from the desks at school, climbing up the brickwork to the second story to do so, or, more momentously, made away with a book from the bookstore (tucked inside the sailor blouse); or, again, come close to drowning at Thunderbolt, under the Yacht Club, while playing hookey from school? And that had been the night, yes that had been the night, when he had returned late, up the back stairs, hoping to escape notice, and had undressed in the dark, putting the wet clothes on the back of his chair; only then that Mother should come in, to say good-night, and all unconsciously place both her hands upon the chair; not to say good-night, however, but instead, in the one tragic moment that had ever trembled between them, to murmur that when he had grown up, he would protect her, *wouldn't* he — ?

And yes, he had said yes — of course he would protect her (hoping that at such an obvious "crisis" she would not notice the wet shirt and trousers); and that had been all. Surely she must have noticed? Perhaps indeed Selina and Clara, who knew all about it, had already informed her? But she had said nothing more, after the strange little speech; during which she had not really so much looked at him, as beyond him, and into the future. And then she was gone. As only a little later, Savannah too was gone. For the first time, a train was taken (which had been a treat in itself), with grandmother, and Cousin Maud, and the Beloved Uncle. A train taken all the way to the north! and Savannah was gone forever, miraculous but gone.

To become itself now, in turn, a mere counterpoint to the north, as the north had formerly been to Savannah. For now the unfamiliar, but firmer, rituals and references, of Cambridge and Concord and New Bedford, replaced those more singular violences with a swifter and deeper notation, a finer and colder texture, a darker sequence of insights and divinations; a world in which loneliness had the greater scope for exploration, both inward and outward, because of its very mystery and obscurity. New schools, new houses, new faces, too many of them; the stream too swift for anchorage. Instead of the long warm twilight, the bats circling, the cicada's plainsong (or to be collected in cigar-boxes), the cry of the children at the evening game of "Run, sheep, run," came the groan of the ice on the shallow pond at the end of Concord Avenue, or, better still, the hiss of new skates on the miniature lakes which never failed to appear along and under the lilac hedges between Longfellow House and the house next door to the east of it: for not only were these little lakes a sort of Virgilian miracle in themselves, so dark, so secret, with narrow paths of ice between the ancient and frozen trees, where one could hear the other skaters passing quite near without seeing them, but there was also the now increasingly important and relevant shadow of the Poet of White Horse Vale. Up there, on the terrace, stood the Poet's great house: one was skating here in the lamplit twilight where once a poet had lived. In this, one was moving definitely closer to the continuing "thing," the continuing dream; this was the shadow of one's shaping, or self-shaping, destiny.

A poet, too, of one's own legendary country, of the Minute Man and the blacksmith (the site of whose chestnut tree was commemorated with a granite slab a little way down the street), of Concord and Salem and Gloucester: for had one not oneself vicariously and antecedently participated in these heroic shapes and events? Greatuncle George had built the Constitution, an achievement which, so it was still said at New Bedford, had "spoiled him." He had shaken

Talleyrand by the hand, after that prodigious launching in Boston, when everyone had been warned beforehand lest the tidal wave caused by the ship should sweep them out to sea, and that transatlantic handshake had unbalanced him: it had rendered him so hopelessly conceited that he had never done another stroke of work in his life, but retired to his estate in New Bedford, and there lived out his days in gloomy dudgeon. And had not another poet written of that ship? that famous ship which one's own ancestor had built? Cambridge, still remarkably like a country village, with its white picket fences, and lilac rows, and tall elms, fed thus one's sense of the past; one could still hear in its streets the tramp of Washington's raw troops; and with all this the poets were clearly involved. What more natural, then, than that with the son of the famous Shaksperean scholar, and indeed in his very study (at those hours when he was lecturing at Harvard), they had edited, and of course, written — for how many weeks? — their first weekly "magazine," and its pathetic imitations of Longfellow and Poe and Hawthorne? From the first odd little poem at Savannah (*The lions had waited all the day*), that solitary "sport" of composition which had crystallized enigmatically out of the rhymed words of the spelling lesson on the scrolled blackboard, now had at last begun to evolve what seemed to be becoming the deepest and most secret habit of his nature. This nature, it appeared, must learn to shape itself in words; words, and the rhythms of words, were the medium in which it seemed most likely, or at any rate most happily and magically, to find the equivalents of being, the equivalents of the still shadowy self. Here was the clearest process, and evidence, of growth; these were the tree's leaves.

And the Frightened Uncle's library, and the books brought home from Gore Hall, where both the uncles were librarians, the innumerable books (not to mention the constant visits to the library itself, and into the cathedral aisles of the stacks), all this back-

ground, this rich and endlessly changing arras of books, whereupon
every form and guise of knowledge was emblazoned, embroidered,
heraldically and cryptically unfolded, this was now, of course, the
river of life itself. This was the great, the immortal, river on which
one was already setting forth. Here one was to choose one's way
towards the already favorite colors and patterns and intricate designs, those first adumbrated slyly and shyly at Savannah, on the
playroom floor, where one had first fingerpointed the words of
Jackanapes and *Tom Brown's School Days* and *Under Two Flags*
and *Pilgrim's Progress,* not to mention the Lang fairy books, whose
ghostly horrors still had the power to freeze him, and his mother's
copy of *The Vision of Sir Launfal,* that first love among books, the
sheer physical beauty of which had caused him to appropriate it,
on leaving Savannah, by pretending to the Beloved Uncle that it
was his own. Those earlier points and spurts of gleam, and outline,
those simplicities, now began to exfoliate, to bud and break into
secondary shapes and coils, more mysterious and haunting still;
ever more arcanely and deepeningly alluring, nevertheless somehow, they still always kept that primary oneness of meaning; as if,
while the statement was always more fascinatingly elaborate, and
progressively extended further in each direction, whether spatially
or temporally, nevertheless the vital meaning — and vital it truly
was — remained algebraically the same and constant. Yes, this was
now the current of living: this would take one anywhere and everywhere: this accompanied one at all times, was already there, and
awaiting one, when one arrived at a new place, had indeed been
already pointing the way to it, if only one had known. At dear
Aunt Jean's in New Bedford (whose ninety-fifth birthday the whole
family had attended only three years before —) the bound volumes
of Harper's were ready for him behind the glass panes on the shelves
in the sitting-room, as also, more esoterically, grandfather's whole
library in the drawing-room, where they filled the shelves of an

entire wall. Not that one had neglected the other rituals of the New Bedford scene, of that most beneficent of houses; nor that indeed they had been forgotten, years later, in the many projects and unfinished or unsuccessful works. No, the two levels of process had gone on simultaneously, were aspects of one evolution, the semantic fever accompanying the explorative action, so that all in the instant became one, and the experience became experience simply because it must at once and inevitably become language. But had justice ever been done to it? To the New Bedford scene? —

Well, there had, to be sure, been the long speech in *Purple Passage*, the long speech to Cynthia, the interminable soliloquy (and good heavens how prone he had always been to the soliloquy — there was something symptomatic in *that* which certainly needed looking into) — the long speech about the voyage down the Bay, down Buzzards Bay almost to Cuttyhunk, on the whaleship: and in this there had been a little of the New Bedford background, but not much. It had not been, of course, too germane; even the whaleship had been somewhat dragged in; there had been a shade too much panache about it, it had been a trifle false. Not that the whaleship had not been important, or the occasion not memorable. But it had been merely a natural part of so much else which had *not* been chronicled: for that matter, the whaleships had long been a familiar feature of the waterfront at New Bedford and Fairhaven, they had always been there, square-rigged ships were a constant sight along the wharves, and to turn from County Street down Union Street, the mile-long street of cobbles, and to look downhill past grandfather's stone church, was to expect to see them there. That the Frances Allen had, however, been the very last of the ships to sail from New Bedford, and that she had been lost (only her sternplate found awash off Greenland a year later), and that she had belonged to the family (Cousin Steve Howland, who took him for the voyage, had owned a share in her), had made a difference.

94

No, the ships, there, of whatever description, had been familiar enough to him. During that whole New Bedford year, at Aunt Jean's, he and Cousin Ed had "collected" ships: they had literally haunted the wharves, and, in a series of notebooks, purchased for the purpose, had noted-down the name and category and port of origin of every vessel larger than a yacht that had tied up there. Tugs, coal-barges, steamers, barkentines, barks, schooners — the latter from three-masters to seven-masters, the one and only, the famous and ill-fated, Thomas W. Lawson — all these had been captured and pinned like white-sailed moths into the little books, some of them many times. He had even — D. remembered — been invited once, by the captain of a coal-barge, to join ship and go to Norfolk, Virginia, if he would pay the price of the passage — namely, an armful of old magazines! for they were short of reading-matter. And then, of course, there was the fussy little steamer that plied daily down the Bay to Nonquitt, and the summers there with Cousin Ed — the dwarf wild roses along the salt shore, the kelp-smelling rocks, the pretty girls on the beach in their gay bathing-suits, and the delicious torments and heat-lightnings of adolescence.

But that was a little later: that was after the death of dear Aunt Jean, and the funeral, to which he had had to travel all alone from Duxbury to Boston, and then from Boston to New Bedford, himself the only child present; sitting for a last time in the flower-packed drawing-room, and in the front row, too, next to Cousin Maud. Dear Aunt Jean — ! Incorrigible, headstrong, delightful Aunt Jean — she had encompassed her own death, as no doubt she would have preferred, by once too often undertaking the forbidden pleasure of trying to carry, unassisted and undetected, a heavy valise up to the attic. And had fallen, and struck her head; and had had to be put to bed, where, of course, her extreme old age had at last been too much for her. He had been there when it happened;

and when she became ill, and delirious, had been packed off to the Frightened Uncle's at Duxbury; only then to be summoned back. But he still remembered the extraordinary feeling it had given him to hear himself called by one family name after another, each a further generation back — as, in that last delirium, her memory short-circuiting an entire century (she could remember the War of 1812), she rehearsed the whole family history: himself lost, forgotten, he had become first the Beloved Uncle, then Aunt Jean's only son, Alfred, who had died in childhood, then her husband, whom she had married against the family's wishes (it had been thought a mismarriage, for he was a wholesale butcher), and at last her father, Cousin Maud's uncle. In this involuntary assumption of so many roles, as if he had become a kind of composite portrait of five generations of the family, he was to feel, as never before or since, the queer ambiguity of one's existence within the *frame* of family, the simultaneity of belonging and of being, of group anonymity and individual identity: tradition and the individual talent . . . as the Tsetse was to say! Aunt Jean, invoking and reviewing them all, for a last time, and in a single *moment*, had bestowed them upon him forever.

But that house, that life, that ritual — he had come to it just in time; there, no doubt, the fates had been kind to him; for, earlier, he would not have appreciated its unique charm and beauty; and later, so very little later, it would no longer exist. Not only because Aunt Jean was to die, but because, at the turn of the century, such cultural holdovers from New England's past, so lovingly preserved, were doomed to rapid extinction. The house in County Street — the then still handsome County Street, and its mile of huge elms and stately houses — was a lesser version of Cousin Maud's: built of wood, instead of stone, but terraced like hers, and mansard-roofed, and, of course, like all the New Bedford houses, with a cupola on the top, from which one could look all the way down the blue Bay to the Elizabeth Islands. Glassed on all sides, and approached by steep stairs from the attic, and of course pervaded by the same delicious odor of old pine, old oak, old silks, old paper, this cupola had become his eyrie, his study, his sanctum: it was like living in a diamond: never in his life had there been a room to match it. Except perhaps the great studio room in the House at Saltinge, whose tall windows opened on the foam of Ushant — ? for that, too, had the same quality of being at the same time secret and exposed: there, too, one could almost literally seem to be drowning in a rainstorm, or annihilated in light, or washed away on waves of lightning. Spectacular it had certainly been, nor was the attic far behind it in wonder: so many boxes of old letters, smelling of sandalwood, to explore, and read, and tear the faded stamps from: love letters, letters of travel, letters from clipper ships; and the treasures, too, forgotten items of trove, brought from Java or China: particularly he remembered the small links of a carved ivory chain. But if these were enchanting, it was the life itself, with Aunt Jean and her companion — Miss Daggett, from Martha's Vineyard — that was ultimately to remain as the true gift of the house to him, it was this that was to stain him with its own soft radiance, and, perhaps, to gentle him with its own gentleness. From the brilliant brutality, the savage glare, of Savannah, the faceted metal flash of the palmettoes, to the sedate quietism of the aromatic house in County Street, the two little old ladies who lived in it, not to mention the perfect "ring" of convention and ritual that encircled them, this was a transition of which the effect upon him was only much later to become apparent. Not unnaturally he had himself, to begin with, more often honored those rituals in the breach than in the observance. *Farouche* he had most certainly been. What a scandal had arisen (and public, at that, for the Tabers next door had been a witness to his infamy), when he and a schoolmate, without so much as a by-your-leave, but at any rate without the least attempt at concealment, had stripped the cherry-tree of its cherries, and sold them! Property — was there such a thing as property? the cherries could not be taken and sold — ? A new concept for the young gang-member from the alleys of Savannah, but interesting; as were now so many other aspects of convention and conformity. But restraints so gently applied — was there not something, *au fond*, that was really *satisfying* about them — ? Yes, the chains had fallen upon him as softly as cobweb. No possible induction into a *formed* mode of life could have been subtler. And when one thought of the courage, the kindness, of these two dear creatures, in taking into *that* hushed house an undisciplined male-child of twelve — !

Not only in their nomenclature had the three little D.'s been, in their turn, affected by this house, these women, this life, this year: for they all, in one way or another, had been named after Aunt Jean; but more important by far was the image of the Aunt herself, whose goodness, and classical beauty (even in death she had kept this extraordinary beauty), had been for him, ever since, like a lamp buried in his breast. That sort of memory became one's body, one's eyes, one's hands, one's life: as much as one could, one simply *became* the beloved person; and thus it was to join the endless succession, the moving hierarchy, of the family image, which, willy-nilly, one must then oneself bequeath. *His* somatic and psychological echo of Aunt Jean had been, as it were, overheard by the three little D.'s, as now their own children would again overhear it — and, if diminished, and now of course combined with his own complex of identity (composed so slowly and patiently out of all the *other* sources, whether family or outside), nevertheless it remained there, that precious lamp was still theirs, still hers.

And with it, all that miraculous perfection of living, that never-since-attainable blend of simplicity and dignity, *rus in urbe*, a calendared and horometrical harmony of days, each with its proper pattern. The tiers of plants must be watered, with the little copper watering pot, in the pantry-conservatory between sitting-room and dining-room, before one could sit down to breakfast; and if Miss Daggett, humorously insisting, was always in the end allowed to do this, it was just as invariably after the ritual protest. And at breakfast, perhaps midway in the meal, which was served by the immortal Irish Maggie (who churned the butter herself in an old-fashioned churn kept in the kitchen, using their own milk, from their own cow, to make it), at breakfast, no matter what the weather, old James D., the coachman-gardener, mutton-chopped and grizzled, would appear at the dining-room window, wearing his bowler hat, to receive the orders of the day. The window was raised softly, and Aunt Jean would lean down for the customary exchange. — Was it too windy for a drive? or too cold? was it likely to rain? or would it hold off long enough, so that they might perhaps get at least as far as Padanaram, past the cotton mills, if not all the way round the Point, by the Point Road, and to Fort Rodman, where — as they all knew! — young D. so particularly liked to go? And, in the season, there was also the question of the garden: there were beans ready, James would say triumphantly, or some fine peas; there *would* have been cherries, if the *birds* hadn't made away with them somehow, a very bad business; the roses should be cut; there were nasturtiums in the usual quantity round the pump; or, later in the summer, there were tomatoes, there were pears. And very well, he would bring the carriage round at ten, and D. (at whom he winked) could sit on the front seat with him. And in the meantime, if it was a Saturday or a Sunday, and no school, D. might like to drive the cow with him out to pasture?

D. would, D. did: never if he could help it would he miss that fantastic drive. For, alone in the city, in the heart of the city, Aunt Jean still kept a cow: since the house was built, some sixty-odd years before, when of course it had stood right at the edge of the countryside, not to say the wilderness, there had always been a cow in the barn, at the back corner of the block-long lot, or rather in the shed that adjoined the barn, just as there had always been a horse, and, in the basement under the barn, or carriage-house, a pig. And, as the estate, like all the original estates in New Bedford, ran in a narrow strip straight out to the pasture and woodlot, half a mile south, nothing had been simpler, to begin with, than to drive the cow out the country roads, or paths, to the walled pasture; but as the city grew, and the intervening lots had been sold off, and the city gradually built its way farther out, the time had at last come when not only did the cow have to be driven along a paved city street, for the entire distance, but also through a growing competition of traffic, even including street-cars. Not that it in the least feazed the cow. Old James D. (who was in fact a distant cousin, which, however, in no way interfered with his being a devoted servant) had trained her somehow; and, no sooner was the gate opened on to the street, than she headed past the High School, with James D. following in his trap, the horse keeping to a slow walk immediately behind the cow. It was in fact one of the famous sights of New Bedford. Everyone was delighted with it, shared in it — it became an institution. And old James D. was just as proud of his sea-going cow as he was of his immaculate coach, and the immaculate broadcloth coat which he donned for the morning drive.

A priceless and beautiful experience, timeless as poetry, it had remained in memory like a delicately colored scene from a period-piece play: the two old ladies playing cards on the marble-topped table under the green-shaded lamp; or together winding the grandfather clock, on Saturday night; Aunt Jean always the first to be down in the morning, to read the New Bedford Mercury with her enormous magnifying glass — the grey curls falling past the soft pink cheeks, the lace ruffles falling over the fine blue-veined hands. And then, of course, the never-to-be-forgotten episode of the piece

of toast. Ah, that recalcitrant, that treacherous remnant of toast —!
For he had been gently but firmly — and often — instructed, at
the breakfast table, that never, *never* should one have any leftovers,
whether of butter or toast: one must so calculate, so prearrange, that
one always "came out even." But on this delicious occasion, having
excused himself from the table to collect his books, prior to his setting forth to school, he had returned, somewhat sooner than he was
expected, only to find dear Aunt Jean furtively dropping the left-
over piece of toast out of the window into the nasturtium bed below!
Naturally, he had retreated at once, to return a little later, after he
had heard the closing of the window. And naturally, neither Aunt
Jean, nor Miss Daggett, had ever known.

Yes, the house in County Street, in the shade of the two giant
horse-chestnut trees, with the bells of the Catholic church reverberating over it, while by no means as beautiful as Aunt Sibyl's
second house, or as grand as Aunt Maud's, was the most haunting
of those that were to have been celebrated *seriatim* in *Rooms,
Streets, and Houses*: a lucent Victorian piece under glass. And to
have gone to it direct from Savannah was to have experienced one
of those rare spiritual immersions, like the dipping of one of father's
sensitive camera-plates in its bath of developer, which, by adding
a clear small image of a clear small scene, was to change his own
outlines forever. The wild young child from the south would never
again be quite the same. Not that his awareness of it was to come
all at once, or uncomplicated with other elements — for hadn't
grandmother's house, the little half-house on Common Street, in
Watertown, the small shabby house of the whatnots, the pear-tree,
father's bad oil paintings and father's organ (on which he had composed, and played, at Savannah, his "national anthem," teaching
them to sing it) — and, above all, the hidden leather portfolio of
father's poems and articles — hadn't this poor house blended by
insensible degrees into the same picture, or joined with it in mak-

ing the ultimate composite? For if infinitely humbler, and even by comparison poverty-stricken, so that to begin with at Harvard he had been really ashamed to take his friends there, nevertheless the houses had much, essentially, in common. If the one was smaller and plainer than the other, nevertheless in character and period it was almost identical. The florid Victorian furniture, of embossed and filigreed curly walnut, the marble-topped tables, the hassocks, the antimacassars, were interchangeable — it was only that the rooms were smaller, the furnishings fewer. Both houses had that faintly sweet *sachet* that seemed invariably to be the perquisite of very old ladies — the faint essence of orris, or lavender, of sandal-wood, that seemed to have saturated their clothes, the curtains, even the thick carpets beneath their feet. And if grandmother, small, heroic, brittle, fierce blue-eyed grandmother, was by no means, when first he had begun to go to the house in Watertown, as yet so old as Aunt Jean, and certainly made no pretensions to that sort of social stature, not to say grandeur (and it would be hard to say, D. thought, just at what *moment*, precisely, he had first begun to make this distinction for himself); just the same she was again, like Aunt Jean, an old woman, or an aging one, she represented the past, she came out of the past. She was a farm in upper New York State; a plain country girl, the eldest of twelve children; she was apple-pie and coffee-cake and homespun clothes; she was a slate-pencil and a slate, little used, for her schooling was brief; she became, with her mother's death, the fury-driven head of a family at thirteen; and this slavery she had merely exchanged for another when, at eighteen, with forlorn hopes of escape, she had married the stern, abstractly intelligent, puritanical but libidinous martinet of a schoolteacher, who was to make her life one long misery of des-potism. Poor grandmother — she had conceived and borne her two children without pleasure, had raised them only that she might store up grief; Deena, the daughter, she had hated, to be hated in return; and the beautiful son, her golden-haired Apollo, her genius, her beauty, was early marked as one of those whom the gods would destroy.

Yes, grandmother and Aunt Jean and Cousin Maud, like Aunt Sibyl and the Beloved Uncle and the Frightened Uncle, all these, the one after the other, in series, or now and then doubled or trebled as in a counterpoint, composed the moving pattern of meaning and design out of which he was himself all the while directing his confused and changing aim or aims: these were the component materials of evolving attitudes, nascent definitions. And if it was Aunt Sibyl and the Beloved Uncle who had first clearly made it seem as accessible as desirable that he should join his own profile, as it were, to the composite profile of family, and to take with him into this joining his own lurid past, and the red raw shadow that walked forever behind it, it was grandmother, as much as they, and in some ways more, who had (by allowing him to see father's portfolio of writings) enabled him at last to accept and recapitulate the agony at Savannah, and in this somewhat secret process (for he often examined that leather portfolio on the sly, when grandmother had gone down to the Square for her morning shopping), he was to discover, while at Harvard, that the staining sense of guilt and shame had been mysteriously exorcised, was no longer there. A singular, and slightly naughty, alliance had grown up between them: they had become accomplices in what was almost admitted was a sort of private vice — the illicit re-appraisal and exoneration of father, and the tacit admission — against the silent family taboo — of his genius. With the others of the family, none of this was ever mentioned or referred to. The reading of the poems — the quails, the punning triolets, the startlingly carnal love-poems, and among them, of course, his own *Lex Talionis*, so high-handedly appropriated and rewritten — together with the newspaper articles on the "shadow-bands," the notes, the letters, and, above all, the newspaper accounts

of the tragedy itself — all this constituted a sort of constantly renewed conspiracy between them.

Odd — come to think of it — that he had nowhere, in the abortive or aborted plays and short stories, done justice to this skein in
the tapestry, or only, yes, once or twice, and obliquely — the death
of grandmother, in the forlorn nursing home on Palfrey Hill, this
had been vulgarized and commercialized in a story, — or would it
be more accurate to say that he had vulgarized himself? True, he
had gone from his last visit to the nursing home by street-car and
subway — the long, dreary semi-suburban street-car ride, through
scrubby fields and vacant lots ragged with wormwood and chicory — to one of his clandestine meetings with Marian, and so to the
Orpheum, to hold her hand, and grind her knee with his, while the
blackface singer crooned above the grinning orchestra; and afterward to dinner, and to the red brick boardinghouse in Brimmer
Street, for an evening of laughter and merriment and lighthearted
lovemaking — for what a sense of humor she had had, and what a
giggle — ! but after all, what was wrong with that? Well, at the
time, the element of contrast had been paramount: it had seemed
to heighten any wickedness, or sense of sin, involved in his secret
liaison with Marian: but hadn't it, more exactly, been the *aesthetic*
shock which he had aimed at in the only moderately successful
transcript he had made of it? It had been, as so much of the writing had been, or attempted to be, an effort at preserving, and thus
remembering, in this case, the horror of the final visit — for he
never again saw grandmother alive — the shrunken body lying motionless under the sheet in the hot room, while the sad head, with
its two little braids of grey hair, turned in misery from side to side
on the pillow, the tears running down the sunken cheeks, and un-
prevented into the toothless mouth. "I can't die — I can't die —
I want to die and I can't — and my teeth hurt me and I can't wear
them any more — "

So she had wailed, weakly and persistently, indifferent to the cluckings of the nurse, and his own halfhearted protests, until she had had to stop out of sheer exhaustion. It was for this that she had been born, struggled so long and hard, suffered, endured, learned, grown mellow in wisdom — for this that she had adored the lost angelic son, and his children, and now the children of Lorelei and himself, that very minute playing in the sunlight on the beach at South Yarmouth — and, above all, little Jean, little Jean!

Learned — ! Good Lord, how she had labored and learned. *That* singleminded heroism was unforgettable. From the moment of her husband's death at the Thanksgiving dinner table (and how this had infuriated her!), she had begun to change and grow: who could have foreseen, except perhaps herself, that as soon as the rock was removed the buried seed would sprout, or take such beautiful shape in leaf and flower? The books read so painstakingly, the books on art, the prints of the world's masterpieces laboriously collected and memorized, so that, when, already turned seventy, she had gallantly sallied forth to Europe alone, it was to discover that she knew her Titians and Raphaels the minute she set eyes on them — it had been an astonishing lonely apprenticeship, she had been indeed for all the world like a little girl going to school: the neglected slate and slate-pencil had at last been put to work, and to good purpose. And now miraculously she had changed! For gradually, as she turned, on the endless wonder of knowledge, the eager young mind so long thwarted and stifled by the impatient brilliance of her schoolteacher husband, himself a thwarted philosopher, and a satellite of the minor literati of his day in New York, it was to find that there was no longer any need for the defensive anger and bitterness which had been her only armor against his condescension and contempt. She had herself become young again — good heavens, she had even, he suspected, on one bewildering occasion, offered to seduce him — for what on earth else could she have been meaning if not that, when she placed his hand on the warm, soft, and still young, thigh, under her lifted silk dress, to show him *exactly* where it was that she had a broken muscle — ? *That* had been of course the giddy and guilty climax of their secret love, their conspiracy to canonize the son and to declare him free of sin. From that moment, she had been happy, they had been happy together. And in this reciprocal catalysis, along with his sudden realization that in the Watertown humbleness and humility there was something genuinely moving and lovely, something profoundly *true*, came without warning his knowledge that now he could bring his friends here from Harvard — the Old Bird first, as obviously and always the most understanding, and then all the others. He was emancipated.

And naturally, with the acceptance of the father, not only as one who had been misunderstood but also as unmistakably the most gifted member of the family, the brilliant but lost one, came more confessedly D.'s long-since tentative, and increasing, impulse towards identification with him, and imitation of him: he must become like him in everything. Grandmother's array of faded brown photographs was examined over and over; and, particularly in those that were taken in adolescence, and as a pale wide-eyed young medical student at Harvard, or in the slightly more rakish snapshot from Vienna, it had been possible to see that there was indeed a very strong resemblance. Not unnaturally either, when it was remembered that after all it had been a marriage of cousins: his mother's surnames had merely, after the marriage, been reversed. And thus, here too, again had occurred that fusion of inheritance — in his own face, the "D." character had simply been softened, and sensualized, by the "P." character; for the father's finer and firmer and longer upper lip had been substituted the narcissistic fullness of the mother's. Was this a kind of physiological disloyalty — ? It had worried him; he had studied this evidence of nature's treason morning after morning, as he shaved, and had practiced a deliberate tightening of the muscles of the mouth, to contract its disturbing softness, the all-too-evident tenderness and sensitiveness, not to say weakness; that mouth was a dead give-away, and must be curbed. And so, it had been curbed: slowly, inexorably, it had been remodelled by an effort of will. And the young face, for so many years too exposedly and transparently mobile, had deliberately stiffened its upper lip, and learned how to mask itself as that of the father. He had acquired not only a second character, but a protective disguise as well.

The *persona,* yes, of the father had thus been adopted — exactly as if those photographs, luminous somehow in the back of his mind, had projected their rays, like father's magic lantern, subtly and prolongedly forward to the face, drawing it, and then re-drawing it, to the earlier genetic image; and together, too, with this, had proceeded a parallel adaptation, the taking over of the father's role as a writer. "The Poet of White Horse Vale, Sir, with liberal notions under my cap — "; no doubt, this had been the first occurrence of the magic, the all-precipitating word or at any rate the occasion for the first explanation of it: poets, there were such things as poets: they wrote poems! And poems were in rhyme, like those chalked words on the school blackboard — *prey, day.* But there was also the further fact that *father* wrote poems; and then typed them on his Blickensderfer typewriter, as, a decade later, the Tsetse was to do; with the fascinating little revolving bobbin that nodded down the printed words on the moving paper: and somewhere, too, it had come to light that grandmother P., the inventor of the smiling pig, had herself written poems. It was clearly therefore a thing that one should be able to do — ? an evidence of something a little out of the ordinary? or, if not that, perhaps a dedication of oneself to some such vocation or avocation? There was also, D. reminded himself, at about the time when he was first allowed to have a room of his own (and a desk to put in it — ah, yes, that desk — which, come to think of it, he must have asked for) — there was also the brief period when, with a small bottle of red india ink, he had, in pious imitation of grandfather P., written a series of sermons. These he had printed out painstakingly with the pen, trying to make them look as much as possible like the printed page. The separate influences had worked together, of course — each contributing to the discovery that "writing," in one form or another, was a family habit, or cloak, which he must himself, naturally, try on. But it was that delicious portfolio of father's, finally, and its wonderful miscellaneous medley of poems, philosophical statements, scientific and medical papers — some handwritten, others in typescript, others yet on the well-remembered prescription pads (one of these was the suicide poem) — that had given the final impetus: he must become like father in this, perhaps even to surpassing him. He would look like father, first, — and after that look like — what? a preacher? a poet?

In *Twenty Thousand Days* there was to have been a long and searching analysis of this erratic evolutionary process — together, of course, with an analysis of the discoverable tendencies in the writing, both early and late, as rooted in these simple beginnings. Or *were* they so simple? From the word "poet" in the epigraph to *Tom Brown's School Days*, thence to the question asked by the child, and so to the school blackboard, with its rhymed words — and thus finally to the first spontaneous poem — *The lions had waited all the day, lying concealed in the grass, for their prey* — the little parable which father was to seize upon and paraphrase, bestowing on it the unintelligible Latin title — this was perhaps obvious enough, if one could say that the spontaneous *writing* of the poem was obvious. Spontaneous it had most certainly been. He had rushed home from school, through the cemetery park, jumping over the sunlit headstones and tombstones as always, but with one thought only — to get to his room, take paper and pencil, and write the poem which was already buzzing irresistibly in his head. It was all already there, the idea was clear, and most of the phrases and rhymes: the lions killed the antelopes, and then the men killed the lions: it was the manifest and irreversible law of things, the inherent and fatal irony of life — jungle justice. And never afterward was he to forget the extraordinary feeling he had experienced as he wrote it, there on the carpet of the bedroom floor, the pencil repeatedly stabbing almost through the paper. This extraordinary thing had come from himself, he knew that — and yet it had also come from somewhere else. It was a new existence, an addition to all that had existed before, it was here on the paper, both his and not his, so that one hardly knew whether to take pride in it or not. If from somewhere else, from where? How had it happened? All very well to understand, years later, the logical sequence of the steps that had led to it, but the fact remained that at the moment of conceiving, and then of writing, it had been a sort of apocalypse, a seizure, the self becoming merely the invisible and nameless lightning-rod for an alien and unfamiliar lightning. And as far as the logical steps were concerned, the precipitant causes, doubtless there had been many more that had not been recalled at all, and perhaps extending much farther back in time than he had imagined. How could one guess how long had been the interval between his first reading of the verse epigraph and his inquiry, of father or mother, as to its meaning? Weeks, months, perhaps even a year: he had known the fragment of verse by heart, indeed it had haunted him all his life; it was, or had ended by becoming, his own epigraph, a key, a shibboleth: and it was therefore possible that he had been in the habit of reciting it, and that *this* had in the end led to the discovery. But no — it was more probable that it was *after* the word "poet" had been explained, and the concept of poet first entertained, that the lines had begun to exert, or to acquire, their pure and singular magic. The poet — the maker of things! as he himself had now made a "thing"!

Which was only the beginning. For then there was the further and tantalizing question involved in that phrase, "liberal notions." What was one to make of that? To begin with, "notions" was itself a particularly slippery and elusive abstraction, as difficult to grasp as father's lessons in grammar, where the definitions had been so much vaguer, somehow, than the things they defined. What possible help was there in knowing that a verb was an action, being, or state of being? where did one get? And then there was "liberal," with a further cluster of meanings and feelings, somehow admirable; and — quaintly enough — to be put under one's cap. And finally, beyond all these teasers, and casting a tremendous and spectral light over them, as it galloped away with them into another country, another world, galloping away with the poet and his cap as well — was the ghostly White Horse. The lines had become pure murex for him, and were to remain so, just as profoundly as any that were ever to be encountered later: just as profoundly as these of S'su Kung Tu, "In the morning I whip my leviathans, and wash my feet in Fusang." And could it not be that the taunting phrase, flung at him everywhere in Savannah, "Red head, white horse" — could it not be that this charm, this folk ritual, had added yet another sheath of meaning, and hence of shaping, to the fragment of verse? —

Yes, all this was to have been tabulated in *Twenty Thousand Days*, the threads teased out in all the subsequent endeavors, whether completed or not: and most especially the many-branching elements and leads, and on many levels, that were to evolve out of that little matter of liberal notions. Liberal — ? Well, it had undoubtedly been early emphasized that grandfather was a liberal, and a great one — a great liberal in the philosophic or religious sense. As so often he was to hear it repeated in New Bedford and in Boston. Grandfather had preached at the Arlington Street Church, and in fact all over the country: he had served as a chaplain in the Civil War, and at the battle of Bull Run had not only been under fire, but had cut out of an oak-tree beside him the whizzing bullet that had barely missed him: his sermon on The Voice of the Draft, accepting the call to arms as a burden that must be borne alike by all men, of whatever rank or class or condition, and his refusal to seek sanctuary in the Union Street pulpit, or in the sombre Sunday cloak of the Unitarian minister, had made him famous; it had led to his ultimate discharge, as more useful out of the army than in it: and he had founded and become president of the Free Religious Association, his pet, his darling, his dream, through which he had worked for a religion "purified of myth and of dogma." He had died, unnoticed and alone, there on the dark doorstep behind the Parker House, in Boston, at midnight, while the Beloved Uncle and Aunt Sibyl, whom he had married only that afternoon, were speeding to New York on their honeymoon — died with little of that dream realized. But was it so? was it really so? For noble ideas, as he himself had declared, have a power to live and generate by themselves: they are man's externalized thought and soul, and therefore immortal. And a century later — D. now considered it with humility — was to come from Harvard a letter for D. from an undergraduate who, for his thesis, had been assigned the study of grandfather's religious liberalism. "And the life, so lived, shone that night like the moon over Sheepfold Hill."

Your ghost will walk, you lover of trees —

And how the dear man, gentle, humorous, and shy, would have loved to consider this; and, even more, to consider the evolution of that courageous thinking in the living terms of D. himself, of his own being as thus extended into other and further dimensions — how that would have fascinated him! Was there not, in that blessed scene under the trees at Buttonwood Park, near the bear-cage, when the teacups and saucers had been made out of the little green acorns, grandfather tenderly stooping over them to work with the tiny pearl-handled penknife, was there not in this scene a kind of dedication, could he not remember it still as profoundly just that? Had grandfather not been saying, the white beard saying, "Thee must now — always remember this, little D. — thee must now and hereafter do *my* thinking for *me*, thee must be the continuance of me, thee will forever, even if intermittently, or if only every so often *consciously*, stand in the ghost of a pulpit, in the ghost of a church, in the ghost of our beloved New Bedford. Our little sacrament, see, is in these beautiful green cups, green because living; and in my hand upon thy head." Yes, this was true. Something like this had really happened — wordlessly, but it had happened. And this implicit and transcendental exchange, subtle as aether between them, was, when one considered it justly, one of the profounder forms of the process of inheritance. As later D. was to mould and extend his own extended being in the new beings of the three little D.'s, launching them into awareness like a little tripartite and independent, but attached, antenna-flotilla of himself, so grandfather had that day set his own immortality into posthumous motion. And in a true enough sense, it was now the grandfather in D., as it was also the three little D.'s (now *where* in war-dark England?), who were all simultaneously engaged in the wonderful formulation and statement of a theme of living — a theme, too, of loving. The journalist, the unsuccessful but undefeated writer and playwright, was not this creature, in his better or more truth-seeking and explorative sense, even now the audible speech of grandfather's unobliterated tongue? Was grandfather not here (and in the little D.'s waiting there in dark England) still thus reshaping himself? And would see it as miraculously such: would see it in D.'s slow emergence into a becoming gesture and shape out of all these ante-

cedent ghosts and essences. This was the stuff from which consciousness was made.

Bells again — *tin-tin: tin-tin* — as those on the P. & O. boat,
rounding the sea-blue corner from Trafalgar and Cape St. Vincent:
bells of time, or bells, the one stroke or two, struck rhythmically by
the lookout in bow or crow's-nest, to note the approaching presence
of another ship, now faintly visible, to starboard or port. Bells far
out in the Atlantic, off Ushant, off the *Raz de Sein*, with all its
invisible shoals and cunning passages — yes, and the bells, strung
like beads endlessly backward in time, of all the other ships, his
long life of ships.

I I I

——— yes, the bells, whether of ship's chronom-
eters or the remembered clocks of cities, or
echoed from one part of a ship to another,
struck by hand; bells that marked off, and then forgot, intervals of time, of life, of desire or memory, or death; the bell in
the church steeple, at Duxbury, which the sexton-barber, after
cutting his hair in the shabby little waterfront barber shop, took
him up the steep stairs, and the steeper ladder, among century-old
cobwebs, to see, and then to strike, with the knotted-rope bell-
pull — to strike just once, the sweet round clang rolling out over
Duxbury Bay, up the hill to the Myles Standish monument, across
the inlet to Powder Point, and over the Frightened Uncle's wind-
mill, and out to sea; a single bell-stroke of which the secret meaning would never be known to any but himself; the quarter-bells, too,
of the Metropolitan Tower in Madison Square, which had so pos-
sessively set the tone, the tempo, of that long hot summer in West
Twenty-third Street, setting in motion, like a summer wind from
New Jersey, from the Palisades, the leaves of grass, and the heart-
shaped lilac leaves in moonlit dooryards; those feverish bells which,
in the early story — Jules's story — of the Fall River Line, had
accompanied the young hero up the gangplank and into the ornate
plush-and-gold of the long-since-forgotten Priscilla, the young
hero, of whom the Tsetse had said, "I think your young man was

not as innocent as you pretend; I think it is highly probable that
he always carried 'rubber goods' in his hip pocket"; the bell of
the white church at South Yarmouth, its thin complaint almost lost
in the endless sibilation of the immense silver-leafed poplars that
brooded over the little house, the little lost ancestral house, the
house of Cousin Abiel, the Quaker; the midnight clamor — twice
repeated — of Santo Spirito, by Arno's side, while he lay, with the
Belgian revolver under his pillow, and listened to the English girls
giggling and smoking on the dark roof outside his window, but
didn't dare to join them; and then, in London, the curious irregular
pacing, the slight rush as of an irregular regularity, in the quarter-
bells that ceremoniously announced the master of them all, the all-
vibrating, all-enduring, voice of Big Ben; bells, too, of trains —
the slow and melancholy *ylang-ylang, ylang-ylang,* of freight-trains
at night, so analogous to the long, curling, valley-filling wail of the
whistle, sounds that took one's body into the air and across a continent to another sea; but above all, for himself, and all his life —
and set like a kind of pattern or rhythm in his consciousness and
memory, his own rhythm — the bells of ships, the bells of voyages,
and the dear people, dear and dead or dear and alive, whom he had
so first encountered, so travelled with — bells for Cynthia, for
Jules, for Bob, for Hambo, for Ebo, for Hay-Lawrence, and all the
others — bells for the eternal ship ——

And the Wild Cousin; the handsome Wild Cousin, dear, ever-
giggling, powerful Del, smashed in a motor-car accident, at the
midnight crossroad in Florida, between voyages, on shore leave
between voyages, his own so many voyages — had there been for
him too, so long unguessed by Aunt Sibyl, that same compulsion?
was there in it, as she and the Beloved Uncle had later maintained,
an element of atavism, the adept and unsleeping hands of the
ancestors reaching yet again to turn a wheel? *His* ships — round
the Horn to Australia, before the mast, and the gun-running yawl

lost on a sandbar off Yucatán, and the powerful bootlegging speed-boat slipping in fog down the Hudson to a secret assignation with rum-runners off Sandy Hook or Fire Island, shot at by coast guards — and at last his love, his beauty, his own brave battered schooner, sunk off the vexed Bermoothes, himself swimming back to it from the lifeboat for the forgotten compass, and so westward to safety after eight days in the open boat with nine men and a mad sea-cook — *his* ships, and D.'s, on their parallel or divergent courses — two lifetimes of ships — how evident now was the cousinship in these, in the necessity for these! It was still only a moment, as the ship-bells chimed and counted, from the morning when he had seen the Beloved Uncle step lightly round the corner of Reservoir Street, agitatedly smoking his pipe, to say that Del had disappeared from school, from Milton, and that as no clothes were missing, and it was well known he was unhappy there (for years he had dreamed only of becoming a naval architect), it was feared he might have made his way to the Quincy quarries and — fallen in? drowned himself? perhaps in a kind of unhappy somnambu-lism? —— And so, came the three days of dragging the deep copper-green water of the granite quarries, but in vain; only then to find the Wild Cousin, "snug as a bug," on a dirty coal-barge in Salem Harbor; and to free him (after a family conference at which D. had spoken the deciding word), for the sea, for his passion the sea.

And now, all those ships to be remembered, theirs, and Hambo's too: Hambo to Kowloon, with his taropatch, pursued by the Chinese coolie from wharf to ship and back again, with the cry of "Beautiful English boy, beautiful English boy!": the Wild Cousin to Cádiz, there to be laid off, for a month of gypsying in Spain, from the salt-hills of Cádiz to the wineshops of Algeciras, dancing in the moon-light, drunk in the fierce Spanish moonlight, drinking from wine-skins, and dancing and sleeping with the strong handsome girls who were never to be seen again — for yes, it was the Wild Cousin, the gentle Wild Cousin, at first so disapproved of by all, who had revived in the family the ancestral knowledge of how to live: it was he who had most of all, as a good animal, and a brave one, truly lived for them: if D. was to adventure for them with the mind (tentatively, anyway) (but let us not pretend that he had not done so carnally as well) it was Del who had lived for them with hands, feet, heart, soul, and sex: he had had a genius for living: perhaps too a genius for loving. And as to the latter, good heavens what a bond that had always been between them, from the first time they had got drunk together, there in Brimmer Street, in the very room (he had sought it out) where, years before, dear lost Marian had lived! They had talked of that, over the bootleg gin. In the summer evening, the green lamplight making Rousseau labyrinths of the ailanthus trees, they had got drunk together; and the kinship, long since acknowledged, but never with opportunity to declare itself, for the wastes of water that so often washed between them, was at last made explicit and intimate. They had talked about Marian, and her bevy of naughty trained nurses, here in this house — the roommate who had a passion for reading Keats, but only at the menstrual turn of time: the little Matron: the nurse, who, abandoned after years by her doctor boy-friend — he had been wonderfully generous to her — nevertheless brought suit against him for breach of promise, much to the disapproval of the entire household: but mostly about gay, demure, passionate Marian, whom he had picked up at the Orpheum, and with whom he had had the serenest, the most unclouded, the happiest, sunniest, and, oddly, the most *innocent,* affair of his life. Under that very ailanthus tree in the back yard, on a warm spring evening — one of the evenings when the presence of the roommate had made it impossible for them to use the room, and the couch with its Paisley shawl — they had stood embraced, with the lighted windows above them, after cocktails and dinner and the inevitable benedictines (which she claimed always made her passionate), and she had clung to him, murmuring, "You are touching — you are touching — the clitoris — the secret of a woman's passion!" Dear Marian, how comically clinical she could be — and how amused at the occasional erotic mishap! How unassuming, too, and how insistent that he should in no way neglect his dear Lorelei and the two (as they then were — for it was from witnessing the birth of Jean, in Watertown, that he had returned for an evening with Marian) little D.'s! The truth was, she had really loved the little D.'s — perhaps it was even true to say that she had loved Lorelei as well: she had loved them all. And so, from this to the Wild Cousin's disastrous marriage: the story, at last, of the disastrous marriage, and of the fatal honeymoon, from which tall, handsome, Amazonian Bea, his childhood sweetheart (returned to after all those years at sea, those nights in port, and the brothels in port), fled back home in dismay, back once more to the cloistered safety of Cambridge, and Brattle Street, and the Sewing Circle. Yes (the Wild Cousin had said, puffing old Reekie, his powerful pipe, and giggling half apologetically, half amusedly), it had been a mistake, he should have known better. He had been too long away, was too long unused to the subtler and tenderer customs and cadences of Cambridge and Boston: it was not exactly that he had been coarsened, was it? — but that he had learned to live more directly and simply and animally: you took a woman to bed, did a job of work, and that was that. And yes, he had got drunk the first night, and taken Bea to call on his former landlady, who was of course an old sweetie of his, and she had appeared in the doorway in nothing but a dirty wrapper, which was unfortunate: and he was afraid poor Bea, unused to such goings-on, had taken a dim view of the company he kept, and the way he lived. And so, after two nights of very unsatisfactory love-making (she was frightened and frigid, he said), when he had had to tell

her that he had been ordered to sea a week earlier than they had
expected, and had then gone off to the ship-chandler's for his oil-
skins, leaving her silent and confused in the somewhat tawdry —
he admitted — Greenwich Village room, it was to return that
evening and find her gone. Not even the conventional note on the
mantelpiece — just packed and gone. Never a word from her
again, either, except through the lawyers a year later, to the effect
that she wouldn't see him, never again wanted to see him, wanted
only a quiet and dignified divorce. And that, he said, was that.
He had giggled again, but in those sea-grey, melancholy, in-going
eyes, under the handsome arched eyebrows (he was without question the most purely "Delanoye" of the family, far more of a
Delanoye even than Cousin Maud), there had been the unhappiest
recapitulative questions — it was the saddest unanswerable Why
of his life, he had lost his one and only true love. What, exactly,
had the tall girl meant to him? The girl who was later to kill herself? He had never tried to say, had never again evinced any desire
to talk about the reasons for it all — though he had always wel-
comed any news that D. might have of her. Was it simply that,
after so rough, violent, bawdy, and promiscuous a life (including
the two Negresses at Santiago), she had remained, or become, the
shining, wave- and wind-purified figurehead, the symbol, the
thought of landfall, that must precede and guide him forever,
everywhere, over all waters? Was this the great, the only sentimental attachment — or love — in his life? Not that he wasn't
affectionate, and devoted: he was. He had always been deeply attached to the Beautiful Cousin, his sister, and to Aunt Sibyl, his
mother: had from now on been greatly attached to D., in an alliance that was to become profoundly important and nutritious for
both of them: attached, later, to the Beloved Uncle, on a plane
that, had she known of it, would have horrified Aunt Sibyl out of
her wits, as betraying a depth of depravity and duplicity in her

menfolk that would have altered her entire conception of life, of reality, of morals: in all likelihood, the disclosure would have destroyed all values for her, and killed her. For if she had a single passion in life, it was Del; and of his central goodness (which was true) she had no iota of a doubt. It was simply that *this* sort of masculine alliance, and for *this* sort of purpose (and what a purpose!), would have been utterly beyond the reach of her understanding. Understandable, perhaps, of the Beloved Uncle, but hardly of D.; and never conceivably of Del. That would have been the final moral monstrosity.

But the ships, Del's and his own, and even Aunt Sibyl's, for that matter, and the Beloved Uncle's — how had it been that they had never, in any of those family conclaves, in the dusky golden-walled drawing-room, with the Chinese carving under the mantel, or on the porch at twilight in the shadow of the sterile wistaria, overlooking the tennis court, and the terrace that fell beyond (where later the Beautiful Cousin was to build her own house), how had it been that they had never discussed, never realized, how vital in all their lives, in the whole family's life, indeed, the ships had been? The Constitution, and its builder, had of course been prototypical. Something had been begun then, in New Bedford and Boston, which would never, perhaps, be ended; the sea was as inevitable for them as breathing. No accident that D.'s father and mother had almost been lost at sea off Cape Hatteras, on their way from Savannah to New York, in the hurricane which swept away the deckhouse — and their cabin — only a few minutes after a human chain had handed D.'s mother to safety, and with her, the embryonic D.! And hadn't D., years later, on one of those Savannah ships, lowered over the side a string, from a ball of string, in order that he might thus measure the height of the ship against the height of the house at Savannah? — to find, magically enough, that they were identical; a fact which had at once had the effect, of course, of turning the house itself, the whole sea-saturated and sea-surrounded house, into a ship — so that in their turns, all the rest of his life, *every* house was to become a ship.

The dark, the war-haunted house at Saltinge, now awaiting them there in the lightless little riverside town, itself lightless and bomb-scarred, this house most of all: for it looked at the sea, and the sea looked at it: the abyss had been gazing into it, searching its stone soul, for the two centuries of change that lay between its dedication in Latin, by the great astrologist, and the birth of D. — that birth which the gaze of the sea had come so near to preventing. But the other houses, too — the cottage at South Yarmouth, that little barnacle of a cottage, salt-soaked with the sea-fog, the sea-dew, its back turned to the tidal river — its existence was half marine, the tides at the foot of the stone wall were lifegiving. Yes, all the houses, Aunt Jean's, Cousin Maud's — and of course, to a degree almost rivalling that of the house at Saltinge, the Frightened Uncle's summer cottage at Duxbury.

Ah, to be sure, that cottage at Duxbury, knee-deep in wild grass and goldenrod, glared at by blue bay and blue sky, lifted almost from its moorings by the savage northeasters, while D., and the Red-haired Cousins, played cards under the swinging kerosene lamp, and listened to the *plink-plunk, plink-plunk,* of the rain from innumerable leaks in roof and walls, dripping into pails and basins. The house of the Indian arrowheads — white quartz, pink quartz, chipped flint — ruled over, alas, by termagant Aunt Deena, the unbearable Aunt Deena, Aunt Deena of the unsleeping intellect and the relentless vulgarity; while the Frightened Uncle (surely one of the most heroic of beings — for it is the frightened ones who are brave) flitted in the shadows. And then that one, terrible heart-felt confession of his to D., on whatever botanical expedition, whether in the White Mountains or at Duxbury (for wildflowers were his true love, and D. had ever since been grateful to him for it), that one illuminating lightning-flash, which laid open the whole unhappy, timid, sequestered, and apprehensive life, the confession itself heroically made in order that D., whose shyness and timidity, if less marked, or more traumatic, or more in the nature of the family *petit mal,* was at any rate analogous — what a magnificent decision that had been! "You must not make, never make, dear D., the fearful mistake *I* made, first as a boy, then as a young man, then as an adult — for these things end by becoming habitual — you must not make the mistake of sitting on the fence. I always sat on the fence. I never joined in. At the Friends' Academy, in New Bedford, I hadn't the courage to join the other boys in their games, I sat on the fence and watched. It was the same at Harvard — it has been the same ever since. As Matthew Arnold said of Thomas Gray, I never spoke out. I'm not sure that I know how to explain it. But possibly some of its roots were in my very rootlessness; for as you know I was orphaned when I was eight, and your grandfather P. became my guardian — but I had no home, I never had a home of my own, I felt unwanted; and in this there might be a similar danger for you — that is why I bring it up. Yes, I always sat on the fence, early and late: it was the same in everything: at no time, on no level of endeavor, was I ever able to take my own proper place, I hadn't the courage to make myself heard, to put myself forward, I preferred (as less painful) to be overlooked; and as a result I *was* overlooked. That is why I failed as an historian — a miserable little monograph or two, and the translation of Ploetz, with the emendations to bring it up to date — and that was all. For, as I was a total failure as a teacher (again owing to that same flaw in character), and as these books made very little money — and certainly no splash to speak of! — and as I had married your Aunt Deena, other ways had to be found; and so I buried myself in Gore Hall, to become a third-rate college librarian. You can see for yourself what became of me, what has become of me. No doubt what I've done is useful; and if three or four people above me were to die — Lane, or Winship, for example — I might even, at the end of my days, become Assistant Librarian, heaven help me! But it's not a man's life: I've lived in the shallows: I've made no friends to speak of, or only one or two, in my whole life: you know only too well how socially meagre is the existence we lead, how little, and on the whole how inferior, is our connection either with Cambridge or the College. Your father and mother were not like that — they took life with both hands, they met it and used it: they lived with their minds, that is true, for they were brilliant creatures, both of them; but they knew that that was not all there is to it, they were social, they were gay, they lived richly, even, in fact — which took courage — to living beyond their means — and not only economically. They *lived* — even if it ended tragically; they lived! And that is just as true of your Uncle A. and Aunt Sibyl. They, too, know how to live, and I have often thought it was a pity you elected to have *me* as your guardian rather than them, for they could have given you a great deal more than we have — as, indeed, anyway, they do; but in the earlier years they would have been better for you. The point of all this is that you must not live as I have lived. But I don't think you will, as a matter of fact, you have already shown enterprise, and, if you are shy, you seem to be outgrowing it; you have many friends, and it seems to me you are already beginning to shape a well-balanced life for yourself. You are a good athlete, and that is excellent, for it brings you the right sort of contact with others: and that is just where I made my mistake. I sat on the fence." —— Poor, dear, kind, gentle creature; — it had been true, every word of it. And D. still remembered with almost its original shame and pain, the dreadful and cruel and unforeseen moment in the summer "show" at Duxbury, when it was jokingly said of the Frightened Uncle that he had been run over by a baby-carriage —

and that in the ensuing operation, by mistake, they had sewed up his mouth! And the uncle had laughed. . . .

Your ghost will walk, you lover of flowers! — on Powder Point, counting all its varieties of goldenrod, *Solidago goldensis,* and the others: to the mysterious little water-lilied pond, under Indian Rock, for pickerel weed: to the marsh for marsh rosemary: to Arlington Heights for anemone and star-flower, snow-white among last year's brown leaves, and bloodroot and Lady's Slipper: to Concord, across the dirt road from the school (Middleclass School!), for the most precious of all, the tiny Quaker Lady. Those walks, those immense summers, those fugitive springs, the dear uncle looking so absurd in the green-visored yachting-cap (for, alas, he and Aunt Deena had never any vaguest notion of what to wear, how to dress — it had engendered an inadequacy in himself which only Wild Michael from Tonkin, him of the "African ancestor," had taught him to overcome) — how enchanting now, they seemed, and how deeply beneficent, in fact, they had been! And D. had learned, thank god, to know this, and to know it in time to acknowledge it. Had this been one of the effects of Aunt Sibyl's famous rebuke, the rebuke for his self-centredness, his selfishness? "You like to come here, yes, I know, and we like to have you come, and as often as you wish, and to bring your roommates and your friends: you know we want you to do this, we want you here, we are very fond of you, and we think you are great fun: you are very clever, too: but just the same I want to tell you that I sometimes feel that although you are fond of *us,* you wouldn't cross the road to *do* anything for us! Now would you? I don't believe you would!" Yes, he had taken them too much for granted; and although he had defended himself by saying that surely it was only necessary to *love,* to manifest *love,* and not necessarily to "do things," nevertheless he had begun to suspect that Aunt Sibyl was right. The gestures, too — the attentions, the observances — were cardinal, and he had neglected them. Merely to radiate good will (if one could assume that one did) was not enough: and if the gift without the giver was bare, barer still was the giver without the gift. He had sent Aunt Sibyl a dozen red roses, after a nicely calculated interval, and at once — at once! — their love had bloomed. And so with the Frightened Uncle, too; it had suddenly occurred to D. that he had never "*done*" anything for the Frightened Uncle, either: not a thing. And therefore, on the third of the returns from Troutbeck Bridge, he had brought him a Medici print, purchased in London, of the Origin of the Milky Way (!), and after that had fallen into the habit of taking him to dinner in Boston, at Marliave's or Jacob Wirth's (for the Frightened Uncle loved German beer, he had been to Heidelberg), and then to the theatre. And that love, too, had bloomed.

Troutbeck Bridge, and its train-bell, chattering sadly in the chapel — and the ships to and from it: the Allan Line ships from Harvard to Glasgow, Harvard to Liverpool, the old Cunard ship from Harvard to Naples: his ships, *their* ships: and the people met on them, known on them: they were his chorus, they had become his Greek Chorus. To Gray's Inn, London, in the footsteps of the Beloved Uncle, with Heinrich, there to stay with the little English spinster, whom the uncle had discovered years before, and who had been so alarmed by their — or Heinrich's — importation of Hawkins for the night — *la la,* what an episode, and what a revelation, *that* had been! For, to the little brick house, just inside the iron gates which were locked at midnight, from an expedition to the British Museum, Heinrich had brought home the extraordinary Hawkins, the small, soft, cherubic Hawkins, the bright pink spots hectic in his cheeks — Hawkins the exquisite from Uster: — neat, tiny, precise, but under all that nicety so amusingly and confessedly "dangerous," so eager to corrupt! He had picked up Heinrich, it seemed, amongst the Roman statuary. "I think" — he had said, almost immediately after the first exchange between them — "that the

variety in the form and size of the penis, in these charming figures, if you will give them your attention, is really most extraordinary. Quite fascinating. So much character, such individuality!"
And, as he had clung to the stunned Heinrich like a leech, he
had had to be brought home (after dinner in Soho) to Gray's Inn,
for an evening of such bizarre talk as neither Heinrich or D.
had ever before encountered. Was it sophistication? was it de-
cadence? A little of each; but it was fascinating; and in the light
of subsequent understanding, it was now clear enough that the
whole pyrotechnical and wicked display was nothing on earth but
Hawkins' love-play, his love-song, which only next day was D. to
discover the reason for. For how astonishingly innocent he and
Heinrich had been! and with what a primal shock came the revelation! "I had to tell him" — Heinrich murmured, with the (as always) infinitely subtle shrug and twinkle — "I had to tell him that
it would really be impossible for me to spend the night both in *his*
arms and those of Morpheus!" For Hawkins had shown no signs
whatever of going home: he had outwaited them; and when, at last,
thinking to precipitate the departure of this entrancing stranger,
Heinrich had said he was afraid they must go to bed, Hawkins had,
all simply, asked whether, as it was so late, they would mind putting
him up — ? Which, as Heinrich had the double bed, was precisely
what Hawkins wanted. And then the unexpected assault, the repeated attempts at an embrace, the first horrifying revelation of the
existence of homosexuality. Had they truly never heard of it before? Perhaps vaguely, tangentially. But until then it had possessed
no reality for them; and Hawkins was as real — or as really *unreal* — as his creels of peat, his poetic talk of whin and heather, and
his exquisitely precious little essays on perfume and color. The room
in Saville Place had soon become familiar to them, the talks
and walks and explorations of London a delight; for once it
was understood that there was to be no further nonsense — of an

erotic sort — between them, Hawkins had happily and generously adopted them — as two nice young naïves from "Amurrica" who deserved to be taken in hand. To be educated, of course; but also to be somewhat corrupted. They must be told all — they must be told everything. And so, Hawkins' entire sexual life was prismatically unfolded for them, all the varieties of his ambidextrous experience — even to a seduction, so he claimed, in a hansom cab.

It was the high point in that summer's adventure, surpassing in mere shock-value even that of the salesman from Detroit, which was to come later. For even in this somewhat noxious and faintly unpalatable adventure (and there could be no question that dear Hawkins was a distinctly unsavory character) had there not been, apart from the strangeness, one of those imperceptible beginnings of an attitude, or an alteration of attitude, the process of transvaluation of values, which was later so greatly to preoccupy him — ? If people like Hawkins existed, and made a kind of brilliance of their existence: if the sickness (always assuming it was genuinely a sickness) could be by a process of secretion and sublimation made over into a nacreous "culture," or even cultural pearl — and certainly by any standards, Hawkins had achieved a refinement of taste, and a logical system of behavior, which made the liberalisms of Harvard and Boston look pale indeed: then, surely, one must widen one's categories of acceptance and tolerance. Yes, there it was, the homosexual thing, which one quite intensely disliked, with an almost animal revulsion, and which, nevertheless, as one was later repeatedly to discover, could produce quite admirable, if almost invariably somewhat unhappy and frustrate, human beings. Of course, there was always the insistence — by Hawkins, by Chapman, by the fabulous Uncle Dracula — that these aberrants, these deviants, these "sports," or experiments, on the part of a mother nature who had finally become bored with the mere proliferation of the normal, were the true thyrsus-bearers, the witnesses of genius, the three-eyed

127

sex of the future of mankind. Just, as somewhat later, too, there was Edward Carpenter (and who on earth had recommended *that?*) with his intermediate sex, his "Urnings," and suchlike, which, even at the time, D. remembered, seemed pretty pallid and spurious: for once, he had not only not been taken in, but had seen the melancholy speciousness and hollowness of it all, the essential defensiveness of the *manqué,* at a glance. He had experienced a feeling of pity, of sympathy — even of sorrow; and it had been possible for him to understand the occasional usefulness to society of this flawed but interesting by-product: but flawed, and a by-product, it remained.

Hawkins, then, had been the first of these, and in some ways the most captivating. But just the same, there was a great deal to be said for Chapman, the most truly ambivalent of them all, the gentlest, the subtlest, the true narcissistic echo-soul, the one who attached himself instinctively to any attractive surface for his happy symbiosis, the delicious relationship (with either sex) in which it was his wonderful role to agree, to say yes, to accept, to elaborate, to extend, to analyze, or, in the musical sense that was second nature to him, to transmute whatever theme was provided by his vis-à-vis into the tender and often exquisite variations, the loving commentary, affectionate and intelligent, which was his natural song of praise. But Hawkins, too, shared that ability: he, too, was the born commentator, the elaborator of the initial perception, the initial feeling, in which sounded the rightness and trueness of his partner: as if, *au fond,* neither he nor Chapman dared trust his own perceptions or feelings as valid, and both must await the announcement of key and subject from another before they could, in the musical art which both made of conversation, "come in." Very curious, this — he had of course felt it early; but he had not fully realized how all-controlling was the mechanism, especially in Chapman, until Jules, the astute dramatic critic from Boston, and an acute observer in such matters (being himself, like D., naturally attractive to such deviants, sometimes embarrassingly so), observed, after one of those marvelous dinners at the beloved Brice restaurant, in Wardour Street, when they had parted with Chapman and gone back to the liver-colored boardinghouse in Bedford Place: "You know, D., that man is very charming, I like him, he is most entertaining, and he gives the impression of being most wonderfully subtle and witty, not to mention exceedingly well-informed. And yet, I couldn't help noticing that in the entire evening he didn't advance a single original idea of his own. I know you have always said that you considered him brilliant, and a marvelous talker, and that you have learned a great deal from him: but just the same, the truth is that it was you and I who launched the themes, the perceptions, and who started things going; and all Chapman did was to come in, as it were, on the second round, and add a little — and I'll grant you, very skillful — embroidery. And you can say what you will, that's not the mark of an original or first-rate mind. His taste, no doubt, is trained and subtle; he obviously knows a great deal about art and music, he's been to concerts and galleries; he's travelled a lot, he's what I suppose you'd call a typical 'public school' and Oxford or Cambridge product, of the more aesthetic sort — perhaps better than average, if a trifle epicene: but I'd like to bet you that he will never accomplish anything as a critic, or anything that isn't refinedly derivative, and quite without force or character. Force, or character — those are the indispensable ingredients of an art that is true because the artist had been true to himself. That is the difference between you and Chapman. Oh, I know, you are young, you haven't done anything yet, maybe you never will: you may not *finish* anything, that seems to be your difficulty — you are always making starts, and getting halfway: but in everything you do there seems to me to be a sound of your own voice, even the faulty work has your own profile, your own gait. You'll fail, possibly, but not for lack of character, or for not having your own thing to say. But Chapman, no. You'll see. It will all be very nice and harmless and pretty; it will have a good many of the feminine graces, charm it will have, and it will be skillful; but it will nevertheless remain a *dolce far niente*. He's essentially the genteel amateur, perhaps in the best sense of the term; and if he wanted to, I have no doubt he'd compose just as prettily as he writes, or paint little gouaches and watercolors as prettily as either. And I don't mean this disparagingly. But I do think, just because you've found him so extraordinarily useful, and such a mine of information about English *mores,* and Continental sophistication, and so on, that you tend to exaggerate his talent. For it's a slight one at best, he's no genius, nor will be. His mind is second-rate. *Voilà!* And now, let us go forth and have a pint of warm beer!"

London in the summer — the "smutty sheep," as Henry James called them, nibbling at the shabby lawns of Hyde Park, where, shamelessly, in the hazy afternoons or livid evenings, the English lovers lay amorously interlocked — "these acquaintances," as Heinrich laconically remarked, stepping gingerly among them, "that might eventually ripen into friendship." London in the blond English summer, and the queer little top-hatted, frock-coated, Unitarian-minister-and-clairvoyant, from California, who had come all the way to it to see his English opposite numbers — William Stead and the others; and who, on meeting D. over the kippers and marmalade, in the boardinghouse in Guilford Street, had said at once, "You want to be a poet, a writer, a playwright? Yes, I see it clearly. Come to my room after breakfast, and I'll tell you what I find in your hand, your heart!"

Which indeed he had done, and with astonishing foresight and accuracy, while he smoked his confetti-colored herb tobacco. "Yes, you will write, but not too successfully. You have, I think, a streak of genius, maybe a little more than that, maybe a little less — the ability, perhaps, without quite the perseverance or devotion — no, it's not quite that either. You have the vision, the primary requisite: you will be a true seer: it is, I fear, in the communication that you will fail. You will always tend to rush at things somewhat prematurely: you will see beyond your years, ahead of your maturity, so that continually, and unfortunately, the immaturity of your expression, a certain glibness and triteness, will tend to spoil your excellent ideas, leaving them to be adopted and better expressed — better organized, because better understood — by others. Oh, not that now and then you may not blunder into an exception! You will achieve a few wonderfully happy incidents, you are of the race of the inspired; and at least two or three times you will have the most wonderful of experiences, the blessed experience of coming suddenly upon a veritable gold-mine of consciousness, seemingly inexhaustible, too, and with the words already hermetically stamped on the gold: perhaps out of some such experience you will even achieve one of those "controlled" masterpieces that are both controlled and uncontrolled, and these are the best, the true artesian water of life: moments of abundance and joy, and the memory of power; but no, not the disciplined knowledge that will enable you to perfect, at will, and repeatedly, true works of art. Perhaps yours is the happier way — I don't know. You are a diviner, a dowser, the hazel twig of vision will tremble in your hands. But — the gift will be capricious, will come and go; and in the end I am afraid I see a sort of final bankruptcy for you, an exhaustion of your virtue, even a debauchery of it. I think you will waste it in frivolities and piecework, in journalism and makeshift, in odd jobs dictated by laziness and indigence — or, worse still, by the need to gratify your baser appetites. You will be devilled by sex, and will not, will *never*, learn to control it; and for its sake you will disgracefully, over and over again, betray or sacrifice all that is dearest to you. A dreadful, if delicious, pattern, here awaits you; and I am sorry for you; and yet I would not be honest if I didn't say that you will have a quite miraculous, a quite extraordinary, life, one that most of us should profoundly envy; for you will touch it at almost every possible point; and, if you do die spiritually bankrupt, you will have known at least nearly everything — known and seen it, even if ultimately without the requisite power, or love, or understanding, or belief, to harmonize it into a whole, or set it into a frame. Even in your decrepitude, your terrible decay into poverty and meanness of spirit — if that should happen to you — you will remain horribly alive; and you will go under the ground thus dreadfully alive. For I am afraid, out of some strange kind of misguided courage, or instinct, you will actually, perhaps, feel this as a moral obligation. You will want to taste your own spiritual death. . . ."

The words had been as fascinating as alarming; but how kindly said, in the dark little Bloomsbury room, and how devastatingly true they had turned out to be! — And could one explain this sort of prophecy? At every subsequent turn in his life he had found the predicted pattern emerging, and, if only fragmentarily discernible, nevertheless all too patently there. A remarkable, and an extraordinarily *good*, little man, and good heavens what a singular pair they must have seemed, walking together along the paved banks of the Serpentine, Shelley's Serpentine — the sparrow-toed little figure, in buttoned shoes, and the shabby top hat, and the frock coat that was too long for him; and the slender young athlete, in his loose Harris tweeds, talking earnestly together, or stepping solemnly into the shining rowboat, himself to row (for the first time since Duxbury), while the owl-eyed little man steered (when he remembered to), and discoursed of clairvoyance and clairaudience. He had heard a child crying, he said, "all the way from Denver to San Francisco": he would tell Stead about it — Stead, who was destined (did he know it?) to drown on the Titanic. . . .

— Had he ever managed to meet Stead? — and what had become of him? For D. had himself, a few days later, been visited by a vision: after thrice — during the summer — dreaming of the sinking of the ship on which he was to sail from Glasgow — the deplorable little Allan line steamer Ultonia — and the very day after writing to the Frightened Uncle that, were he inclined to be superstitious, he would be tempted to change his passage, he saw before him, outside the Holborn tube station, the newsboy's apron-like placard, and on it — solely — the words "Atlantic Liner Wrecked"; and, proffering his penny, he had read, as he knew he would, of the loss of the Ultonia off Halifax — and in a fog, just as in the dream. And so, on another ship, and at an earlier date, he had set sail without seeing the little man again.

Your ghost will walk, you lover of ships —

Curious, now, to think of that young Widsith, that young Far Traveller, weaving his innocent design of journey across and across the Atlantic — on the Paris, the Empress of Britain, the Empress of Ireland; the lost Ultonia, the wrecked Haverfordian; as later on the Celtic and Cedric, with the chess-playing bar-steward and his ukulele Lady — D., with his omens and keepsakes, from the Old Country, bearing them preciously back to Harvard and Cambridge and Aunt Sibyl's drawing-room: or was it perhaps a mistake to consider, as he sometimes had, that there was no discoverable aim in this, no conscious purpose? For hadn't he been genuinely aware, on each of these returns, of the new items of love and language, as of heather-mixture socks, and the famous green hat — the new "currency," to be traded with Tinck, from Calcutta and Quetta, with the *Hound of Heaven* on his tongue — or John Davidson's "Forty Bob a Week"; or with the Tsetse, the fabulously beautiful and sibylline Tsetse, and his newly found treasures of Krazy Kat, and Mutt and Jeff, and Nell Brinkley? It was true even of the first of the returns from Troutbeck Bridge — but increasingly true as they were repeated — that he had invented for himself, or was inventing, and quite consciously, an "equivocal" existence: he was beginning to lead a double life: bi-lingual, bi-focal, he was deliberately learning to be two slightly different persons, to speak two languages, and to live simultaneously in two places: a secret dualism that profoundly suited him, since in a way it was the inevitable recurrence of the bi-polarity of his childhood, the seasonal swing from south to north and back again, from Savannah to New Bedford, or Boston, and from the language of the one to the language of the other. And just as then he had known at once how to adapt himself, or his tongue, to the basic need for inconspicuousness, shedding one sort of accent or vocabulary for another, and back again, experiencing in the process a sense of combined duplicity and power (like those lizards in the south which were reputed to change their colors, but so disappointingly never did, when transferred from brick, or board, to green leaf, or sheet of paper), so now it was with a sense as of a hidden reserve of knowledge and power that he made the voyage either to or from his Ariel's Island. To come back to Cambridge, and the sanctum of the Advocate, with its "rum teas" and punches, at the top of the Union, the winter walks and talks, the drunken philosophical debates, the long marvelous afternoons of reading in the Union library, where first Arthur Symons and the symbolist poets had been encountered and rifled, or the stolen mornings of reading at the Signet — Ibsen, and Tolstoi, and Turgenev, and Shaw, and Maeterlinck, devoured in the light of falling snow, while Paul, doomed to die, improvised Debussian variations on the dark piano in the dark corner — to come back now to this was in effect to come back to taste its comparative innocence. The shadow of Hawkins, and Gray's Inn, and Saville Place, but above all the shadow of Hawkins discoursing of perfumes and colors, of the Irish nobility, and Helen's Tower, and the Abbey Theatre — this shadow, for D., supplied an extraordinary counterpoint for so much in America that was still virginal and tentative. It was the shadow of the Old Country falling with a disturbing and revealing suggestiveness on the simple planes of the new: it asked questions that were difficult or impossible to answer, made statements that were difficult or impossible to deny. Dear enthusiastic Hindu Tinck, with the Persian profile, and the delicately sensuous mouth, like that of the death-mask of Keats, and the exquisite English diction — "a cup of chocolate — one farthing is the rate — you suck it through a straw, a straw, a straw" — dear Tinck, who was destined for tragedy — even he could hardly, despite his own emanations of London, avoid the singular dissociation which the shadow of the monstrous Hawkins seemed to induce in everything. No, there was no doubt about it: there was a destructive element in the Old Country in which one would have to immerse, which even here, at this distance, was already operative like a catalyst, and to which he now knew he must deliberately submit. He would have to go on submitting, as to a kind of delicious and intoxicating poison, perhaps to the point of becoming himself a saturated solution: only then, perhaps, could he become free of it, or free, should he then decide to do so, to enjoy the American scene wholeheartedly again. In this, if Hawkins' "immorality," or unmorality, played a conspicuous part, it was not really paramount. The decadent refinement, the weary sophistication, the serendipity eclecticism, were in their way even more vitalizing. This was a richness, taken altogether — if one threw in Troutbeck Bridge, and the wholesome Dixons, and all London, with its dark backward-reaching into the racial origins — a richness which he would have to assess, and amass, and make his own.

It had become, therefore, this duality of awareness, an ever more pressing constant in all that went on in Cambridge, and at Harvard — even penetrating, of course, into the Fayerweather Street drawing-room, and those at New Bedford — it followed him to the Chicken Hops at New Bedford, and the Egg Leaps, as to the

135

Buckingham Hall and Brattle Hall dances, to the dreadful little formal dinners (which had begun at New Bedford, where his shame had been bared, and his first dress-suit provided by Cousin Lew), but also, even more persistently, to the editorial conferences at the Advocate, the midnight arguments and debates, the exchanges of one's little poems and stories with those of Tinck and the Tsetse, and with Freddie, the Giant Sloth, the Colossus of Rhodes Scholars (he too with his omens and keepsakes, his letters from Balliol — ah, and that lamentable misreading of the crabbed handwriting, which filled a whole number of the Advocate with the repeated use of the term "Otonian," as meaning the denizens of Oxford) — in all these, though by now the details were lost, the English echo had become increasingly obvious. The green hat had been disapproved of — by all the roommates, by everyone, and had finally and unaccountably "disappeared." The preoccupation with that England, that London, that Lake Country, that sea-going bicycle (by this time put in storage, never to be seen again, at a bicycle shop just outside the gates of Gray's Inn) — all this was attacked as snobbish and inimical, if not indeed plain treason. What? There was not enough cultural background, or humus, or milieu, or history, or mulch, in which the new native roots could thrust and thrive? What about Hawthorne, and Poe, and Whitman? what about Dickinson? Thoreau? If Poe and Whitman could stay in New York, why not oneself? If the dear, pale, yellow-green, shadowless American landscape, lit everywhere by a blaze of light that was untamably indiscriminate, was different from that of Europe or England, did that necessarily make it unusably provincial or sterile? And the landscape of the American spirit, was that too so wholly without its native virtues and saliences, its clarities, its humilities and simplicities? Hawthorne, it was true, had momentarily succumbed to the insidious poison, had tried to warm his hands at that *ignis fatuus;* he even called it "our old home," and had had to admit — as Luke Havergal Robinson was to admit many years later — that the English, as Robinson was to put it, were in every sense of the word a "*superior people*." But that was hardly the end of the matter, was it? No, there was much more to it than that. The new civilization, the new culture, were still in the process of formation, of evolution: a new language, the language of a new biological and social continent, a new biological and social climate, was this minute in its most fascinating stage, the stage of concrescence and emergence: you could feel it on every side of you, in the wonderful new comic strips, in the Charlie Chaplin and Mack Sennett movies, in the magnificent flights, the inexhaustible inventiveness, of the American smutty story. The very language of the street had genius in it. Hadn't the Tsetse and D., just the moment before, been revelling in the latest slang word for Negro, "dinge" — ? Could one find in England any comparable fecundity, or, for instance, anything remotely like the delicious lingo that every day the sports writers were evolving for baseball and football? And could it turn out to be anything less than suicidal, spiritually and morally, if one were to abandon this for the outworn refinements, the tarnished subtleties and snobbisms, of a society which was visibly dying on its feet, and from which one's ancestors had come away precisely for that reason? Was it for nothing that William Blackstone had left the banks of the Cam for those of the Charles, to be alone with his books, and the Indians, and his own concepts of goodness and truth, and above all for his own invention of freedom and innocence — freedom from the enslaving bonds of society, and hierarchy in society?

The battle had been joined, the battle that was in some ways never truly to find issue. For if D. was himself to solve it, in the end, by exactly the foreseen necessity of saturation, and thus to be able at last to "accept" the American scene by himself assisting in the genetic process of simultaneously altering the scene and himself

— changing by realizing, and accepting by changing — so that, ultimately, there needed to be no semantic gulf, no Atlantic, between Savannah (or New Bedford) and London (or the dear house at Saltinge), nevertheless, for the three little D.'s the solution was not to be so simple. For them, the holdover was to remain, to persist: for them, the White Horse still galloped over the moonlit downs, the variable still approaching, but not arriving at, the limit. *Jackanapes*, and *Tom Brown's School Days*, and *Pilgrim's Progress*, and *Alice in Wonderland*, these, through D., still had them in their power, from which it was indeed even possible that now they would never escape. D. himself, whose problem to begin with it was, had successfully analyzed it out of himself, because at last fully aware of it: but in the process, he had so conditioned the little D.'s that perhaps now only by a miracle — and the miracle only perhaps to be performed by himself — could they ever escape. They had been sops to Cerberus.

Well, to be sure, there had been the problem of their education: it was thought, by Lorelei as much as by himself, that the Cape Cod or Cambridge public schools were not good enough: little D.1 had begun coming back from the South Yarmouth grammar school with an accent that lacked a good deal of the lapidary perfection of County or Hawthorn Streets, and with words unknown to Brattle Street, too. In this growing crisis, was not England, was not Ariel's Island, where the pound sterling was at a post-war bargain, the answer to the enigma? The few dollars which D. could earn by his wits might there be supplemented by other, perhaps journalistic, means: the short stories and book reviews would perhaps find another market. The Tsetse was already (somewhat with D.'s assistance, via Rabbi Ben Ezra) strategically established there, as D., on his first post-war expedition thither — the expedition which had also discovered Cynthia, and provided the ship, the *mise-en-scène*, for *Purple Passage* — well knew. Chapman, too, was there, in the exquisite panelled rooms in Queen's Square, writing musical criticism in the shadow of the Children's Hospital, while the long forlorn queues of silent women listened to the wailing of the lost children from the windows above them. *In Ormond Street the children cry* — what had become of *that* fragment of verse, the little uncompleted poem which still, for D., like those other lamentable verses which he had perpetrated during the 'Cynthia' summer, and in these very rooms, echoed faintly, deliciously, with Cynthia's voice? Yes, Cynthia had come there: she and the professor's daughter had come there, had stood there, astonished and admiring, while, in the bedroom, with its view of the chimney-pot (the one which in moonlight always reminded him of a whale balancing a harpoon on its head) he was changing; and the golden-haired Lily knocked at his door to tell him. Two ladies, two young ladies, to see you, sir — thank you, sir! Breathless, too, she had been, and no wonder: no two such visions of grace and beauty had ever before entered Mrs. Stagg's extraordinary little lodging-house, or come past that majolica urn, on the marble column, which proudly bore, in the entrance hall, its splendid aspidistra. Yes — but to remember this was to remember also the deliberate ambivalence with which the entire scheme for the education of the little D.'s had been engineered: for not only was it still, to all intents, the siren call of Ariel's Island which lured him back, but now there was more than that: the tall, the beautiful, the incredible Cynthia, the Cynthia whom he had foregone so unhappily for the sake of the three little D.'s and Lorelei (to whom he had precariously returned — and how narrow the escape had been!) — the Cynthia whom he did not yet know was wholly lost to him, still in a sense stood there, in the exquisite room, still murmured there, turning to look from wall to wall, "But *how* did you find *this* — ? Who would have thought, here, to find *this?*" And so it was therefore to an Ariel's Island and a Miranda, too, that he had proposed to return — ostensibly for the sake of the children!

Had Lorelei suspected? If she did, she hadn't said so. Not that it would necessarily have much mattered: the abyss had long since opened between them: years had passed since the halcyon morning, in the Green Mountains, when he had suddenly known that Lorelei had fallen in love: she had stood there before him, radiant as a summer tree in her innocent, her unconscious, happiness, the sudden and wonderful light that a mere look from Jacob had, like a wand, struck from her. Yes, like a tree in ecstatic bloom, she had stood there before Jacob, no longer aware of D., letting the raincoat fall a little from the shoulder of her bathing-dress, the simple and beautiful gesture of surrender. She was gone, she was lost: never again would their glances truly engage. The cold mountain brook, from which they had created with the mountain rocks their cold little swimming-pool, became, in a twinkling, in an eye-glance, an abyss over which intimate speech would never again be possible. He was wounded: if not mortally, then at any rate *im*mortally, with a kind of wound that thrice again he was to know: with Cynthia on the Celtic, Cynthia encountered for a second time on a ship (and good gracious, what *dea ex machina* had conceived *that* little irony!), Cynthia more dazzling than ever, in the same Hindu-striped jersey, as she told him that she was engaged to be married; and with Lorelei Two, on his return from the last the farewell visit to Lorelei One, the last time she had ever been seen (and how angry she had been!) in the house at Saltinge; and now, once more, at the wanton hands of Faith. Faithless and Pitiless —

But how much, how fantastically much of all this, come to think of it, had been, willy-nilly, left out of the plays, the stories! In *The Quarrel*, that only partially successful essay in classic form, partial because slight — but still, with its mild and argentine grace — the problem of the education of the little D.'s had indeed been pivotal, and was dealt with; but then, the little D.'s had ruthlessly been reduced to one, Lorelei's mother rendered as absurd as untrue, and the

whole erotic situation between Lorelei and himself not only completely falsified, but subordinated to a mere accident, the visit to
South Yarmouth of the professional fur-thief, and his stable of
poets. No mention of that abyss: not a word. No mention, either,
of his own — by that time — many divagations. No mention of the
years of sex-obsession, when, haunted by that animal, that feral
hunger, the unappeasable desire of the nympholept, he had hunted
women, in the swarming jungle of the city — London, Boston,
New York — as others, in another sort of jungle, hunt the tiger.
Purple Passage, it was true, had been a shade more honest about
this. But here too were the central, the fatal, omissions. Why have
suppressed, for example, the fact that the philandering D. was married, and had children? Why throw away, and at the outset, the
very element in the situation that made for tragedy, and thus irre-
mediably rob the poor play of any possible extension towards the
classic, or power? Without those inestimably precious children, the
nuggets, the rubies, of his heart, what possible dignity of motivation
could there be for D.'s self-control, his abstention, his flight from
London and Cynthia, or, for that matter, the abortive attempt at
substituting Helen Shafter for Cynthia, and that astounding train-
journey with her from New York to Boston, and to the Hotel Victoria (she had signed the telegram Victoria Cross) — none of which
was mentioned, either! Compromises, compromises — again and
again that telltale cowardly compromise, the failure to excavate the
core of the pain in its entirety, to tell the whole truth, and all for
the sake of keeping up appearances! All that long rain-and-sea-swept
winter in the great room at Saltinge, volleys of hail and sleet and
the channel foam flying across the tall windows, which looked out
to sea, past the castle on the marsh, he had patiently jointed and
joined — and so confidently, too — what was from the outset condemned to be a piece of work with a central fault in it, another
Jamesian 'golden bowl,' and why? simply that D.'s character, as

rendered in the play, should be a little more respectable, and that as an unmarried man his freedom to fall in love with his divine Cynthia should be unquestioned. That, and somewhat, too, of course, the fear of offending Lorelei. For if the true situation had been deployed and examined, it would have led inevitably to a casting of balances between Lorelei and Cynthia: he would have had to admit that Cynthia was recognized at a glance, once and for all, at the very first glimpse of her on the ship's narrow gangplank, as his since-the-beginning dedicated angel, his nonpareil, his four-leafed clover; and that his agonized abnegation was caused not in the least, or very little, anyway, by his concern for Lorelei, but primarily by his concern for the children, and his all-vitalizing love for them; and, after that, by a deep fear of public opinion. And it was his failure to do justice to *this* that had made the play essentially makeshift. As so many times before and since, he had simply funked it.

Just as he had funked — or avoided, anyway — the Ariel's Island theme, and Cynthia's crucial role in it. For had she not been the final precipitant in the decision to make the break, to cut loose from the fatherland, in order that — crossing wide water — he might rejoin the motherland? She had herself resembled him in sharing the same predicament: bi-lingual, bi-racial, and, like her famous uncle, bi-cultural, shuttling restlessly between Beacon Hill and Cheyne Walk, aware in turn of the virtues and defects of each, she had been the first to warn him of the danger that he might not so much find himself as lose himself. "One misses in it" — she had said of New England, and America — "the hand of man. How sad, how melancholy, a country it is! It haunts me, I am unhappy in it — as at Tamworth, or Jaffrey, or in the beautiful Berkshires — but with an unhappiness that is quite wonderful, because disturbing; you feel alone in it; and that is something that England or Europe cannot give you. There, it is finished, shaped, complete: and it is beautiful and satisfactory. But *there*" — and she had pointed to the western horizon — "you have a sense of freedom that is priceless. To give *that* up might be a profound mistake."

In this, she had echoed somewhat, to be sure, the many discussions between the Tsetse and himself, both at Harvard and later in Paris and London, the prolonged debate as to whether one could, or should, lay siege to one or another of the European countries, or cultures, and with what prospects of success, and which one. The Tsetse, early inoculated by the subtle creative venoms of Laforgue and Vildrac, looked rather to France than to England: an editor of the Advocate had returned from Paris, after a year, in exotic Left Bank clothing, and with his hair parted behind: it had made a sensation. But for D. there could be no question that, if anything at all, it must be England. The pull towards it had been steady and unintermittent, the signposts that pointed towards it, even if sometimes barely detectable, had been everywhere. Aunt Sibyl painting at Broadstairs, the Beloved Uncle cycling through Dorset, Cousin Maud stopping at Garland's Hotel, in London, for the opera, on her way to Paris and Weimar — or the Wagner Festival at Bayreuth: the Beloved Uncle bringing back his briar pipes and baggy tweeds and English tobacco, the Aunt her sunshot landscapes, which were somehow so much more fascinating than other much more successful paintings, with a centripetal whorl of light and life all their own: and then, of course, his own increasing investment, culturally and experimentally — now beginning to be quite a sizable sum — in the bewitching island: all this, in combination, without his wholly realizing it, had already shifted his center of gravity well over halfway across the Atlantic. The number at the Army and Navy Stores, in Victoria Street, was entered in his "Coop" notebook — it was there he had bought the two chuddah shawls, one as a commission for Aunt Sibyl, the other, on the spur of the moment, for poor dear astonished grandmother — who had considered it much too precious ever to use. From the little village

near Perth, in Scotland, and the dark weaver's cottage, where the
weaver sat over his loom — the uncle, to whom Wason, the carpenter, met on the Empress of Britain, had sent him — had come
the shining linen tablecloth for grandmother, too. To these rooms,
alleys, roads, and landscapes there was now a steady compulsion to
return: they must be seen again, the essences must be retasted, repeated, for confirmation and further analysis. This was a part, certainly, of something basic which he recognized very clearly: the
need of a rapidly growing awareness to match itself with other such
awarenesses, and more particularly those that were subtler than his
own, or different. It was this process, for example, that at Middleclass School and Harvard had automatically and insidiously di-
rected his activities progressively away from the friendships which
had arisen out of mere good fellowship, or a shared love of baseball, or tennis, or mountain-climbing, or other such sports and hob-
bies, to those young men who, like himself, had begun to look
round them at the inexhaustibly magical worlds of the arts and
sciences. Through the Red-haired Cousin, the Frightened Uncle's
ever-kind and ever-kindling son, he had been permitted to meet, a
year or so before entering Harvard, two or three of the editors of
the Advocate; had felt, reading their poems and stories, a foretaste
of the excitement of the adventure to come, the attempt to make
one's way into that world. And sure enough, step by precarious step,
from the illegal entry into Copey's English 12 to the printing of the
first bad poem in the Monthly, it had all come about as planned.
And with the knowing of Paul, the genius of his time at Harvard,
Paul, so early doomed to die, and then Tinck and the Tsetse and the
others, and Heinrich, whose love of music and painting it was that
first aroused in him a curiosity about those arts, and a love for them,
that were never to die, this process of selective advance, for a creative matching of wits, had been accelerated. The hunger of the
mind for adventure, and knowledge by adventure, led him every-

where, was unappeasable. It led him, among other things, into a selective shedding of friends — such was the hurry and pressure, with so much to be learned or discovered in so short a space of time — that had not always done him credit. Decisions had to be made, and choices, as nimbly and swiftly as the choice of eye and foot in the crossing of rapid water by stepping-stones, and the losses, the neglects, the omissions, had in many instances been as unkind as improvident. It had been too absorbing, too animating, too intoxicating for balanced judgment, even if at the time he had been really capable of balanced judgment. The very good Charles, from Kinderhook, for instance, with the charming and luminous asymmetrical face, and his infectious love of Shelley — that precocious anticipation of the later *annus mirabilis* when, with Wild Michael from Tonkin and the others, they were to spend a whole cerulean winter reading Shelley with Santayana, that Merlin, that Prospero, with his wizard's mantle from Spain — the very good Charles had been undeservedly forgotten, for he had been generous with his love, as of his gift. And there had been others. *Arriviste?* Must one, in such a venture, inevitably be *arriviste?* At any rate, the process had been compulsory, and in effect his behavior had simply been a tropism; he had merely, like a fly, ranged himself with the light. In this regard, one was merely an insect.

And the same tropism, naturally, operated with regard to Ariel's Island. The air there, and the whole complex and profound cultural *modus vivendi,* were an elixir of which one simply could not have enough. To read Wordsworth's *Intimations,* or *Prelude,* or Coleridge's *Biographia,* on the green west bank of Rydal Water, after a swim, or Thompson's *Anthem of Earth* in the sea-green light of St. Paul's, or on a bench in Leicester Square, or on the grubby (as Cynthia had said) marble-topped table of an ABC or Lyons coffee shop, in a smell of Bath buns and wet mackintoshes, this was altogether a more rooted experience than the reading of the same poems in America: if the figure — the poem — didn't in a semantic sense actually *need* the landscape, could there be any doubt that it was incomparably the better for it? and for the feeling, too, that the poet's veritable somatic presence, the sound as of voice or footfall, was still manifestly there?

Just as, for the sake of that still reverberating presence, those footfalls, those dying voices, and the echoes of death, he had fared forth, resigning both from college and the office of class poet, to Italy. The dean's office had done him an injustice: for spending two weeks on a verse translation of Gautier's *Morte Amoureuse*, during which he had absented himself from all classes, all lectures, he had been dropped from the dean's list to probation, and, affronted by the indignity, had resigned. Vain the appeals, relayed to him by the school grapevine and the Old Bird from the god-impersonating headmaster, the Boss: he had merely asked the Old Bird to justify the ways of man to god. Vain, too, the pleas of that other, that angelic Dean, the ageless seraph of English Five, after the meeting of the class in Sever. "I know you feel that the college has been unfair, and perhaps it has, I myself don't know all the circumstances, and it's not in my province anyway. But I would venture to suggest that in such an action, no matter how good the reason, you might be just as unfair to yourself. I won't insist on the fact that morally there is much to be said for obeying the rules, or fulfilling the terms of an agreement, just as, for example, in a game of tennis, although you might serve better if you could stand a little nearer the net than the baseline, nevertheless you refrain from doing so: it might be that this discipline, if it were self-imposed, would be good for you. But from the other point of view, that of your own career, if you should continue to want to be a writer, as I assume you do, and considering, too, that your *academic* career has been, may I say, a trifle random, in spite of your obvious gifts, and, in some quarters, your success — I mean, in your writing for the Advocate and for me — from this viewpoint I think you might be sacrificing a great deal, and will later regret it. You are very close to finishing — you have a post of honor to fill, a responsibility, even if, as I suspect, you don't relish it: in three months you will have done this and taken your degree, you can go out with a small but definite achievement behind you, and the feeling that, adversities overcome, you have come through, you have accomplished something. I hope you will think it over. I hope so perhaps a little selfishly, for I enjoy the work you do for me, and you are one of the half dozen in the class this year who make it lively. . . . And it wasn't a *rat*, I think, as you suggested a moment ago, that was rustling in the wastebasket, but a mouse."

How characteristically gentle and offhand and forgiving had been the little rebuke for his impertinent interruption; and the more effective, as admonition, for the fact that the interruption had been simply ignored, without comment, until the real business at hand should have been attended to! The humor, as he well knew, had gained point by the delay, the timing; and the correction was the more overwhelming, when it had come to be properly understood, and with the proper embarrassment, for being a correction of fact as well as of manners. "My dear D.," the kind voice had said in effect, "you should not have interrupted me in the middle of a statement, least of all in the middle of one that was intended for your own good, and volunteered by your elder and mentor, even if he were the last to lay claim to any virtues as either: but still less should you have interrupted him for the sake of making an observation that was, if not exactly facetious, at any rate in error. To leave it only on aesthetic grounds, let us say that a writer must be a better observer than *that!*"

How true, how generous, had been the advice, and how luminous, how "through-shine," as the dear Dean had been so fond of quoting from Donne, that miraculously wrinkled face, as he rocked his shoulders against the scrolled blackboard, imprinting, as always, the chalked words on the back of his coat. And was it true — he had remembered wondering, during the quiet talk — that he had been hopelessly in love with Cousin Lou from Plymouth, and that she had broken his heart? In which case, it was conceivable, had it all happened otherwise, that he might this minute be the adoptive father of K. and R., and the lost brothers would not have been lost, but here in Cambridge, and perhaps even — how could one know? — the Dean would have been his *own* adoptive father, the very role that he was now so beautifully playing! And had the Dean been aware of all these possibilities? did he know about the family at Boxley, the tall *porte-cochère* behind the immense hedges of box, which William Penn had planted, and Cousin Ted, defying all precedent, had successfully moved? and the family hidden from D. behind all?

Probably.

But it was to no avail, could not be invoked, anyway, and D.'s mind had been made up. Not only because of the injustice at the hands of the college: it had been considerably more complicated than that. That class poem had filled him with horror. Had he been more honest, or more courageous, he would have refused the nomination, for he half knew, in advance, that if elected he would run away rather than go through with it. But no, he wanted his cake both ways, he would indulge his vanity in allowing himself to be elected, then to resign, in order that P., who had so desperately craved it, should take over. Into this situation had fallen the episode with the college, so conveniently that one might almost suspect that he had in some degree fomented it. And of course there was the imaginary love for delightful long-legged blue-eyed Anita, the gay, vivacious, dance-loving Anita, which had come to its preposterous conclusion in the cloudburst by Fresh Pond — there, and on the rain-soaked front seat of the open street-car, as it rocked its way

148

back to Harvard Square, the wet canvas curtain flapping against them as they strove, in their distress and confusion, to find something to say. The imaginary love had reached its inevitably imaginary end in an imaginary heartbreak — perhaps now one should imagine oneself into a decline! One must drink too much, dissipate in every way, go morbid, shun Anita entirely: toy with the oh so very attractive idea of an early death: or even — why not? — fly from one's heartless Fanny Brawne, and join Keats in Rome. The Piazza di Spagna — it was high time one got to the Piazza di Spagna, and saw those flowers round that fountain. Rome in the spring, the Judas trees in purple bloom, and the Colosseum in moonlight — and after that, the grand tour leading, naturally, to London and Troutbeck Bridge —

The colored maps unfolded before him, the little antique Cunarder and its parading bedbugs (thanks to which he saw the sunrise over Gibraltar) dropped him into the orange and lemon groves of Naples and Capri, Wild Michael from Tonkin accompanying him (a very unsuitable plot on the part of friends, relatives, and teachers, to "save him from himself"), and the comic pilgrimage to death — and love — had begun.

I V

"—— and in Hong Kong those tiny little ponies they use for polo, they're only twelve hands high — they take them alive in the hills — you just send a message, 'Send me twenty griffins'; then they bring them in and you draw lots for them. That's the way it's done. Wonderful sight, too! Run like rats, they do, the riders' heels kicking the ground — "

The sergeant-major, turned bar-steward, clicked his own heels, the polished boots, smartly over the tiled floor towards the Punch-and-Judy-Show bar, his white-jacketed shoulders concavely erect, every five-foot-six of him still a soldier, still in North Africa with Monty; the bartender opened and poured; the isobars of blue cigarette smoke wavered and descended over the green baize tables, the grouped heads or the heads in rows; behind the heads, on the dirty wall, the war-neglected wall, a row of greasy headmarks, the marks of the innumerable heroes who had gone this way; but now, instead of those heroes, the old trouts seated in chairs and on the lounges, knitting, and gossiping, or writing letters. The pig-tailed little girl in the typical pink starched dress picked out Wenceslas on the querulous piano with one tireless finger. And once more the Old Toad, in the fat moleskin coat, approached the bar on neat low-heeled Oxfords, the tam-o'shanter pulled down over the glazed green eyes and puffy cheeks, on the prowl for the fifteenth time; while the tall beautiful Canadians, those two of the unearthly and Olympian beauty, the sort of beauty that is marked for early death, sat, as always, over their books at the center table, reading, talking and not talking, observing, and then forgetting, the human horrors around them. The hideous little Baby Russell, for example, playing his secret little game of "hand-mouse" along the edge of the card-table, ignored by the peroxide mother, the thickly powdered pachydermatous face staring stonily at nothing. Pity them — ? Must one pity them? These helpless ones, torn up by the roots, on their way to broken houses, broken cities, broken lives, broken minds and hearts, to resume, or try to resume, some fragment of a lost or forgotten pattern, to remake, or try to re-make, some bruised little remnant of a former existence, in a scene that would all too probably be wholly unrecognizable, and itself heartbreaking — well, were they not heroes too — ? Even the Old Toad and the peroxide mother? And as for Hardie, heroic and wonderful Hardie —

Difficult to read *Bubu de Montparnasse* (with the Tsetse's intro-duction) when one thought of Hardie, saw Hardie passing the porthole in the southwest rain, followed by the two boys, for Hardie's extraordinary reality made those violences and purpurate poisons seem the flimsiest of falsehoods. His perpetual astonished eagerness when told anything whatever — "Is that right? — Is that so? You don't say!" — literally singing the phrases in his ecstasy, his positive ecstasy, of surprise and joy at coming into possession of a new fact or idea, the face lighting intensely, and thrusting for-ward a little, the torso advancing a little too. "Well, I never thought of that — no, honest to God, I never thought of that!" There was an extraordinary sweetness in him, an almost excessive reasonable-ness, which was in odd contrast to his animal violence and the loud-ness of his voice, his boisterous high spirits: it was the signal that he was facing death, that he had come to terms with death. Already in a sense *d'outre tombe*, although not admitting it for a moment, he relished life, every brilliant instant of it, with a rapture that was purely lyrical: the prospect and immediacy of death had made him a poet. And along with this facing of death, or knowledge of it, and perhaps because of it, at intervals a strange and rare and profoundly touching modesty appeared to come softly over him, as if he were afraid lest, through some excess in his own tastes or notions or judgment, he might be momentarily blinded to those of anyone else. "Now here's a funny thing" — he had said to old Blimp, getting his word in edgewise — "here's a funny thing. While I was at the hospital in Pittsburgh someone sent me a couple of dozen oranges, sent them *anominously*. I never knew who it was. And I passed them round to the patients — Christ, that hospital was like a veterans' hospital, no toes, no feet, no legs — and there was three left. Well, I started to peel one, and I was just about to put my mouth into it, I'd peeled it all nice, when the nurse she came in, and oh didn't she snatch that orange away from me! . . . No, sir — bad for the *pancrease* — the *pancrease*, that's to distribute your energy. But *mine* doesn't. They told me how to get out of an insulin coma — and how to get out of a reaction coma. And I've got a card — look, here it is — that says I can urinate anywhere — anywhere. I had to urinate in an alley once, and a cop started to arrest me — all I had to do was show him this card. Wet feet — that's my enemy. But I've got it licked, I've got it beaten, *I know it.* Your life's in your feet — your feet has to be cleaner than your hands, they has to be immaculate. If they aren't — gangrene. *I* know I've got to have two toes lopped off — and when the time comes I'll go and do it. But as long as I can hop along on two feet, I'll hop! Course, I haven't been able to *do* much. That's why I'm taking the lads to my sister — she can do for them what I can't. But *I know* I've got it beaten. . . ."

Convincing? Self-convincing? But before Blimp could comment

the younger of the two boys had interrupted to ask for his money.

"Daddy, the candy shop's open again. Where's my money?"

"You've got it."

"No, I gave it back to you."

"That's right, you did. Fifty cents. . . . Funny thing, too —
when I was packing my box in Pittsburgh, there I found this little
purse, my dead wife's purse — I hadn't see it for four years. Four
years."

"God-damn — god-damn — god-damn — "

"Daddy, would a swordfish cut this ship?"

"No."

"Would it cut wood?"

"O aye, de aye, de o — "

". . . Yes, that's the hard part of it, that's what's hard." The
Blimp was off again. "To outlive the passing of the ones you love. I
was the youngest of thirteen, I was. And now there's only three of
us left, myself and my brother and sister in London. That's what's
hard. And it's peculiar, it gets harder as you get older. To see the
others passing on — your friends, and brothers and sisters — very
hard that is. You'd think it would get easier, that you'd get used to
it, but you don't. It began early for me — my mother died when
I was two. My sister mothered me. And when I was thirteen I
went to live with my uncle, who was gamekeeper to Sir George
Wetherby, in Surrey. In those days the laws was strict, if you went
poaching you took your life in your hands — yes, sir. You could
be 'anged for stealing a sheep. You could be 'anged for robbery
with violence. Or for selling a loaf of bread that weighed under
two pounds. Just to show you what could happen, take my great-
grandfather's cousin, this was in the days of King George the
Third. And in those days, you know, there was fops and dandies,
and they used to walk up and down in Birdcage Walk. And they
wore loud handkerchiefs, 'angin' out of their coat pockets. And

just for a kind of joke, you know, or to play a trick, as you might say, this poor chap took a handkerchief from one of these dandies, and damned if they didn't send 'im to Australia for it. My great-grandfather's cousin. . . ."

"How'd you sleep?"

"No, not too good last night. But that first night, after that train, I was ready for it, I slept like a fish. Hearing those wheels click, why, every blessed rail reported itself."

"I slept pretty good, and when I woke up — it was 'im, the gentleman from Boston that woke himself up with that bloody great gasp, and woke us all, it was 'im, by Christ, and I'll tell him so — it was 'im that was snoring — but when I woke up, oh my, wasn't I hungry. I did justice to that breakfast. Guess that's the last egg we'll see for a while. Though they say you can buy baby chicks in the Old Country now — two weeks old."

"Yes, a cockerel for five-and-six, so they say — "

"Won't be buying many at *that* price, by god — !"

"No, buy the feathers and make a soup! — "

"Toreador — "

"Shut up."

"Toreador — !"

"Shut up."

"Toreador — "

"Shut up!"

"Yes, Lord Brampton gave him twenty years' penal servitude and thirty lashes of the cat for robbery with armed violence — "

"God-damn, god-damn, god-damn."

"And in Montreal those bloody French-Canadian policemen, you ask them how to get somewhere, to the C.P.R., and all they can say is *were, were,* at you, *were, were,* like bloody idiots — "

"Drink your water now, Hanky, and go to the bathroom, and maybe you can go ha-ha — "

154

"Aye-de-o-de-aye — in Vancouver, in Montreal, those bastard, they rob, they rob, they rob, and tree year, four year, tree year, four year, tree year, four year, Jesus Christ, that's all they geev — tree year, four year — "

"*Rah, rah, rah, rah, rah* — " The hoarse animal bark of the loud-speaker, with its unintelligible gibberish, deafened the room with an announcement of a cinema performance in the recreation room, while the bedroom steward dropped the blood-stained twist of ab-sorbent cotton, Hardie's, into the slop-pail, and rinsed the blood-smear, Hardie's, from the thin green cake of soap, while Hardie, patiently, slowly, with conscientious pale fingers, picked at the caked and stiffened socks of his two boys, devotedly bending over them in an attempt to crack the dirt out of them and to restore shape to the shapeless. Hardie, up since five, when D., waking, had seen him prepare and use the syringe.

"Is it five o'clock?"

"Yes, it's five o'clock. I'm afraid I woke you."

"No, it's all right, I was awake anyway."

"I woke up feeling a bit jittery. Insulin, you know."

"Yes, I know."

But the feeling of guilt persisted, and rightly; for his inquiry about the time — is it five o'clock — had been intended as a rebuke to Hardie (as Hardie had well known) for getting up at that un-godly hour and disturbing the eleven other occupants of State-room 144; and his ignorance of Hardie's reason for it could serve as no excuse. It was Hardie's apologetic kindliness about it that had in turn, and all the more incisively for being wholly unintended, rebuked D.; and that now, over the opened pages of *Bubu de Montparnasse*, made that book, and the Tsetse's introduction to it, seem so remote, so factitious, so profoundly untrue to the *Ding an sich* of life, its real current and bloodstream. False was the bright green flamboyant jacket, the translation was unspeakably vulgar, and conspiring against the sordid and touching little story were both the vividness of Hardie, in that scene, at that hour, or later picking at the filthy socks, and D.'s equally vivid recollection of the meeting with the Tsetse in Paris, that summer, so many years before, when Bubu and Charles Louis Philippe — and all the others — had just been discovered. It was the good Grolier who had given the book to him, knowing his lifelong interest in the Tsetse; the Grolier, who, like a sort of beneficent spider, glowed over that incredibly confused cobweb of a bookshop in Boston; and now once again time worked its circuit of visual magic. From the green jacket and the bad translation, and the careful precise prose of the Tsetse's preface — ("I am learning to write reviews and criticism directly on the typewriter," he had said, "and I find it tends to compel one to use periodic sentences rather than loose. Has that been your experience — ?") — and across the sounds and shapes and vibrations of the ship, the Grey Empress, with her hubbub of a cargo, her Blimps and Hardies and Geordies, not to mention the Mad Swiss — slowly and tentatively began to emerge, under the corrosive fluid of the developer, the shapes and sounds of that spring, that summer.

That spring, that summer: they had been crucial, pivotal, all-generating, in the shaping of his destiny: the decisions made (like his resignation from college and the resignation as class poet) and the actions taken (his unerringly aimed flight to Naples, and the waveringly aimed fugue to lodestar London, in order that he might there, at last, rid himself of his tormenting virginity) had fixed the course of his life's voyage indelibly on the chart forever: Ushant, and all that it stood for, the hoped-for and miraculous light that guarded the subtle and treacherous approaches to the most dangerous of coasts, the most rewarding of landfalls, the vision beyond the shoals and rocks, had now begun to form itself as the place and idea, the spiritual locus as well as the *genius loci,* towards which all his life he must inevitably move. Reading *Bubu de Mont-parnasse,* he had become himself the gorilla-like figure of Bubu, the pimp, he had become also Bertha, the sentimental syphilitic whore, and Charles Louis Philippe as well — the sometimes too rhapsodic author, with his extravagant and violent Goyaesque images, who existed there, beneath the surface of the prose, like a pale crab, with sentimental blue eyes, which held on, with all its hard claws, to a raw human heart. One had become all that, and the ship, too, with its genius of a Hardie, its genius of a Geordie, but in addition now to this complex of complexes there was the identification with the Tsetse, the letter from Paris which first made mention of Bubu and Philippe, and then, at last, the actual meet-ing with the Tsetse in Paris, at 9 Rue de l'Université, for the first visit to the *pâtisserie* and then *sirop de fraises* and soda at the side-walk café. But this meeting was itself just as equivocal and am-biguous and incidental, like a stepping-stone from which one could go either forward or back: or a milestone which was equidistant from two goals. And everything, no matter how fortuitous or trivial, which had gone into it. The midnight arrival at the Gare de Lyon, when, too shy to try his French, and therefore to attempt to cope with buses or subways, he had walked, by dead reckoning (having worked it out of the map torn from Baedeker), all the way to the *pension* behind Notre Dame, and rung the night-bell prolongedly and apprehensively to wake the porter. Equivocal, ambiguous, but also germinal and central, a swift recapitulation (of all that had gone on during the year at Harvard, on the one hand, and the Sor-bonne, on the other), synthesis followed by thesis, and then the casting of runes, the making of plans. Bergson, and *L'Évolution Créatrice,* and the Tsetse's intention to return to Harvard for a study of Sanskrit, but behind these the target-practice with the revolver (bought at Wild Michael's instigation) on the beach at Capri, and Wild Michael's arrest and imprisonment in Rome, the hissing of the prostitutes from dark Roman doorways, and a bottle of warm Lacrimae Cristi on the hot lip of Vesuvius. The graves of Keats and Shelley had been visited. The revolver had been fired (by accident) through the hotel bed at Naples. Titta Ruffo had been heard in the huge Neapolitan Opera House, Pompeii explored solitarily in a cold April rain. The graves of Keats and Shelley had been satisfactory? Yes, very moving. He had presented a copy of an early "Moxon" Keats to the Keats Memorial Library, in the little building, on the Spanish Stairs, where John Keats had died, and in consequence had become privileged to read or work there whenever he liked, and this had been a delight: the identification with Keats had there reached its bathetic and pathetic apogee, and, after one more atrocious poem, suggested by the extraordinary view of San Castiglione del Lago seen from the train, had begun to decline. The arrest of Wild Michael did he say?

Wonderful, unpredictable, sentimental, romantic, violent Michael — "Travel not by the way with a bold fellow," he had read to him from the Apocrypha later in Florence, and this had really begun the end of a strange and in its way delightful, if a shade unnatural, friendship, a trifle infantile, and disapproved of by Wild Michael's mother, who thought D. an unsuitable companion, and far too sedate, for her lion cub. Lion cub indeed: he was perpetually knocking people down and beating people up; had had to run for his life in a Berlin train after assaulting a Prussian officer; had come perilously close to causing the deaths of D. and himself on Mount Washington in a scatter-brained ascent, in midwinter, without proper equipment or precautions; and was all his life to extricate himself, with extraordinary difficulty and bravado, from one mishap after another, which he had brought upon himself by his peculiar blend of courage and foolhardiness. It was typical that in the snowfilled hut on the shoulder of Mount Adams, which by a miracle they had found, and by another, with axes made habitable, they should have read *King Solomon's Mine* by candle-light, waiting for the snow to stop: he was a born adventurer, he wanted things, violent things, to happen to him, and they *did* happen. Was it true, as some thought, that there was a streak of murderousness in him — a sadism, and cruelty, that made him capable of calculated murder? There had been those, on his return alone from his honeymoon in the Canadian Northwest, with the story that the canoe had capsized, and his wife had been lost in the rapids of the Peace River, who believed her loss was intentional. He had married the girl — they said — unwillingly, as a result of pressure from her mother, for he was rumored to have compromised her. There were those who had in fact actually made the prediction that she would not return alive. But an investigation, and inquiries of the Hudson's Bay Company, proved nothing. Another party which had passed him on the river, going the other way, had warned him that the rapids were near, and dangerous, had advised him to make a portage around them; but apparently the advice was not heeded. He had seen his wife swimming strongly towards the shore, he said, and then, he thought, rising from the water — this while he tried to right the canoe — but he had himself been swept downstream (how far he couldn't guess) and had lost consciousness. When he regained consciousness, it was to find himself washed up on a spit of beach, *sans* canoe and *sans* wife. With the help of another party, which came along later in the morning (and in this he had been lucky — for weeks might have passed), the woods and shores, on both sides of the wild river, were scoured for days. The canoe was recovered, many miles below. But of the lost wife no trace was ever to be found.

It had therefore come as no great surprise that Wild Michael had kept him waiting all that halcyon morning in the Borghese Gardens: one always had accepted these eccentricities and irregularities: he was an extreme individualist, a most engaging nonconformist in all things; and for this reason, although an excellent athlete, and enormously powerful, he had never more than intermittently, or casually, played football or baseball, for all discipline was abhorrent to him. One expected him, as like as not, to be late — or more exactly, one expected nothing. And in this instance, the fact that he was once again so tardy — (in fact, he had never appeared at all) — proved, for D., to be a piece of curious good fortune; for without it, and his prolonged wait there on the park bench, under the Judas tree, he would not have been picked up — and picked up he literally had been — by the extraordinary monk. It was only later, on his return, finally, to the hotel for lunch, that the spectacular events of the morning had been made known to him. He had no sooner seated himself at the table in the dining-room, and looked, as always, to see if the pale English girl and her mother were there, than he was told by the headwaiter that he was wanted on the telephone. Wanted on the telephone — ? This struck him at once as manifestly improbable — neither of them knew anyone in Rome, not a soul — and that Michael himself should be calling seemed unlikely, to say the least, considering his deficiency in Italian. But of course it wasn't Michael, it was Michael's lawyer, an agitated Italian, appointed by the police (so he said), who began to explain, or to try to explain, what had happened, and what would probably happen next. Michael, it seemed, was in prison. He had assaulted a custodian at the Borghese Gallery, and had, in fact, broken his jaw. When arrested, he had claimed — said the lawyer — that the custodian had threatened him with a club — there had been some sort of misunderstanding, not to say dispute, over a matter of some photographs, or postcards, which Michael said he had paid for, and the custodian said he hadn't. And from the charge of assault, the lawyer said, he might conceivably have got off, on the plea that he had thought he was being attacked. But unhappily there was another matter. It seemed that on the way to the prison, in the patrol wagon, Michael had remembered that he had his revolver in his pocket (he had maintained from the outset of the voyage that travel in Italy, at that time, without a revolver, was absolute madness) and he remembered, too, what was worse, that D. and himself had never got round to applying for permits: he had no *permesso*. He tried, surreptitiously, to cover it with his handkerchief and drop it out of the car, and was caught. This — added the lawyer — was a most serious offense. The other thing could be dealt with, probably — but this, no. It meant two weeks in prison, at the very least, as well as a small fine. There was nothing D. could do: nor would he be allowed to see the prisoner. In fact the prisoner — Signor N. — wished him to explain to D. that D. might just as well go on to Florence the next day, as planned; and he would in due course join him there.

Which, of course, was just what had happened. Even during the talk on the telephone he had begun to feel that this sort of thing had now gone too far; a genuine annoyance with Wild Michael, which for some time had threatened to replace his admiration for one who was so much more forthright than himself, now effectually did so: and the next day, leaving a curt letter for him, with his Florence address, at Thomas Cook's, he had set forth on that journey which, he was now explicitly aware, was aimed at carnal knowledge: he must somehow, by hook or by crook, god help him, get himself seduced.

And it had been the monk, there in the Borghese Gardens, under the purple Judas tree, who had been, miraculously enough, the *deus ex machina*, or perhaps rather the *machina ex deo*, in this decision, since a decision it now quite definitely had become. Not that before then he had not been in perpetual torment about it, obsessed with it, miserable and guilty about it. But the singular interview with the Franciscan monk (as he turned out to be) had turned the trick. What a beautiful little irony, and how the Beloved

Uncle in later years, after the establishment of that wonderful intimacy between them, had relished it! "You mean to say you had to wait for a *monk* to tell you? You mean to say you couldn't have thought of it for *yourself?*" Which was exactly what he *did* mean to say. It was as if destiny, with the finest possible sense of design, and of the true fitness of things, destiny with the sure ethical and aesthetic hand of the artist, had chosen for him this form of annunciation, in order that not only the sense of guilt might be exorcised, but that it should be even accompanied by the blessing of the Catholic church. And if Wild Michael had not seen fit to go to the Borghese Gallery, in that dedication of his to art which was such an unfathomable mixture of spurious and genuine, and had not there flattened out the gesticulating custodian with one melodious haymaker (D. had seen it done on other occasions, and was himself, and in Rome itself — and only a little over a year later — to receive a letter from him threatening death with that same lethal left), then none of this would have happened. He would not have sat there all morning under the Judas tree, and, reminded by it of Savannah, as he looked up the Italian words in the little dictionary, and crept his way into the enchantment of Leopardi for the first time, he would not have caught the eye of the promenading monk, or the monk's would not have caught his, as he passed and repassed from bench to fountain, from fountain to bench, his head bowed as if in meditation, but in reality (as D. was subsequently to realize) to observe that astounding phenomenon, the blue-eyed and blond Anglo-Saxon young man, who sat there reading his book. For so it had been — for so, comically, it had been. Unable to resist that temptation any longer, the monk had at last dropped down softly on the bench beside D., and had at once plunged into that fantastic conversation, that macaronic conversation, with its alternations of Latin, English, Italian, and Provençal French. "*Non Angli sed angeli,*" he had begun, with the hackneyed old Latin saw, and eyeing D. a little lecherously: "Not English, but angelic, yes!" Had he heard that — ? Had he ever heard that? Oh, he had. Well, anyway it was true, the young English had an extraordinary beauty, and an extraordinary appearance of innocence. And skipping back and forth from one language to another, in his eagerness to make himself understood by D., who limped lamely after him, he managed at last to get out the burning question that had, it appeared, always haunted him. They *looked* so innocent — but *were* they? That heavenly and incredible look of innocence and purity! Could it possibly be true? — The full import of the catechism was not at once apparent to D., though he had begun to feel a shade of embarrassment, and a little like the bird that is being approached by the snake. But he was not for long to be left in any doubt: for, fixing him with that kindly, but also hawklike, eye under the brown cowl, he came out with it. *"Tu es virgo?"* And then, while D. sat dumfounded (for among other things he had never heard the word applied to a male before), he had repeated it in Provençal French and in bad English: he was taking no chances.

And of course D.'s admission of his virginity, and at the age of twenty-one, well, this had really set off the fireworks, the Roman candles. The monk viewed him with a mixture of incredulity and pity, not untinged with awe. Could such a thing be? was it truly customary? was it *generally* true of the American and English young men? For here in Italy, good heavens, here in Italy — and while he was not precisely cynical about it, he was at any rate calmly, matter-of-fact — the young men, or boys, lost their virginity at twelve or thirteen — yes, twelve or thirteen! Perhaps the northern races were more cold? the southern and Mediterranean races more passionate? or could it be a question of self-control?

They had, to be sure, discussed other things as well. Literature? Yes, Leopardi was a great poet, but a pessimist, and misguided.

And the great American novelist, Marion Crawford, was a personal friend of his, and came once a year to stay in their monastery. And he himself travelled annually from Italy, all through northern Italy, going from one monastery to another, and so into southern France, and even to Spain, preaching everywhere. For — he had repeated it slowly, emphasizing the words with one finger — "*Je suis le premier prédicateur de mon ordre.*"

And so, that had been the good man's gift, his unwitting spiritual viaticum; and it was from that singular and very disturbing conversation in the Roman park, in a Roman spring, that D. set forth, now consciously and deliberately, to find his Irene. To find his lovely Irene, in Leicester Square.

The grand tour, indeed, had from that point onward become pure fugue, the two themes, the two voices, pursuing and over-taking and overlapping each other, the twin and ambivalent themes or voices of sex and art. Nothing could have been more magical, nothing ever again would be quite so entrancing. Nothing ever again, either, would be quite so funny. But how fortunately it had all turned out, worked itself out — or could he claim, himself, the vaguest of hands in it? Perhaps. His resignation as class poet, he knew deeply, had been wise: not merely because that sort of ordered and factitious poem, for an occasion, was almost automatically doomed to falseness and dullness, nor only because its effect was apt to be stultifying, as the Tsetse had been inclined to agree, over the *sirop de fraises,* but rather because — and in this it was the forerunner of many such crucial decisions and avoidances — it was the first time he had been forced to measure, and respect, the dis-turbing force of his share of the family *petit mal.* He had known, instantly, that this kind of public appearance, and for such an occasion, was precisely what the flaw in his inheritance would not, in all likelihood, be strong enough to bear. This was the kind of 'public' trial — and to tell the truth it was something he had been pretty acutely aware of even as early as his last year at Savannah — which he must learn how to circumvent: otherwise, the penalty might be tragic. Not that the *petit mal,* or whatever, hadn't, and repeatedly, manifested itself in other ways, as it had continued to do for the whole of his life. That rhythm, that almost predictable rise and fall in one's sense of moral or social or aesthetic or psychic 'distance,' was all too familiar to him. He knew those days, those weeks, when the interior imbalance was perilous, when chaos had come again, and the machine of consciousness, and of controlled living, was all but vanquished. The mind was as if unreachably suspended in a vacuum, it did not respond as ordered to, or responded at random, disconcertingly, or even not at all. On these occasions he had learned to absent himself as much as possible from all social contact, for the slightest unusual pressure was likely to produce unhappy or embarrassing consequences. A schizophrenic *manqué?* Or must he accuse himself of a lifelong self-indulgence, and was it, *au fond,* a weakness which he might, with a shade more courage, have overcome — ? No — the evidence had been more than convincing: he had always had those days, and had even been able to name them, to those he loved, when he knew himself to be insane, or on the brink of being so. And in his recognition of this crankiness in the otherwise excellent machine at his disposal, and of the angles, as of a crotchety clock, at which it simply would not run, had been his salvation. The decision about the class poem was, with the resignation from Harvard, the first of these to be made quite consciously and deliberately, even if he had not been able — at the time — to say so to anyone. It was going to be too much for him — he had known it and avoided it; and in this sense it was perfectly true that he had himself had a hand in the shaping of that magical spring and summer, which had had, for him, the effect of finally opening all doors, everywhere. It was his decision that his life must be lived *off-stage,* behind the scenes, out of view, and that only thus could he excel (as that morning in Savannah when he had been afraid to jump down the twelve-foot wall in the ruins of the old post-office, with the others watching, but had come back later to do it alone), that had now established for the first time his freedom to maneuver as he wished to, and as he knew best he could. And this freedom, for him, must be inviolable.

He had it, at all events, and he enjoyed it, he hugged it rapturously, he was precipitated into it like a musical chord, which in turn, by its very presence, seemed to open an endless succession of vistas of beauty and life. The series of shapes and symbols — and it was odd to reflect, as Arnault, the editor, had noted, how the idea of 'series' had always attracted him — which constituted life, or the language by which one understood life and thus lived it, had suddenly become apparently inexhaustible, extending and exfoliating in every direction. Dogs and horses in one world, indeed! But what about a world of symbols so geometrically and psychologically complex, so shimmering with ambivalences and ambiguities, and algebraic extensions or equivocations, that one's dazzled awareness simply hadn't time to take them in, and was on the run, on the gallop, merely to get a fleeting glimpse of them? The semantic richness involved in merely *being* thus aware, and participating, made him feel as if he were himself the perpetually but logically, if unexpectedly and unpredictably, shifting pattern of prismatic hues and forms under the scrutinizing eye of the kaleidoscope: he was the watching and the watched, and the Law was in both, and alike in both. He had, of course, many years after that golden spring, written a brief essay using that very kaleidoscope, at Savannah, as the basic symbol, and comparing *that* progression, or series, of statements and patterns, first to the astronomer's view of the cosmos, or the ship navigator's, the moving ship on the moving water of a moving world taking its course from a cosmic chronometer of stars which was itself in visible motion, and then drawing a parallel be-

tween both of these and the comparatively uncharted cosmos of
the human mind, with its own Denebs and Rigels, Rolando's fis-
sure and the island of Reil, in which, as in those others, the straying
of a single particle of neural matter might change, or create, or
obliterate, a world. But no, that unfathomable, and yet to-be-
fathomed, pluralism, the plural mind in the plural universe, must
forever partly escape the flung net of symbol. That eternal problem
of language, language extending consciousness and then consciousness extending language, in circular or spiral ascent — as in his remarkable dream (partially translated into a poem) of the two sages,
the first of whom had discovered the most astounding of all languages, one in which, he said, meaning had been so fragmented
into particles and surds that it would require a thousand years to
assemble enough of them to constitute a single statement; only
then to hear the other sage reply that this was nothing, for *he*
had discovered a language in which meaning was so concentrated
that a single syllable, a single sound, was itself the equivalent of a
thousand years. *Vitam impendere vero,* naturally: but the process
would have to be empirical and slow, one would have to improvise
with the expedient, one could not possibly keep up. The dogs and
horses were too many. No, not too many — that was exactly what
made it so inestimably precious, the one pursuit to which one must
undeviatingly devote oneself, if only because only in this could one
fully realize the joyful dance, the *gaia scienza,* the gay wisdom,
of being. To bring it all into one solar or lunar and shining parenthesis, one expanding synthesis — the grave of John Keats, the monk
in the Borghese Gardens, the thunderous *fiat* on the ceiling of the
Sistine, the pitiful dyed flowers of the Piazza di Spagna, or that
admirable fresco, on the wall of the lupanarium at Pompeii, which
showed the young Roman's penis so emphatically outweighing the
heap of gold on the other side of the balance — to bring all this
together, well, wasn't that precisely what one was there for? Wasn't

one's own *existence* the synthesis, if one used it properly? Wasn't even the Wild Michael, now languishing in jail, and sharing his cell for the first night (so he reported two weeks later) with a Sicilian murderer, doing exactly the same thing — even if sometimes he *did* draw the long bow? —

The thing, of course, was not to retreat, never to retreat: never to avoid the full weight of awareness, and all that it brought, and above all never — and this was the undaunted grandfather, speaking from his plain little pulpit in the plain but beautiful little church in New Bedford — never to seek refuge from it in the comforting placebos of religious or mystical myth or dogma. The pressures would become, for some, too great to bear: the temptations, too, would be insidious. The security in conformity, in joining and belonging, was to prove to be too seductive for many a better mind than D.'s. Including that best of all, the Tsetse's.

But now the Tsetse was waiting at the marble-topped table in Paris, the chestnut blossom fell from the lamplit spring trees into the bock or the *bière blonde,* or onto the hair of poets; and, in the Luxembourg Gardens, the marble head of Verlaine looked downward, behind his marble screen, with exactly that half-abstracted, half-musing look, and a little complacent, of a man who is urinating. Irene was setting forth from Kennington for the nightly prowl through Leicester Square and to the Leicester Lounge (ah, that fabulous Leicester Lounge), while in Florence the tall, saturnine Chapman sat silent and discreet, his chin lowered, in the midst of that long table, that Last Supper table, in the Lungarno *pensione;* and in Venice, at the *traghetto* by the steps of Santa Maria della Salute, the gondolas knocked and chafed against the slimy stone. He had disgraced himself, on the train from Rome, by breaking the leather window-strap, and by his subsequent inability to get the window — of a variety unknown to him — shut: smoke had poured in: an Italian giant had been summoned from the next compartment, and after shutting it with, as it were, one finger, had dropped his freezing insult, "*Poco bravo*"; so that D.'s paralyzing shyness had been re-intensified a hundredfold. But he was on his way. London was there, and so was Troutbeck Bridge, and perhaps Alice Dixon. And women, there were women everywhere, there was a whole continent of women to travel through, and what might not happen — what? That *something* would happen he had no doubt.

> The Pillars of Hercules go down
> Like clouds beneath the sea:
> O that man's griefs went down so soon
> In Time's immensity!

How far back, and how unreal, already, was the sentimental little poem which he had left unfinished in the back of the *Golden Treasury*, that copy of the *Golden Treasury* which had twice been with him to Troutbeck Bridge, and which now he would have bound in Florentine leather, with gold stamping on the cover. *That* sunlit deck, east of Gibraltar — a deck which a day out from New York had been two inches deep in snow — where he and the Wild Michael had sat together, reading Chaucer, and studying Italian, was now like something from another constellation. And long-legged, blue-eyed, giddy Anita, she too had suffered a sea-change, and in this new light, whatever it was, the whole absurd preoccupation, not that it hadn't been in its way delicious, seemed now to be the purest moonshine. And what *was* this new light? Obviously it was nothing so simple as the mere change of scene, brilliant as the Italian scene had turned out to be: if a mere unfamiliarity, or an extreme degree of beauty, had been the secret, then the same thing would have occurred when he had first voyaged to England. No doubt the beauty and the strangeness had a part in it: and so, for that matter, did the unexpected 'references' to the south, to Savannah; for here again were Judas trees, the green lizards threading through vine-tangled walls, and that small daisy in the grass, smaller than the English daisy, and paler, which had brought Savannah back as into his very body. That had been an unfore-seen catalyst of a kind, it had added nostalgia to the brilliance of a hard sun on a hard landscape and hard pure architecture; just as, in its different way, was the abortive expedition to Paestum, when they had taken the wrong train, and got lost in the Abruzzi Moun-tains; and so, instead, had driven by carriage from Vietro to Posi-tano, and thence by *barca*, manned with brigands, had rowed and sailed, under a stupendous lemon-yellow moon, along a Cyclopean coast to that fabled *Toteninsel*, Capri. But no, the change was in himself, and the roots of it were in that decision of his — to leave, and to come; and to begin, so to speak, his *own* education. He had begun to look at things for himself, to read the text, for the first time, by himself, and to measure what he saw by what he wanted to do: a somatic change, which was a mere inheritance — a *moment* of change, like that at which the pupa emerges — had taken him in hand; and it was this simultaneous alteration of both outer and inner landscapes that had made the difference. The difference was, that he now knew where he wanted to go, and where he was going. It was no longer a game, or an exercise, or a study: it was the real thing, it was the beginning of a conscious life.

That ridiculous revolver — what a sensation it had made on the beach at Capri! Unaware of the need for a *permesso*, and having nothing to do while the Wild Michael lunched with his grand friends at the grand villa, D. had all innocently climbed down to the beach, at the foot of a cliff, had set up targets of old tins or bits of driftwood, and for an hour had entertained a growing audience of Italians with an exhibition the like of which they had naturally never seen. The whole thing was illegal; but as it had been so blatantly public, no one, not even the police, had thought of interfering. If the mad foreigner did such a thing, then clearly someone in a very high place indeed must have authorized it. They stood at the cliff's edge and admired: they admired, at last, in such numbers, and with such a steady, silent, animal stare of uncomprehending and unconcerned satisfaction, that it was at last only his own discomfiture that had made him break it off — that and the need to save ammunition against those potential dangers of travel in Italy which had so concerned Wild Michael.

And it was these potential dangers, at Florence of all places, and his habit of sleeping with the bright beautiful thing under his pillow, that had brought about his meeting with Chapman. The only males at that long Last Supper table, flanked on both sides by incredible specimens of spinsterhood — German, English, American — in search of culture, he and Chapman had sat opposite each other three times a day for a week without speaking. Each had been too shy: both had perceived that to speak at all would lead at once to a general involvement which would be only too painful. No step, therefore, was taken, and in all probability they would never have become acquainted at all — least of all after Wild Michael's arrival from Rome — had it not been for the revolver. For one morning at breakfast, over the pale coffee and *croissants*, and curly chips of butter, and honey, one of the waitresses addressed herself to Chapman, at some length, and with great agitation, in Italian, now and again glancing almost angrily in the direction of D.; with the result that Chapman, blushing a little, and kneading a bit of *croissant* between two fingers (a habit of his with which D. had soon become familiar) had then leaned a little towards D., and said, with some embarrassment, but with an evident appreciation of the humor of the situation, that the poor waitress, who was also D.'s chambermaid, had found the revolver beneath his pillow, had been at once seized with panic, and now didn't dare go near his room, much less make his bed. And would the young American gentleman please therefore be so kind as to remove it — ?

The young American gentleman said he would, the young American gentleman did; peace was restored; and in no time at all D. and the leonine untidy Chapman were reading each other their poems (after the usual protocol the admission being made on both sides) and delving into each other's histories. Chapman was five years older, had been to one of the lesser "public" schools, and to Exeter College at Oxford; had briefly studied music, with the idea of being a pianist-composer, but had decided that he was without sufficient talent for it; put in two years in a publishing house, in which his father owned an interest, but was bored with it; and had now, for the second time in two years, come to Florence for a refresher course in Giotta and Piero della Francesca and Perugino. To write — well, yes, he would like to write — in particular, criticism of music; but for that, too, he feared — and was frank about it — he had no genuine vocation, it was simply that it gave him pleasure. But so did looking at pictures, and especially here, in the shadow of the great Berenson. Berenson — ? The Wild Michael had talked of Berenson, and of getting a letter to him. Perugino? D. was taken to see the great Perugino triptych, and the Michelangelo *abbozzi,* and everything else; and the appetite which Heinrich had whetted began now to learn the first rudiments of discernment and taste under a guide who was catholic in his likes, a gold-mine of knowledge, extremely *simpatico,* and gifted with a fine sly sense of humor. For a few weeks, the year before, he had tutored an American boy, and his delight in American accent, and American slang, and Americana, was endless and, for D., very instructive. Here at last was someone from whom he could learn what *not* to say, and what *not* to do: it was precisely the final course in "English" that D. had been looking for. And in the blue-morning walks to San Gimignano, or the Certosa, or Fiesole, or to visit the *priore* at Settignano, who regaled them with scabrous stories of D'Annunzio and his white horse, or described with most unclerical glee the casting-out of a devil from a young girl in his parish (he had slipped a little picture of the Virgin under her pillow, when she wasn't looking, and instantly a fiery pingpong ball had flown out of her mouth), D. had learned in a few weeks more about the areas of reticence, and the areas of committal, of the upperclass Englishman, than in all his previous visits to England. He learned, too, that the New Bedford diction and language were a sure defense against anything. How often was he subsequently to be told that he could not possibly be an American, nor have acquired that speech anywhere but in England — as on that occasion, at the Savile Club, when the not-so-famous husband of the somewhat famous English authoress had drawn back and said to him, as if almost in reproach, "But you're an American! And you speak English!" — and he had replied, "Oh yes, at will."

The truth was, as D. could now reflect once again, that Chapman had been a veritable lifesaver: the debt to him could never be repaid. And his appearance had occurred at exactly the right moment. Perhaps, as George Moore had said of books — that they' fell into one's orbit, one's hands, just when they were needed — so people did, too: — they were there, waiting, in the requisite shape adumbrated by one's necessity, and ready to be found by that necessity, as if created by it. The Tsetse, and Tinck, and Freddie the Giant Sloth, the Colossus of Rhodes Scholars, had performed this friendly office for him, this office of creative response, as indeed the Tsetse was destined to do, in the future, with an influence so close and consanguineous, or fraternal, as sometimes to be paralyzing, or eclipsing; but poor Tinck had been expelled from Harvard, for cutting too many courses (he had asked D. to walk round the Pond in the rain, that classic Cambridge walk, and had wept in the rain as he told him about it, shocked, shaken, and incredulous), and had therefore, after that, departed; and the Tsetse had wafted himself to Paris, and Freddie to Oxford; Paul had been stricken, and was in hospital, writing his last short stories, as he watched the crews at practice on the Charles, and waited to die; suddenly, all that fine little literary scene had been disrupted by the onward processes of life and death; and D. had found himself once again alone, and without that so-much-needed competition of elders and betters. Competition — to be sure, Ned Holt, at South Yarmouth, in the famous argument with Jacob, had denied categorically that the competitive instinct (as asserted by D.) played any part whatsoever in the workings of the scientist's or artist's psyche, and therefore in his productivity, or the level of it. But could there be any the slightest doubt that he was profoundly mistaken? That matching of wits, that exposure to the brilliance of the rival, was there any doubt that, as with the runner, one did one's best, and even exceeded it, against opposition? The literary *milieu*, at Harvard, had for the time being, with those absences, become stagnant. The Old Bird was still there, and from him, during the year, had come in fact one of the sources of influence, hardly as yet recognized as such, that was to prove momentous in the shaping of his *Drang*, his career, his work — in fact, the "motor set" of his whole life: the Old Bird's discovery of Freud's *Traumdeutung*. The implications of *that* "Passage to More than India," which they had debated at such length (D. remembered arguing that *fear* should have its place in the motivation of the dream, just as much as the wish, or desire), were as yet perhaps too recondite for them; but there was no dismissing the fact that the magical bucket had at last been lowered into the only, the infinite, magical well. Out of this, and the reading at the same time of *The Origin of Species*, and Nietzsche's *Zarathustra* and *Beyond Good and Evil*, was to evolve (since one spoke of evolution, whether of worlds or morals), but so imperceptibly and slowly that he found himself possessed of it before he knew he had been thinking about it, his own late concern with the evolution of consciousness. . . : as being, for *homo sapiens,* or *homo incipiens,* the only true teleological "order of the day," his share in the great becoming *fiat* in the poietic of the great poem of life, his share — if one preferred to call it so — in the self-shaping of godhead, or the only thing we knew it by, the mind of man. But this was as yet a seedling that had not even begun to germinate, it was simply there; and it was the lack of the other, the cultural and literary side of the humanist tripos, that D. had found frustrating, and which now Chapman, in Florence, and later in England, both in London and at Inglesee and Saltinge, was to satisfy. Through him was to come the first genuine "social" foothold in London and England, the continuing *pointe d'appui* from which he could make his sallies of exploration and adventure.

It was to an address in Beauchamp Place, therefore, and to an engagement for breakfast with Chapman there, after the Channel crossing and the early train from Newhaven — an arrival unannounced and previous, which had caught Chapman by surprise, already at breakfast, in his charming little digs, with the handsome young peer's son, who was on his way to India — that D. was this time to make his return in Ariel's green Island; and to the discovery, as well, that this was a somewhat too American way of doing things, though Chapman hadn't said so in so many words: the surprise, which amounted almost to distress, on the parts of both Chapman and his friend, had made this abundantly clear: but, in the meantime, the fugal flight, which was so grotesquely in the nature of a nuptial flight, with its alternately urgent voices of sex and art, had to be accomplished through Europe — from Florence to Venice, from Venice to Milan and Como, on foot over the St. Gotthard Pass, and so through Switzerland and France to Paris. Vision and soundtrack — it was hard to say which had been the more rewarding and disturbing. "Ye Gods, I am in Venice!" — so D.'s father had written

ecstatically to grandmother, on *his* way to the medical schools of
Vienna: and ye gods, how dazzlingly and cornucopiously true. Wild
Michael — the rift between them now tacitly admitted as in the
process of deepening (and to this D.'s established friendship with
Chapman had of course contributed) — had gone ahead, and was
staying at the Danieli, which he well knew D. could not afford —
it was his way of saying "Let us now go our own ways" — and so it
was to the pension on the Grand Canal that D. had come by the
canal steamer at midnight, along the silent quays, and to the conversations at breakfast, while the water-lights oscillated on the blue
ceiling, with the Viennese art teacher, who, as she was making a
study of Tiepopo — Tiepolo? — naturally persuaded him that in
Venice that was positively the only thing, the only truly esoteric
thing, to do.

Tiepolo, in consequence, it had been. Every Tiepolo in the guide-
books had been dug out, and tracked down, by gondola or on foot
— from the agonized and earthy realism of the Stations of the
Cross, at the little church behind the Academia, to the most melt-
ingly diaphanous of clouded ceilings or cupolas on the farthest
watery fringes of that Aphrodite of cities. The kind Fräulein gave
them lists, and they obediently and joyfully did as they were told.
And it was on this relatively happy note that the queer friendship
had ended, for Michael had decided that the comparative placidi-
ties of Switzerland — that smug little nation, as Ebo called it — or
of France, and certainly of England, were not for him (implying a
little too that in *those* countries, at least, poor D. would really be
safe enough by himself) — and that as he preferred a somewhat
racier dish, he would go to the Balkans and Constantinople. To the
dangerous East, and by the famous international train — the Orient
Express — this suited his Byronic pose, on the one hand, and his
love of grandeur on the other: it was a natural exit. They were to
meet only once again in their lives. After the winter in Rome with

Lorelei One, where the first bad plays had been written, and where Kay had been told of Wild Michael's philanderings (with the inevitable result, and Michael's threatening letter) and after the Old Bird's transparent stratagem to keep them apart, on D.'s return to America, they had, despite this plot, encountered in the underground shoeshine parlor, in Harvard Square. "One of these days" — Michael had then said, the cruel little mouth thin as a safety-razor blade — "I will appoint a time and place for a reckoning with you." "Very well — I'll be there with bells on." And Michael, picking up the professorial "green bag" of books, which he then affected, and which D. had removed from the chair beside Michael's, in order that he might himself sit there, lunged up the stairs to be lost forever.

But now, the parting was, if offhand, and airy, amiable enough: they had had a good time with their gondolas and Tiepolos: a good time in their friendly rivalry of aquatic prowess at the Lido, for both were strong swimmers: a good time even at the Berlitz school, studying Italian. And how completely typical had been his final legacy of danger, the inaccurate and casual instructions about the crossing of the St. Gotthard, the bland assumption about the snow conditions there, at this season, which, as on the earlier adventure in the White Mountains, might so easily have had serious consequences! It was the last casual wave of that perilous hand.

Sex and art, art and sex: the twinned and ambiguous voices chimed harmoniously or discordantly everywhere, denied each other only then to embrace each other, or so naughtily mimicked each other as to be at times quite tantalizing, indistinguishable. If the dream was all sex, rooted all in love, was art therefore, too, nothing but an instinctive love-song, a song of glory, a praise of the life-force in its very essence, the becomingness of sex? Could it be anything but a compulsory — if infinitely elaborate — celebration of the will to live? and in that case, had the individual, the artist, any say in the matter, any freedom at all? Bewildering questions, one was for a long time to be caught in that logical predicament, and to feel that there were only two possible alternatives: either the individual was a 'healthy' or true child of nature, of the *natura rerum*, in which case he was automatically and helplessly her servant, her unconscious spokesman and celebrant, her predetermined victim, her slave, and incapable therefore of assuming any pride of identity or originality or virtue; or he rebelled, and ascended magnificently into the empyrean, out of time and space, like Lucifer in starlight, for a treasonable and independent view of the *primum mobile*, in which case he was forced to admit that he was *ipso facto un*healthy, and from nature's point of view defective. D. was not for many years to see beyond this somewhat specious 'either or' dilemma, with its fine use of logical exclusion, although the comprehensive vision of an evolving consciousness in an evolving world — a synthesis which could accommodate healthy and unhealthy alike, finding use in all — was already implicit in his very awareness of the problem. For a long time he took pride in saying of himself that he was a yea-sayer — in Nietzsche's phrase — but a yea-sayer who found nothing to say yea to. But now the furious dialogue was too immediate for resolution in anything but experience: the insidious debate was all very well, all very brilliant and spell-binding, but what was needed was action. One must live, first, by seeing and being: after that could come the translation of it into something else. This constant state of his of 'falling in love,' falling in love with all of life, this radiant narcissism, with its passionate need to emphasize and identify, this all-embracingness, must find something to do with itself. Subject and object must be brought together, and brought together in an apocalypse, an ecstasy, a marriage of heaven and hell.

More easily said, or dreamed of, than done. For the sake of economy, he had moved into the lodgings of the Famiglia Ghezzo, in a flagged alley behind Santa Maria, where the dear old ladies, delighted to learn that he intended, or hoped, to be a writer (and what a difference from the *American* attitude), insisted on bringing the cup of morning chocolate to his bedside; and from this he went forth daily to his lessons at the Berlitz school and his tours of Venice. To the Berlitz school, after the early-morning crossing of the Grand Canal by *traghetto,* the gondola ferry, in the slant Canaletto light of pale gold and pale blue, not only for exercise in speaking Italian, but, more excitingly, for speaking it to the delightful dark-eyed little Signorina, whose name he never knew, for he was too shy to ask it. The two hours went by in a twinkling: each day he would have memorized another of Oscar Wilde's little fairy stories, which he had bought in the Tauchnitz edition (along with Arnold's essays, in three volumes, and Wells's *New Machiavelli*), and these she was delighted with. It was obvious — wasn't it? — that she liked him: she was always, he thought, or almost dared to think, a good deal more pleased to see him than would have been occasioned by a merely professional interest: she liked his sense of humor, he was able to make her laugh, and she liked to laugh. His imagination, too, she clearly enjoyed, and the whole 'literary' tendency which he gave to their talks; and as they sat opposite each other, every morning, at the narrow table, searching each other's eyes, was it not for something else that they had perhaps been searching? But the conversation remained literary, rarely became personal; she lived alone with her mother, at the other end of Venice, and walked to work every morning; and she liked to paint, but wasn't very good at it; and this of course led to Tiepolo, and to her endless amusement at the idea of his making, all alone, and at *his* age, so serious a study of him. Just why Tiepolo — ? Just why, when there were so many others, and so much else to see? — She had very nicely pulled his leg, she made fun of him, teased him, enjoyed making him blush (which he did all too easily), and this in turn had led to questions about his life in America, and at Harvard. He was very serious, she said. Perhaps too serious. Perhaps he ought, as he was young, to have a little more fun. Did he ever go to the Lido? Oh, he did. Well, that was good, very good. And she knew he went to the cafés, in the Piazza San Marco, for she had seen him there, and she had looked right at him, and smiled, but he had not recognized her. But why — he said, horrified at the disclosure of this lost opportunity, in which the whole relationship could so naturally and easily have taken a more personal turn — hadn't she spoken to him? She should have spoken to him! He had said this almost miserably: it was a real disaster. But oh, she said, she couldn't, for she saw that he was 'thinking'! "*Lei pensava!*" And when he denied this, laughing, on the ground that he *never* thought, that he was incapable of thought, she too laughed, shaking her head, and repeated it — "*Si, lei pensava!*"

And that, alas, was as far as the subterranean little idyl was ever to go. The tension of his shyness, and of his fear to attempt any change in the tone of the relationship — for how should he go about it? — and his sense too of having betrayed himself as hopelessly and shamefully incompetent, *poco bravo*, an inadequate lover, in short, and no man at all, all this had the effect of frightening him off. He didn't dare see her again, finally, and sneaked in, on the last morning, simply to pay the manager and depart. What was his horror when, as he stood there in the hall, counting out the notes, his thirty pieces of silver, her classroom door had opened, and she stood there, silent, confused, hurt, incredulous — he would never forget that look of pain and shame — and he had then walked past her, too diffident to explain — for how could he ever explain? — simply murmuring, or mumbling, the words, "*Grazie — e 'rivederci!*"

Thanks — and till we meet again!

But there would be no meeting ever again; she was to stand there in that doorway forever; and that momentary and tangential meet-

Grandfather (The Reverend
William James Potter).

Grandfather. The bust in the
Unitarian Church, New
Bedford.

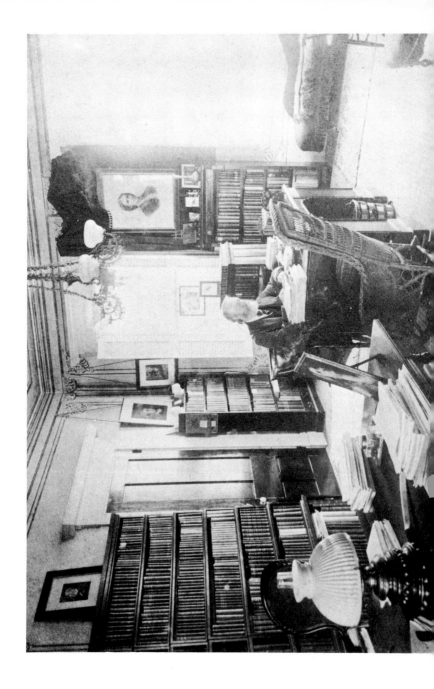

◀ Grandfather's study,
New Bedford, 1890.

The Beloved Uncle (Alfred
Claghorn Potter) in costume,
aged 5. Painting by Lorelei
Three from a daguerrotype.
Photo Waldrop.

Aunt Jean (Jane Delano Kempton).

D. (Conrad Aiken), aged 2.

◄ D.'s house
in Savannah.

Mother (Anna Potter Aiken).

Father
(Dr. William Ford Aiken).

D.'s mother with her children and Selena and Clara in the Colonial Cemetery, opposite D.'s Savannah house.

D., aged 3, with wheelbarrow at Cousin Joseph Delano's house, New Bedford. Cousin Maud Delanoye (Julia Delano) is on horseback.

D., aged 6.

D., President of the *Advocate,*
Harvard, 1910.

The Tsetse (T. S. Eliot),
Harvard, 1910.

D., aged 25. Painting by Aunt
Sybil (Edith Van Duzee
Potter), 1915. Photo
Waldrop.

The three little D.s
(Jane, Joan, and
John Aiken).

Hambo (Malcolm Lowry),
Cuernavaca, June 1937.

Hambo and his first wife, Jan Gabrial Lowry, Cuernavaca, July 7, 1937.

D. and Lorelei Three, Saltinge (Rye), 1941.

Bassett (Gordon Bassett).
Painting by Lorelei
Three, South Dennis,
W. E. Phelps collection.

Nicholas (Edward Burra).
Painting by Lorelei
Three, Saltinge, 1938.
Photo Paul Cordes.

D. at Saltinge, 1941.

Paul (Paul Nash). Self-portrait from a letter to D. 1939. Photo Waldrop.

D's study, Saltinge. Painting by Lorelei Three. Mrs. Robert J. Bender collection.

The Tsetse. Painting by Lorelei Three, 1952.

D. in 1968.

ing, which had promised the tenderest of blossoms, was to remain sterile, one of those exquisite — perhaps the more exquisite for that very reason — meetings of eyes that, through mischance, or folly, or timidity, lead to nothing. And what mightn't it have been! Venice, and summer — he could have changed his plans and stayed in Venice all summer. A letter to the Tsetse in Paris, another to Chapman, a third to the Old Bird (on his way to London), and of course a careful explanation (*omissio veri* in the highest) to the Frightened Uncle — it would have been as simple as that. But no, he had been afraid. The complications were too many, too real. There was the language barrier. There was the mother. And how could he be sure that it wasn't marriage she was thinking of — ? How, otherwise than fatuously, have made it clear that marriage was out of the question? How?

And so, the disgraceful flight, the feverish flight, had been resumed. Sex and art, sex and art, from train to train, city to city, frontier to frontier. From Da Vinci's Last Supper, and the pitiful cries, the anguished cries, of the insane woman all night in the hotel bedroom next to his, in Milan, "*Aiuta, aiuta!*" — Help, help me! — all night long, cries which he had not dared to inquire about — and how could he be so certain that it *was* a case of insanity? and that it was not someone beating her? and was there not the sound of a whip? — from this and Piero della Francesca northward, away from the landscape of the open or closed umbrellas, the cacophonous and deafening streets of Rome and Naples, to the orchards above Bellagio, the icy swim in Como, and the all-day climb, on bleeding feet, over the St. Gotthard Pass (for Wild Michael had been wrong again, the pass was still filled with snow, the chalet at the summit had not opened, he had to continue on, exhausted, and with the wrong shoes for snow, all the way to Göttingen) — from all this, reading Matthew Arnold on Keats and Shelley, and the touchstones of poetry, and *The New Machiavelli* on the nice conduct of *liaisons dangereuses* (extremely pertinent information), he must make his way to Irene. Over the crooked wooden bridge at Lucerne, and the *memento mori* of Holbein's Dance of Death, and past the Siren of Interlaken, dear Elsa — ah, dear pretty blonde Swiss Elsa, of whom Alan had reported, on a picture postcard, "I love her false teeth, every one of them — she loves me, she loves me not" — (a detail which was to be used in *Purple Passage*) — dear attentive Elsa, in the empty hotel at Interlaken, where he was the only guest! It had come pretty close to happening there — yes, it had been a near thing. For, alone in the long dining-room at every meal with dear Elsa, and emboldened by the lessons learned from the sacred Wells, he had nerved himself to flirt with Elsa; but how clumsily, and how as if instinctively on the wrong foot! Very fine to have a flirtation, conducted with a heart that hammered itself almost out of his breast, but why drag in marriage, why tell dear simple Elsa that she ought to marry and have ten children? No wonder she had begun to look at him with eyes like pale blue saucers, and to climb on a chair, ostensibly to put away silver or napkins, but really in order that he might see her very shapely legs, and to lean against his shoulder, ever so slightly, as she served him. The wrong attack altogether, the wrong approach, by no means Wellsian. And so it was in vain that he dropped his little hints about his habit of taking a stroll every evening, along the wooded road to the mountain, and in vain too, that, with a supreme exhibition of nerve (a milestone in his progress), he had told her the number of his room, and where it lay, and suggested that she come at night and knock on his door. She didn't say no — she didn't say yes. Nor did she appear to be in the least shocked. She hesitated, she frowned prettily and noncommittally, she smiled past him; she leaned against his arm again, showed him her lovely legs again; but then she wanted to know why he thought she ought to marry and to have so many children. Ten? Must she really have ten? —

182

The fatuous conversations repeated themselves almost verbatim from one day to another — it was really remarkable that a situation could be at the same time so fascinating, so agitating, and so silly — but no progress was made, he got no forrader; it became more and more apparent that the dreamed-of Wellsian *liaison* was not going to come to pass at Interlaken, or with pretty blonde Elsa. Elsa was not going to be so easy. She was as willing to flirt as ever, she would go on displaying the pretty legs indefinitely, but it was becoming clear that what she had in mind was — exactly as he had himself suggested — that little chalet on the mountainside, and the cows, and the bees, "and roses peeping in, you know, and babies peeping out." Would the young American have said all that if he hadn't meant marriage — ?

And so, as *The New Machiavelli* had been finished, and a week had been lost, which might better have been spent with the Tsetse, and as the local mountains had been climbed, and the glacier inspected, the fugal flight was once again resumed, but only after a quite ludicrous re-enactment of that anticlimactic scene at the Berlitz school. He hadn't had the courage to tell Elsa that he was leaving, and by the morning train. There was the usual arch conversation, but now becoming a trifle flat, for it had been kept up too long; and after breakfast he had gone to the office and asked for his bill. The manageress looked a little surprised, he thought; and this somewhat puzzled him, for he had made no commitments. But she made up the bill and brought it to him, after going to the dining-room to confer with Elsa, to make sure there had been no extras, and it was then that the reason came out.

"I'm afraid" — she said, very soberly, on her return, and looking at him with a curious attentiveness — "that our Elsa feels very sad about your leaving us. Yes, she is feeling very sad!"

It was a rebuke, and he began to feel deeply ashamed. Was the poor girl in love with him — ? had she told everyone? had the entire hotel been watching, as they believed, the budding of a beautiful romance, the Cinderella story all over again, with their own little Elsa cast in the heroine's role, and about to enter the transformation scene? The revelation was dumfounding, he blushed miserably, but there could be little doubt that it was true. He was being reproached: for in what was to have been this touching little fairy story it was D. himself who had turned out to be the villain, the ogre. He had trifled with the girl's feelings. His intentions had been dishonorable. And now he was leaving her, callously, with a broken heart, and without even so much as a warning or a farewell! —

He turned away from the grave eyes, unable any longer to endure that sorrowful appraisal, and it was then that he first realized that something far worse was to come. He had not been able to leave a tip for Elsa before he left the table, for he had unhappily not had any change, or the right notes: he must go at once and give it to her, for his bags were in the vestibule and the coach was at the door.

She was standing, silent and motionless, and with a look of heartbreaking humility, in the corner by the pantry, and her eyes, although filled with tears, looked at him with nothing but tenderness.

"This is for you, Elsa," he said, putting the notes awkwardly in her hand. "And good-bye. And thank you. You were very kind."

"Thank you. Good-bye."

She appeared as if totally unaware of the notes in her hand; they were obviously the last thing in the world she wanted; they were there in her hand, but without meaning; and he turned and left, for the coach, the train, and Paris.

For the coach, the train, Paris — Tsetse, Irene, and life: the centripetal and then the centrifugal dance of landscapes and cities, the flow of telegraph poles beside the train, the viaducts, the cry of the locomotive's whistle amputated, stifled, by the tunnel, and lost behind them forever, like all those other voices, the voices of the schoolmates in Savannah and New Bedford and Cambridge and Concord — the voices of the four geniuses of Middleclass School: Avvy, of the unforgettable Etruscan beauty and nobility, who had nicknamed him Candlepower; Penny, who had called him the Noox; intrepid, enchanting Jack; and the Old Bird, who was the whole world's conscience — these, and the chorus, the everlasting chorus of the voices remembered already from the ships, to which so many were yet to be added — but no, none were truly lost, they were still there, and still, in the heart and mind, could exert their magic, their magnetism, and the more magic and magnetic for his acknowledged sense of having abandoned them, his sense of guilt. Choice — yes, one was forever having to make choices; or, to be more exact, the inherited 'character,' that peculiar impulse so evident in the ancestors to make of themselves a 'writer,' this made the choice *for* one, the need of the ancestors finding its own necessary way. How much would yet be sacrificed to this ancestral need, in order that they should at least have their chance, their opportunity! even if, in the somewhat unsatisfactory persona of D., nothing very much was to come of it. Sex and art, yes, for those two twin divinities — unless indeed they were one and the same, a Janus god, who turned first one radiant but imperious face and then the other — his whole life was to be a perpetual series of forced marches, forced moves. But was art, in the end, to have rather the better of it? Yes, there could be little doubt of it. That virus, in the imagination, was a doom, a dedicated and delicious doom, in itself. Here, for example, was the Tsetse, writing, so many years later, the lucid sentences for *Bubu*, distilling, a generation after the event, and under compulsion to do so, the essence of a literary experience: there was no avoiding it, no evading it: the vision might remain for a long time unvoiced, but it was lodged there, it burned there, slowly, surely, it clarified there, and in the end it would stammer itself into speech; and in order that it might do so, everything else would be swept aside. Art,

185

and sex, or art and love — that was the primary order, for if one could sacrifice love for art, or one love for another, one could never — could one? — sacrifice art for love — or only momentarily, and with an eye over the shoulder, the unsleeping knowledge that this, like all experience, but more than most, was the indispensable raw material of art; for everything, and finally one's heart itself, went into that alchemist's alembic. Poor little Elsa, would she not some-day take her turn, her pathetic turn? Just as the oh so precious, the oh so exquisite, Madeleine, the Jamesian lady of ladies, the en-chantress of the Beacon Hill drawing-room — who, like another Circe, had made strange shapes of Wild Michael and the Tsetse — was afterwards to be essentialized and ridiculed (and his own pose with it) in the Tsetse's *Portrait d'une Femme.* Just as, again (and again on a ship), D.'s inconclusive encounter with Margaret Mc-Carthy, the demure little Irish maid from Boston and Tralee (and how nice she had been!), was destined, after years of imperceptible incubation, to make itself into an inconclusive short story.

And just as, in a different way, the meeting with the Tsetse, in Paris, was to be commemorated in the hauntingly beautiful recur-ring dream, while the more mundane details, apart from the *sirop de fraises,* had long since sunk into oblivion. Had a poem been read aloud in a Paris attic? or had there only been talk about it? It was years before he was to acquire in London, at the little Meynell shop in Museum Street, the Steinlen lithograph, with its pale mauves and saffrons, of the young girl on the balcony against the striped Parisian sunset; but it was invariably of this sky, this sunset, in Paris — and as if it were at first merely the sound of the poem being read aloud by the Tsetse, and then, like the genie mounting from his magic jar, becoming the whole diffused enchantment of a Paris sunset in the spring — that the dream spoke to him, sang to him, in the most disturbingly nostalgic of colors. Invariably it began with the poem, the cadences of the poem heard in the bare Parisian attic, and just as invariably then, like a camera, it dollied up to the high little window, and, all sound and rhythm falling away, became nothing but the unearthly beauty of an unearthly evening sky. There had been no other dreams of Paris — nothing else in his experience there, either on this occasion or a year later with Lorelei One, had exerted any comparable pressure to be remembered. No trace, for example, of the pretty little American coquette, and her mother, at the *pension,* who had taken him under their wings and guided him about Paris. No trace, and this despite the fact that he had thought he might be falling in love, or perhaps had even tried to, and despite the fact, too, that Hots — so he had called her — met him decidedly more than halfway, and with visible and audible maternal approval. Difficult to judge in retrospect just how serious in the end it might have become: she was charming, and pretty as a picture, she was vivacious, she dressed beautifully, she had tiny hands, and tiny feet in tiny expensive slippers, she carried a parasol (it was the era of the parasol; he remembered her carrying it over her shoulder in Trafalgar Square), and she wore a very clever little bracelet from which depended a heart-shaped pendant, and on which the enamelled letters, when it was spun rapidly, spelled the message I LOVE YOU. But that was in London, in the little "secret" sitting-room, at the hotel in Russell Square, to which she had led him alone, and with intent. From Paris he had had to flee, and ignominiously too, and just as the little affair, the dalliance, was at its gayest: with a trumped-up explanation, too, for how could one confess to so delicious a creature, and at so critical a moment, that — as the simple truth was — one's trousers were worn out, or as nearly as made no difference, in another day the seat would have gone through, and that he had no others? It was clearly impossible, would have introduced altogether the wrong note in the pretty little Watteau scene, or so he thought; and therefore, in some dismay lest his motives be misconstrued, he had had to cut and run. Not that he really needed to worry. They were themselves coming to London, and did so, and by this time he had the new Harris tweeds, and they met at once, and resumed the happy flirtation, not just where they had left off, but in reality, as so often happens after an enforced separation, a little further on. Yes, they had met at once; and after dinner she had guided him to the secret room; and the heart-shaped pendant had duly delivered its message. Perhaps too abruptly? Perhaps it had seemed a shade calculated? Was it too soon, too obvious? At any rate, although he had had the impulse, naturally, to embrace the sweet creature, and kiss her, he had been too embarrassed to do so. He had gone back to the digs which Chapman had found for him, in Trevor Square, excited and elated, and with the definite feeling that the next time would be the time, would bring the climax. Delicious! Marvelous! And what would it be like, to embrace this lovely being — what? —

But meanwhile other wheels had been turning, other footsteps and voices had become audible: the Old Bird was coming in the morning to share the Trevor Square rooms (with that odd bedroom which was really a backyard under glass); and although he did not know it, Irene Barnes, of Kennington, would appear at the corner of Wardour Street at precisely the moment when he and the others had emerged from the Gourmet, after a suitable champagne reunion, on the next evening; and, as a consequence of the meeting, he would be relieved at last of that bothersome virginity of his, and never would see dear Hots again.

For of course, after that momentous evening with Irene — Irene in the cool white muslin dress, and the black slippers, silver-buckled, which still, after a lifetime, he remembered as standing close beside the blue-and-green chalk drawings of the pavement artist, while the first light conversation between the four of them took place — after that, in a way that he could not possibly have foreseen, everything was to be changed — chemically, somatically, psychologically, spiritually: in effect, it amounted to a revolution of the soul, and nothing, not the light of day, or the shadow of night, nor sun, moon, and stars, and his own infinitesimal orbit beneath them, would ever look quite the same again. He had put on a new body and a new mind: it was as if suddenly he were clad in sunlight or dressed in gold: he could rejoice in his own radiance, like a fountain that knows its source to be unending. He had come to life's very center, and stood there with a feeling of precarious and impossible security, and as happy as a blossoming tree anchored in wind and light. How many things, now, that there would never be any going back to — ! How many incomplete patterns, unfulfilled designs, that had now, as with the slight click of the kaleidoscope, been completed and fulfilled! The many-colored map of life, stretching away backward to his own jungle of horizon, which for so long had seemed confused and confusing, without north or south, and roadless, now lay as in a bird's-eye view far below him, every detail in it perfectly clear, and everything predetermined and intended. How miraculously one knew what one was doing without any conscious formulation whatever! One's deliberate life, in this, was analogous to the dream in its precision of self-shaping, its beautiful ordering and composing of opposites, its glittering sleights of translation and elision, its globed and shining synthesis of the unknown into the known. And how comically exact, and aimed, as now he reviewed them, had been his own footsteps towards this *dénouement,* this transfiguration: even from the stone parapet of Monte Scenario, high among the trees, where he and Chapman sipped the cordial which the good monks had distilled from the pines, the *Gemma d'Abete,* and watched, far away, the first airplanes ever to fly over Florence, over the Duomo, even from that improbable eyrie, which at Harvard had had no preexistence at all, Irene, like a magnet, was already drawing him to London, to the pavement artist's chalk colors, and to the little gaslit hotel bedroom, off the Tottenham Court Road, where she had given him, with her love, and with her father's ring, his heart, his life, and his courage. What recompense, beyond the pitiful half-sovereign of gold on the windowsill beside the bed, for a gift so princely? What recompense for Irene? That he had loved her, truly and tenderly loved her, and told her that she was beautiful — which she was — or, what had so astonished and delighted her, told her also that her breasts were beautiful? — It had pleased and flattered her, too, to know that he had taken such pains to find her again, when he had seen the others to their hotel; for the first meeting had soon broken off, after the idle bantering and bartering, and the proposal by Irene's companion, of hiring a cab for a drive in the Park; and so, the minute he was alone, he had set out to find her, threading quickly through the crowds that circulated idly round the triangle formed by Shaftesbury Avenue and Charing Cross Road and Coventry Street, through Leicester Square. He *must* find her — he must: for his very first sight of her had been a finding, their separation had been a wrenching loss, they had instantly, in an extraordinary way, known each other. And if she and her companion were still together, how face the embarrassing necessity of making known his choice — ? But when at last he found her, in Shaftesbury Avenue, she was alone, she recognized him at once, she stood still as he approached her, and smiled, and said, "Hello!" And then she had taken his arm, as if they had known each other forever, and they had walked, slowly, slowly, through the June evening, to the blessed hotel.

Yes — her father's ring — he was in the army, stationed in India — with the Islamic inscription on it, which meant "good luck," she said — he could have it, if he liked: it was brass, merely, and of no value, but handsome; and she would like him to have it to remember her by. She had never — she added — thought of giving it to anyone before, but he was nice: he kissed her as if he meant it, and *that* was nice: and she was sending money to her mother and brother in Australia (they didn't know how she was earning it): and saving up to go there herself, where she hoped, she said simply, to marry. And since he was on holiday, wouldn't it be fun if they could go to the sea somewhere? It would cost him nothing, nothing but the hotel, and maybe, *maybe,* a new little hat, something pretty but not expensive, for the summer — ?

A seaside honeymoon which was not to be, never to be, though it echoed and sparkled before him, with its colored boats on the shingle, its crowded piers, and the bathers and the bad music and the cockle stalls, more intimately and vividly than many subsequent expeditions which had actually been made. Clovelly, with Avvy and the Old Bird, to which they had gone, Chapman seeing them off from Victoria, could not possibly compare with it in veridity. From the midnight swims off the breakwater, the phosphorus bursting in pale blue-green stars and Milky Ways around them, to Llanelly and the solitary walk through Wales, he carried that dream, that unindulged vision: beside it everything and everyone seemed unreal: and yet that was not quite true, either. For landscape and figures alike had now acquired an intensity of being like that remembered from early childhood: the walk through Wales had the same magnified immediacy that had characterized the walk with his mother (on that famous winter day) to the telegraph office, with the news of grandfather's death. Each tiniest detail asked for separate and loving attention. The idiosyncrasy, the precious idiosyncrasy, of each grass-blade must be saluted, the individuality of the pebble acknowledged. And as for language, the world of words, the books in the knapsack on his back, and that ancestral hankering to set about making one's own sibylline or hermetic onomasticon, out of which was to be architected one's own prismatic instant (if it came at last) of vision, whether of acceptance and wonder, or of denial and despair, as the logic of one's evolution might determine, *this* world suddenly had become as if possessed with a kind of mad erethism, exfoliating autonomously, word creating word, and mean-ing meaning, in an uninvoked parthenogenesis of galaxy that fol-lowed or preceded one even into the dream. Everything translated itself miraculously into language, as if that translation was the im-manent necessity of its being: its natural inheritance of the ideal. Lucky words, lucky language: perhaps that ring had — as Hambo would certainly have said — been a talisman, a secret sign: the well-wishing that was inherent in all things for oneself, and in oneself for all things: and what more mysteriously and divinely appointed than that Irene should have been, as it were, the Sibyl? She had given him a world. She had given him the word, the password: love.

What recompense for Irene? From D., none. He had sought for her again, on his return to London from Troutbeck, and for many evenings, but in vain. Round and round that tragic and dusty tri-angle in the blue London lamplight, and even up the Tottenham Court Road to the shabby side street that led to the little hotel: but in vain. Had she got her holiday by the sea, after all — perhaps even her honeymoon, with someone else? Or found her way to Australia to start a new life? No, no recompense for Irene: and from D., in all his life, no worthy celebration: only incidental refer-ence, but in terms of dream-compensation, in the *Gigue*. A complete falsification, lest poor Lorelei One realize that it had been no in-vented dream at all, but the truth of truths, the essence of essences.

And the more extraordinary, too, when one considered how radi-cal had been the influence of that single meeting, and how rami-fying. It was not enough to say that the entire summer had been illuminated by it. For hadn't it really been his entire life? That year, he had thought of her everywhere. She had been with him in the Garbourn Pass and on Dollywaggon Pike. Her shadow had fallen between his and the Welsh miner's, when, as they trudged north towards Conway Castle, the miner, asked for specimens of popular Welsh poetry, had come up with that alliterative curio, but in English: "You can manage my money — you can make me pure and happy — well-met, you are almighty — Mary, will you marry me?" — And at Troutbeck Bridge, with the good Dixons, and Chapman playing the Chopin Mazurka on the tinny piano, or walking in the soft rain to Orrest Head, she had been as present as himself. Was she already in the process of becoming, for him, the veritable symbol of his love for Ariel's Island, and, in this sense, of his conquest of it, his successful invasion — like another William the Conqueror — ? Had she become its *anima*, and had he, with the gift of that unwithholding love, at one and the same time recovered his lost mother and escaped from her? The *freedom* to love was at last unlocked in him.

It was of this that he was thinking, on the train from Windermere back to London, of this that all his life he would think whenever he remembered that train, and his encounter with the Wounded Face. For without Irene, that lesson of love and goodness would not have been learned, he would not have been ready for it, or more accurately he would not have been ready for the partial perception and acceptance of it which was all he could really claim. The man had got in at Kendal, and the face was a thing of horror. It was not a face at all. It sat opposite him, they were alone in the compartment, and he could not bear to look at it. But for five hours, on their way to London, how could he possibly continue the evasion? To get up and take his knapsack from the rack, and move to another compartment, would be too pointedly cruel: but perhaps he could wait for the next station, and, on the pretext of leaving the train, walk back to one of the rear carriages — ? He fixed his eyes on his book and thought of it with shame. He thought, too, of the cake of chocolate in his pocket, his lunch, which now, in these dreadful circumstances, he would simply not be able to eat. What on earth could he do? But just as he was deciding that at the next stop he would pretend to get out, the train began slowing down,

was gliding into a station, and before he could move the man with
the wounded face had himself risen and was going to the corridor
door, leaving his luggage in the rack. D. realized with dismay that
his ruse could not be made to work: he would be detected. He remained where he was, therefore, and waited helplessly for the
Wounded Face to return.

The return was not as expected, however. For the man came back
in a few minutes from the station buffet, bringing two cups of tea,
one for D. and one for himself; handed the cup to D., with perfect unconcern and unself-consciousness, remarking merely that it
helped to pass the time, didn't it? and began telling D. about the
explosion in the foundry, and the history of the operations on his
face, which had now been going on for a year and a half. It was
lucky, he said, that he had kept his eyes: yes, that had been lucky.
But the rest of it, as you could see, had been pretty bad — fourteen
separate operations there had been, and now the fifteenth — the
first he'd had in London — coming up. To build up the nose, this
one was, and to put some bone — or a plate of some sort — in his
lower jaw, so that there'd be something to support teeth. Then there
would probably be one more, and it would be over. Or so he hoped.
And did D. know where the Middlesex Hospital was? And, as he
wasn't familiar with London, could he kindly direct him? —

D.'s humiliation was complete, his shame abject. The offer of
chocolate could make no amends for that profound betrayal, that
meanness, that violation of humanity — yes, the very sense of one's
humanity, of 'belonging,' which Irene had all simply and all humbly revealed to him. But now, thanks to Irene, the springs were
there, the pity was there, and the shame, and the love — yes, perhaps, now, at last, there could be a little love. The chocolate could
make no amends, nor the insignificant act of putting the poor man
on the right bus — off he went, with a final wave of the hand and
an unspeakable grin — but perhaps, now, Irene had had her recompense.

V

"Upon Action Stations being sounded, everyone, except those on duty, will immediately
double below decks and proceed directly to
their cabins. DON'T STAND IN DOORWAYS OR ALLEYWAYS. GO TO YOUR
QUARTERS. Put on your life-jackets and see that all ports are securely
closed. If an attack develops while you are on deck: lie down prone
behind the nearest shelter."

—— war, and the echoes of war, disaster, and the echoes of disaster. Yes, don't stand in doorways or alleyways, little man, but go
to your quarters, hide in the dark crevices of corners, under stones
or grass-blades, like the miserable little insects, under a sky of tempest, that you are. Did you think there was any escape for you? that
the blast of searing wind, the tongue of forked lightning from the
divine dragon-mouth, or the all-dreaded thunder-stone, would spare
you, not find you out? Did you believe there was still privilege, for
such as you, or sanctuary anywhere, outward or inward, behind
walls of manmade but aspiring stone, or walls of vision and conviction? You will lie down behind the nearest shelter, but in vain: in
vain will you tie the futile cords of the life-jacket: useless, too, to
clamp and bolt the black eye of the porthole: the sea will have you,
has already, under your innumerable other names, sought you out
and embraced you, whether behind the sheltering deckrail, or in
the smashed lifeboat, or picked out of the alleyway by the green

triumphant wave, or sealed up forever in your dark cabin, like a bee in amber. Look at Hilloran, there, in the frayed Chief Engineer's jacket, on his way home from the lost ships, his hair whitened in the five minutes of agony in the engine-room, hanging on to the steel ladder under the closed trapdoor, as the sea, the Mediterranean, rose over his ankles, his knees, his thighs, his breast, before the footsteps rang on the metal overhead and the remembering hand lifted the ringbolt: did he not die then, drown then, only to perish again in the icy waters of the Arctic, off Norway, as the flaming ships went down all around him? It was really only a ghost of Hilloran (typographical error for Halloran) (and this had amused him) who walked urgently along the deck, the perpetual deck, one fist lightly clenched, and swinging backward and outward as he moved, while he talked in a rapid rush of half-intelligible words, and with short bursts of self-entertained laughter. Browning — did he know Browning? had he read *The Book and the Ring* — ? and he winked with the automatic left eye, the tears oozing down the side of his nose. He, like all the others, had been claimed by the sea, he and D., and all the others: the aproned kitchen-hand, strolling, cigarette in hand, out of a cul-de-sac, obviously from a passenger's stateroom: the tipsy blonde devoured by the three strangers, indifferent as to which it might be, so long as the contact came quickly and all over, overwhelmed as she was, and made helpless, by the pianist's hand, which was on her thigh: and the bright-eyed, soft-haired little Jewess, with the colored cord of torn necktie knotted carelessly about the slender waist, leaning forever over her interminable list of names, the names of the lost people, in Germany and Czechoslovakia and Poland, the lost relatives, the thousands, the hundreds of thousands, who were lost in Europe and must be found, whom she and the others were credulously and bravely setting out to find: yes, were they not *all* lost, like these, and somewhere on a list of names, like this, to be checked as missing? —

196

War, and the echoes of war.

"Law sets the boundary of war, and war of law: where the one is weak, the other is strong."

He had said this, quoted this — was it lifted from the article on war in the *Scientific American Encyclopedia?* — in the somewhat pedestrian and synthetic little essay on soldiering which, peculiarly enough, had been his sole comment on those gigantic parentheses between which his life had had to run the gantlet (like all mankind) from beginning to end. The echoes and shadows of war had been brilliantly present, excitingly present, at Savannah: the Beloved Uncle had arrived by ship from the north through the perils of minefields: and the battles of San Juan Hill and Manila Bay had been re-enacted, with lead and paper soldiers, and cardboard battleships, in the great long room at the back of the house, while the tropic rain beat at the windows. He had lived with the soldiers, when they camped before the house, he had messed with them in the improvised mess-hall, or tent, in the jail yard (the jail to which he would one day return with his message of death), he had marched with them, armed with a bayonet from someone's Krag-Jörgensen, the brass band playing Sousa up ahead, when they had removed their camp to the fields and chinquapin woods outside the city: he had even had long letters from them from Cuba. A game, only: but had he known it, the pattern was already set, the dreadful pattern which was to recur at intervals all his life, and to enforce his goings and stayings as it had those of the innumerable others. Take cover — double to your quarters, whoever you are, or lie down behind the nearest shelter (if there is any): live, if you can, or *as* you can: make the best of it: and die, as you must, with the deaths of those that die. With Sergeant Williams, drowned at Havana. With Alan, in the Foreign Legion, the gold chaplet still on that rebellious hair, and the phrases about the "beauty" of war still on his lips, as in the famous debate with old Yeats at the *Petit Pas* (he had swept in, tossing back that hair, with the announcement that war was beautiful, and old Yeats had sprung at him like a mastiff) — with poor deluded Alan, still in effect carrying that taboret, inlaid with mother of pearl, for his Monthly initiation, dead in the trenches at Vimy. And with little Bruce, one of those he had forsaken at Harvard, dead in the provincial French hospital.

A few out of many. Pawns that had been taken, sacrificed, and to what end or purpose neither they nor anyone else could say. "In the last war of all, we conquer ourselves" — so he had argued, the wish perhaps father to the thought, in that little essay on evolution, himself exiled again by war from the house at Saltinge, but exiled, this time, to Cape Cod, where the voices of the ancestors floated down to him, teasingly, nostalgically, perhaps even reproachfully, from the hills of locust and tupelo. Just as, a quarter of a century before, in that gay summer when Félice had appeared, parasol in hand, at the window in London, he had been driven back from his attempt to establish himself in Ariel's Island, Irene's island, with the idea of then sending for Lorelei and the little D.'s. Could one say that these interruptions, or postponements, or diversions, or influences — for himself, any more than for anyone else — had made any profound difference? How could one tell? If something precious was lost, might there not have been compensatory accidents of contact or accretion? The nice freckled English girl, in Brattle Street, had given him notes of introduction, and these he had presented, or some of them, and out of these tentative approaches it would now be forever impossible to gauge what might have developed. Brooke had knocked at his door in the Bedford Place boardinghouse, the front room to which he had moved in order to escape the feverish eye of Félice, and at the Vienna Café they had talked of the theatre and playwriting, for Brooke — so he said — had decided to give up poetry, thought it was not his true *métier*, felt he was not in the same street with Abercrombie, had been soaking himself in Webster — did he admire Webster? — and wanted more than anything else to write plays, to have a damned good whack at seeing what could be done with the theatre, or with poetry in the theatre. Shaw was all very fine, social comment was admirable; but one needed a deeper statement of values and feelings, the philosophical standing-off, individualism in the best great sense, Tamburlaine or Faust measuring himself against his world, wasn't it something like that — ? He had been to Tahiti, he had had a royal time in America, but now he wanted to settle down and have a good go at it. Would D. come up to his room in Gray's Inn, in the Raymond Building, and talk about it some more? D. would, D. did, and was a shade embarrassed by being asked to look at a great many very large and handsome, if somewhat posed, photographs of this extraordinarily beautiful young man. But the sherry was dry, and the talk excellent, and how was one to guess that the next time he was to see that godlike creature was to be the last — seen from the top of a bus in Fleet Street, making his way past the Cock Tavern, the bare head golden in the pale sunlight? He had not been able to catch his eye, he was soon lost in the crowd; it was the third of August; and although he did not know it, the poet was already making his way to the Aegean. To Antwerp and the Aegean.

August the third, and the fever of war mounting: the great city literally boiling with it. With Chapman and the Noble Lord (who was Keir Hardie's secretary) he had gone into Parliament, into the rotunda between the two houses, and listened to the inconclusive fragments of excited talk, and afterwards back to Gray's Inn (in the same building with Brooke) to play a Brandenburg Concerto (the second) on the player piano: ("If you have ears," he remembered saying, "prepare to shed them now"): and to look at the Noble Lord's collection of posters. But the sound of that excitement from the city, the feeling of that mounting tremor, was disturbingly perceptible even there, high up among the plane trees: and to the Noble Lord's anxious and unhappy question, "Do you think, do you *really* think, the people want war?" he had been constrained to reply, though he knew the reply would be distressing, that he was certain, he was convinced, they did. It was unmistakable; and by the next day there could no longer be the shadow of a doubt of it. The whole city had been seized by a kind of madness, a crowd frenzy, in its way comparable, but with a different intent, to that, so many years after, of the time of jubilee. The crowds coalesced, amalgamated, like an animal force forming itself instinctively out of its constituent cells, in a passionate need for union and direction: and once thus united, poured themselves, now to the Mall, to sweep up to Buckingham Palace, where the prolonged cheers brought out the little figures on the high stone balcony, and again to Whitehall and down to Downing Street, and, without knowing it, past the spot where their dead, their own countless dead, and themselves among them, were to be commemorated. The crowds dissipated, broke up in fatigue, fell away in remnants, shredded out into side streets, only then to rejoin, reform, renew their vitality out of new elements, new recruits: cars were commandeered: taxis were swarmed upon, the roofs climbed: flags waved: all day and late into the evening that human sea grew wilder, beat higher against the city's walls, as if in a kind of terrible joy, a dance of death. He had himself many times gone back to the house in Bedford Place to rest, only then to find that the excitement made it impossible to stay in, he must go and see it again, join it again, it was irresistible. And so with Chapman, and the young American composer, and the teacher of music, and organist, at Groton, they had once more left the crowd of Germans who listened, silent, frightened, and unhappy, as the Consul periodically came to the window to address them; and, after a late and hurried dinner at the Brice, had been swept to Buckingham Palace and Downing Street, not once but many times; and had even, thanks to D.'s brashness, got into Parliament again, for D. had noticed that the Noble Lord's procedure, on entering between the two giant bobbies who stood guard there, was simply to murmur, "Mr. Hardie"; and persuading the others to follow him, he did precisely that, and walked in. Rumors, rumors of rumors, rumors of late wires and ultimatums, of zeppelins shot down over Paris, over the Channel, of troops already clashing on borders. Grey was speaking to the House, someone said. And it looked like the real thing, yes, it looked like it. The faces, unlike those in the streets or before the Palace, were grave and drawn: no such hysteria here, these men knew what it would mean, were already thinking ahead. But in the streets, again, the human tidal wave roared down Whitehall more fiercely than ever, and rocked itself off its feet round the narrow aperture of Downing Street, in the lamplight, just in time to press hungrily round a dark limousine which crept out, and in which was visible, for an instant, the pale profile of Asquith, leaning forward a little as he replied, to the vociferous and choral cry from his people, "It is war."

War. And all night for many nights the rumble of caissons and tramp of feet down Woburn Place and Southampton Row, from the northern stations, Euston and St. Pancras, to the southern, Cannon Street and Charing Cross and Waterloo, the bands playing at measured intervals (one of them had played the Harvard tune, "Up the Street"), the cry of command floating intermittently over the dusty lilacs in Russell Square and up against the Byzantine minarets of the Hotel Imperial, where, only a few weeks before, he had lunched with Rabbi Ben Ezra and the representative of that newly founded magazine, the New Republic — who, it turned out, was no other than Walter, from Harvard, the darling of English 12. And the Tsetse, also seen a few weeks before, but now in Germany — what about the Tsetse? So little while before, and they had all been so full of plans for the immense, the wonderful future, the future which it was theirs to create into such unforeseeable and iri-

descent and illimitable and inimitable shapes and designs for themselves — in Paris, or London, or Rome, or wherever — like Brooke,
setting out on their individualist Faust-Tamburlaine conquests of
the inner and outer worlds: but now all was electrically changed.
The Tsetse was already endeavoring to make his way out of Germany (and this, after the endless complications and difficulties, and
the many letters, about that confounded suitcase, which D. had had
to forward to him from London); Lorelei and the Frightened Uncle
were cabled to; and the formidable task of trying to find a ship for
the return to America was undertaken, to be successful after a
month. But all that new beginning, which had been so gay and
promising, that prospect of an ever-widening life, through the renewed contact with Chapman, and now all the others — all this
must be foregone, postponed: he would once again have to retreat
to Cambridge and Boston, which, in the light of so much that had
happened in these two months, now began to look a trifle pallid. But
yes — there were compensatory advantages. For the Tsetse, the retreat would only be as far as England: but the accident would prove
to have been decisive, and in England he would remain, exploring
and consolidating the new cultural terrain, and beginning the la-
borious work of marking out what was to be his own domain in it.
Rabbi Ben Ezra would stay, of course; and so would Arnault the
editor of *Drama*, at whose bookshop, in the little square, D. had
met some of the *Pleïade* of new English poets: and Davies, the
tramp poet, would cling stubbornly to his diggings in Little Russell
Street, limping out to the corner, by Mudie's, for his morning newspaper. "It's not my habit," he had explained to D., "to read the newspapers, they are too literal, and I think they have a bad effect on the
imagination. But now with a war on, I read two a day — two a day!"
He had said it apologetically, and with a kind of sad amazement, as
they made their way to the little second-story room for tea and a
smoke — the room which one day he would line, from floor to

ceiling, with turves of peat (someone having told him that it was cheap), with the quite foreseeable result of the famous fire, from cigarette or whatever, and the astonishing sight of Davies, at the window, hurling turf after turf of smoking peat into the street below. The room, too, in which had occurred the wonderful battle between Davies and the prostitute next door. For the prostitute's hours, not unnaturally, were very different from those of Davies, and irregular, to put it mildly; and Davies, aroused at all hours by unseemly noises of one sort or another, and bursts of alcoholic merrymaking, which he could hear through the walls, decided that something would have to be done about it. As the good lady did not live in the same house, but next door, and was not even known to him by sight, and as she made her exits and entrances before Davies ever had time to catch up with her, hampered as he was by the wooden leg, and the start that she had of him, the problem took a good deal of thought; but at last he solved it. He would keep *her* awake, in his turn, until she had been taught the lesson. And so, from two or three in the morning for a week, he banged with his stick on the intervening wall, and she banged back in a fury, the two of them at it hammer and tongs, until both fell asleep exhausted.

It was the freckled English girl, from Bedale's and Cambridge, who had sent him to Davies, as to Brooke and Thomas and Flecker; and it was curious now to consider, when all of them had long since been dead, this accidental little nexus, not without its pathos and irony. Davies, like Brooke, had replied at once, but with a note; and, when seen, had said that he didn't in the least know who the woman was, but that perhaps he had met her at a literary gathering of some kind. Thomas had replied, too, from Petersfield, to say he could not come to London, but would D. like to come down? and this, of course, the war had prevented — as, too, it had prevented their *ever* meeting. Most touching of all, however, had been the little note, in the tiny envelope, written on a visiting card, and never sent to Flecker, never delivered (for of course he had learned in London that Flecker was in Switzerland, and dying) — the little note which he had come across in a wallet, years after, and at last opened: for by this time the writer too was dead, had drowned herself during an attack of puerperal fever: the little note which simply said, "Do you remember the girl at the dance in Cambridge whose brooch you lost, I wonder? Anyway, I am sending you a young American, from the *other* Cambridge, who wants to write — do be nice to him!" That was all. And the meeting between Flecker and D., which was to have been blessed by that little reminder of the party, the dance, the music, the Japanese lanterns, and the lost brooch, was never to come to pass; and even if it had, could not have been reported on to the one whom it most concerned.

Diversions, postponements, frustrations; the giant detours marked out with the red flags of war; the ship putting out from Glasgow, but at sea, off the Giant's Causeway, ordered by wireless to put back, on its own detour, waiting without escort (for none was available), to see what the invisible enemy would do; and then again ordered, just as mysteriously, to proceed. But despite the postponement, the diversion, like that which would befall him a quarter of a century hence, how much of the *mise-en-scène* of the second removal, the background, and all that it implied, in way of life, in its concerns and circumstances, and even the people, how much of this was already made inevitable and implicit by the events and encounters of this brief interlude! In the halcyon summer of Irene, so luminous, and so short a while before (before, too, his accidental meeting with Lorelei by the autumnal, the chicory-starred banks of Fresh Pond), his 'situation' in England, in London, if delicious and enriching, had been as yet pretty precarious: perhaps it was simply that what had been needed was a mere passage of time, the addition of a sense of the past: a sense of perspective. Yes, partly that, and the interval had provided it; Irene, and that summer, could now be looked back to, and with the feeling of continued and matured possession, and this in turn folded into the *new* summer, the *new* people, the experience as of deliberately widening one's circle. The scene at lunch with Chapman and Uncle Dracula, when the latter, bristling with delight in his self-assumed role as the most evil and corrupting of men, had kept wagging an accusatory finger at the embarrassed Tsetse, and repeating over and over, "I think you are a very wicked man" (the last thing, of course, that could possibly have been said of him), and then subsiding into that incredible croon of glee, so rich in diabolic insinuations, the Dracula moustaches arched, the little eyes almost shut — or tea with Rabbi Ben Ezra, tea with the Meynells (where the precious archpriestess had dismissed poor Brooke's "squamous, omnipotent, and kind" as "So stupid, so very stupid"); and the expeditions, from Rabbi Ben Ezra's triangular flat, and his Gaudier-Brzeskas, on the uniformly unsuccessful visits, whether to Yeats or Ford Madox Hueffer, for they were never, never, in: all this, and the meetings with Davies and Arnault, the evenings of music with the Noble Lord, had at last, somehow, fixed the evolving pattern out of which, for the better part of the rest of his life, his feet would hardly stray. He had his "place," now, in Ariel's Island: he was conscious of having acquired his own right to it. His feeling of security in it was as definite as any he felt in New Bedford or Cambridge, perhaps even more so; but given an edge, a danger, by the fact that it constantly challenged him, and that his right to it must be constantly re-asserted. Now, in effect, he lived there.

The diversions, therefore, would after all prove to have been quite literally postponements. The train of action, of events, which had now been set in motion, would unfold its *a* to *b*, its *y* to *z*, undeviatingly; and the great house at Saltinge, though as yet, like

Saltinge, unvisited, awaited him as appointedly as the successive Loreleis, who would, in their different ways, brighten or darken it; or the two other little D.'s, as yet unborn, who would forever add their glad ghosts to its beauty. Yes, it stood there, at the foot of the cobbled street, or near the foot, drawn into itself under its green hood of creeper, and with that wonderful appearance of serene self-sufficiency, as if it led a magical interior life all its own. It had been waiting, it could wait: as now, once more, it waited, after yet another war, for D. and Lorelei Three to return again. Already, up and down that cobbled hill as the ship bore him to Quebec, passed faces that he was destined to know: the Foetus-Face, invariably accompanied by the Boston terrier, and invariably wearing the knee-length lacquer boots: the man with the wen: the shrimp man, his basket under his arm, walking rapidly, the gold rings shining in his ears. The postman, too, whose footsteps could be heard clumping round the corner at the top, by the little greengrocer's shop (and the cat in the window), on his way downhill, in a zigzag progress, announced by the various sounds of the knockers, flat or resonant, loud or slack, until the sudden thunder sounded on their *own* door, and indeed in the heart of the house itself — those footsteps, once muffled by a mirage of snow, which had given him the idea for a story. And with the knock, and the fall of letters through the brass slot, which one could see if one peered round the bend from the top of the stair-rail (that moment of delicious appraisal), lying on the doormat in handsome dishevelment, what echo might not be repeated once again across all that crowded parenthesis of time — ? Rabbi Ben Ezra, for example, in an angry letter which opened with "Jesus Gord, D., you poor blithering ass," and went on to reproach him, after twenty years, for not attending the "Blast" dinner, as he had been instructed to do, with Amy Lowell and Wyndham Lewis and the rest — that first, and tell-tale, evidence of insubordination: adding, too, that he had been informed that D. (literally speaking) had not been too 'discreet' in his choice of friends! Or the Noble Lord, in a note from the Reform Club, inquiring whether, as he was approaching the end of his life, and lonely, they would consider accepting him as a P.G.

All this was postponed, merely, by the first of the many compulsory returns to America, whether to New York or Boston (for how often economic pressure was to drive him back, on the one hand, or a sudden need for reimmersing himself in that more vital, if more vulgar, solution, a touching of earth, on the other): and the war years in Boston, on Beacon Hill, had been simply a kind of exile in advance, and the work done there was done as if in preparation for the ultimate removal, the return to what was now clearly accepted as the chosen base. There would be, of course, in the meantime, the sally to South Yarmouth, also at the dictates of economy, but partly too in order that he might join the composer and Jacob there: the sally to the little ancestral house (though they hadn't known it until long after the house had been sold) by the river, on Cape Cod, where also, it was agreed, life in the country would be good for the children. Cape Cod — of course, grandfather had taught school there one summer, to help defray his Harvard expenses: and it was from that very cottage in South Yarmouth, then a Quaker settlement, that Cousin Abiel had written the teasing letter to grandfather at Harvard. "It is fashionable down this way" — it was something like this he had written — "to go and live with the girls, instead of finding them a home — for a while, at least. *Thee* might get married on those conditions, I should think, and not always make the *world* thy home!" It was a family stamping-ground; the streets, like those in New Bedford, bore the names of the ancestors; and had not the good Bassett, the great Bassett, been born and raised there, the Bassett who had been his alphabetically ordained *vis-à-vis* in Spanish 5, in Emerson Hall, and his wonderful mentor then (for D. had privily elected an advanced course

207

without the slightest previous acquaintance with Spanish) and his wonderful friend ever since? The Bassett to whom he had said, in the Cambridge apartment, just before they had moved to the Cape, that the Marsden Hartley "Blue Mountain" (bought with the proceeds of their solitary Liberty Bond) needed more perspective than so small a sitting-room afforded, and would be better seen if hung in the tree outside the window; the Bassett who walked over the country roads from his mother's house in South Dennis, past the village church, where his own ancestors were buried, and Jacob's cottage, opposite, for their first Sunday of housewarming, and Lorelei's first scallop stew. Had the Bassett, in fact, perhaps exercised some influence in their choice of the Cape, with his profound and inexhaustible knowledge of family lore there — D.'s as well as his own? It was more than likely: and it would turn out to be more than fitting. For together they would make it, at last, and rightly, with the truest of poetic justice, their own country; as grandfather, and Cousin Abiel (how the Bassett had relished that impish letter!), and all the other dear people, would have wished.

The apartment in Cambridge, with its all-dominating blue mountain, had succeeded the eyrie above the roofs of Beacon Hill, for the year between the war's end and the departure for the Cape; it was here that delightful Marian had come, on the memorable night before prohibition, while Lorelei and the two little D.'s (for Jean had been born that winter) were visiting in Montreal; here, alas, that he had seen her for the last time. What extraordinary nonsense had come over him? What had possessed him, what momentary folly of self-delusion? Disenchantment — it was that notion of the composer's, derived, he said, from a passage in Strauss's *Don Juan*, the theme of sexual disgust (*post coitum tristis est*) which again, as so many times before, had interposed its poisonous self-consciousness; and by the mere act of prediction, or of foresight and fear, had brought the predicted feeling to pass. As simple and ridiculous as that. He would never — he had been absolutely certain — want to see her again; it was finished; and his distaste and embarrassment had become so acute that he had not even seen her all the way home: he had put her on the last car from Harvard Square, the only woman in a bedlam of drunken rowdyism, for the terrifying midnight ride to Boston, and then walked back to Craigie Street with a feeling of relief which amounted positively to elation. Small wonder that she had refused to see him again, when, a year later, he had written her from the Cape, or that, when she married the lawyer whom she "liked, but didn't love," she should have concealed both the event and his name. He had found out, but only by tracing the nurses' home, which had moved; and by asking her roommate, who had finally told him, but reluctantly, and with disapproval — (obviously she thought he had behaved very badly); and only then, when he had assured her that he had no intention of trying to make trouble. She had, in effect, warned him to leave poor Marian alone.

Which he had done. Once only had he written to her, simply to say that he would like to give her a wedding present: she had not replied. And once only, years later, during a summer return from Saltinge, had they met by chance, in the North Station, and she had half hidden her face in her handkerchief, and tried to duck past him unrecognized, but he had caught her and turned her round, the same merry and pretty and giggling Marian, hiding her mouth, as always, behind the crumpled handkerchief, in a kind of delighted embarrassment. And he had urged her to meet him for dinner. They would go, as they always used to, to the Avery, and have martinis, and listen to the music, where that astonishing girl had sung — did she remember — M-i-s-s-i-s-s-i-p-p-i; and after dinner the benedictines. And after that — ? But no, she said no. They mustn't. No, they shouldn't, he knew that as well as she did, she said, but looking at him, just the same, as enchantingly and provocatively as ever. She was very happy, and hoped *he* was, and they had had a good time together, hadn't they? — but they mustn't try to resume it. And he had acquiesced, of course, for she was right. And did she have any children? No? That was too bad. And he, had he had any more — ? One, little June. And yes, he liked living in England, but it was difficult making a living there, he was back looking for more hackwork to do, more journalism, more reporting of tennis and horse-races, god help him, more book reviews, more articles. And how were Jean and Jed? Jean and Jed were fine. Jed knew more at ten than D. had at twenty, so much better were the English Schools: he played chess — think of it! — with the mayor of Saltinge: he was learning tennis, too. And Jean was a ravishing redheaded beauty, and just as funny as she'd always been. Still made those staggering remarks that came, like lightning, out of nowhere. As, when D., at breakfast in Inglesee, had delivered a comic tirade on the high cost of living, wildly exaggerating the cost of everything — the food, the rent, the coal, the paraffin for the lamps, the typewriter paper, the matches, the buses to Saltinge, the trains to London, the food for the cat (whose name was Nettle), and the clothes, the clothes, the clothes — and at the end had turned to Jean with what was intended to be the ultimate and devastating question: "Yes! and do you know what *you* cost — ?" — and she had replied instantly, "A marriage!" Or, as when he had somewhat sententiously observed that "Yesterday was today and today was tomorrow," she had at once triumphed with "Tomorrow today will be yesterday!" It was like that — it was still like that. And Marian was entranced, as she'd always been, by the intimate details of family, in which she so loved to share, and to which — for she so visibly enjoyed it — he habitually gave a slight twist of farce-comedy, of the ridiculous, himself a mixture of victim and clown. She had truly loved them; she still did; she had truly loved *him*: perhaps that too she still did; and that he had himself loved *her*, far more than in his easy complacency he had ever paused to guess, and still loved her, he knew now, as he took the white-gloved hand in his, for the last time, and she said good-bye, and turned smiling away.

Love, indeed: how humiliating that one knew so pitifully little about it, was so often so cruelly unaware of it, unaware of its beauty, its strength, its generosity, its wholeness! How often had the shadow of Eros passed by unrecognized, unhonored, the ethereal wing-beat unheard, or, if heard, mistaken for something else! Once — the poet — Rimbaud? — had said — 'If I remember rightly, my life was a feast where all the hearts opened, and joy flowed like wine. How was it all lost, and where find again the little key to that divine banquet?' The key was charity: *caritas,* the love of loves! — But charity had been asleep, on that as on too many occasions, and the god had passed him by. To no avail that he had made 'copy' of that beautiful episode, in an unsalable story, or that (in order to make himself suffer a little, like Sentimental Tommy) he had actually rented her room in Brimmer Street, chancing to find it available. This was self-indulgence, nothing else. But trust — ? had he trusted her, as he now knew he should have, and could have? No. Instead, there had been the miserable and shameful episode of the book, the one and only gift of himself that he had ever made to her, the little privately printed volume of essays, which he had inscribed for her. How pleased, how flattered she had been! How proud, too, as if now she shared in him! But no, he had repented it. He had worried lest somehow she might use it, take advantage of him. How could he be sure — how? And so one evening — and he had planned it all carefully, he knew just where the book stood — he had torn out the incriminating page, while she was out of the room, and crumpled it in his pocket. And had never known — to add to his misery — whether she had ever noticed, or guessed.

And of course, as any idiot *could* have guessed, she had been the golden core of those war years in Boston and Cambridge, whether in the eyrie on Beacon Hill — with its Steinlen on the wall, the girl leaning out pensively into the Parisian sunset, and the back windows overlooking the roofs and walls of Boston, the sunsets over the Esplanade, the Basin — or at the flat in Craigie Street. From the passionate literary quarrels and debates with the farouche John, next door, or the choleric psychoanalytic discussions with Jacob, at the epicene flat in the Fenway, where aromatic pastilles were burned before the bronze Buddha; or from the club, and bawdy talk with all and some; it was always to the bow-windowed room in Brimmer Street that he had gone, it was only to Marian that he could talk with his whole being, and *of* his whole being. It was to her, first of all, that he had hurried with the news that he had been summoned before his draft board, the war summoning him down from Jaffrey, and his summer vegetable patch, to show cause, under the Work or Fight Act, why, as one not usefully employed — for a writer was not usefully employed, was he? — he should not either seek other employment or allow himself, although married and a father, to be drafted. Drafted: the prospect was not pleasant: it was even a little disturbing; for how could he be sure that his share of the family *petit mal* would endure that sort of regimentation? But to allow the writer to be thus degraded, and classed along with doormen and soda-jerkers, this could simply not be permitted; and he had therefore pointed out to the somewhat baffled draft board — who hardly knew what a writer was — that so far as he was aware there was no mention of writers in the terms of the Act. And, if that were, as he assumed, the case, he would not change his occupation: perhaps they would give him a ruling? They examined the text of the Act, and sure enough, it contained no reference to the writer: but still, was a writer useful — ? They had eyed him suspiciously with the question, but in the end had felt that they had no authority themselves to interpret the law, it must go to the board next higher above them, and in the meantime he could — they supposed — go back to his writing, whatever it was, though it was pretty obvious that they took a decidedly contemptuous view of it. Back to his writing — the attempt to make a modern adaptation, in terms of modern psychology and psychoanalysis (for he was then deep in Freud, Adler, Pfister, Ferenczi and Rank) of *Punch and Judy* — he had gone, at Jaffrey, in the shadow of Monadnock; back to his useless writing, and the more profitable hoeing of his hills of Golden Bantam corn, and the proud rows of beans. And did it mean — Marian had wanted to know, as they lunched under the awnings at the Westminster Roof Garden — that he would be drafted at once? No, simply that, if he refused thus to change his work, he would cease to be in a deferred class, as a married man with children, and would be reclassified as in Class I, and therefore draftable as soon as his number came up: that was all.

A curious reversal, in a sense, though he had been unaware of it at the time, of grandfather's decision, in a somewhat similar situation; on the surface, at any rate, it looked like a reversal; but on careful analysis wasn't it precisely the same *kind* of moral problem? Grandfather, when actually drafted, had refused to ask for exemption from military service, although he had been encouraged by some of his parishioners to do so: at a moment when opposition to the draft was widespread, and had led to dangerous outbreaks of rioting, he had made the point that in a democracy all alike must obey the voice of the draft, the ministers of God included, and that he would therefore go, and gladly, and of course. A noble decision, and doubly so, for it not only added lustre to patriotism, it also added a new dignity (if it needed any, indeed, in *his* church) to the office of minister. D.'s decision (which had really cost him no effort, for the issue seemed to him plain as a pikestaff) was quite without any such heroism; and yet he could feel, and perhaps rightly, that it was one that grandfather would have made, or in fact was himself, even now, making. The writer, the poet — and above all the poet, for the poets were the indispensable evolutionary fuglemen of mankind, the extenders of awareness, and therefore of control, and therefore of wisdom — was this high office, the highest, to be thus publicly and officially, and by the government itself, degraded and denigrated, posted on the bulletins as "useless"? No, it was a point worth making, worth taking issue about, and D. had all plainly, as he saw it, done his duty. The irony being — as later he was to say to Marian — that the ultimate decision in Washington, and by General Crowder himself, that the writer was in fact "usefully" employed, was not quite as noble as it seemed to be: for somehow the newspapers, and the policy-makers of the newspapers, had got wind of the question: it had become instantly apparent that if the decision went against the writer, then the entire newspaper world, from top to bottom, could be put in Class One, and be liable to draft at once. The attention of the authorities was called to this rather serious aspect of the matter, and its probable consequences; and so, for the sake of the journalist, the poor poet was saved. The editorials that greeted the official announcement were a little mocking, a little condescending, a trifle cynical: for America had yet a long way to go if it were ever to overtake the European, or for that matter, the Asiatic, countries, in its evaluation of culture. So, the writers, the poets, those long-hairs, were useful, were they? — Well, well, what next! The last twist of the knife: but perhaps, just the same, it was the last knife.

War, and the diversions, the postponements, of war: but, viewed in retrospect, could one not now say that the compulsory deviations, from the chosen 'line,' the chosen purpose, had been so slight as to have been almost negligible? He would have lost, it was true, six years that otherwise might have been spent in England, in London; there would have been the continuing and developing closeness of contact with the Tsetse, and Rabbi Ben Ezra (though this was perhaps inherently less probable, for Rabbi Ben Ezra a shade too much resembled the Old Man of the Sea, and, if a good teacher, was also something of a tyrant); there would have been Davies, too, and Chapman, and Arnault; he would have found entry, possibly, into the Egoist, and the little group of people who revolved around it; and out of these tangential grazings and contacts and human explorations it was of course impossible to imagine just what thematic evolutions and enlargements might not have come to pass. He would not, in that case, have returned to find Rabbi Ben Ezra already departed, or the Tsetse so rootedly established, both socially and in the "politics" (as it were) of literature, not to mention personally, as to have achieved what Emily Dickinson had called 'overtakelessness': he had built the splendid ramparts round that rare new domain of his, and behind them he had become all but invisible, all but intangible: the affection between them was not to have been diminished, but the distance between them was sensible, and would increase. But was it so certain that this was in any degree a misfortune, or that it might not have occurred anyway? From the Tsetse's brilliantly analytic and destructive thesis in epistemology at Harvard, in the year when D. had come back (in order to take his degree) to the colonial house in Church Street, from the windows of which he could observe the Tsetse, with that newly acquired Malacca cane of his, on his way to Sanskrit, or the humanities discoursed upon by Irving Babbitt — that year of the dinners at the Greek restaurant — from this remarkable thesis, which had contributed much to the 'fixing' of D.'s implicit intellectual or philosophic position, adding, as it did, the basic "why" as to the values of knowledge, the Tsetse was gradually to retreat, as if that magnificent vision, into the apparent chaos which blazed and swarmed and roared beyond the neat walls of Eden, was one he found insupportable. Thenceforth, like the salmon, leaving behind him the outrages of ocean, together with its wilder freedoms, he would ascend the ancient river of a more peaceful culture, where the banks were trim, and the views symmetrically landscaped; and, mounting from cataract to cataract, or hierarchy to hierarchy, of accepted order, would at last achieve what no American ichthyolater had achieved before him, and find himself, at Canterbury, after the pilgrimage of pilgrimages, in the very presence of the Ichthos itself. That the achievement was unique and astounding, and attended, too, by rainbows of creative splendor, there could be no doubt. Indeed, it was in the nature of a miracle, a transformation. But was it not to have been, also, a surrender, and perhaps the saddest known to D. in his life?

And of course, as D. could hardly flatter himself that his presence in England, during the war years, or a continuance of the intimacy between them, would in the least have affected this tragic metamorphosis, this transubstantiation in reverse, or even retarded it, it was perhaps idle to speculate on the hypothetical loss to D. He had *thought* himself frustrated, to be sure: and a victim of privation: he had even regarded himself as an exile. But what he was not yet perceptive enough to know, or wise enough to understand, was the fact that the enforced banishment to Boston and Cambridge and South Yarmouth was the best thing that could have happened to him. For not only was he not really exiled at all — such, already, was the transatlantic closeness of contact between the two countries, in a literary sense, and the immediacy of communication — but there were elements in the Boston scene which were to prove invaluable to him, and which would have been irreplaceable. To "keep up" with the London scene was easy enough. The Imagist movement was from the outset international in character, and remained so, with London and Boston as its two centers. It was the beginning, if one had only had the prevision to see it, of a profound change, a profound and permanent alteration in the cultural balance between the Old Country and the new; as the economic balance was already beginning to shift westward, so now the cultural balance had begun to do so: and if it would not have gone far enough, in the early twenties, to prevent the wholesale migration of American writers and painters to Europe, and mainly to Paris, or indeed to prevent D. himself from then, at last, anchoring himself at Saltinge, nevertheless the reversal of the process was already a dynamic and inevitable potential: the time would come, and far sooner than anyone could have imagined, when not only would the American artist or writer find in the American scene all that he needed, whether as a sustaining solution in which to exist, or as the material for observation — the requisite "Fitness of the environment," as the wise and kind Lawrence Henderson put it, in that admirable, if forgotten book — but when, for the first time, there would actually be a reversal of the current, and French and English writers would select this new scene as now more conducive to work, more liberating, or more fecundating, than their own. The time was past when the solitary giant needed indeed to be a giant if he were to withstand an almost fatal solitude, or the restrictive, and even crippling effects of lonely soliloquy — as with Hawthorne and Melville and Dickinson — or when the young Henry James could lament, for Hawthorne, the absence of the sort of social or cultural 'reference' which would have enabled him both to widen and deepen his view.

And the signs of this change were present in Boston in the war years: for had not Amy Lowell returned thither from the famous "Blast" dinner, which D. had not attended, and from the inaudible reading by Rupert Brooke, at Arnault's bookshop, where she had shouted from the back row that she couldn't hear a word; and hadn't the farouche John also settled himself there, that together they might insure the nice conduct of Imagism? They were both in touch with Rabbi Ben Ezra and H. D. and Aldington: a Boston publisher was found who would publish them: and if D. had retained his independence, venturing to voice his own scepticisms as to what he thought narrow or extreme or absurd in some of the new theories and experiments, nevertheless he was as much immersed in the thing as any. Boston reverberated with it. Boston might not be London, but in a very real sense London was now in Boston. The eagle scream of Rabbi Ben Ezra was audible across the Atlantic at regular intervals, and was relayed by Amy Lowell to the farouche John, and so to himself. The Poetry Bookshop had opened its simple doors in Pemberton Square, poetry was everywhere, battle was in the air, and the poets seemed suddenly to be coming from all directions at once — penniless, but all of them on the move, and making the regular rounds from Chicago to New York, New York to Boston, and Boston to Chicago. Chicago: ought one to go to Chicago? or New York? He had gone to both, like all the others, and like all the others had blithely rung strange doorbells and knocked at unknown doors, sometimes with unhappy consequences, as when he had made the profound mistake of calling on the editors of The Little Review, had sat stiffly with them and discussed Marsden Hartley, and, on leaving, had heard behind him, as he descended the stairs, peals of uncontrollable and derisive female laughter. An era of legend and myth-making, of cutthroat jealousies and vendettas, of gossip and wild parties, of murderous exclusions, and, of course, of the all-too-eager joinings and belongings as well. An era of the picturesque, and picaresque, too, when the improbable was the order of the day. And the era, the first era, of the "little" magazine, "Others," and all the others, for they sprouted on all sides, quarreled, debated, made their own little private and esoteric splashes and died.

In all this extraordinary activity D.'s position had not been precisely central, but near it: perhaps a little to the left of center. For if, on the one hand, Rabbi Ben Ezra was to credit him, in a letter

many years later, with the "discovery" of the Tsetse — as if anyone but the Tsetse himself could have accomplished that bright
and arcane invention — as his only contribution to the age (contrasting this, to D.'s disadvantage, with his own so innumerable and
repeated "finds"), on the other hand he had kept firmly to his own
slightly conservative bias, in the persistent belief that form must
be form, that inventions of form must keep a basis in order and
tradition, that a mere surrender to the pleasure (which was undoubtedly to be had) of chain-making in the bright colors of the
colloquial and the colloquial cadence was not enough, not a substitute for the dark and difficult and, yes, painful process of cryp-
topoiesis, and that this, in turn, must, like a compass, have its true
North in the shape of a conscious and articulated *Weltanschauung,*
a consistent view. The consistent view had shaped itself slowly and
intermittently out of the incredibly rich pour of new discoveries,
new ideas, the miraculously rapid expansion of man's knowledge,
inward and outward, whether into the ever farther-reaching astro-
physics of the heavens, or of man's mind. Hadn't Henry Adams, in
The Degradation of the Democratic Dogma, predicted that the
early years of the twentieth century would witness the flowering
of an ultimate phase (if Brooks Adams's theory of the rule of phase
as applied to history was correct) in man's thinking, a final brilliance of consciousness, as of the world itself coming to self-knowledge, even to the point of then coming apart, dissolved, dispersed,
in its own sense of series — the series, like relativity, beginning in
man's own mind to show at last its wonderful and profoundly disturbing seams? Hadn't Flinders Petrie said something of the same
sort as early as 1911 in his *Revolutions of Civilization,* although
without making any predictions? The church, the churches, would
undoubtedly make a last forlorn attempt at a *redivivus,* there would
be a period when they would whip themselves up to repeated
spasms of resurrection, as spurious and unveridical as that on which

they had been founded, but they were visibly moribund, and religion, in the old sense, with them. *Gnowthi seauton* — that was still the theme, the open sesame, Freud had merely picked up the magic words where Socrates, the prototype of highest man, had let them fall, and now at last the road was being opened for the only religion that was any longer tenable or viable, a poetic comprehension of man's position in the universe, and of his potentialities as a poietic shaper of his own destiny, through self-knowledge and love. The final phase of evolution of man's mind itself to ever more inclusive consciousness: in that, and that alone, would he find the solvent of all things.

In his only partially successful work during the war years D. had, as it were, walked round this "consistent view," he perhaps only partly knew it was there, or only saw it in angles and fragments, and not all at once for formulated statement, but rather for intermittent and musical reference, by counterpoint and implication. His interest, a holdover from an almost unanalyzable complex of literary influences, and the bright shadows of music and painting as well (for these increasingly pressed him for attention), was still primarily dramatic, fictive, analytic, poetic, in the sense that what most concerned him was the making of a "shape" out of these components, and that in the finding of the "shape" would be his immediate satisfaction. There must be, of course, a constant fidelity to the consistent view — which lay there, in the somewhat too musical design, but interfused with the possibly too insistent sounds and colors, and therefore, for anyone who was not actively looking for it, out of sight — but the presentation of the "view" was not as yet the paramount concern, it was treated rather as thematic material, something on which to play variations. So persistently musical for a time had been the preoccupation, in these attempts at shaping, that he had often wondered whether after all it might not have been the 'musical' echo, in his inheritance from his father, or from the *am-*

biente at Savannah, that he might more profitably have listened to:
perhaps those piano lessons, dropped after one winter at Middleclass
School, should have been kept up: and it was not without interest
to remember, too, that in that other winter, the winter of honeymoon at Rome (where the bright snow had spangled the camellia
tree one morning), he had actually begun to study — in Italian,
too! — a handbook on counterpoint. But was there any turning
back? or any assurance that his gift for improvisation, on the piano,
a pretty limited one, indicated the presence of anything more, or
anything now recoverable? It was most unlikely. It was easier and
lazier to indulge that musical hankering in an approximation to
musical structure, a kind of algebraic play, but in terms of language;
and to take his music straight — with Jules, or the farouche John
— at Symphony Hall or the Opera House. Not for another decade,
not until he had been moored safely at Saltinge, and had lost it and
refound it, with Lorelei Two and Hambo, in that miraculous return
when he had discovered the beautiful house empty and forlorn, with
a FOR RENT sign in the stair-window to proclaim its shame; and had
then arranged, in effect, to rent the house from his own children
(for whom, under the terms of the divorce, it was held in trust) —
the arrangement so disapproved of by the Old Bird, as being unfair
to Lorelei One — not until then was the consistent view at last to
receive his consistent attention, and to find at last its own expression
in the two volumes of *parerga*, the serial essays towards attitude and
definition. The preoccupation had been prolonged and deep: and
perhaps it had only needed the shattering disequilibration which followed the fatal interview with Lorelei Two at Aunt Sibyl's house in
Fayerweather Street, and the resultant wrenching of himself away
from the three little D.'s, and Saltinge, to bring it up, into full and
clear consciousness, as now discoverably the very heart of such conviction as, in his moment of greatest distress, he could hug to his self-
inflicted wound.

It was to prove, in fact, a veritable life-line. Even if — on the one inevitable and predestined occasion — he was to let go of it, and drown, and only to have been saved, for a renewed hold upon it, by the most ludicrously fortuitous of accidents. Predestined, yes: for had he not always admitted, almost as a kind of necessity, if he were to achieve identification with the father, the need of emulating him even in self-destruction? Was it going to be enough that he should rival him, or even surpass him, in the role of writer (and how was one to know that one had): must one not also rival him in the other? If *he* had dared — and twice, too, the first time unsuccessfully — should not one dare oneself? An insidious doctrine, well-rooted in narcissism, and rooted too, in that early identification with all such writers as died tragically and young, the whole romantic picture; and now, of course, given a sudden and unexpected force by the self-inflicted wound, the abandonment of the little D's, and the house at Saltinge, and, with them, all the sense of security which it had taken him a whole lifetime to build. And the abandonment — hadn't that too been a compulsory repetition of the family pattern? as, indeed, had been so often discussed with the Beloved Uncle and Aunt Sibyl? As if, now and then in one's life, one must bring one's courage, and one's disregard of law and order, to the very highest pitch, and venture on the outrageous, deliberately commit an outrage. Was there even a queer kind of heroism in this? a setting forth, as Zarathustra would have argued, beyond the pale of good and evil? Must one dare the lightning, invite it to strike one's heart? and thus deal it oneself, at the same time, to others? If *he* had been thus abandoned, flung overboard, should not they? —

All these elements had been present as background for the sudden action, but others too: the remorse, and the sense of loss, which were almost inextricably blended, had been, just as Aunt Sibyl had predicted, so dazzling a pain that he had not been able to look at it.

He had sought refuge from the Gorgon vision, which hung there pitilessly before him, in alcohol, on the one hand, and what was more remarkable, for he had not cried since he was five (when he had decided that he never would cry again), in tears. Tears: there had never been such tears. It was as if he had abruptly discovered that he had an entire life of unacknowledged suffering, agony, humiliation, and despair — and of cruelty and shame and deceit as well — to atone for, and to make oblation to. He had not — till then — really known what it was all about. It was as if he had needed to test the reality of his feeling for the little D.'s, or could *only* test it, by losing them. Was this perhaps true of everything, and everywhere — and was it perhaps only in the profoundest experience of annihilation, and of the dissolution of all hope and pride and identity, in the great glare of cosmic consciousness, that one could regain one's power *to value?* It certainly looked very like it. And as the dreadful feeling of personal exposure, of being lost at sea, corresponded quite preposterously with the feeling of intellectual exposure with which now for years that "consistent view" of his had been confronting him, but of which he had heretofore never quite accepted the true consequences, the effect on him was revolutionary. What had been merely an idea till now, or a system of ideas, which he could contemplate, or disregard, with complete detachment, had now become a terrible and tangible and wonderful world again, like that of which he had learned the first vast and shocking syllables at Savannah; and what, in the realm of personal relationships, in the nexus of society, had been easy and light and habitual, had now, just as suddenly, become fearfully and brilliantly alive, an endless profusion and confusion of every shape and shade of the progressions of love and hate. Values! — The values began a Heraclitean pour such as he hadn't known since he first crawled on his hands and knees. The lesson partly learned from dear lost Irene, of Kennington, and the Wounded Face in the train from

Windermere, was this time to be learned for good. One was now naked again, and in the open.

But if it was good, what at first blindly he began to see of it, it was also difficult: for a world so new, a new language would have to be discovered, or rediscovered, and for this, one's own muscles readapted and re-educated. The improvised return to Saltinge, with Hambo and Lorelei Two, and the reoccupation of the house, as if he were a hermit crab returned from an almost disastrous foray over the sea-floor, had immensely assisted in this: it had given him perhaps the requisite sense of security and continuity, of hanging on, which he needed. The shell still fitted his back, fitted it better than ever. He could again make himself available for the little D.'s. He could pick up the innumerable dropped threads at Saltinge, with Hambo now adding his own bright gold. And he could work, and did, in the intervals between potboiling, at the consistent view, for his own satisfaction — even if, as in so many other of his projects, he was never to find quite the time or patience or vision (alas) to bring it to a proper conclusion. But it was difficult; and the prolonged, if shadowy, difficulties with dear Lorelei Two — for their steps, their gaits, after that first magical moment when their every most random movement was that of the dance, had gradually ceased to be parallel — these had added to the burden, already pressing, of consciousness; and to the need, for rest or insulation, of alcohol. Insulation: yes, there was no question that he had needed a long period of insulation, and that in the well-freighted tray on the dining-room sideboard; — where, like Paul, the sunflower genius of English landscape; or poor Edward, of Inglesee, forever on the lookout for new "bits of fluff"; or the Noble Lord, in the old days of the Raymond Buildings — he kept the whiskies and the sherries and the vermouths and the gins, and the siphons of soda, with the green Viennese glasses always ready; — in this tray, and in the fifteen glorious pubs which Saltinge boasted, but especially in the beloved Ship, with its beloved host, Old Tom, he found it, he took it. Perhaps at times too generously? How was one to know? And didn't the organism itself, intuitively, know and prescribe what was necessary in these matters? The family *petit mal,* which in the case of father had by no means been so *petit,* wasn't this (as in many families, where, over a period of several generations, there has been a perhaps too rapid development of consciousness, and at the expense of stability), wasn't this a clear enough indication that the neural insulation was worn a shade too thin, and needed cushioning? He had experienced, and was experiencing, the shock as of an enormous exposure: as if he had been placed on a cosmic table, *en plein soleil,* for a cosmic operation, a cosmic intrusion: the light became at times so cruel as to be insupportable: and was there to be no anaesthetic? no refuge, at intervals — from that self-imposed glare of isolation, which so burned the eyes and heart, — or from the more normally human and social problems in which his departure from Saltinge, and return to it, had so pressingly involved him? The tray on the sideboard became that escape, that and the regular, the ritual, nocturnal visit to the grained-woodwork altar (of which Old Tom was so proud) at the Ship. The half-quarterns of White Horse — and how appropriate *that* had been — or Booth's yellow gin, were the libations for the god of forgetfulness; if simply in order that the next morning, from the great window of the great room, overlooking the Salts and the castle and the sea, he might again look, through lightning, or fog, or squalls of southwest rain from the Channel, towards the invisible, but forever challenging, cliffs and shingles, and obscured lights, of Ushant. Paul, too, had shared with him, on such mornings, that not desperate, but nevertheless somehow so exigent view, that visual imperative: giving back to it his own sea-hawk genius, his own wing-swiftness and perilous certainty of perspective. And powerful young Hambo, down from St. Cath's at Cambridge, after their bizarre meeting in the 'other' Cambridge (to which he had come for study with D. after reading *Purple Passage*) — Hambo, down for the Christmas holidays, or the 'long vac.', bringing the lyric ukelele, or bringing Hugh and his concertina, his squiffer, for the fine and giddy concerts at the piano in the front hall, Hambo, too, at that great lens of a window, took from it his own prismatic lights and mysteries, his own long spirals of sea-flight, as to Kowloon and back; or later, and with D., past Ushant to Cape St. Vincent. It was dear Lorelei Two, alone, who could not — and perhaps rightly, who knows? — share in that vision.

But despite the admirably prescribed insulation, and the many fine drunken comedies it had provided for them (as when D., hurling his javelin in the pitch-dark of a Channel fog across the little river at the foot of the cobbled street, in competition with Hambo, had also launched himself into space, and had fallen ten feet down into rich Saltinge mud), despite these libations to the god of forgetfulness, the moment had at last supervened when such temporary rests from the vision seemed not enough, and when a more famous sleep had suddenly appeared, one evening, as the ultimate, the only, desideratum. If one had learned, all dangerously, to live, should not one also learn, as dangerously, and of one's own purest volition, to die? And therefore, Lorelei Two having gone off for the evening to the cinema, so that she would be absent for more time than he would require for his purpose, and after a cheerful, but for once quite moderate, offering to the god, he had sat himself down to read Wyndham Lewis, under the electric light in the little subterranean kitchen, with the gas-rings and gas oven fizzing softly behind him. He was perfectly serene: he had made up his mind with absolute calm: it seemed to him that he had no, or few, regrets: he thought he had done what he could, with his volatile oddment of a share of life — that trick horse on the roundabout — and that he had now had perhaps as much of the vision as he could bear, and more than — obviously — he could find any adequate expression for. The flies dropped one by one from the ceiling and window, on slow wings, fell to the floor, spun, and died. And just then it was that he remembered the unfortunate letter from Ee, which lay under a pile of handkerchiefs in his chest of drawers in the bedroom — the only thing he had forgotten to destroy. He would have to go and get it.

Up from the gas-filled kitchen, therefore, painfully hauling himself up the stairs by clinging to banister-railings and the rough edges of stair-carpets — for he had begun to feel faint — up the two flights to the bedroom he had managed to go, and had retrieved the tell-tale letter; and then, without any second thoughts whatever, so deep, apparently, had been the impulse, or need, back he had returned to let himself into the closed kitchen; which now, however — presumably because his own lungs were by this time saturated with it — no longer smelled of gas. The Wyndham Lewis article was excruciatingly funny, one of his best satirical pieces, an attack on political leaderwriting. "As I was wandering alone this morning over one of the northeast slopes of J. L. Garvin's leader in the Sunday Observer — " That was the last thing D. could remember; and the next thing he knew, he was lying flat on his back on the dining-room floor, and trying to sit up for the drink of straight gin which Lorelei had poured for him. She had come back an hour earlier than he had expected — for it turned out that the second feature, on the cinema program, was one that she had already seen. And where had she found him? Not at all in the chair by the kitchen table, where he had been laughing his head off over Wyndham Lewis — not at all. No, that impulse, that need, had not been as profound as he had supposed. Not as profound as the will to live, anyway — for Lorelei had found him lying against the kitchen door, the door that led to the corridor. His last act, although he could not in the least remember it, for he hadn't known what he was doing — or *had*

227

he — ? — had been to crawl to the door and attempt to open it. He had, after all, wanted to get out and to live. And live he did, even if only by accident.

An extraordinary, and, curiously enough, a profoundly *releasing* experience, the end of one chapter and the beginning of another; and if he had no particular 'moral' feelings about it, no feelings of regret or shame — for wasn't his life his own, to do with as he pleased? — he did feel, for a long time afterwards, a Lazarine superiority to death, and a Lazarine astonishment at finding that, through no fault, and certainly no virtue, of his own, a second existence now lay before him, a whole dazzling and unexpected existence. Release, yes: for if the past had by no means been expunged — in fact, it was vivider than ever — just the same, it had been, in some uncanny fashion, finished. That part of his life was definitely over and done with, that book was closed. And the pages to come, would they not now be richer than any hitherto, and more rewarding and surprising, if only because they were the pages he had himself tried to tear from the book, the pages he had decided never to read? Grace abounding for the chief of sinners! no doubt about that. The sense of largesse, of bounty, of an immeasurable gift, which he probably didn't deserve, surrounded and elated and overwhelmed him; but with it, too, came a new feeling of obligation. If he had been weak, he could perhaps now be strong: if he had been wrong, he could perhaps now be right. And hadn't the refusal, the abnegation, by some subtle sort of alchemy, actually refreshed and strengthened him? The choice of darkness having been made, brightness was incomparably the brighter. Once again, and this time with an incredible gratitude, he could call the roll-call of his loves. The delicate lace of the blackthorn, along the path by the Channel shipyard, was past its prime — was already passing it, when he and Paul had gone that way to photograph the up-ended baulks of half-hewn timber, like those *abbozzi* of Michelangelo's which he had seen in Florence with Chapman; but the white hawthorns in his garden, and the pink, and the red; and the three golden laburnums interspersed with them, which he had himself planted there, his gift to Ariel's Island; and the crooked old pear-tree by the schoolhouse wall, which flanked them; all of these now hosannaed in the paved garden as if it were the first of all springs and summers, to be celebrated by the first of all thrushes and blackbirds; by the roulade of the chaffinch, the bubble-and-squeak of the starling on the chimney-pot, and the skylark's mounting spiral of *O altitudo!* — an invisible pinwheel of pure rapture in the purest of skies. Time was again striking; the golden Quarter-Boys on St. Mary's Church, pivoted stiffly, in turn, to smite the bronze bell; and the soft *ting-tang* floated down, over the hill-town of red-tiled roofs to the open window, which looked away over a halcyon Channel to Gris Nez and Ushant. Time was still striking, to measure one's love.

To measure other things as well: and Hambo, of course, with that sixth-sense mysticism of his, and his eternal, and so often verifiable, adduction of cabalistic correspondences — the evidences, to him, of a mystic pattern — would have been the first to point out that it could surely be no accident that the same year had witnessed D.'s attempt at *felo de se* and the farouche John's also. Time, the long slow waves of time — was it simply that those waves, for D. and the farouche John, had at last, and at the same moment, worn down the headlands of their strength, their resistance, and dropped them into its devouring sea, there to be once more analyzed into the elements? It was indeed a long time, in the endless explorations and adventures of thought and feeling — not to mention what John had once called, in a burst of fury, the wear-and-tear of "sheer domesticity" — since the war years on Beacon Hill, and the almost fatal quarrel over free verse — of all things — ! — and John's departure, to England, to be married. That quarrel — how ridiculous the little episode had been, and yet how moving! And if it had not happened that the farouche John, only a few days before, had narrated in detail, and with gusto, to D. and Lorelei One, the circumstances of his final quarrel with Rabbi Ben Ezra, there might have been no reconciliation, and the entire post-war era, in London and Inglesee and Saltinge, and especially at Saltinge, after the purchase of the house (which John had loved almost as much as himself), all this would not only have been different, it would have lost a vital part of its character. How much can depend on how little! Had there been no story about the quarrel with Rabbi Ben Ezra, there would have been no lifelong love-affair with Japanese prints and Chinese painting: the great Hiroshige triptych, Snow on the Kiso Mountains, would not have stilled to its own stillness the long, beautiful room at Saltinge — or, later, the dark magic of the kitchen at Brewster, on Cape Cod — from which he was this very minute *en voyage* to Saltinge; nor would the aquamarine purity of the Leech bowl — which John had given, and then retaken, and then given again — have signalled upward, for emphasis, to the resonant darkness of the Chinese *kakemono*, the God of Longevity Blessing a Child, which hung in the same room, and which Chapman had truly said was as fine as any Giotto. But these treasures were not to be lost, after all: for when John knocked at the door in Walnut Street, that winter evening, and asked for the return of his books, the Henry James and the others, D. had at once recognized the symptoms. It was precisely this that had been done on the occasion of the quarrel with Rabbi Ben Ezra — John had gone at once to demand his books. The books, accordingly, were once again handed to him, through the door — for he wouldn't come in — but in addition, D. had insisted on his accepting a small phial of Rhinitis tablets, for his cold, and this he displayed the utmost reluctance to do, squirming in embarrassment, but at last — if only that he might get himself away — thrusting the detestable object into his pocket, and vanishing silently down the stairs.

And, in the morning, he had vanished from the breakfast-room as well, leaving the little brown phial on the table, without comment; but with word to the landlady — so she said — that he was unexpectedly moving away, that he was leaving. What — in those days — would one not do for free verse! It was evident that D.'s strictures on the article in the New Republic, by Edward Storer, and his proposal to write a crushing rejoinder (which would in part be praise of the Tsetse) had hurt the dear man much more than D. had intended — if he had indeed intended any hurt at all; and something, therefore, must be done about it. He went up to John's room, in the house next door, and sure enough, he was in the midst of packing; he greeted D. monosyllabically, and with averted gaze, and carried shirts and socks gloomily from chest to suitcase; while D., leaning against the door-jamb, and after a prefatory disclaimer about his intentions in the proposed article, began to outline it in detail, and to demonstrate that it was by no means the unprincipled assault that he might have imagined, did not in the least invalidate the common ground between them (which had already become very precious to both) and in fact was going to be — if he could manage it — a very moderate, and carefully *raisonné*, inquiry into the whole question of free verse — its origins and possibilities, its very obvious achievements, but, to some extent, its limitations — and a comparison of these with the more traditional forms which employed rhyme and metre; and, perhaps at the end, he would suggest that the Tsetse, in such things as the Portrait, had already adumbrated a form which might be exactly the solution they were all looking for — something freer, certainly, than the strictly stanzaic, or the monotonies of classic blank verse; with varying length of line, and, to some degree, a substitution of cadence for metrical beat or measure; but using both these and rhyme, too, when it wished, or when it suited. Something, in fact, which would combine the best features of all. Wasn't it — after all — a reasonable idea — ? D. thought so: it would be presented as calmly and dispassionately as that: it would merely suggest that Edward Storer's view had been a shade circumscribed, nothing more.

The packing, which had gradually been slowing down, now came to a standstill. John was at last facing him, shirt in hand: he grinned apologetically, with that fascinating satyr-like leer of his, dumped out the suitcase on the bed, and suggested that they lunch — where he well knew D. and the Tsetse had for years been in the habit of going — at the Greeks'. There they could discuss the whole thing over martinis and a bottle of wine.

And it had therefore been, in a sense, from that table, that bottle of wine, and that mended quarrel, that discussion — or that now forever-settled-between-them *willingness* to discuss — that they had begun to move on their separate paths to London and England, the farouche John first, with instructions to get in touch, of course, with the Tsetse, and D. later. And the wonderful decade or more was to unravel itself as predestined — in the Arnault bookshop, at Soho restaurants, in the Bloomsbury tea-shops, Lyons or ABC's, and at Sydenham and Saltinge. A time of blooming, of profusion, of hard work and endless debate; of good food, good drinks, and good living. But a time of competitive stress also, of unceasing literary *sauve-qui-peut* — as the farouche John had himself many times observed, with cynical and somewhat ghoulish glee. Which of them would survive? which of them wouldn't? The various cliques formed or fell apart, new coteries rose and fell; but central among them, and in the end omnipotent, was the group that erratically and fluctuatingly arranged itself, or rearranged itself, round the Tsetse's quarterly, and the luncheons and dinners that intermittently celebrated its appearances. In these rituals and observances D. and the farouche John had both shared, but perhaps a little humbly and peripherally: their roles or offices were minor: they were permitted to review books, or even, when an assassination was in order, invited to place the tormenting banderillas, or use muleta and sword. But on the whole, they had not been permitted to feel secure, or as if in the superior circles of the constantly shifting hierarchy, nor that they themselves quite had access to the sacred pages with their own writings; or only semi-occasionally and, so to speak, on sufferance. An uneasy situation, which neither of them had much relished, and of which the farouche John was angrily and outspokenly critical: he disapproved of what he considered to be a deliberate and Machiavellian practice of power-politics, of reputation-making and reputation-*un*making. "You'll see" — he would say — "that it will be X's turn next, the writing is already on the wall, the Word had gone forth, and at the next meeting X will be publicly, and as cruelly as may be, thrown to the wolves. Or should one say that the wolf would be thrown to X — ?" For they had both been themselves witness to *that* particular literary murder, or attempted murder, and a messy and unpleasant affair it had been, quite without credit to anyone present. The carefully picked quarrel had been public, prolonged, and pointless: and if it exhibited anything, it was that evident streak of sadism in the Tsetse's otherwise urbane and kindly character, which now and again, as D. well knew, he enjoyed indulging. "You don't know the meaning of words," he had once remarked to D., in a sudden such thrust; and on a subsequent occasion, when D., acknowledging from his hospital bed in Fitzroy Square the Tsetse's latest book, and, writing in great pain, the morning after an operation, and with his head still full of ether, had praised the book with that kind of drunken fulsomeness which can perhaps sound a little false, even though based on genuine and envious admiration, the Tsetse had replied, not with a letter, but with a printed page torn out of *The Midwives' Gazette*, on which he had underlined in ink certain words and phrases — "*Blood — mucous — shreds of mucous — purulent offensive discharge.*" That was all — no comment or signature. The bite of the tsetse, and no mistake.

233

Had the farouche John perhaps taken too hard, and too seriously, all this semi-political, or personal, concomitant of the literary 'scene'? It seemed likely. He had more and more withdrawn from it, at all events; and the more unhappily, as time went on, and as his own career seemed, with each new book, not quite to achieve what had been so brilliantly promised. Even his best work — which was yet to come — was not destined to receive the attention it deserved: the sense of failure dogged him, was becoming habitual: he appeared to be striking no roots in England, and in this an unhappy marriage was by no means helpful: and D. was later many times to reproach himself for not having earlier perceived how very much the dear creature was in need of assistance. But could anything really have been done? Probably not. When at last John had suddenly sent him the frenetic wire begging him to come up to London — as he was ill, had left home, and needed guidance — it was already too late. D. had sped up to town, of course, and had seen in one horrified glance that the haggard and unkempt man before him was desperate, and almost totally without will or desire. Like a child, submissively, he did everything that D. told him to. From Paul's flat, opposite St. Pancras — Paul's *Northern Adventure* — he had rung up his wife, to say that he would go down to Saltinge for a week or two of rest, staying with D., that he would come and collect his things that afternoon, and go down in the morning.

But what to do with him in the meantime?

It was then that D. had had what amounted to an inspiration.

For in the vacant lot between Paul's flat and St. Pancras was a newly arrived Fair, with roundabout and swings, and the liquid squeals of a calliope; but more importantly, something that had taken D.'s eye at the outset, a switch-back, a genuine nerve-shattering Coney Island roller-coaster. The gay little cars swooped down the dizzy inclines, teetered round banked curves, shot up to another crest to swoop down again, the occupants screaming with terror and delight — wouldn't this be the very thing? Wouldn't the sheer shock perhaps help to bring the poor man out of his dreadful lethargy? It could be tried, at any rate: and it was, and it did. John had never in his life been in any such contraption before: in that strange, remote blue backwater of a lagoon — as Chapman had once put it — which was his intense inner life, there had never been time for the sports, for games, for fun, least of all for the giddy devices of Coney Island or the White City: it was doubtful whether, in his childhood, there had even been a merry-go-round: and it was therefore with some evidence of alarm that he permitted himself to be persuaded by D. to step into the little boat for that fantastic and perilous voyage. He was afraid — and why not? — but determined to give no sign of it; and it was perhaps this very fear, the fear of something else, something real, something objective and physical, and wholly unrelated to the private world of misery and pain in which he was stumbling like a man hypnotized, that began to shake him out of his trance. The change in him was electric: he started to smile, he grinned, he laughed: the thing delighted him, he could not have enough of it; and they must have spent more than an hour in that extraordinary occupation before they decided to go on to the Café Royal for dinner.

But of course, although the evening was pleasant enough, and the farouche John had recovered some of his spirits, and a little of his sense of humor, and although he had managed to keep this up on the train from Cannon Street the next day, to Ashford and Saltinge, it was clearly not going to last much longer, and it didn't. The man was too ill; the agony — whatever it was — was too great. And no sooner had they got into the house — where they were to be alone, as Lorelei Two was in Normandy — than the furies once again took possession of him; he paced like a ghost up and down the long room, looking at nothing; descended or reascended the stairs for no purpose; went out into the garden, climbing the stone steps to the terrace, under that miraculous and motionless waterfall of laburnum and hawthorn blossom, only to return then to the dining-room and hall, there to stand speechless with misery, and now so far lost in it that he seemed to be beyond the reach of even the kindest of questions. To leave his wife, if he dared, or could: to join this other woman (of whom D. had never heard before), if he dared, or could: but was there any choice? or was one any better than the other? wasn't it all hopeless and useless, and himself done for? Either way, he would be devoured, they would devour him. And he thought — he at last got it out — that it was an imposition for him to stay with D., for D. could see how it was: it would be perhaps better if he could be alone somewhere, maybe in a room at Inglesee, there to work it all out by himself, since it was clear that nobody, not even D., could help him. . . . Yes, he would go to Inglesee.

By bus, therefore, in the golden evening, to Inglesee, past a mile of may in bloom, the skylarks rising from the salts, and to the room they found at the Castle Inn, where D. saw that he was comfortably installed, made sure that he had everything that he needed, and left him, after arranging a meeting for dinner the next day. And how, how, was D. to know that this unhappy parting, this unhappy "goodnight," in a stuffy hotel bedroom, just round the corner from the tiny cliff's-edge cottage, where, years before, John had first come to visit them — that famous occasion when, on leaving, he had forgotten all his luggage in the train at Ashford, all except his umbrella! — how was he to know that this would mark the end of that long intimacy, begun in Boston and continued in London and at Saltinge? and the end, too, of the farouche John's life in England? —

For so it was to be. There was no meeting for dinner the next night, or any night thereafter. A note, instead, very distraught, the handwriting more chaotic even than usual, to say that he couldn't bear it, he must go and face it out, he was on his way to London, for better or worse, and that he would write. And after that, the silence, the disappearance, the unanswered letters — the silence becoming at last ominous — and then the rumors. That he was ill. That he was insane. That he had tried to kill himself. That "friends" were taking care of him, in Kensington. But who? Which friends? No one knew. Only, at last, to someone brash enough to telephone the house at Sydenham and ask for him, the statement — by one of the stepchildren — that he wasn't well, and was in fact in a nursing-home, but that it was nothing really serious.

None of which, sinister as it was, had adequately prepared D. for the shock that was to come, and that would, through the inter-mediacy of D., have the effect of sending the farouche John back to America. For the letter, when at last it came — and when D. had found it, on answering the postman's knock, lying on the doormat — was the longest he had ever had from John, and the most terrible. It was his farewell to the world, to life, to love, to his friends, and to sanity. And it came — it had been smuggled out — from Bed-lam — Bedlam, to which he had been committed, after hurling himself out of a window at Sydenham, in an unsuccessful attempt to kill himself, and where now he was doomed to stay forever. His existence — he said — was that of a ghoul: it was subhuman: it was fitting that he was given every morning a pail of water and a scrubbing-brush and set to scrubbing the foul floors of cells and cor-ridors, for he no longer had any semblance of a mind, nothing was left but a chaos of horror and darkness: there would be no escape, ever, for the simple reason that he could not escape from himself. To begin with, he had gone to stay with his friends the Johnsons in Kensington, Johnson the sculptor; but he had soon discovered that his behavior, which was becoming more and more monstrous, was beginning to unhinge both Johnson and his wife: he could no longer dress or undress, his habits had become unspeakably filthy: his teeth were breaking off in his face: and he could not go out on the simplest errand, to buy his tobacco or postage stamps, without taking the wrong turning and getting himself lost. He had realized at Paul's flat, at St. Pancras, that he was on the brink of some such disaster: but at Saltinge he had finally known the worst, known the infernal depths to which he was doomed to sink; and it was to spare D. any further distress, as D. had been kind, and he was grateful, that he had decided on the desperate return to London. But it had been, as he had foreseen, no use. His vampirism, both at the Johnsons' and when he had returned home, had had the terrible effect of reducing all those around him to his own ghoulish level, he was gradually making idiots of them all: and so he had flung himself from the window. But, incompetent even in this — and how typical of a life of failure! — he had not succeeded in killing himself, had merely injured his back, and was now, thank god, where he belonged, and resigned to a horror that he richly deserved. And would D. be so kind as to make his farewells, his adieux, to the few people who had genuinely cared for him? —

An appalling letter, a desolating valediction, but D., despite his dismay, saw at once that it was itself the key to the locked door; for, if it was a fearful document, it was also, in D.'s opinion, the letter of a man who was unmistakably and demonstrably sane: it could be used to get him out. By the merest accident D. remembered the name of the farouche John's doctor, in London, the surname only; and by patiently calling the dozen or so doctors of that name in the telephone directory, he was at last rewarded. The doctor happened to know who John's solicitor was, copies of the letter were taken to him — the poor man was horrified and incredulous — and the train of events was set in motion which was to rescue the wretched John from what was virtually a burial alive. American relatives were notified, the Commission for Lunacy appealed to, and two months later, from Southampton, on the well-known Cunard notepaper, with the little triangular red pennant, came a brief and noncommit-

tal note from John to say that he was off to America, and that he
would stay there for good. And D. was never to know for the rest of
his life — for how could he inquire? — whether the dear fellow had
ever discovered by what process he had obtained his release. The
episode was never again — in the two or three meetings in America,
or the semi-occasional letters — referred to by either of them.

Yes, Hambo would undoubtedly have made an attempt to link
these two abortive suicides: perhaps indeed he had done so, at one
of those bibulous and eloquent sessions at the Ship, or in the dining-
room at Saltinge: or even on the voyage to Gibraltar, at a time when
already the strain imposed on them both by D.'s pseudo-guardian-
ship — for Hambo's despairing father had in effect placed D. *in
loco parentis* — was beginning to elevate and illuminate the friendly
rivalry between them into something else. For hadn't Hambo already, or at any rate D. and Hambo together, analyzed the necessity
that lay there in hermetic pattern between them, that in some sense
and inevitably the son must 'destroy' the father, castrate or crucify
him? And hadn't D., like the farouche John, tacitly admitted that
this death was already within him — working itself out to the surface — in this attempt at suicide? Beyond the pleasure principle! —
hadn't it, in both instances, been just this need of the organism to
die, a secret, or even explicit, confession that the cycle had been
completed, the semantic statement finished? To be sure, in these
discussions, which, D. had often thought, since, had sometimes
achieved a quite astonishing pitch of divination — and a kind of co-
operative, and hallucinatory, alcoholic brilliance of statement unique
in his experience, the two minds and psyches complementing —
and complimenting! — each other in a moving braid of analysis as
closely woven as the serpents in the uraeus of an Egyptian king —
in these competitive flights of semi-mystical dialogue, as between
his projected 'Dr. Quicksand and Mr. Tattletale,' or 'Dr. Saltpetre
and Mr. Joyprong,' there had been, as time went on, a steadily and

perceptibly increasing pressure, on the part of Hambo, to hasten this very process of 'death,' on the part of D.; and no matter how far out into the empyrean they might soar, in their joint pursuit of 'truth,' or how diaphanous might be their analysis of its apprehensibility, or how sacred and Daedalian and dedicated must be the office, *vis-à-vis* mankind, of the writer, the poet, as they vied with each other in envisaging it, nevertheless almost invariably at the end they would come back to that question of the creative *moritura* in D., and, from dear young Hambo's viewpoint, the obvious desirability of D.'s getting on with it. Was the attempted suicide, *tout court*, a confession of failure? And had Hambo been quick to seize on the fact, and to try to take advantage of it? Not that it wasn't all brought up, or dropped again — between drinks and the pyrotechnical ping-pong games on that splendid "refractory" table so beloved of Squidge, the cat of cats — always with the utmost of urbanity and good humor, not to say hilarity: it was a game, a ritual, an exercise, and a debate, all in one; but also, as in that weight-lifting at St. Cath's of which Hambo was so proud, it was a deadly serious testing of strength, in which the steel was occasionally, for a flash, just visible, and now and then the blood drawn.

The element of confession, confession of failure, had certainly been present, and had been voluntarily offered up by D., in these discussions; and of course this had quite contradicted D.'s easy assumption, at the time, that there was nothing to be ashamed of, and that he had no regrets, no feelings of remorse. The truth was that D. had himself not yet begun to understand how comprehensive had been his betrayal of all that he most profoundly and integrally set store by, the very light by which he had proposed to live. What sort of priest of consciousness was he who would himself be the first to take flight from it? and hadn't this been a double betrayal? For, quite apart from the failure in his career, his work, wasn't there also that obligation, as pointed up by grandfather — both to the ancestors and the descendants — of transmitting the preciously learned inheritance? Weren't the three little D.'s, and his work, in this regard, practically synonymous?

There was no doubt of it; and it could hardly comfort D., when later he had begun to realize it, that it was only the title of a film at the Saltinge cinema that had enabled him to undertake those neglected obligations anew. One could make excuses: as in his citing of the family *petit mal*, the wearing out of the neural sheathing: it was even arguable that in this sense what had happened was predestined, and inevitable, and that the act, in the end, and as it had so fortunately worked out, provided its own cure. Weren't his dreams, his whole lifetime of dreams, that unparalleled parade of monstrous fantasies and malformations, convincing enough evidence of this? The obsession with death, with abnormal sensibility and death, informed them everywhere: the reek of decay and dissolution and corruption arose from them every morning of his life. The solitary dark tombstone, for instance, on which was merely the inscription SACRED TO THE MEMORY OF ARKOMON AGAIN. That pitiful sensitive pig, as reported in *Purple Passage*, with the oh so tender and transparent wings, bitten by the dog. The tiny wounded and discolored pig (ah, that pig of grandmother's) creeping timidly along the curbstone, for shelter against the terrible dangers of the street, and with one eye so luminously sensitive that it continuously, in response to the light, expanded itself like a bright bubble and burst in sparks of agony, only then to reinflate and burst again, while the pathetic creature stumbled blindly from one fearful peril to another. Or that other, that dream of the 'comic strip' series of drawings; a dream in which D. was himself rapidly making the drawings, which then as rapidly became the thing itself, the real thing; a series of portraits or cartoons, of D. — D. in the process of dying; D., hurrying towards his death, into death; in each new panel the figure becoming more gaunt and skeletalized, the eyes further

sunken into the hollow eye-sockets, the ribs more nakedly promi-
nent, as it ran, stumbled, and fell, towards the sea — desperately
trying to get to the sea, with some obscure notion of then swimming
out into the sunset, into the light: until, in the final panel of all,
the skeleton, at last bare, now lay prone, with empty and outstretched hands, on the beach at the water's edge; disclosing, within
the rib-case, where the heart should have been, but itself rotten and
falling apart, and with crumbling amulets among the perishing
pages, a copy of *The Book of the Dead;* — what was one to make
of *that* little comic-strip-tease, which was to have been entitled, a
trifle sardonically, "*D. Gets Going*" — ? And they had been as innumerable as dreadful, those dark spoutings from the foul unconscious: to fall asleep in the evening was automatically to submit
once more to a lethal flooding by those bitter and mortal waters.
What would breakfast have been, all these years, at South
Yarmouth, or Inglesee, or London, or Saltinge, whether in the con-
sulates of Lorelei One or Lorelei Two — or now in the blest consulate of Lorelei Three — without those dreams, the ritual narra-
tion of those dreams? They had become as indispensable a part of
the order of the day as the punctual arrival of Squidge, or Squarry-
ongs, the Cat of a Hundred Names, with a skidding slide up onto
the *Times* at the end of the refectory table, or the endless variations,
for the children, at bedtime, of the never-ending — and never-ended
— serial story, *The Jewel Seed.*

Yes: it was perhaps interesting to consider the waking life, the
conscious life, and in all its multifoliate ramifications, too, as merely
paralleling, in such improvisational fashion as it could, this deeper
and darker force which lay there forever below, a constant and coefficient, a measure and reminder. The pressure of this towards
death, and the hesitations, the pauses, the deviations, the avoidances — and even the acceptances — which this unceasing pressure
must incessantly be evolving for *it*self and *him*self: as if the con-

scious and the unconscious were engaged, had always been engaged, in a dance, the most intricate and surprising and involved and contrapuntal of dances, and this dance, in which light and darkness were the partners (or all and nothing) was one's life: it was against this pressure, and out of it, that his work, his loves, his hatreds and fears, his gettings and begettings and losings, his fruitful or fruitless travels, his visions and his mischiefs, had found their — as now it appeared — implicit self-shapings. For now, how preordained it all seemed to have been! as if, from the very outset, from the shadow of the first palmetto leaf at Savannah, and from the first stammered syllable for the first raindrop seen darkly descending against the limitless sky, or felt warm on the hand, the already-conceived design had begun to unfold itself with stealthy purpose and foresight, and with entire command, into an incredibly increasing complexity of meaning. That shape, which was to be the shape of oneself, and the shape of one's 'view' from the little headland of oneself, was immanent, was already there: that map had already been drawn: inward, or outward; one would follow those contours and travel those roads, those seas, make landfall of those shores: they were there, waiting, below the horizon, those houses, those countries, to be lived in and loved: even to the perhaps unattainable — or approachable only at peril of shipwreck — Ushant.

In this sense the casual weekend visit to Saltinge with Chapman, that first summer, after the 'Cynthia' voyage; and the lunch at Inglesee; and the walk to the sea, where, it was said, you could hear the bells of the 'lost' Inglesee (which had been drowned) when the sea was still — the bells of the *Cathédrale engloutie*; or, at last, the ascent of the cobbles of Strand Hill, past the house itself, the blessed house, even although it could not as yet be recognized as such: all this, so seen in retrospect, was as ordered and precise and simple as a recital of the alphabet. What could have been more natural than that they should have wanted to see that other house, at Saltinge,

where the Old Master had lived, and where he had wrought those
fabulously involute symphonies of his, those multiple palimpsests,
in which, as in the changeable signs of one's childhood, each new
angle of approach revealed a different shade or nuance of moral, or
immoral, meaning? Wasn't this merely tantamount to a return, a
revisitation — a renewal of inspection of an area, a province, which,
like Chapman and the farouche John, he had long since been possessed of, or had been put in possession of, by the Old Master himself? To see, in the pale summer sunlight, the soft red brick of the
quiet façade, and the little white stone urns above the cornice, or to
look in through the tall studio window, at the turn of the wall,
where one could glimpse the edge of a piano, and a gloom of books,
was merely to read again, as one had just now been doing on the
voyage with Cynthia, or at Arundel with Chapman, or at South
Yarmouth with Lorelei One, by lamplight, under the Golden
Rooster that flamed over the mantel, one of those lucid masterpieces
of exploration which in every generation are the gift of a great
writer — the gift, indeed, of a new country. And wasn't Saltinge,
symbolically now, that country, the essence of it, the very *Ding an
sich* of D.'s lifelong search — wasn't this perhaps the very center,
so that, although he didn't yet know it, he had at last come home,
and all the more fittingly guided thither by a tutelary genius, the
genius loci, who had himself made his way to it by a lifelong process
of need, and analysis of need — the need, too, of an American? Yes,
this was going to be home, it had seized him, it was inescapable: it
had been home from that very moment, on the bedroom floor at
Savannah, when the poet of White Horse Vale had first beckoned
to him, and the mystic white horse had begun his soundless gallop
over the moonlit or moonless downs toward that other mystical
figure, in the south, the Long Man of Wilmington; who waited,
staff in hand — although D. didn't yet know it — only a few miles
away from Saltinge. Here too was the same beckoning, the same

feeling of being beckoned to on all sides: everything was at once familiar: the mysterious familiarity of the *déjà vu*, but this time on a transcendental, and overpowering, scale. The tiny blossoms of the Mother of Thousands in the crannies of the churchyard wall: the jackdaws circling the Tower, and speaking, as he pointed out to Chapman, their native French, their *"tiens, tiens,"* which no doubt they had brought over with William the Conqueror: the pint of beer at the King's Head, or the Ship Inn, and the narrow cobbled street that took him, down the hill, past the house that was still invisible, still under the snow of the future, but already, for all that, his own — all this, under the *ting-tang* of the golden Quarter-Boys, and in the center of the immense Marsh, that vast and intricate map of green, with its numberless canals and dykes and tree-bordered fields, where, as far as the eye could see, grazed the numberless sheep, all this had been here all his life, to be sure; but now, by some miracle of temporal transformation, it was as if all his *own* life, every instant of it, had been spent at Saltinge; for as long as he could remember, he had been leading a double life.

And no matter how ineffectually he had worked here, after the house had found him, and little June had been born in it — the only one of the births to which he had not been a witness — there could certainly be no denying that he could not possibly have made the attempt under better auspices. The attempt had at least been made — that much could be said: and if the Old Master would not have applauded the end-result, he could have approved of the aim. That great consciousness, wouldn't it have found something to bless in D.'s 'consistent view,' the notion that consciousness was itself the chief of blessings? and this despite D.'s momentary betrayal, and his backslidings? For he had tried. Along with the multifarious work, most of it ephemeral, for the innumerable magazines and newspapers — from the Chicago Daily News and Tribune to the Dial, the Freeman, the New Republic, the New York Post, the Athenaeum, the Nation, the New Yorker — a gamut that ran from the reporting of tennis at Wimbledon, or the launching of the Queen Mary, or the Grand National at Aintree, on the one extreme, to a dissection of Croce, for the London Nation, or a polite murder of Osbert Sitwell for the Tsetse's quarterly on the other — along with all this had gone, if intermittently, or incompletely, or unsuccessfully, his persistent effort to find for himself a literary *modus vivendi* which would keep that consistent view of his as its constant center. And there was even more to it than that. Consciousness, yes — one was automatically enough implicated in that, from the outset: but there was another aspect of it which had early begun to concern him, as early as the war years in Boston, in the psychoanalytic discussions with Jacob: for if it was the writer's business, or the poet's, to be as conscious as possible, and his primary obligation, then wouldn't this impose upon him the still deeper obligation of being conscious of his *own* workings, the workings of his psyche, and of the springs and deficiencies and necessities and compulsions, the whole subliminal drive which had made him a writer to begin with, and along with the work itself, to present, as it were, the *explication* — ? Wouldn't this be the next mandatory step, the artist's plain duty? that he take the machine apart, and show how it worked? He had discussed, with the farouche John, and with the Tsetse too, the notion, for example, of presenting a poem, or a piece of fiction, complete with the formative matrix, the psychological scaffolding, out of which it was in the act, the very act, of crystallizing: he had even once made the attempt, in a curiosity which the farouche John had facetiously entitled "Brain Fag," and of which, with competent irony, the Tsetse had accepted, for his quarterly, only the ultimate and rather pathetic little 'crystal,' not the matrix: the mouse, but not the parturient mountain. And at Troutbeck Bridge, on the honeymoon with Lorelei One, hadn't there been, along with the lost fragment of verse about Browning's lover of trees, that other fragment — or could it even have been part of the same attempt at a sort of fugue-form in verse — about the poet?

> *Was this the poet? It is man.*
> *A glass-cased watch, through which you scan*
> *The feverish fine small mechanism,*
> *And hear it ticking, while it sings:*
> *Behold, this delicate paroxysm*
> *Obedient to rebellious springs!*

That little fragment, which had been emblazoned on the wall of the Harvard Psychological Clinic Memorial Bathroom, in the old farmhouse at Brewster — whither they had been driven from Saltinge by the second Great War — scrolled there by Lorelei Three, and calligraphically, too, in the design of an hour-glass, in homage to Harry, their *primum mobile* of loving-kindness — wasn't that visible now as the first succinct and lucid statement of what was to turn out to be the all-gathering preoccupation? even if, as seemed likely — though how could one be sure — ? — one hadn't so conceived it at the time. But wasn't the fact that this fragment alone remained in one's memory, after upwards of three decades, and so many summers, so many loves, indicative of something at least prophetic? And in this had Jacob perhaps been right in his suggestion that an author's writings were very often in some degree an anticipation of attitudes yet to be formed, definitions yet to be made, actions yet to be taken? the work of art, of whatever category, itself, therefore, the conscious-unconscious process of arrival at this new point; and, when completed, itself in a sense the catalyst which would precipitate the new attitude or action — ?

Clearly, it was another definite facet of the whole disturbingly beautiful mechanism; and another aspect, therefore, of the off-and-on project, of all those years at Saltinge, or to and from it,

driven by the twin winds of love and economics, the project of adding, to such work as he might undertake, or ever succeed in finishing, an exact statement about the nature and contents of the author,
like the bill of lading of a ship. Santayana had mentioned, during
the discussions of Shelley, that it was probable that the individual's
'range' of thought, or imagination, his reach, or capacity, was already
adumbrated by the time he was twenty-one; and that the ensuing
years could only be devoted to deploying, or expanding, this potential, on the one hand, or defining and refining it, on the other. And
D., looking back over his own somewhat zigzag course, had long
since perceived that the zigzags were by no means as random or
capricious as they looked, and added up to an at least partial veri-
fication of that slightly depressing theory. Wasn't it all, for instance,
implicit, and kernelled, the tiny wrinkled seed all there, in that
fragment of sententious verse? And why, in that case, hadn't he
pursued it, gone on with it? Presumably because, from the psychological viewpoint, so much, at that time, was still exploratory and
heuristic and tentative: there was even, as D. had often since had
occasion to remember, a quite considerable period when the findings of the new psychology — and what findings there were, and
what troves that were not always treasure! — appeared all too
damningly to discredit the artist or writer completely: it had been
difficult, in that esurient shadow, to keep up one's *amour-propre*,
and difficult, too, and frightening, in such a situation, to venture
further with one's own speculations and explorations. How was one
to know, as the work of translation proceeded so slowly, that the
great Freud himself had already stated that 'before the work of the
poet he simply gave up'? One didn't; any more than one foresaw
that one would oneself come very close, one day, to going to Vienna
to work with that genius of explorers. And so, the self-doubt under-
mining his faith in the social role of the writer, he had deferred, and
temporized, had shied off, and gone round; he had waited, so to

speak, to see; and, while waiting to see, had too often, alas, written with his eyes shut. Too many years had passed between the fragment of prophetic verse and his somewhat halting attempt — rejected by the Tsetse as too metaphorical — at finding, in terms of this psychology, a relativistic basis for criticism, a sliding scale of social measure, from simple to complex — the X solution (in terms of art) as perfectly suited to the x audience level, as the Y to the y: a thesis that had left D. himself *en plein air,* and had attracted no attention, when published, but which had at least had the virtue of preparing and priming him, when the time came, a little later, for that most golden of opportunities, the reviewing of the *Principles of Literary Criticism* for the Nation; a review which was in turn to lead to the meeting of D. and Richards — of all places — at a bullfight in Spain. Here, in this brief review, he had been able to clarify for himself something of his central concern, but only a little; in the experiment which John had called "Brain Fag" he had carried it a trifle further; but of course it was in *Purple Passage* that he had at last, but with too many adulterations and lost directions — his own intentions a trifle obscure as yet — made the attempt to put down, for that crazy voyage, its true bill of lading.

Which, as Hambo was to say — when, on the strength of having read it, he had crossed the Atlantic, himself no mean voyager, bringing with him the script of his own unfinished drama, *Aquamarine,* in order to work, to study with D. — a singular *façon de parler* — was as good as far as it went. But did it go far enough? A just criticism. The idea — of putting all the cards on the table, all the writer's marked cards, of whatever nature, and his whole disgraceful (if it was) accoutrement of sleights of hand and sleights of mind, not to mention all that dubious apparatus of the illusionist, the self-debunking Houdini, but still up to his old tricks, just the same — that slightly soiled apparatus, a little stagey, of the *suggestio falsi* and *suppressio veri* — the idea was all right, but it had not found its objective correlative. In order to make a go of it, in the sense that it should be dramatically effective, or have a beginning, a middle and an end — or, as he had pointed out to Hambo in the case of *Aquamarine,* the ascending and descending curves of form which would supply direction — too much extraneous matter had been added. The minor characters, while perhaps well enough blocked in, were really there for the purpose of adding verisimilitude, not because they psychodynamically belonged. Too much Cynthia and Smith, and too little of the bare-assed truth about Demarest; as, for example, in that matter of the suppression of the fact that Demarest was a married man with two children. No, it had been a compromise in which the voice of Joyce had been too audible; and the best that could be said of it was that, psychologically, the long soliloquy was skillfully placed — the action flowing first into it and then out again; thus making for a true resolution.

And so, it remained there, that unfulfilled project, as something still to be done, if indeed it now ever could be: as something which the life, in Saltinge, and in that house, had always promised, and never given. Should he now reproach himself for that inability? or was it enough that the life itself, during all those years, and all those erratic comings and goings, had been a sufficient justification? It had been incomparably rich. It had been — there could be no doubt of it whatever — exactly what he had wanted. And he had himself been the prime agent in bringing it to pass. Just as surely as the great astrologist had laid his foundations of Caen stone, and built the beautiful house, with the carved serpents under the eaves, he had himself built the life there, and slowly but surely enriched it. Not that good fortune had not attended him throughout, for it had. The strange little town was itself a veritable cornucopia of wealth, on whatever conceivable plane one looked for it. Hadn't the great Queen called it her little London — ? or, as someone else had naughtily amended, her little Soho? For if the town itself was quite magically situated on its little hill, in the triangle formed by the three "baby rivers," and looked, when seen against the sunset, like a ship setting gallantly out to sea, out to the channel, it also had the singular power of attracting to itself the most diverse company of human beings that surely was ever gathered in any place so tiny. It looked so innocent, so tender, so humble and true, in the evening light: as the Vicar, Mr. Birdlime, stopping D. one night on the Marsh, had somewhat intensely indicated, with a wave of his claw-like hand, "You can hear its little heart beat!" But also, as D. had refrained from replying to that gaunt figure, which was forever flapping about those windy streets like a jackdaw, you could hear its little tongue wag. The window-curtains stirred as one passed, stirred and were still again, and one was aware of the watchful eyes behind them. Hadn't the Mayor himself, living and writing in the Old Master's house — and what a desecration! — had his own satirical fling at its inordinate propensity to gossip and snobbery and social backbiting? All too true: and D. had often thought that it bore a sinister resemblance to that dark little walled town, in a story of Algernon Blackwood's, which was haunted by cats; where, every night, as soon as the moon was up, and its golden swale of light on the vast marsh, the inhabitants all came out on the walls in the form of cats. It would not have been in the least surprising to find this so at Saltinge — there was undoubtedly a sense of evil in it, and this had been repeatedly drawn upon, both by the Old Master and by his successor in the house — which, of course, had been that of a murderer. Was it this curious combination of beauty and evil that perpetually drew to it such extraordinary people? so that the variety of its characters, whether well-known, or simply encountered by chance in the narrow streets, was as extravagant as that in any Elizabethan play? To those who remained there long enough, like Paul or Nicholas, or Edward, or D., this became of

course a joke and a commonplace. Sooner or later, everyone was
sure to turn up, and not always mere human flotsam or jetsam.
Mrs. Q., whom everyone thought to be a murderess, but who had
miraculously got off, came down to Saltinge at once, after the trial,
as a matter of course. But so did the Bengal Lancer. So did the
Roaring Girls, that astonishing pair — and extremely entertaining,
too — who could be heard almost any morning bawling out the
wretched little tailor in the High Street, or flinging back at him,
all publicly, a badly made pair of breeches. What more natural than
that the incredible, the fascinating Ruts, with the bright vermilion
mouth, and brown stumps of teeth, and the foot-long cigarette-
holder, should, all unknown, knock at the door and ask them to a
party? as, all unknown, she had asked all Saltinge? or that, at the
party, or near the end of it, being asked by her what he thought of
her, he had told her that she was like a particularly fine sunset, and
she had crowed with glee? Those streets — what would one not see
in them next! The Foetus-Face, following the Boston bull terrier
slowly, slowly, down Strand Hill, the mask of self-devouring evil
closed and blank like that of one in an opium dream: old Clinker,
their celibate neighbor, with his pathological mania for cutting
down trees — in a weak moment they had indulged this vice, and
had allowed him to send over his manservant and strip the house,
and forever, of its Virginia Creeper. Mr. Birdlime, with his invet-
erate sense of the dramatic — it was said he had wanted to go on
the stage — pointing abruptly upward to the balcony of the George
Hotel and asking: "Do you see him up there? — No? — Why, it's
Wellington, just back from Waterloo, and about to throw down
pennies to the boys!" Or Captain Pyx, with his obsession about operations, pausing on his way from one pub to another, and tapping
on the cobbles with his ash-plant, to say ominously, "Yes, they're
going to open me up like a herring — open me up like a herring!" —

"You seem" — Aunt Sibyl would almost invariably say, in the brief letters from California, whither she and the Beloved Uncle had retreated — after selling the beautiful house in Fayerweather Street — "you seem always to enjoy life there so much, you seem always to be having such a good time, and to see so many people! I don't know how you do it, and with so little money!" It had been the recurrent theme of those sad little letters, in which there was also what seemed almost to be a note of envy, and of opportunity lost. And indeed, how she would have loved that life, that little town, that intensely organized and conscious little social complex, which so often, in moments of levity, he had compared to a cheese full of mites! If the social waywardnesses and intrigues and backwaters of Cambridge, or Boston, or New Bedford, the patient cunning employed in the manoeuvres of inclusion or exclusion, not to mention the murderous deadfalls so cunningly contrived of paper roses and *papier-mâché* trellising as to deceive any but the most hardened frequenters of the pergola season, if these had so amused her in the house at Cambridge, for endless sly comment and analysis, how much more would she have relished the devious and Daedalian ways of Saltinge, and its mere human variety, since it was this that above all she most loved. Was there anything she enjoyed so much, or so fastidiously, as the entrance into a new 'scene,' a new society — as in the winter at Florence, for instance — with the preliminary survey, the establishment of contacts, followed by the mapping of strategy, the brilliant skirmishes on one or the other flank, to conceal the true purpose, and then, at the chosen moment, and on her own chosen ground, the general engagement — ? Nor was it in the least necessary that this should terminate in fanfares of victory. It was the game itself that was the fun, the stratagems and protocols, and what people did or didn't do. And even from Fayerweather Street she had from the outset taken an enormous, and penetratingly observant, interest in D.'s English adventure, and particularly after he had settled himself at Saltinge. There was nothing she hadn't wanted to know; nothing, down to the tiniest detail, that she hadn't inquired about. What people did they see the most of? And what did they all do, and where did they live? And did he and Lorelei dine out, or go out to tea? Had they been, so to speak, "Received"? In Inglesee, for example, had they met Lady A.? Or at Saltinge, Lady R., who, it was reputed, had been one of King Edward's — King Edward the Seventh's — favorites? One could have — she had agreed — too much of that sort of thing, and the more particularly if there was work to be done. And it was therefore perhaps wise that they had preferred, on the whole, the company of writers and painters. But how had it happened that there seemed to be so many painters, and D. himself no painter? Had he really become so interested in painting? Of course, she remembered his saying that he had gone all over Venice searching out the Tiepolos, and that in London he had done much the same for Hogarth, and she could to some extent share his enthusiasm for Hogarth, though she herself preferred Romney; she remembered, too, his saying, while she was painting that little unfinished portrait of him, that he had always liked daubing, and had occasionally toyed with the notion of taking it up; but how had it come about that so many of his friends were painters? These Harolds and Lauras and Pauls? In his "London Letters," too, he seemed so often to be talking about them, and going to exhibitions — she thought his little description of the surrealist show very amusing; it must have been fun; and that other one, she couldn't remember which, where the artist's wife had appeared with bright green hair, at the opening, and all the drinks, too, had been green, various shades of green — but hadn't he perhaps been a little hard on the poor old Academy, and was the conservative always, or so invariably and inevitably, dull? She didn't think so, if you looked carefully. But if he saw so many painters, and Saltinge seemed to be full of them, what with Paul there, who of course, she knew, was very fine, and Nicholas, who, she took his word for it, was even finer, how did he find time to see the writers he knew, or to keep in touch with them? In fact, he seemed to be so busy, how did he find time for anything? But he certainly — she admitted — enjoyed it, there was no doubt about that! — And for instance, did he nowadays see very much of the Tsetse, or Chapman? — And Nicholas; whom of course she remembered very well, for he had been to dinner in Fayerweather Street, and she had thought him most unusual, a really remarkable person, but so fragile — and not too well, not too strong, was he? — and Nicholas, whose paintings were said to be so completely *sui generis,* and certainly they looked it, in the little Penguin booklet of reproductions, a bizarre and fantastic and beautiful and terrifying world of his own, and a savagely satirical, but also exquisitely poetic, commentary on *our* so increasingly monstrous world — did he still see as much of Nicholas as before? or go up to that Victorian house on the hill, outside Saltinge, with the beautiful sloping gardens, and the little rococo Greek temple under the trees, and that unbelievable chaos of a workroom, where he painted (with spit!) the brilliant panels of water-color, patiently pasting each to the last, until, with the completion of the final corner, the great vision opened its translunar and as if death-stilled infinitudes of vista, and of motionless violence in vista, for superhuman, and subhuman, joys and despairs, or loves and hates — ? And did he still play the gramophone unceasingly as he painted, the unceasing American jazz, which, according to D., he so liked? Of course, they had all been to Mexico together, hadn't they; Nicholas and D. and Lorelei Three; but that was after she and the Beloved Uncle had withdrawn to San Clemente, to be near the grandchild; and so they had never heard much about it, or only that Nicholas had come close to dying there, had barely managed to drag himself all the way back to Boston, and all alone, where the great and good Bassett had nursed him back to health. So, she supposed that Nicholas and Lorelei Three must like each other, despite the fact that they both were painters, and in such different styles — but then, *anyone* would like Lorelei Three, as she had done herself, at a glance; otherwise she would not, there in the Boston hotel, by the Muddy River, have given her the roses. For once, he had been as lucky in his wife as he had been with his friends — ! and lucky in his friends, he ought to remember with gratitude, he had phenomenally been.

Yes, Aunt Sibyl, there could be no question of it, would have loved Saltinge just as much as he had loved it himself, would have brought to it just the right sort of connoisseurship — just the right palate, and the right palette, too. "You really love Saltinge, don't you?" — So Paul had abruptly asked D., on one of those precarious and improbable returns of his, by the skin of his teeth, with a new wife and no money, to a house emptied of its contents, and to friends who were beginning to be a little bewildered by these changes, and by the necessity, which they so heroically undertook, of adjusting themselves yet once again. Not that there hadn't been one or two exceptions. The young Jed himself — as Aunt Sibyl, then just back from London to Boston, was the first to report — had formed a somewhat sinister alliance with Lorelei Two, there was a definite attachment there, something about which, she had taken pains to warn D., he had better be extremely careful. What with the love of music which they shared, and playing the piano so much together, was there a possibility of — what did they call it? — an emotional displacement which might make trouble? They were even thinking of taking a flat together, in London, and didn't D. think that would be most unwise? A danger which had been averted, thank goodness, and the good Jed had in due course recovered his balance; recovered, too, from the hostility to D., or disapproval, and the indifference and condescension towards Lorelei

Three, which had led him so profoundly to underestimate her. It had been hard on dear Jed: harder, perhaps, than the previous divorce had been, when, in his adolescence, he had found himself — during the three-year absence of D. — willy-nilly *in loco parentis*, as regards the two younger children, with the unhappy result that when D. *had* come back, to Saltinge and the blessed house, there had developed that curious and shadowy, but temporary, rivalry between them. Temporary, however, it had been; and in this their love of Saltinge and the house — and *all* their loves, Jean's and June's as well, and, of course, Lorelei Three's — had been decisive. That house, and its rituals, that wonderfully but so lightly intricate continuum of living and loving — in which their tutelary genius, or *genius loci*, the benign inquisitive ghost of the great astrologer and mathematician (with his zenzicubes and zenzizenzicubes and zenzikes!) had become quite indispensably the symbol of the family — all this was now established by their communion as something which they would share forever: it would die when *they* died, but not before.

And by how many noble or beautiful or delightful spirits had it been lighted and blessed! Lighted by love, lighted by laughter, the kind of light that never goes out; Paul, bringing into it not only the feline grace and Persian eye, or the arched light-years of his Hanging Gardens, the ethereal vanishings of The Mansions of the Dead, but also the unsleeping and amusedly affectionate and immortal watchfulness of a mind half man's, half satyr's, the love of beauty that was oddly both animal and mineral, and could be as soft as a cobweb (as in his drawing for The Garden of Cyrus), or the flesh of a woman, or as hard as one of the flints in his Nest of Wild Stones. And Chapman, even if in the end he had disappeared, their interests dividing, what subtleties and nugae of humor and good humor, the grace-notes of talk, he had dispensed there. Yes, the sense of humor — it had been remarkable how often, and with

what instinctive felicity, one of them would, almost as if deliberately, set up the inviting opportunity, the *donnée,* of the joke
as the Old Master would say, for the other, so that it would then
come out as pat and pink as the magician's rabbit. As on that occasion, one winter's evening, when they were walking past the façade
of the British Museum, ghostly in the moonlight, and heard from
it, high above, the shivering chatter of starlings; and Chapman had
played the 'straight man' with his "It must be cold up there in the
metopes," so that D. could reply, "Of course. They're doing the
Parthenon Frieze." And Arnault — stubborn, crotchety, perverse,
and difficult Arnault, down from his bookshop for the weekend,
with his latest kinky poem, and the latest news of the Tsetse's quarterly, or of the Tsetse himself, and ready for the libations of Bristol
Milk and the stubborn rearguard defense of Georgian Poetry — or
some of it, anyway, he would say belligerently: for although in the
course of time he had come to acknowledge the Tsetse's genius, it
was usually with reservations, and it amused D. to remind him, now
and then, of his rejection, when D. had first offered it to him, of
The Love-Song, and also of La Fanciulla; and this always embarrassed him. Even the famous *Blick ins Chaos,* wasn't it destined —
he said — to become a twentieth-century *Kubla Khan,* with the
same sort of romantic and talismanic glitter, but fragmented or fragmentary, and perhaps without final profundity in scale or idea, a
broken bundle of mirrors, an anthology of vivid reflections, a tantivy
of vivid scenes — and therefore minor? Paul had once happily
described Arnault's own poetry as an "interesting fumble"; and
nothing could have been truer. There was a kind of angry desperation in it, and in its dogged insistence on the literal truth, nothing
less, and every inch of it, it tangled itself in the contingent, got
helplessly in its own way, and suddenly came to an end exhausted.
But his talk was searching and invaluable, or at any rate till the
later collapse into illness and alcoholism. For, never, no, never,

would D. forget that final dinner in London, over the bookshop, where, after meeting the Tsetse at the door — who was just coming out, and who warned him that Arnault was "not altogether himself" — he found the unhappy man seated at the table, his head in his hands, all but speechless, or his speech reduced to four-letter words of imprecation, imprecation from the last depths of loathing and disgust and despair. Incapable of serving the cold collation which had been laid out on the sideboard, he rolled his head in his hands (while D. served himself) and cursed his existence, cursed everything, cursed everyone, but above all cursed the utterly meaningless caprices and bad jokes and filthy connivings of a destiny that would compel one to fall in love, for instance, with a dishonest little tailor's assistant, who was utterly incapable of fidelity; and thus to destroy all that one had believed in, or been faithful to, in one's life, all that was good. What was it for? What? And the muttered imprecations would begin again, round and round and over and over, in an ecstasy of self-loathing. Better — thought D. as he let himself out, unnoticed, at last — to remember an earlier visit, when Arnault, not yet so obsessed with his need of death, described so amusingly his encounter, at the ballet, with his divorced wife. How long since they had seen each other? A long time — enough, it appeared, for the rancors to have been dissipated; they were glad, they were delighted, to see each other again, and began to talk animatedly, almost as if it were a first meeting, or even a flirtation. But then, Arnault had said, a curious thing began to happen: in the space of something like half an hour, they had begun to disagree, then to wrangle, then to look at each other with mounting dislike and distrust, in an accelerated recapitulation of the whole marriage, the long years of marriage: and suddenly they had again reached identically the same end in identically the same silence of hatred, the long hard look of hatred: and realizing that he still had more than an hour to sit beside this terrible woman, he had got up abruptly during the next curtain, the next interval, and departed without another word.

Yes, better to think of that, or of the brave pathetic last letter, from the hospital at Brighton, dictated to his nurse, full of cheer, although he obviously knew he was going to die, and ending with the final humorous admonition — a reference to D.'s confession, during Arnault's last visit to Saltinge, that he was suffering from a collapse of morale, of which it was perhaps symptomatic that he could no longer bring himself to shave every day — a reminder of this admonition, and a command: his final, his farewell, gift, to D. and the house, the gift of courage: "Remember, dear D., to shave every day, as you promised me you would do!" And then, only a few days after, the notice, in the *Times,* of his death.

The sorrows, the agonies, the despairs, such as Arnault had brought there, or the farouche John, or brave little Ee, or that other and gentler John, the quietest of poets and kindest of friends, stepping softly from one room to another, as he made his confession, the confession that he must face death daily, that he never knew, when he set out for his office in the morning, or for a business trip to Leeds or Liverpool, whether he would return alive: hadn't these, both of family and friends, added most to the enrichment of the spirit which, for all of them, so palpably, so almost visibly, informed the house: even more than the gayety, the laughter, the good times, the mad games of ping-pong, the riotous concerts, the birthday mint-juleps in the terraced garden, or the semi-occasional passade, or flirtation? hadn't these contributed an essence that was perhaps the most precious of all? Just as one could say that no house is wholly and forever a house until there has been a death in it, until it has had its first death! Yes, it was these that gave it dignity, the requisite echo or overtone of sorrow, of sadness, the reference to Virgil's *lacrimae rerum;* the far-off sound, barely audible, of the axe striking its first musical but murderous blow in the doomed orchard. Not least the anguish of Lorelei One, left alone there with her sense of betrayal and shame, her grievously wounded pride, waking every morning, as Aunt Sibyl had said to him, to find there was no longer any floor beside her bed, no floor at all to step upon, nothing, nothing, to sustain her. And wasn't there also, in one of his many tattered note books, where the all-too-many unfulfilled projects lay cryptically buried, the title for a story, or a meditation, or at any rate a reminder — "Sunlight, Cuckoo, White Clouds, and Thunder" — ? To remind him of the day when the doctor had diagnosed a cancer, for D.; and had added that he would not be doing his duty if he failed to warn him that it might well prove fatal. And as he had sat in a deck-chair in the garden, under that waterfall of blossom, in the May morning, looking up at the blindingly white clouds in the bluest of skies, he had heard, in quick succession, the first cuckoo call of spring, the first cuckoo from Spain, soft-voiced, double-voiced, in the distance, and then the mutter of the approaching thunderstorm in the darkening west over Inglesee; and he had thought, what a marvelous synthesis it all made, the incredible beauty with its incredible core of death! Yes, death must come to a house, and the house at Saltinge had added to its ghostly treasure those of the gentle John and the stubbornly honest Arnault, and his own recollection of the shadow, in May, which turned out to be only a shadow, after all. The diagnosis had been incorrect, so the London specialist discovered; it was not D. who was to die in that season, but Amy Lowell; and that shadow, too, the moment of fear followed by the moment of incredulous resignation, was blended into the ever-deepening chiaroscuro.

But never put to any use, any more than poor ultra-poetic Edward had been, with his own agony in Inglesee, Edward bursting in on them all as they sat at luncheon — for it was during the school holidays, and all three of the little D.'s were there; and weeping as he told them that Frances had left him, his wife had left him, saying that she was at last fed up with those innumerable bits of fluff, of which he was perpetually boasting, he admitted it, and gone off. He deserved it, he said, weeping, but what was he to do? How was he to live without her? How could he possibly live without her? He strode up and down the long dining-room, a grotesque and somehow El Greco figure, in the faded shorts and Tyrolean stockings, and carrying a shepherd's crook as tall as himself; and poured it all out, while they sat embarrassed over their uneaten luncheon. No, he couldn't blame her, he knew that: he had done it just once too often, just once too often. It was that Canadian girl who had torn it; it was that honey-colored darling, whom he had met on the dike, as he had told D. the week before — he had revelled in the honey-and-amber breasts, the honey-and-amber shoulders and thighs — it was she who had proved fatal, the one too many; and Frances was gone. And while they still sat in astonished silence, off he shot, banging the front door behind him; and, as D. was later to learn, had then rushed to Maxwell's, the dentist's, and had burst in on *him,* and in his office, too, to repeat the performance all over again. Poor, improbable, frustrated Edward, whom he had first met in Chicago, in Chicago's poetic heyday: only the week before, it was all too true, he had admitted at dinner in Inglesee (he had had his man-servant blow an Alp-horn to guide D.'s footsteps through the rolling sea-fog) that he could think of nothing but fornication. He sat there all day thinking of nothing but fornication. It would get him into trouble, he knew it, Frances wouldn't stand it forever — or would she? But no, she was gone; the good and patient and heroic Frances was gone; and with her, as it was to turn out, his own strength, his own will to live. He had loved her more than he dared to know.

A lost man, a man overboard, and the sound of that despairing cry was still audible in the house, to arrest one in the midst of diurnal duties or pleasures; the needed contrast, for example, to the comic, the exaggeratedly comic, spectacle of the Tsetse, all knees and elbows, and with a maniacal leer, crouching at the end of the 'refractory' table for his first game of ping-pong. But it was those cries of the lost, those valedictions of the dying, that in the end did most to give the house its character, its profound and secret meaning; and in this connection it was fascinating to reflect on the extraordinary similarity of poor Edward's outburst, or inburst, and that of little Julian — so exact a repetition (although with a different cause) that it had seemed to Hambo completely, by whatever obscure metaphysical powers, prearranged. They had heard, D. and Lorelei Three, the queer sounds outside, in the cobbled street of Strand Hill, the queer sounds, as of somewhat hysterical laughter, approaching rapidly up the hill, and had looked out from the stair-window and seen the strange little figure of Julian, with one arm over his face, running blindly, with a sort of waddling rush, on the extremely short legs, towards their door; and before either of them could move, he had burst in, just as Edward had, and hurled himself on Lorelei's breast, and into her arms; burying his face on her breast, and, they thought, laughing. But no, not laughing: he was crying hysterically, he had been crying in the street, all the way up the hill from the telephone kiosk by the weigh-bridge, he was crying convulsively and inconsolably. But for what? What new tragedy between himself and his beautiful but wayward Gloria? What disaster in the Cottage on the Marsh? They waited patiently for the convulsion — which it really was — to wear itself out, and gradually it did, and he began to ejaculate, in broken phrases and sentences, the awful, the tragic, thing that had happened to him, that he had only that minute learned, over the telephone, from Gloria. Gloria had been away again, that was it; that was the only explanation of it; if she had not been away again it could not have happened, it was all her fault; and when he thought of the dear creature, lost like that, and of all that could happen to her, and such a sensitive and gentle little thing, out there somewhere on the great Marsh, and all alone — it was at about this point in the sobbing narrative that the name of Gretel was first mentioned, and D. and Lorelei had first realized, or begun to realize, that it was the little Airedale bitch, at the Cottage on the Marsh, Julian's favorite, his love, his sweetheart, who, through some neglect of Gloria's, was gone, was lost.

By degrees, thus, it had all come out; and by degrees the unhappy little figure permitted himself to be consoled and somewhat reassured. It was not, surely, as hopeless as it looked: Gretel might yet turn up: she had only been missing overnight. But if not, they could put up notices in the villages round the Marsh, they could even advertise in the local papers, and the chances were very considerable that Gretel would be found. And perhaps it was not as much Gloria's fault as he supposed: hadn't Gretel strayed once before? Well, that was true, she had: he admitted that: she had strayed, to be exact, from his cottage at Angchurch, which was the very reason why they had decided, Gloria and he, during their divorce proceedings, that it would be safer if Gloria would keep her in the Cottage on the Marsh. But now, when he had phoned her from the kiosk by the weigh-bridge, to report on the divorce proceedings, and to inquire about Gretel, to learn that Gretel was lost — !

As to be sure, she was to be lost again, but in a very different manner, and this time finally; lost again, when pretty much everything else had been lost — including the Cottage on the Marsh. What a saga it had been, and for how many years, going and coming, appearing and disappearing, that astounding and truly unbelievable pair had been building, and so amusingly, with such high good humor, such generosity and high spirits, their Elizabethan tragicomedy! The disparity in ages, in appearance, in habits, in dress, in tastes, could not possibly have been greater. "That extraordinary little man!" — so Paul had said, after his first glimpse of him, at the Ship, the tiny squat figure in the baggy plus-fours which enveloped him from chest to ankles, and the enormous, and very fine, Roman head, with the profile of Herrick the poet — was it the latter that had attracted beautiful Gloria, who so revelled in the bawdy of Herrick, as indeed in all bawdy? He was twice Gloria's age, he didn't like to drink, he didn't like to read, he was a claustrophobe, and couldn't ride in trains, least of all such trains as ran through tunnels; he was an anarchist, a furious hater of capitalism and capitalists, which included, for him, nearly everybody, but reserving a particular ferocity of hatred and contempt for the Royal Family, about which he was so uninhibitedly outspoken that he had many times been thrown bodily out of pubs, and once, even, out of a bus in Piccadilly. But no, even more than the Royal Family he hated his father and mother, the vicar and his wife, those two monsters who had indulged themselves, and without the means for it, to the extent of begetting ten children — or was it eleven — and bringing them up, as they had to, hit-or-miss. An atheist, as well as an anarchist, an individualist à l'outrance, he had gone to St. Paul's School, and had lent his piping voice to St. Paul's choir, a fact that it afforded him a kind of perverse pleasure to remember; and he made his living by any method that came to hand, from selling eggs to 'following the dogs.' In making a living, as a practicing anarchist, he had, of course, no scruples whatever. Every man for himself; it was a battle of wits between himself and society, this rotten society; and so, although in theory he backed the poor against the rich, and would have abolished the landed gentry, and indeed all the upper classes, with one drastic edict, this by no means prevented him from making the poor his victims. What was wrong with that? Consequently, while he was staying in Angchurch during the divorce — for he and Gloria had agreed that it might be expedient if they ceased to live together in the Cottage on the Marsh, for this period, just in case the King's Proctor *should* come to call, and this despite its other and obvious advantages — consequently, to eke out some sort of living for himself and poor Gretel, to supply the ground wheat-germ on which they both lived, he had hit upon a most ingenious scheme, that of buying imported, cold-storage, New Zealand eggs, obliterating from them, with patience and pumice, the tell-tale purple stencil, in the shape of an oval, which proclaimed their origin, and then, placing a dozen or two in a neat basket, in a nest of green leaves and grass, selling them, from door to door, as new-laid country eggs. It was a huge success, as long as he kept away from the same doors, always moving on from one district of the town to another; and he and Gretel had never had to do without their bread and milk and porridge.

This was all the more helpful, too, for there were the divorce costs to be met, and the payments to the bank on the mortgage — which increased almost hourly, as beautiful Gloria borrowed more and more on the cottage; not to mention the high cost of keeping Gloria in gin, and with enough cash so that she could indulge her passion for antiques and books. A sorry end to the adventure seemed to be in prospect: but not tragic, somehow, for the two gallant creatures quite simply refused to take it as such. They had had fun — hadn't they? — in buying the condemned little cottage, and in getting it un-condemned, and fixing it up, Julian and Gloria doing much of the work with their own hands. They had made it beautiful, too, with Gloria's antiques, her old china and old pewter, and had given it a garden; they had defeated the threatened invasion of water from the Marsh — for two days they had had a foot of it in the dining-room, and had to live in rubber boots; and they had had fun, too, in trying to breed and sell Airedales, even if it had been a financial failure, and had merely been the means of further impoverishing them. And the divorce; well, it had been inevitable.

They had always known it. When they had married, years before, as the result of a chance encounter at Inglesee, and of their shared love for Inglesee and Saltinge — which they regarded, they never tired of repeating, as their 'spiritual home' — it had been admittedly a marriage of arrangement: everything had been discussed, and with the utmost candor: she wanted a father or a father-lover; and as it was obvious that the inequality in their ages must prevent this from being an entirely satisfactory relationship, it was agreed that she should have such lovers as she wished, provided this was conducted with due decorum, and at a distance. And for a long time it had worked very well. "*You* love Saltinge, too?" — Gloria had asked D. the question during their very first meeting at the Ship, and this had become an instant, and a lasting, bond between them. Not that there hadn't been other bonds as well. For Gloria had been nothing if not frank in her liking, which was a great deal more than liking, for D.; and this, he was bound to admit, and did, he reciprocated. But those other fellows, those other chaps, who were perpetually turning up — even in the days before they had bought the Cottage on the Marsh — there were, well, just too many of them: he didn't wait to join a parade: she ought, he had said, to think a little better of it than that, and a little better of himself and *her*self. And for a very brief period, it had appeared that she was, in fact, attempting to initiate a season of celibacy, and of fidelity to him, in the hope that, after a suitable interval of purdah, he might consider her no longer defiled, and agree to a surrender. It was during this odd interval that she had ridden down from London on the motor-bike with the embarrassed and nice, but very unwilling, young man, the young man who had *thought* he wanted to be seduced, or ought to be, but who, with every mile they put between themselves and London, became more woefully and guiltily attached to his dear mother. Gloria had taken D. aside, while the young man brooded in the Private Bar, and told him about this, with tears in her eyes; she wanted D.'s approval, thus tacitly admitting that it was D. she would rather have had, if only he hadn't been so deplorably moral, or selfish, or whatever; and she wanted his advice. He could see that the poor young man was unhappy, and desired nothing so much as to go straight back to home and mother: but what about herself? She too was unhappy, she declared; she had so looked forward to it; she had wanted the nice young man so much, and especially here in her beloved Saltinge, her spiritual home; and to have it all come to *this* grievous, and so utterly unexpected, and unflattering ending, this appalling, even if it *was* funny, anticlimax! — What was to be done? — She laughed, through her tears, for her sense of the ridiculous was unfailing; and on occasion she could be extremely witty; and, then, after her third or fourth half-quartern, and tearful farewells to Old Tom, with his endless repetitions, as he leaned in the doorway, "I say, I say, yes, I say — " she got on the motor-bike, behind the young man, waved ruefully, but comically, at D., and shot away back to London.

But of course the divorce had at last become inevitable. It was decided that they were no longer good for each other, or at any rate while thus living together; that they would be freer and happier apart, for in that event her chances of remarrying might be improved; but that naturally they would be as close as before, and that he would come to visit, and stay as long as he liked, and whenever he liked. They had cried over it, not once but many times; they both cried over the dinner-table at Saltinge, when first they had informed D. and Lorelei Three of the desperate decision, for they loved each other, as anyone could see, with a truly extraordinary depth of tenderness, they adored each other; and this tearing of the moss from the rock, or the rock from the moss, was almost more than they could endure. Just the same they were agreed that it must be done; and now the only question was, *how*. How to go about it? Everyone knew, of course, that the classic, the easiest method, was that of going with a prostitute to a hotel — one of those cheap hotels, for example, that so conveniently and expectantly and furtively surround the Charing Cross station or Paddington — and registering with one's own name, so that the lawyer's spies could in due course investigate and obtain the necessary evidence. But poor dear Julian, with his claustrophobia, was plainly terrified of this idea: it was too far from Saltinge, too far from his indispensable Gloria, he would funk it, something was sure to go dreadfully wrong, he simply couldn't go through with it. No, something else would have to be devised. Couldn't it be accomplished right there in Saltinge, he asked despairingly? Couldn't something like *that* be managed, be made to work? —

And it was; for Gloria rose magnificently to the occasion. She would herself arrange the whole thing. She would herself engage a prostitute — and why not? — by offering her a very handsome fee, and by dangling before her the prospect of a quite giddy and luxurious week — a holiday, in fact — at Angchurch. But where was she to find a desirable prostitute? This, she confessed delightedly, was something a little out of her line. There was the Café Royal, to be sure; but wasn't it true that ladies without escort were not admitted? Still, in that neighborhood; or in some of the bars there; or simply by herself picking up a nice-looking girl in the street; and you could always tell them, couldn't you — ? — she was sure she could do it! — And she did. She returned in triumph from London to announce that she had found an extremely nice girl, the very thing, who was pretty as a picture, blonde, and not too much made up, or bedizened; and she was simply delighted with the whole idea, and was coming down by the five o'clock train the next day. A room had been booked at the Lynton, for a week; and now there was nothing more to worry about. Julian would meet her at the train, she had been given his description, and would know him — as indeed who wouldn't — the minute she set eyes on him, and off they would go for their bizarre little honeymoon. In fact, it would be jolly, they would have fun; and if anything *should* go wrong — though she couldn't see why it should — he could of course ring up the cottage, and she would advise him.

And ring up, of course, he did. He had done nothing but ring up. She had hardly — she reported to them at lunch the next day, helpless with laughter — got a minute's sleep; for poor dear Julian, who had never in his life even so much as spoken to a prostitute, apparently hadn't the foggiest idea of how to go about it, how to treat one or what to do. To begin with, he had driven to the wrong station, the High Street station, heaven knows why, for she had been perfectly explicit about it; naturally no such person as he was expecting had alighted there; and it was not for some time that he had thought of the other, the central station, and had hurried off to it, very late, and in an awful panic. Would the creature still be there? And, in that vast and rambling edifice, how could he possibly find or identify her? He had rushed in, by now in a state of extreme agitation — quite needlessly, of course; for the sensible girl had planted herself and her luggage bang in the middle of the rotunda; and, as Julian himself had admitted with horrified glee, she was unmistakable, to put it mildly. The entire station was in fact already actively aware of her, every eye was upon her: and upon poor dear Julian, too, as he embarrassedly hustled her out to the car.

But that was only the beginning.

For — as Gloria reminded them — he had been particularly alarmed, from the very outset, by the question of whether he would be expected to sleep with her — in the Biblical sense, she meant — and whether, if he refused, her feelings might be hurt. He had been quite comically upset by this problem, and only partially convinced by Gloria's reassuring argument that the poor darling would probably welcome nothing so much as a much-needed change and rest, and that anything else would be, so to speak, coals to New-castle. All he had to do was give the girl lots to eat and drink, and a good time. They could visit the Art Gallery. And the historical museum in the castle. They could go to the movies — she probably loved movies, they all did. And there was always the beach, and the pier, and the cockle stalls, and the miniature train, and the lift to the cliff-top. There was even — she had added, mischievously — a Punch-and-Judy show, and a very good one, too! —

To all this he had given a somewhat glum and reserved assent, shaking his head, and adding that it was going to be pretty bloody expensive; but of course, as they had agreed, there was nothing for it, they had to go through with it. Expensive! Oh, yes, expensive, there was now no doubt about that. For the very first of his tele-phone calls was to tell Gloria that the girl was demanding cham-pagne — and should he allow her to have it? champagne with her dinner? Yes, by all means let her have a little champagne with her dinner; after all, Gloria said, that was part of the bargain, wasn't it? Julian, although he wasn't so sure, reluctantly consented, and trotted off to provide the champagne. But there was a second tele-phone call, an hour later, to say that she wanted *more* champagne — this time to be sent up to the bedroom — where she now was, he was phoning from the lobby — and what about that? Was it really, did Gloria think, necessary? And he wasn't certain, but he *thought* perhaps she was getting a little tipsy, a little silly, and she seemed to want to flirt with him (if you could call it that); and suppose the situation got out of hand — ? Gloria told him not to worry. Any-thing to keep the child happy, that was all: let her get tight, it might even be the best thing, she would probably then fall asleep, why not? — But alas, no. It proved to be the wrong move. For the third telephone call — at midnight — and she could hear his poor voice trembling — was to say that, just as he had feared, dammit, the girl wanted him to make love to her, and what should he do? She was insistent, too: and quite tight, though not unpleasantly so: and he was afraid, if he refused to comply, that she would be angry, and do something rash — perhaps even sweep out, just like that, at midnight, which would be most embarrassing. Well — Gloria asked — was she attractive? wasn't she in the least attractive? — Oh, yes, she was quite attractive, really *quite* attractive — he admitted this dispassionately — but he couldn't help thinking that it was so unnecessary, so cold-blooded, didn't she think? Did he really *have* to — ? And Gloria, giggling over the phone, had told him that in the unfortunate circumstances — and indeed they were deplorable — she was afraid he must gird up his loins, and go, like the lamb, to the slaughter.

And so, the divorce was had: and the Cottage on the Marsh was lost, swallowed up at last by the bank: and Julian, now alone, had established himself and Gretel — who of course had eventually been found — in Angchurch, where he had gone back to the selling of eggs. Poor Gretel — she was to run away again, and once too often — and wasn't it on this occasion that D. had seen Julian for the last time, as the giant shadow of the second war piled its thunder-heads across the Channel? He had ridden over to Angchurch by bus; and, dismounting at the top of the High Street, had walked down the hill, through the narrow and winding lane, to Julian's cottage, which stood on a terraced sidewalk, five or six feet above the level of the road. The door was ajar, the windows open; but to his knock there came no answer; and on walking in, and then into the steep cliff-side garden at the back, he found no one. Odd, and unlike Julian, who invariably closed and locked everything, even if he were only going round the corner to the tobacconist's or to the Middle Street pub for bread-and-cheese and a pint of beer. But perhaps — yes, of course, he must be at the garage, which was only a few steps further down the hill, in an alley across the way. Sure enough, the garage door was open, and the ancient little car standing in the alley; but what D. saw in the garage, when he looked in, was hardly anything he might have expected. Gretel was lying on the garage floor, very still, and in a slightly unnatural, slightly straitened, position; and — which surprised D. — a small billet of wood lay across her eyes. And above her, leaning against the whitewashed wall, his face in his arm, and his shoulders shaking, was Julian. At the sight of D., he burst out, as before at Saltinge, into a fit of hysterical weeping; embracing D., desperately, as before he had embraced Lorelei; but at last he permitted himself to be let out of the garage, and back to the cottage.

Yes, dear little Gretel had run away once too often. She was on heat, of course; and the carpenter, who was mending a broken window, had gone off, leaving it open; and out she had flown, and down into the Old Town, where only by a miracle had Julian been able to find her. But it was too much. He couldn't, he simply couldn't, go through all that misery again. He had never so loved an animal, she was an extraordinary little thing, but that made it all the worse, all the harder to bear. And so, without a moment's hesitation, on an impulse that was irresistible, he had driven her straight to the vet's, and had her put away — had her put away. And there she was. The vet had very kindly offered to dispose of her, but no, she must be buried in the garden, he would bury her himself. And he had done — he said to D., slowly, and incredulously — an astonishing thing: perhaps D., with his knowledge of psychology, and psychoanalysis, could explain it: for D. knew as well as he did that he was an unbeliever, an infidel, an atheist: and yet, as he was passing St. Peter's — the Catholic church — he had suddenly stopped the car, and gone in, and up to the altar, with all that bloody gimcrackery around it, and the lighted candles, and he had dropped a penny in the box, and put up a candle, and crossed himself. And then, feeling a little

273

less guilty, had driven Gretel back to the garage. — But if only her *eyes* weren't open — ! — Those eyes! Those eyes — ! —

However, an excellent lunch at the Queen's Hotel did much to dissipate his grief; the grilled steaks, and the pints of Bass, could not have been better; and if for once the Royal Family escaped censure, the English race, the English themselves, came in for plenty. Oh, yes, D. would see; Hitler would walk in absolutely unopposed; for the English were by now completely degenerate, a nation of fops and homosexuals, there was no longer any guts in them, not one of them would be found to lift a finger: they wouldn't fight, not even for their own lives. D. didn't believe it — ? D. thought they would fight? Well, D. would see! And so, to the Gayety for a film version of the Mikado, which Julian enjoyed hugely; after which they drove to the station in time for the five-ten to Saltinge. They didn't shake hands — for how were they to know they would never meet again? They waved instead, said, "Cheero," and began the separate journeys that were to take D. across the Atlantic, after a month of war, to a new dwelling, and a new life, and the discovery of America; and Julian, over-age, claustrophobia, flat feet and all, into the British army. He had himself, wonderful fellow, been one of the first to disprove his own contention, one of the first to prove yet again — as D. had predicted — that the English were a race of heroes.

A race of geniuses, too — for hadn't someone observed that of certain races, in certain periods, one can say that genius informs them all? and hadn't the English had it, as a common heritage, ever since the time of Chaucer, a shining inheritance in which they all, to some degree, participated, even if only by loving it? The facets and fragments of it sparkled everywhere, on every level and in every corner of life, one never knew where it would discover itself next, or whether it would disguise itself as humor or poetry. It was in the hod-carrier's earnest remark to his mate, as they looked up at the marble frieze over the columns of the new building in Trafalgar Square, "It's a lovely bit of work, Bill!" It was in the statement, printed in the *Times,* of the witness at an inquest, the inquest of a suicide, who, finding the body of his brother-in-law hanging from a tree in the back yard, and wishing to break the news gently to his sister — so he said — pulled down the window-shade in the kitchen, and then, when she came downstairs, in the morning, "ran it up smart-like, and said, 'Oo's that remind yer of?'" It was in the exchange between the two dear little old ladies, the two bombazined spinster sisters, in the train, in the spring, when they saw the lambs frolicking in the green fields: "Oh, aren't they little darlings?" — "Yes, and wouldn't they be good with mint sauce!" It was in Old Tom's endless inventiveness on the subject of weather, for which he had a whole private language all his own: "A bit clumb, this morning, I say, I say, yes a bit clumb"; or, "A lovely morning, just like a mouthful of cloves!" It was in the Noble Lord's fortissimo exclamation of annoyance, at Westminster Cathedral, where they had gone on Easter Sunday hopeful of music, and were treated, instead, to a sermon in Latin, "I think this fellow is going to be a *nuisance!*" or in his musing aside, "There's communion, that's *another* dirty business!" Or again, when Chapman had mentioned, in some connection or other, the pathetic story of St. Mary of Egypt, who, in order to cross the river, in her pilgrimage, and having no money for the ferry, gave herself to the ferrymen, in lieu of payment, the Noble Lord, throwing back his head with delight, commented, pertinently, "I suppose she thought there was no use kicking against the pricks!" — And Julian and Gloria had this genius too, and shone with it: in them, it was rather a physical thing, the glow of the peach or the nectarine or the rose: it was in the somatic character, their inexhaustible vitality and love of life, their eagerly discriminating love of life, and the vivid intelligence and gusto with which they were ready for any and every new adventure, every new exploration.

Not that they couldn't be witty, too. For hadn't Gloria described herself, once, as the *"pièce de non-résistance"*? Dear people, where were they now in war-ravaged England, war-darkened England? In the project of the novel — if it could be called a novel — about England, *Ariel's Island,* they would have been central, their story would have been the central story, the strand of continuity on which all else would have depended. And if one reflected on this, wasn't it right that it should have been so? If one's theme was "Englishness," weren't they obviously "Englishness" at its unforced and natural best? the natural voice of the English genius?

Which reminded him, of course, of the famous rebuke, by Rabbi Ben Ezra, to D., for having been somewhat remiss, or unfortunate, or misguided, in his choice of friends. "I hear that you have not been altogether wise in your choice of friends, in London." Yes, there it was again, the party line; one mustn't on any account stray from the chosen circles; *a* and *b* and *c* were all right, or even *de rigueur,* but if one showed the least signs of dallying with other groups, or persisted in the attempt to remain independent of *all* groups, choosing one's literary friends simply where one found them, or liked them, and regardless of political sides or currents, one was at once suspect. Had D. been humbly obedient to these fanatical tenets, he would have been compelled to drop Chapman immediately, and he would never have been allowed to befriend the "gentle" John, himself an independent, at all. And how preposterously solemn, at times, they had all been about it! How wary, how suspicious of each other, how unsleepingly cautious! *Au fond,* did anyone trust anyone? D. remembered the grave warning from the Tsetse, shortly after D. had established himself in England, that he should never, under any circumstances, in English literary society, discuss his "first-rate" ideas, lest they be stolen, and rushed into print at once, by those jackdaws, those magpies: one should restrict oneself to one's "second-rate" ideas, as the loss of these wouldn't so much matter. Admittedly, this could happen, and did; as when a certain editor took D. to lunch, which flattered him immensely, and proceeded to flatter him further still by his intense interest in the American literary scene, asking D. innumerable questions about it all — the Chicago group, the Boston group, the New York group, regionalism, and so on — and of course, the week after, embodied D.'s analysis of it, lock, stock, and barrel, in a leading article. D. had even been so brash as to make mention of this, at lunch with the Tsetse and Aldous Huxley and J. W. N. Sullivan, and there had been a moment of silence, of embarrassed consternation; but then, the ice being broken, all three admitted having suffered at this editor's hands; and all three offered to supply D. with well-documented instances, if D. would like to expose him, as he should be — an offer, however, which D. had been wise enough to decline.

Fanatical it had all too often been, too precious and purist altogether in its socio-literary dictates, and D. had strayed too early and too far to be regarded as wholly reliable or safe. Had this perhaps been a mistake? Ought he to have taken it all more seriously, and had he somewhere lost ground because of his unwillingness to do so? Probably not, in a sense that too much mattered, and besides there were compensations: after all, it was the "Englishness" of England that he had come for, that he wanted to immerse himself in, and this was a vastly more complex and comprehensive affair than could be afforded by literary groups or currents or circles: what he had wanted, he had known it from the outset, was to dive into the English countryside as into a sea, and to discover what thus he might come up with; and this, too, quite without any of dear Aunt Sibyl's 'plan of campaign,' or stratagem, but all innocently and exposedly; if nevertheless with every confidence, that the sea would be a sustaining one, and that it would provide, in one way or another, every social element that one could possibly desire, and very likely far more rewardingly than one had dared to hope for. As, of course, it had precisely turned out to do. The ready-to-hand, and random encounter, in that ancient sea, the flotsam and jetsam, had proved to be pearls without price: Inglesee and Saltinge were veritable treasure-houses of the rare, the strange, the naturally and unaffectedly and unself-consciously and beautifully indigenous; specimens, moreover, which approached one without the least alarm, and accepted one without the least question. The supply seemed to be inexhaustible, too, and as varied as inexhaustible: it had a way of feeding him exactly what was needed and just when he needed it. What would the New Inn at Inglesee not turn up next, or the Ship at Saltinge, where indeed had appeared Julian and Gloria? Hadn't Paul similarly swum up out of nowhere to knock on the door of the cottage at Inglesee, through the merest of accidents? But what a princely accident, and what an unparalleled gift, of aerial flowers, and hanging gardens, and sunflower sunsets, it was to prove to be! Wasn't this, again, the "natural" voice of the English genius; the English genius, loving, and scrutinizing with love, tenderly but explicitly, and with a fine-principled deliberate narcissism, its own landscape, both outer and inner? And Paul was to lead to Nicholas, and that farther extension of range, into yet dizzier and headier vistas. Weren't those two visions, alone, worth infinitely more than anything, in the literary scene, that his relative indifference to it might have cost him? Perhaps, after all, for the writer, the would-be writer, the painter's steadier eye and steadier mind are ideally useful, since they fecundate but without the least stain of literary influence. In those two visions, which looked into and beyond the house at Saltinge, there had been wonder enough, and plunder enough, to outfit a dozen poets with all the subtleties and magnificence they wanted. And as it suited D.'s needs, psychologically, to live in the country, and to work off-stage, and *sans* literary embroilment, the presence, in Saltinge, of Paul and Nicholas, had been of incalculable

278

value to him. They had provided two more windows from which to view the wonders of the invisible world.

As England itself, of course, all these years, had been a window, the window which it had been his imperative need to find and to open: the window which looked into his own racial and cultural past, and thus bestowed upon him the sense of belonging, of being part of a moving continuum, the evolving series of civilized consciousness. But had that function now been, at last, performed? It was with love, naturally, and loyalty and gratitude — and pride, too — that he was returning, to the broken country — summoned, after five years of war, by the threat of the authorities to requisition the house at Saltinge, "for the purpose of housing homeless persons"; but he was bound to admit to himself that this time there was a difference. And had this difference really begun to be felt even before the outbreak of the war, and the month of blackouts, and the wail of sirens for the air-raids which always turned out to be false alarms? It was the sort of psychic change that is not usually apparent at the moment; one is walking in the new country, and well into it, too, a long time before one becomes aware of it: but suddenly one is there, and easily, and at ease, and as if it were the most natural thing in the world. And the truth was, that he had been walking in this new country, which was his America, and with possession, for many years of the stay at Saltinge. Those periodic returns, for the purpose of "touching base," and that pressing need for a kind of revitalizing in its more electric air, and for renewed draughts of its racier idioms, and the sense of its wilder violences, not to mention the need for contact with the friends and the family, and particularly with the Beloved Uncle and Aunt Sibyl and the Bassett: hadn't these, and very soon after his installation in the house, meant that he was already embarked — although unconsciously — on the return? — To arrive in Boston, all unannounced; and to pick up the telephone and call the house in Fayerweather Street, and hear the

279

Uncle's voice, the upward inflection of the soft "Hello?"; and then to take the taxi from the Club, and, on dismounting, to tap with two fingers on the study window, through which the back of the Uncle's head was visible — the unvarying ritual, as if he had only been away for a day or two: this had early assumed an importance for him that had not been quite acknowledged. Here was a root, and a radical one, which had been growing without his knowing it, and which was already far deeper than he supposed. Those evenings, whether in the little study, over the gin, which was produced from the right-hand drawer of the desk, under the photographs of librarians, and the color-print of Uncle John's Constitution; or at the Faculty Club, or the Club in town with the Bassett; were beginning to remind him, with ever widening and deepening echoes, of the something that, if not yet exactly lost, *might,* with neglect, be lost, and that was manifestly becoming very precious indeed. For if England had given him the requisite sense of "belonging" to the remoter historical past, wasn't it now New England's turn to bring that process of discovery up to date — New England, and the ancestors, the ancestors whom one shared with the Aunt and Uncle, and the Wild Cousin; and with K., practicing his surgery in Cuba and Panama, and R. in Buffalo, or Bethlehem, or Pittsburgh? Those ancestors had quietly come closer, and the New England landscape with them, as in the game of "Still Pond, No More Moving." And both they and the landscape had, in his absences, but not wholly because of them, become subtly richer, subtly finer and darker, like portraits putting on the patina of time, the "color of old violins." Had the American scene itself, just now, at last, begun to come to flower? Was it just now, after three hundred years, that — in the East at least — it was maturing? A simultaneous action, as a matter of fact: it was really, as one looked back at it, a "double" action: it was simply that the scene, the landscape, had become *ready for acceptance* at precisely the moment when its occupants had become conscious enough, aware enough, to be ready to accept it — and to accept it completely. She was their land, and they were hers, at last.

In this subterranean reversal, or exploration, the intermittent summer visits to the Beloved Uncle were pivotal, and not least the one that led to their infamous carouse together, and the final breaking down of all barriers between them, as the result of the phenomenal, not to say the supernatural, coincidence of the taxi-driver. For the taxi-driver, driving D. from the Club to Cambridge, confessed that he didn't know Cambridge, had in fact been there only once before, and asked D., therefore, to direct him. What was their astonishment, then, to discover that the farther they proceeded the more exact became the repetition of the earlier expedition: and when finally they stopped at the identical red-brick colonial house to which, said the driver, he had driven an oldish man with moustaches, after dropping off a young girl, previously, somewhere in Massachusetts Avenue, the driver was almost as dismayed as D. was delighted. The disclosure had led, of course, to the Uncle's complete confession — D.'s suspicions, of many years, were gleefully confirmed. It led, too, to a particularly glorious celebration, with the clouded prohibition gin, in the study, and on the piazza, under the sterile wistaria. The Aunt was summering in New Hampshire: and her long-stemmed rose, her little oil portrait of a single red rose, stood, therefore, on his desk; as it always symbolically did, when she was away. But this was not to prevent the Uncle from ringing up Old Mary — as he called her affectionately — at midnight; or another taxi, at midnight, for another purpose. Nor, for that matter, the unforgettable, and delightful, and somehow touching, sight of the dear Uncle, in his shorts, leaning his back against the wall, in a forlorn attempt to pull on a sock, and abruptly collapsing to the floor; from which he beamed up at them to assert, with a child's innocent surprise, "I fell down!" —

War, and the echoes of war: disaster, and the echoes of disaster.
And in the shadow of war, of the first year of war, after their enforced return to America, without a penny; and after the life-saving
gift which had made it possible for them to buy an old ruin of a
farm, of an unmatchable beauty, on Cape Cod; it was in this
shadow, and in this house, to which of course the shadow of war
had driven them, that the last of the Beloved Uncle's letters was to
come one morning, and, as so often — for his dream-life was as rich
and as vivid as D.'s — it contained an account of a dream. He had
been D.'s guest at the Harvard Club, he said: they were sitting in a
corner of the bar having a drink: when suddenly D. had caught
sight of someone he knew, had rushed off to speak to him, and had
never returned; and in consequence the poor Uncle, who was no
longer a member, after his retirement to California, and who badly
wanted another drink, was unable to sign for one. Tommy Hunt
offered him a ginger-ale, which he spurned, and properly; whereupon Tommy somewhat nastily asked him how long he had been
drinking. Fifty years, replied the Uncle, proudly — fifty years; and
glad of it; and he couldn't see that it had shortened his life, either!
But as Tommy Hunt seemed disposed to be belligerent about it, he
got up to leave the Club. He went to the door, therefore, only to find
that it was pouring with rain, and that Myles, the doorman, who
stood in the vestibule calling taxis, looked at him wholly without
recognition: he had been forgotten. He returned to the darkening
reading-room, and sat down, alone, feeling very reproachful indeed
of D. And — the letter went on — he had many times dreamed
variants of this theme since leaving Cambridge — usually to the
effect that he was in Boston, and thought happily of the Club, then
to realize that he no longer belonged to it. Only in this final dream
had he managed — at last — to get inside; and only then to be
abandoned by D. — it was all very sad. — And how was the farmhouse? And the gentleman farmer — ? And would he take time off,

from his hoeing and scything — it all sounded extremely professional — to let him know how things were going?

But before the hoeing and scything were to be finished, for that
season, the whisper of another scythe was to be heard, and that wonderful life had indeed been shortened; and although none of them
could have foreseen it, or desired it, least of all the Uncle — or was
it just possible that he *would* have — ? — the Uncle was to pay
them a visit, the most extraordinary of visits. He had died — wrote
Aunt Sibyl — in his sleep, and without pain. It had been sudden
and unexpected, there had been only a brief illness. And she had
decided — she said — on cremation. And as the family burial plot
was at New Bedford, would D. be so kind as to attend to it? The
ashes would be sent East, but she didn't say where: in her distress
and confusion she was a little vague: but after a week, word came
from the express office in New Bedford that a parcel awaited D.
there, and would he please call and collect it.

The Bassett was staying in Brewster for the weekend: with them
also was the young poet who had come to study with D., prior to
his entering the army: and as the Bassett had always liked nothing
so much as the periodic excursions to New Bedford (witness the
celebrated occasion, in the Charlestown year, when with Lorelei
Three and Nicholas they had repaired to the South Station, in midwinter, with the notion of taking a train, *any* train, into the country,
and had wound up at New Bedford instead): and as he had been
almost as devoted to the Beloved Uncle as D., and in fact had always called him "Uncle"; it was at once decided that a festive expedition was in order, and a celebration, with suitable libations,
such as the Uncle himself would have wished. Accordingly, it being
a bright, cold, December day, and the Model A Ford being heatless,
or, as the Bassett preferred to put it, cold as a witch's tit, a stirrup
cup was had, and was drunk to the best of uncles; and they set off
down the Cape, and over the Canal, past the blue inlet of Buzzards

Bay; and in due course collected the small, square, paper-wrapped parcel, at the express agency in the old New Bedford station, to which D. had so often come by train in his childhood. All very well thus far. But at the office of the Rural Cemetery (and nothing less rural was imaginable) — and this after they had got themselves completely lost in the wildernesses of South Dartmouth, not far from the doomed family woodlot — at the office, when they inquired as to the whereabouts of the plot, and explained their purpose, they were somewhat taken aback by a request for the burial certificate. Burial certificate — ? There had hitherto been no mention of a burial certificate. The Aunt hadn't referred to it at all, there was no such thing as a burial certificate — and what, therefore, were they to do? The manager, the watcher of the lots, was as surprised as they were themselves: it was most unusual: but surely they must realize that you couldn't have a burial without a burial certificate? It wasn't merely irregular — it was illegal! — But had they thought that perhaps the certificate might have been sent to the proper authorities at the City Hall, in New Bedford? They might inquire there, at all events. Or *could* it, perhaps, have been enclosed with the ashes, the remains? That was sometimes done, in such cases as this, where cross-country shipment was necessary.

With this somewhat daunting thought in their minds, they returned to New Bedford, drew up beside a likely-looking Bar and Grill, opposite the City Hall, and conferred as to procedure. Should they go first into the City Hall and ask questions? or should they try opening the parcel, just in case? The young poet looked a trifle pale at this suggestion, but it was decided that it would be sensible to open the outer coverings, at least, of the little box, and thus make sure whether the missing document mightn't be there. With the Bassett's pretty little pen-knife, therefore, the many cords and wrappings were carefully undone; layer after layer tenderly laid back; until at last, with silent astonishment, they found themselves looking at the cardboard box itself; which, with its watered-silk design of lavender and rose and mauve, resembled nothing so much as a candy-box. What they had all, for whatever reasons, been expecting, of course, was a small metal casket or urn. But *this* incongruity! this prettifaction, which needed only a bow of red ribbon and a sprig of holly to be put under a Christmas tree, so remote was it from suggesting anything mortuary; was it possible that the metal urn, or whatever it was, lay inside *this* — ? or that the certificate did as well? For there was no sign of a certificate, no sign of anything at all; no clue, no writing, no nothing, not even a name. — And, in dismay, and bewilderment, they agreed that perhaps they had better postpone the opening of the box itself until after they had asked their question at the City Hall.

Which they did, and which elicited nothing; the authorities had no knowledge of the matter whatever, certainly no such burial certificate had come to them; as, in view of the date of the death, there would have been plenty of time for; and in their opinion, consequently, it was quite likely that the missing paper was, as the custodian at the cemetery had guessed, somewhere inside the parcel. So, the box was brought up from the car; and solemnly placed on the immense, and beautiful, and official, mahogany desk. This time, slipping up the lid as gently as possible, while the commissioner and his secretary gazed down at it with fastidious horror, they opened the cardboard box itself, D. himself lifting the lid softly away. But not softly enough. For, from the very delicately tinted ashes within, almost the color of pale coral or dried rose-petals, the suction had drawn into the air a few tiny flecks: and these settled as lightly as pollen-dust on the polished surface of the desk. The Uncle's eyelid? the lobe of an ear? Whatever it was, D. blew it softly off the desk, and it vanished, dispersed, forever.

But no certificate; and therefore no burial that day. They would have to wire the Aunt and wait: they would have to carry the Beloved Uncle back to the Cape with them, in the Model A Ford, and wait. D. picked up the box again, noticing with embarrassment that somehow in the proceedings it had very badly scratched the exquisite mahogany surface, and, thinking it better to say nothing about this, he led the way back to the car. And then, leaving the Uncle in the car, they proceeded to the Bar and Grill, and to their libations, as planned. There were Fairhaven oysters: there were Ward Eights: there were lobsters; there were toasts to the Uncle, toasts which were to be prolonged all week, toasts to one who, as long as *they* lived, would be immortal. All week, to the acute embarrassment of the young poet, the Uncle sojourned in the house at Brewster, although neither he nor Lorelei Three nor the Bassett knew where — for D. had quickly and quietly stowed him in the little Dutch oven beside the drawing-room fireplace. And could anything have been more appropriate, would anything have pleased him more? And all week, while they waited for word from the west, they did homage to this man whom they had so dearly loved, and in the truest way possible they remembered him. They remembered the time he had got backwards into the taxi, outside the club, sitting down on the taxi floor, and drawing up his knees under his chin, the cane entangled in his legs, as always. They remembered his ritual jokes. Of his handwriting, that wholly indecipherable scrawl, he would say, laconically, "the hand of the potter shakes." And one could *putter* about, but never, no never, could one potter. And best of all, most miraculous of all, the never-to-be-forgotten dinner at the Club, with D. and the Bassett, when the Uncle had so instantly capped D.'s own witticism with one that was better. For, describing to them a recent amatory adventure, which had ended in entire physical frustration, despite the joint and earnest endeavors of the lovers, D. had concluded his narrative by saying that he had finally given up; remarking, resignedly, to the poor girl, that he was afraid it was no use, it was a case of synecdoche. "Synecdoche — ?" — She had looked up at him, startled, to inquire — "What on earth's that?" And he replied, "It's 'when the part is greater than the whole.'" "And" — said the Uncle instantly — "did she take it in?" —

A farewell visit that was unique and beautiful, and was to bestow a new dignity on the house; and that was to end, of course, with a second pilgrimage to New Bedford, this time armed with the lost certificate. In a pouring southeast rain, through sheets of water, they had come, at last, among dripping and deserted tombstones — where not a soul was to be seen — to the family plot; and to the little square excavation which had been neatly incised in it. But as D. stepped forward to place the little box on the trestle, suddenly the cemetery was no longer deserted: suddenly, all round them, in every direction, and as far as they could see, the workmen, who had before been invisible, behind stones or monuments, had risen to their feet, motionlessly at attention, their arms at their sides, to face them. It was a resurrection; and more moving, in its silence, and their own departing silence, than any service could have been. The Uncle had been well and truly laid.

Disasters, and the echoes of disaster: war, and the echoes of war. And it was humbling yet again to reflect on the benefits to Lorelei Three and himself which had followed in the train of that human cataclysm; for had the war not driven them back to America, where they had arrived on Columbus Day, the house at Brewster would not have been found, and would not have been thus blessed by the Uncle: nor perhaps would the voices of the ancestors, in whip-poor-will and pinkwink, in the cries of quail and sea-gull, become so soon or so clearly audible. Audible, at any rate, they had now become, audible and insistent; they were voices, borne down from the pasture, or up from the sea-wall, or over the fog-veiled cranberry bog, which would have to be attended to; and the figures which had begun stirring in the shadows, as far back as the *annus mirabilis* in Charlestown, when he had worked on the Massachusetts Guide, had begun, if obscurely, to take shape.

V I

And, of course, prototypically (rediscovered
in the *Memorial History of Boston,* during
D.'s research for the Massachusetts Guide,
and an article on individualism in Massachusetts literature) — that
most individual of all figures, all ghosts, William Blackstone, stepping quietly forward amongst his 'humilities and simplicities,' the
wild roses and samphire, or over the massive oyster-beds that all but
blocked the mouth of the Charles, to tend his spring on the west
slope of Shawmut Hill, or to fetch water from it to his orchard of
apple-trees, and his English roses, newly set out in the wilderness —
William Blackstone, Bachelor of Arts from Cambridge, England, in
search of that virgin solitude in which he might, by there hearing
echoes of his own soul, find God — yes, thus again, punctually to the
moment of need, came the spiritual *desideratum,* in this rediscovered
and haunting solitary, this most exquisite predecessor and antici-
pator of the half-wild individualism that was to be so characteristic,
for three hundred years, of all that was most integral in America.
At the back of D's mind for twenty years, but now found again, and
made vivid in that admirable history; appearing, and disappearing,
and reappearing, only then to disappear once more, and forever;
taking with him his books into the cathedral of the forest, in order
that he might there escape the Lords Bishop, as before he had fled
to escape the Lords brethren; this magical figure seemed to D. to be

288

the 'open sesame' not only to a truer understanding of the American scene and character than any hitherto available, in its rare combination of purity and singleness of purpose, its entire naturalness, and the complete unself-consciousness of its love, but also to be a revelation of something unsuspected in himself. Those apple-trees, tenderly set out by the young divine from England, on the three-pointed hill purchased from the Shawmut Indians — and how this young man must have fascinated them — those apple-trees had roots, somehow, he began anew to feel, in himself. Many times in that winter at Charlestown, waiting for the divorce which never came, and which eventually they would have to seek in Mexico, they had discussed this: D., and the Bassett, and Lorelei Three, and Nicholas; while the gramophone squawked its "Any Nuts, Hot Nuts," and Nicholas added one vermilion or purple cubicle after another to the infernel tiers of his opium den, his opium dream, in the chaos of shirts and shoes to which he had already reduced Lorelei's little front dining-room. Many times as they had themselves crossed the Charles, in February snow or sleet, Nicholas thrusting blue hands, gnarled with arthritis, up his ragged sleeves for warmth, they had talked of this singular being; as of course D. had talked of it, years before, to Hambo. Had Blackstone, or Blaxton, actually written his book? Were those "ten paper volumes," which the flames were said to have destroyed, the first great religious book, the first Revelation, to have been written in the new world — ? He had crossed to this very shore, in Charlestown, where the company of Gorges had encamped, and where the swamp water was making them ill, to offer them the use of his spring: he had come down to the water's edge, riding a bull, and had signalled to them — his humanity, for the moment, overmastering his love of seclusion: and on joining him they had found him to be living in the comfortable house which the Indians had helped him to build, and in which he had already installed his books, his library, from Cambridge. But of that momentary humanity he had soon enough repented. He had sold his land to Edmund Quincy — ancestor of Lorelei Three's land-lord — and the other founding fathers, and moved on. The Lords brethren were bad enough — they were, simply, too much company; but the coming of the Lords Bishop, and the first rearing of the multiple head of theocracy, had put the lid on it — he would become the first settler of Rhode Island, as here he had been the first of Boston. And couldn't one — D. had suggested — use him as a symbol, take him as the spiritual key, or center, of a book on American individualism? Wasn't he the complete and unmistakable forerunner? Yes, this was the thing itself, the American character *in excelsis,* the pure archetype from which all the rest would logically descend. Couldn't one say that every outcropping of American genius, in the centuries to come, was to follow this pattern? weren't they all to be in this sense frontiersmen, pioneers, solitaries, outlaws? those who preferred to seek, and find, alone? Yes, it was a true, and workable, notion. One could preface such a book with a tribute to this enchanting explorer, and then proceed to the variations on the theme, the essays on his grandchildren and great-grandchildren: from Crèvecœur to Thoreau and Emerson, from Anne Bradstreet to Emily Dickinson and Melville and Hawthorne; nor should one omit, to be sure, the Daniel Boones, the Audubons, or even perhaps the Kit Carsons.

But that undertaking, like so many others, had been overlaid by more immediate preoccupations: the notes had been made, the reading outlined, even a preliminary paragraph or two (in the back of a life of Kit Carson) set down: but that was all. Would it now, would it still, be possible to do it, would it be possible at Saltinge? Perhaps, as the Bassett, the great Bassoon, had speculated, it would be all the better for being done in England, provided one had the requisite books and notes, the documentation; for wouldn't one find there a possibly sharper perspective? such as D. had mentioned as being surprisingly useful for *Purple Passage* and *Dead Reckoning* — the very insulation from the American scene, the distance, acting miraculously as a magnifying-glass, so that one recollected with an astonishing, a hallucinatory brilliance of detail, every moment, for example, of a train-ride from New York to Boston, for *Dead Reckoning;* or the storm scene at Powder Point. It was true; he had in a sense been better able to write of the American scene at Inglesee and Saltinge than ever in America, or at any rate for a long time: not till he had begun (alcoholically, and in full retreat) the *Parerga,* the serial notations on attitude and definition, in Cambridge, after the separation from Lorelei One and the first transatlantic visit from Hambo. But then, these were hardly to be characterized as in any way American — and in any case, he had been able to resume them, and with a unique acceleration of both possessiveness and possessedness, on that quite unforeseeable return to Saltinge with Hambo and Lorelei Two. But the Blackstone theme; which had so fascinated Hambo, and with which Hambo had so early begun to build for himself a mystic identification — for wasn't he destined himself to be another rolling Blackstone, and from Cambridge, Eng., too? — moving to his own southwest and northwest mystical frontiers, his own barrancas and estuaries of good and evil — ? — the Blackstone theme, wasn't this perhaps uniquely suited to the house at Saltinge? From that magic window, one could gaze straight across the Channel to Ushant, one's spiritual balcony, and from there, by a secondary plunge of vision, look into the opalescent heart of the west — where at this very instant, William Blackstone, the prototypical "kid" of American slang, was still in the act of disembarking from the little English schooner on the marshy banks of the Wessagussett River. Disembarking amongst his beloved humilities and simplicities, the unknown and delicate jewel-weed, the blue trinity of the spiderwort, and the tiny pimpernel — and who was to say that he had not himself been the first to give them their names? —

To think of this, and of the pleasure of writing such a book, if the time afforded, in the war-scarified house at Saltinge; with Nicholas once more arriving silently, in his plimsolls, every evening, in time for the ritual pub crawl, and dinner; to think of all this was, of course, willy-nilly, to think again of Hambo, and of the long, curious, intermittent, and wandering association with that most engaging and volatile and unpredictable of geniuses: for surely of all the literary folk whom D. had ever encountered, there had been none among them who had been so visibly or happily alight with genius — not that the Tsetse hadn't manifested something of the same thing, to be sure — controlling it, moreover, to better purpose; but in Hambo it had been the more moving, and convincing, and alive, for its very *un*controlledness, its spontaneity and gay reckless-ness, not to mention its infectiously gleeful delight in itself. And why — he had always seemed to be in the act of asking — shouldn't genius damned well enjoy itself — ? what was wrong with that — ? Enjoy itself his genius did; here, there was never any secret hoard-ing, all was communicable and communicated, life itself was a picnic of genius in which everyone could share alike. Nothing here of the Tsetse's caution to D. about mentioning his "first-rate" ideas: nothing here of that first meeting, of which D. had been a silent witness in London, between those two other geniuses, Katherine Mansfield and Virginia Woolf, when the two women, seated stiffly on either side of him, at a dreadful Athenaeum luncheon, had meas-ured each other with a locked gaze of feral enmity while they ex-changed honeyed phrases of compliment and question. Hatred — ? was there a place for hatred, this sort of fiercely animal hatred, in genius? It had certainly, on this unique occasion, been sufficiently evident to be as embarrassing as painful: it had made D. ashamed. Nor would he ever forget, either, the tea in Hampstead, the next day, with Katherine Mansfield, the two laburnum trees, at the back of the walled garden, glowing through the solid London rain; and their talk of rain, their shared love of rain; but all the while the question hiding behind the talk, hiding and biding its time, and at last making the softest and most guileless of entries. Had D. met Virginia Woolf before? Oh, he hadn't? And of course she herself hadn't either. And her work, that so curious work of hers! Had D. seen much of it, had he read it — and what did he think of it? It was interesting — oh, yes, there could be no doubt about that; very adventurous, intellectually quite adventurous; and wonderfully skillful, too. But was it, perhaps — did D. think — just a *shade* self-conscious — was there perhaps just a *little* too much taking of thought? And she had purred, she had audibly purred, when D. acquiesced in these grace-notes of animadversion, and added one or two of his own; but it was when he had at last used the word "sterile" that she had sprung to her feet like a panther, her eyes flashing, and cried — "*Sterile!* But of course — ! — *Sterile!*"

Envy and hatred, alas, yes; one might as well admit it. The rivalries became too intense, and inevitably, and perhaps rightly, occasions arose when there must be a fight to a finish. One must view it — D. had early observed to Hambo — as a jungle scene, simply, this literary forest; and here, as elsewhere, and of vital necessity, the same law must apply, that of the survival of the fittest. The lion *might,* some day, lie down with the lamb, but it would be as well if the lamb were to view it — for his part — as a calculated risk. Hadn't D., in the Beacon Hill era, with the farouche John, the era of the Poetry Journal, written an essay on this very subject, the lethal warfare between literary groups or movements — contrasting, for instance, the aims and methods of the Imagists with those of such psycho-realists as Robinson and Frost and Masters, and pointing to the all-too-natural alarm that each must feel in the alien presence of the other? And could there be any the least doubt that this merciless warfare, in one form or another, had been proceeding, both in England and America, ever since? Alliances might be formed, for a time, or for a limited purpose, between the most un-likely of partners — to make, for a moment, a common front against a common enemy; but that purpose accomplished, or that enemy lamed, the alliance came abruptly to an end, and not infrequently with unhappy consequences for one or the other of the partnership. And hadn't dear Hambo himself, and early, avowed his intention of absorbing all he jolly well could of D., in that curious and ambiva-lent relationship of theirs, as of father and son, on the one hand, and teacher and disciple on the other, absorbing him even to the point of annihilation? Wasn't it quite plainly, if all these things were true, his duty — the duty of the young and strong, the new and healthy, as against the old, or aging, and its diminishing valors and vigors? And, from this point of view, what more natural than that Hambo had at once, and without so much as a by-your-leave, taken over the Blackstone idea as his own. It was, if regarded in the proper light, complete poetic justice, and preordained; it was all quite simple, too, and in the scheme of things; D. could have been, so to speak, 'invented' in order that he might re-invent, or discover, Blackstone, and thus release him, like a catalyst, once more into the creative stream; but wasn't it also true that he, Hambo, was pre-cisely this creative stream, ready and waiting, and himself thus 'in-vented,' into which D., the mere transmitter, must hand on an idea which was not his in fee simple, but merely on loan? Entirely logi-cal, perhaps; and D. had to confess that he had himself been the first to advance the doctrine, or to envisage it: as far back as the summer of Hambo's first arrival, in Cambridge, Mass., with broken suitcase and dirty socks and taropatch, and the much-thumbed blue-covered exercise book in which were the neatly pencilled first frag-ments of *Aquamarine*: as far back as the celebration for that casual arrival, and the all-but-fatal wrestling-match (for the possession of the porcelain lid of the w.c.) between Hambo and D.; from which

D., although triumphant, had emerged with a concussion, and a permanent scar — in the shape of a cross — on his brow.

And what a summer that had been, of all those summers and loves! D. lying helpless and in pain, day after day — for Lorelei Two was away in Connecticut — as the gay, the gentle, the vague, the ever-humorous Hambo drifted in and out of the sunlit room, twiddling the taropatch — *ain't got no money, ain't got a cent, ain't got a house, he can't pay the rent* — drifting in and out again with the more-and-more battered exercise book in which *Aquamarine* struggled to take shape, drifted in and out for D.'s painful efforts at concentration and creation, the throbbing transfusion of his own creative blood into that as yet amorphous embryo of a play: sitting up at half-hour intervals to hear the new passage, the new flight of ship's dialogue, the new patch of recollected matter that was somewhere, somehow, by those two symbiotic sailmakers, to be stitched in. Drifting in and out, too, with a bland perpetual forgetfulness of the fact that D. had no food, nothing to eat, even the bottle of milk was forgotten in the alternating devotion to *Cacoethes scribendi* and the ukulele, the uke-bloody-lele, which he had taken to Kowloon and back; and which, though now getting "a bit knocked-oop," could still fill the bleak corridors of Hampden Hall, and even its whuling elevator, with a hauntingly beautiful flow of American jazz, and as only a haunted Englishman, a young Blackstone, could render it. If music be the food of love, play on — but now and again the bottle of milk, if D. reminded him persistently enough, was actually purveyed, from the Greek shop round the corner; and now and again, too, the good Grolier, the beneficent spider, would ascend from his cobweb of a bookshop, belowstairs, bringing the loan of an armful of books and a ham sandwich, in exchange for a snort of gin; and the work progressed, the play took shape. A summer, indeed, which, in its Bacchic creativeness, was not unlike the winter at the little eighteenth-century brick house in Charlestown

295

— in the shadow, almost, of Uncle John's Constitution, which was moored only a few blocks away — that winter in Lorelei Three's house, into which D. had strolled — and to stay, it seemed, forever. For Lorelei Three, he had seen just as instantaneously as later Aunt Sibyl was to see it, was to be the final answer to the great question; through her the unhappy chord was at last to find resolution; here he would remain. And here, too, to this house, he would import Nicholas, from Saltinge, for a winter of work, and with Bassett here found a new life. All it now needed, indeed, was Hambo: with Hambo, they might here re-enact (but let us hope not in all particulars) the passages of Spain: when Hambo and Nicholas and D. and Lorelei Two had all had balcony rooms round the blossoming patio, and its sprawling pomegranate, at Granada, and where, at almost any hour of the day or night, one could see, protruding from beneath Nicholas's bed, Hambo's feet, as he there thrummed away — four years later — on that very taropatch; while Nicholas, on a broken-legged table, glued his papers together, and smoked, and painted.

But Hambo had departed into Mexico, as for a deliberate variation on that passage in Spain: substituting, for the Sierras, Popocatepetl, and for the gorge at Ronda (with its three hierarchical bridges) the vipers and dead dogs, and the human corpses, and human filth, or jakes, of the hideous barranca that cleft the town of Cuernavaca like a hairy and festering wound. Hambo was there reliving those other violences, those other initiations: for the aguardiente, at a penny a *copita*, on which he had so ingeniously managed to keep himself drunk when D. had cut his allowance, evading the daily pursuits, through all the bars of Granada, of Nicholas and D., or, if at last found, enraged by what he thought (alcoholically) was persecution, he was now substituting tequila and pulque: in the shadow of the volcano, and the sound of Nita's clicking heels, those merciless and hard little heels, clacking along the tiled veranda —

the Nita to whom D. had introduced him, in the Alhambra, in the hope that the beautiful and swift little creature might be just the prescription he needed — there, this *Doppelgänger* of William Blackstone, and of D. as well, was engaged in simultaneously forging his own apocalyptic vision, everywhere veined with those mystic correspondences of his, and the intricate resonances and cadences of language with which, one day, he would make it voluble. And it was wholly typical, too, that already in those tentative pages, the disordered heaps of scrawled scraps and reminders, he had incorporated William Blackstone, made him his own, taking him in his spiritual voyage even as far as that barranca — while D., so many years after, was to carry his own poor notes, and the half-formulated original concept, once again by ship to Saltinge.

But carrying how much else — how much else! For the notes, the notations, had themselves, during all these intervening years, while they lay there, as it were, in the living darkness, been subtly changing in color and outline, adding iridescences of lustre or patina, and accreting yet other ancillary clusters of design or meaning. Not for nothing had been those compulsory war years at the Cape Cod farmhouse, and the prolonged reimmersion in the ancestral scene — nor for nothing, either, that curious need which Lorelei Three and himself had both felt, at first obscurely, but then with growing awareness and glad acceptance, of identifying themselves with Rufus and Amanda Clark, those excellent people whose house it had once been, and whose love of it had made it so beautiful. What the astrologist's ghost had been to the house at Saltinge, the ghost of Rufus had now become for this: and Amanda's too: but these good people were nearer and clearer and dearer: in effect, they had ended by becoming, to all intents, truly ancestral: they were the genius of tradition and inheritance: and it was with a feeling almost of baptism and dedication that Lorelei Three and D. had set to work to repair the torn fabric of the old house, long since deserted by all save rats and squirrels, to mend once again the spilled walls of abandoned farm and pasture, and to restore the terraced gardens, which, first outlined by the massive forefoot of the glacier, had then been carved into such an extraordinary symmetry by the patience and industry of Rufus. Hidden and overgrown, nevertheless it was all still there: the cedars and spruces and willows, set out by Rufus and Amanda and their children, and given the children's names, needed only to be cleared round, and trimmed of dead wood, once more to assert themselves: the old-fashioned flowers, set out a hundred years before by Amanda, reappeared now as if by magic: yellow and purple iris, columbine, matrimony vine, spiderwort, and *Kerria japonica;* and the trumpet-vine, and mock-orange, for the hummingbird. The little yellow-shelled snails, delicate as glass, strolled in the patches of celandine, along old cellar-walls, and under lichened apple-trees, to remind them of their grosser cousins, in the garden at Saltinge, which Jed and Jean, years before, had raced on the concrete roof of the coal-shed; and which could be heard, on a still evening — if you listened on the lower terrace, beside the swing — champing, literally champing, among the leaves and flowers — a steady, soft, rhythmic susurrus, the munching of the innumerable little mouths. And the waves of wildflowers, asking now to be remembered, as they also asked him to remember the Frightened Uncle, and those enchanted botanical expeditions, these too added to the wholly unexpected feeling of homecoming, of profound homecoming — the rediscovery of the past, and of belonging to it — which now so deeply intruded on D., and so pervasively, as to constitute, in the end, an experience of conversion. "I've just had a conversion — !" — so Lorelei One had cried, one summer morning on the mountain road in Vermont, giving a little awkward skip of glee as she did so, that charming and rather coltish habit of hers, which he had found so touching — "I've suffered a conversion!" For she was walking between Jacob and D., and she

had been reading *Varieties of Religious Experience,* not to mention
Freud; and, the day before, she had confessed her love for Jacob;
but now she wanted to feel that she had dispossessed herself of
that so inconvenient love, and, by an effort of will, to reconvert
herself to D. Other summers, other loves — but that was no such
conversion as this, if it had been any conversion, in fact, at all:
here, there was no discernible element of foresight or calculation,
no weighing of values, and to begin with, indeed, nothing but a
sense of loss, if not a sense of betrayal. For, had they not abandoned
Saltinge? and the house at Saltinge? and Ariel's Island? Ought they
not to have stayed, war or no war, where the three little D.'s would
stay, and everyone else — Julian included? Even in the first of the
world wars D. had felt that he owed an immense spiritual debt to
England, he had many times considered going to the English re-
cruiting station in Bromfield Street, in Boston, and offering to enlist;
and all his life he was to feel that in truth he should have done so.
And it was small comfort to him that at the beginning of the second
war he had wanted to stay, and said so to Lorelei Three, for he had
allowed himself to be argued out of it. As aliens, of course, they
would not have been allowed to remain in the house at Saltinge, a
military zone; or at least, not without naturalizing; and without
naturalizing, again, the possibilities of D.'s obtaining suitable or useful work to do, or work for which he had any aptitude, appeared
pretty remote. And so, it had seemed sensible; and they had farewelled Nicholas, and the children, and the others, and closed the
dear house; pasting protective crosses of paper on the windows,
winding the grandfather clock a last time, for another week in
which it might stammer out the hours of silence — or six days,
rather, for this was one of its many eccentricities — and then they
had come away, driving guiltily southward to Southampton. And
therefore, to begin with, there had been no sensation but the soreness of a great loss, the sharp shadow of loss piercing even into the

house at Cape Cod. How to get back, how to get back! And what —
if anything — would there be to get back to? "Thank you" — the
air-raid warden had murmured, when they turned in their gas-masks
on the dock — "we can have them decontaminated and use them
again." It was the final comic footnote to a leavetaking that sent
them forth penniless and homeless.

But not for long, and it wasn't wholly true, either, to say that it
was merely because of this sense of loss, this spiritual vacuum, that
the house at Brewster had cast such a spell upon them. No, the
conversion was clearly, as one could realize after the event, a resolution of feelings and attitudes of long standing, perhaps lifelong:
perhaps it was now possible to say that it was only by obeying the
ghostly summons of the poet of White Horse Vale, and going to
Ariel's Island, and accepting it and being accepted by it, that he
had been able to accomplish what essentially and profoundly all this
time he had most wanted and needed to accomplish, the retention
of that nursery floor, that room, that house at Savannah, that house
and the vivid life in it — father and mother, and the tremendous
parties downstairs, which D. could watch through the banisters of
the curved staircase, and the deeply satisfying sense of belonging to
it all, whether there, or at New Bedford, or Cambridge. Hadn't he,
ever since, every time he set sail for England, actually been setting
sail for that carpeted floor, on which the copy of *Tom Brown's
School Days* still lay open at the luminous fragment of verse?
Hadn't time stood still, ever since, at that echo of a moment, that
phrase of incantation? And hadn't his entire life been simply a
locus bending itself again and again, after no matter how many
interruptions and diversions, as of wars, or storms at sea, to this
limit, this perhaps unattainable limit, this imperative and imperish-
able Ushant? And of course the layers of meaning hidden in the
bright talisman of verse were susceptible of endless further analysis; it lay there cryptically prismatic at the very center of his being.

Because of it, he had had to try to become a writer, and a liberal one; but in addition there was that White Horse, that spectral White Horse, carved out of chalk on an English hillside, and so the question of England, and of the English poets; one would have to identify oneself with all of these; one would therefore, obviously, have to go to England, to hear them speaking, to hear them all wonderfully speaking — as if one were in fact listening to the English birds on a summer's day — ! — speaking in their own landscape, and in their own language. In one's devotion to this singular necessity, one would find oneself over and over again unfaithful to pretty much everything else in life — one's wives, one's children, one's friends, one's loves — even, at times, one's practical interests; and just the same, all this astonishingly intricate come-and-go, this maze-like pattern of persistence and devotion and infidelity, which seemed to be perpetually leading him farther and farther afield, and in everwidening circles, whether outer or inner; all this was really the quite incredible equivalent of one very simple little thing: it had been the stratagem by which he could remain forever on that floor in the room at Savannah, reading, for the first time, a passage of verse; a passage, which, like Paul's sheathed arches of eternity, unfolding and receding endlessly away, was indeed a passage, a passage to everywhere; but from which he would return, at last, to find that he had never in effect gone anywhere at all, and was still, exactly, *there.*

Fascinating to consider the machinery of all this, and the undeviating precision with which it had worked itself out: fascinating, too, to consider how the entire life had thus in a sense annihilated time, and remained, as it were, in a capsule, or in a phrase. And if one followed the radial threads of logic to their innumerable terminals, wouldn't it end by explaining everything, even to explaining himself away? and hadn't that, the explaining of himself away, been central to the purpose from the beginning? For among other things the fragment of verse (in dictating a course of action of which father and mother would have approved, and which therefore saw to it that he *thus kept them*) had meant not only that he must become and remain a devotee of the word, making his daily and all-sacrificing oblations of translated experience to it, but that also the whole tenor of his life, the signature in which it must be played, was inalterably indicated from that moment. As in Lawrence Henderson's crystalline synthesis, the fitness of the environment was the thing, was the primary concern; but with a difference; one would have to see to it that the environment *was* fit, or *make* it fit; that mysterious fellow from White Horse Vale must be provided with his White Horse, and his vale, and his liberal notions, too; and not these alone, either, but everything else that they could conceivably imply. And this was to introduce an element of the double agent, an action on two simultaneous planes. One was, at one and the same time, retaining the house at Savannah, and the gay card-parties, and the timeless walk to the telegraph office, and the extraordinary quarrels — as in that mysterious episode which he had introduced into an early story, when he had looked down over the banisters to see his father sitting on his mother's knee, with his arm around her, and had heard him say, as he softly repeated, "Yes, if you don't stop this insensate round of party-going, with the inevitable neglect of your children, then there's just one way to put an end to it: I'll have another child! — " — He was retaining all this, and re-enacting it, even to the final scene of all: when, after the desultory early-morning quarrel, came the half-stifled scream, and then the sound of his father's voice counting three, and the two loud pistol-shots; and he had tiptoed into the dark room, where the two bodies lay motionless, and apart, and, finding them dead, found himself possessed of them forever. He had kept all this, on the one hand, in obeying the precept of the two lines of verse, and all the *modus vivendi* that it still

302

represented, as in an album of faded photographs. But, also, even
as he looked back at these, and at their immobility, as of artifact,
he knew that he was irrevocably dedicated to a lifelong — if need
be — search for an equivalent to it all, in terms of his own life, or
work; and an equivalent that those two angelic people would have
thought acceptable.

And, of course, nothing could be more obvious than that thread,
in the developing design of his life, that ever-increasing need for
finding in his surroundings, and for making sure that it was there,
the artifact of civilization, the artifact that was its sign manual. The
finished forms and rituals of a fixed and conscious society, a society
of fine lives in fine houses, in a social frame that was elaborate,
finely elaborate — it was this that he had perpetually been searching for all his life: from Savannah, northward to New Bedford —
and that was still perhaps the best — from New Bedford on to
Concord, and Cambridge; and so, following the footsteps of Cousin
Maud and the Beloved Uncle, finding the logical end in Ariel's
Island, and climactically at Saltinge. And, paralleling this search for
the civilized artifact, in all its forms, had been the unremitting quest
for an equivalent *finesse* and logic in understanding, a quest which
had led him from Darwin to Nietzsche and Bergson, for instance,
and Santayana, and from these in turn to Petrie and Freud. An
ambiguous thread, a two-voiced theme: following simultaneously
the precept of the parents to live as consciously as possible (as they
themselves had done) but also to live as richly, and beautifully, as
possible, as well. Would they have approved of the enormous English digression — if digression it was to turn out to be? At all events
they would have understood the necessity for it, and for his there
securing for himself, for the time being, at least, that fitness of
environment which might be conducive to such "work" as he could
ever find time for. As for their approving of his remaining there for
good, or the three little D.'s doing so, that was perhaps another mat-

ter. To remain there for good had certainly not been his original intention: they would bathe in it, breathe in it, expand in it, give the little D.'s a fine deep soak in it, and then, at whatever convenient moment, return again to South Yarmouth or Boston. But alas, events had turned out otherwise. The fatal interview with Lorelei Two had intervened; the house at South Yarmouth had been sold; the house at Saltinge had been lost, and then found again; and now the three little D.'s were fixed in Ariel's Island forever.

But the intentions, the intentions, these they could certainly, even now, and after so much failure or adulteration in the execution, approve of; the 'line,' at least, was correct, was the continuance of the ancestral line; and if the life hadn't always been exactly beautiful, and sometimes downright ugly, or tawdry, or shameless, or shameful, in its subterfuges and makeshifts, its denials and escapes, its failures of nerve, and its failures in love — or (most importantly) its failure to make a useful co-ordinate, in terms of work, of the *other* failures — nevertheless the attempt to do so was one that they could have endorsed. And how, how, in heaven's name, was one to achieve that so-much-desired will-of-the-wisp of a co-ordinate, in a world of awareness in which all was in motion, the values and meanings changing their names and faces at will, and the personality itself — if it could be called such — constantly dissolving into the discontinuous and inapprehensible discreteness of causal or temporal series — ? Well, they would themselves have been the first to admit that they had had a hand in this. That voracious egotism, to which so much had been sacrificed, and which one must ruefully confess had been a nuisance and a menace, socially speaking, and of an appalling vitality too: this was one of their gifts to him; their own *égoïsme à deux* had become a thing of astonishing power, and complexity, and beauty, even to the point of self-denial and self-destruction; and if in their lives, their

living, they had managed to achieve a beautiful resolution, or co-
ordinate, of the disparate elements which moved in them, or in
which they moved — the loves and hates, the knowledges and
divinations, the possessivenesses and jealousies, and now and
again the vaulting imagination that could build its rainbow arch
out of such material — unhappily it must be admitted that, unlike
grandfather, they had nowhere achieved, and nowhere left, the
perfected artifact which, on their own admission, was the ultimate
good, and the ultimate obligation, of the creative mind, and of
creative civilization. The egoism they had had for it: but not the
synthesizing power. And, granted that the egoism, as in his own
deplorable case, was a nuisance and a menace, wasn't it also the
very material for the all-transforming smithy of artifaction? and
wasn't D.'s own formidable egotism still theirs? It was the adverse,
if you so considered it, of the insecurity and *petit mal* with which
they had endowed their children: it was what they, and the ancestors before them, and D., had collaborated in making. This was
what they had done, this was what they were. And even D.'s intermittent effort to translate this inherited egotism, and the rimless
world with which its greedy sensorium provided him, into something that might be useful to mankind, even this was theirs, their
all-giving and anonymous bequest. This 'thing' of the family's, this
accumulated awareness, this evolving consciousness, even with its
taint of insanity, this it was their duty, and D.'s most of all, as now
for the moment their ephemeral spokesman, to put at the disposal
of society — even, if necessary, on the chopping-block or the dissect-
ing table. And in order to do this, as grandfather had clearly seen,
the individual spokesman must himself remain completely neutral,
the mere servant. The artificer, in the very act of deploying himself
in the new shape of the artifact, must remain wholly neutral to that
part of himself which is his subject — which is to say, his all. Just
as biologically the individual is an anonymous tarnsmitter, the mere

305

nameless link, so the writer, if he were to do his duty, must discuss himself, *qua* material, as if this were merely an object to which as yet no name had been given: and in this sense it had been D.'s obligation, and one that he was aware of, to distinguish at all times the "narrating" D. from the "subject" D., and to approach the latter with relentless and unsleeping objectivity.

Unsuccessfully — of course. The observed-observing was an internal partnership that all too often fell out of step with itself, inventing semantic confusions, and vanities, too, of its own. Yet the attempt must be made; had been made: must be made again. And had D., when one considered it from this angle, ever done sufficient justice to the importance of the sexual behavior, and the loves, the loves, the loves — whether sacred or profane — as precisely the dynamic coefficients of the love of the work itself? the love of his work and the energy, and vanity for it, which arose from these — ? Hadn't those sacred or profane loves, the fly-by-nights and fall-by-nights quite as importantly as the great exaltations — the Agnes Fatuous just as vitalizing as the *Ewige Weibliche,* the nymphomania vying fruitfully with the nympholept — hadn't these supplied not only the creative valor for the work, but the substance of it as well — not to say its veritable heartbeat? One could say of them that one neither approved or disapproved, perhaps: or to some extent, anyway, in the interests of objectivity: and yet that was not wholly accurate. Of some did not not approve more than of others? or for different reasons? if not better? It was more complicated than simply Faubion against Cynthia, the gorgeous fleshpot against the stained-glass-window untouchable: for in these matters there were virtues even in vices. And if one could say unhesitatingly and unqualifiedly that the great exaltations, which were precious few, were undeniably the best, and were in a profoundest sense identifiable as the highest-reachings and re-synthesizings of one's love of life itself, one's affirmative cry of "glory!" to the great

Why, and therefore perhaps identical with one's religious will; just the same the humbler and naughtier, even the nastier, of the sister-episodes, no matter how brief or false or empty, had made their own contributions — if not of subject-matter, at any rate of a sort of low-value self-esteem. They fed the voracious ego — they could even be described as a base and basic necessity for it. Hadn't the elaborate conquest, for example, of Amabel, the Kensington Blue-stocking, the slow and painful breaking down of all those frigid barriers and defenses, and the manner, and the manners, and the snobbery, and the intellectual puritanism, which wanted nothing so much as to castrate him, to belittle him — hadn't this, even if it had ended in a disaster, contributed something invaluable? — even when the poor creature, all resistance at an end, and her prolonged spinsterhood with it, had become the most utterly abandoned of sensualists, the ugliest of parched earth, wholly given up to its need, and with no longer the minutest semblance of pride or dignity, crying, crying, for love? — A disastrous, a shocking, a hu-miliating experience; and a curiously debasing one; and neverthe-less with its saving gift of pity. For can there be anything more pitiful or pitiable, anything more miserable, than an ugliness which finds itself helplessly in love, an ugliness finding itself ineptly and impotently in love, hopelessly incapable of making itself attractive to the loved one? He had broken down those defenses, those glacial defenses, as if in a kind of ridiculous game, or obstacle race: he had given her fair warning that there could be in it, for himself, no conceivable element of genuine love, that it would be nothing but a *passade*, a momentary sensual indulgence; and that she had therefore better see to it that her own feelings didn't become in-volved. But what he hadn't foreseen was that the poor inexperienced creature, from the very beginning, from the moment when she had agreed to meet him for dinner, and again from the moment when she had agreed to go with him to Hyde Park in the evening — "like a servant-girl," she had cried, contemptuously — was out of her depth; she was lost, she was going to drown. As drown she did, as drown she did. Drowning, poor hapless woman, in her own tears. And to the accompaniment of what scenes, in the sordid hotel or lodging-house rooms — the room in Woburn Place, the room in Brunswick Square, or in the deplorable Hotel Canada, by the Paddington station, where he had so often, years before, gone with little Sara, the lady's maid — what scenes of abject pleading and weeping, the pitifully unattractive body demanding its due of love, and his own mounting disgust and anger, ending in a silent departure, the hotel door closing once again on the sound of sobs. For she had loved him: among the aspidistras, in the shabby rooms, sleepless in the nightlong din of the streets outside, the horse-drawn lorries clattering on their way to Covent Garden, she had wept and loved him. She had even — in final desperation — sent him a warning signal (a copy of the Spectator) and come down to Saltinge, where, by prearrangement, he was to meet her in the Gun Gardens. Infuriated, he had indeed gone to the Gun Gardens: but only then, finding her seated forlorn and mute on a bench, to tap the toe of her slipper, twice, with his stick, and to tell her that she must take the first train back to London, that he would not see her again.

A dreadful episode, and one which had haunted him for years; here again, in a way, was the Wounded Face, the rejection of the Wounded Face; for that base and basic need, the need for the low-value self-esteem (which could be extracted, like a vitalizing juice, out of the mere feeling of conquest), he had taught the poor woman how to love, but at the expense, to her, of heartbreak, and, to himself, of a fearful complex of pity and guilt, but mostly pity, which had made him physically and morally ill. It had given him a new concept of the terrible — almost evil — power of love, its power for destruction and horror. One could not witness such suffering, such a depravity of suffering, and ever be quite the same

308

again. To see it, week after week, and in those always so dreary surroundings — the yellow fog in the third-rate hotel bedroom, the feeble electric-light bulb hanging over the unleavened English bed, the sooty fans of folded newspaper in the fireless fireplace, and the grained yellow can of hot water in the wash-basin — to see it was, although he couldn't know it, to have a foretaste of his own agonized sense of loss — as Amabel was herself to predict — when he abandoned Saltinge and the three little D.'s. And just the same, the cruelty had been inevitable. To love her had proved impossible; he had felt, as he would always feel, the profoundest of compassions for her, but as he could not, could never, give her the kind of love she needed, the only thing for him to do was to extricate himself, and with a terminal brutality that would make it final.

Discreditable — ? Possibly. And the episode was only one of many on which the insatiable ego had fed itself, and almost invariably at the cost of nightmare hauntings in which the animal disgust and self-loathing must analyze itself down into its hideous components, in order then to reassemble them in parables of pity. Hadn't the poor woman reappeared, in "Brain Fag," as the starved cormorant, of his terrible dream, met at the cliff's edge, the cormorant who had in vain tried to speak to him out of her despair, and who had even attempted to write it for him, with bird-claw-marks, in the sand, as she died? As she died, at last, on his breast, where he had held the wretched creature, trying without hope, and without love, so to warm it. One of many: but perhaps the saddest of them. And whose fault it was, it was perhaps impossible to say. Happier, anyway, to reflect on the lighter and gayer ephemerids, like naughty little Sara, the pert lady's maid of Cavendish Square, who was always so angry with him when he called her "Creature" — "as if I were just an *animal*, indeed!" — or the Southampton Row prostitute whom he had taken to dinner on Christmas Eve, in the snow (for he was alone), and with whom he had spent the

most delightful and innocent of evenings, in her elaborate establishment in Ormonde Mansions, while the couples came and went,
were ushered by her discreetly into the various bedrooms, the door-
bell ringing or the telephone ringing, after which she and D. would
resume their flippant conversation, and (to some extent) the story
of her life. She had been a milliner in Liverpool, or rather, had
worked for one, but then she had got into trouble, the boy-friend
had got her into trouble. She had had a baby, a baby boy, and had
sent him to live with some good people in the country, where he
still was. And for a while the boy-friend had been very decent
about it, he had set her up in a shop of her own. But did such
things ever last — ? No, they never did. And what with one thing
and another, and the shop not doing too well, and a friend of hers
writing from London to say that life was pretty good there, pretty
easy, she had decided to try it. And as he could see, she had done
very well for herself, she no longer needed to go out if she didn't
want to, she had this nice place and it was profitable. And it was
nice of him to have taken her to dinner at Malzy's, she had enjoyed
the oysters and the Pouilly, but now, she was afraid — unless of
course he wanted something else — she would have to ask him to
go, for there was someone at the door, and all the other rooms
were in use — !

A brilliant Christmas Eve, and he was glad that he had obeyed
the impulse, when he had seen the young woman, through the
slanting snow, standing in the shadowed doorway, and heard her
murmured "Hello, darling!" and had at once gone back to her. For
his own door, at Saltinge, was closed to him, that Christmas; the
marriage was broken past patching, and perhaps just as well; Lorelei Two was waiting for him, or not waiting, in Cambridge far-away,
and now he would recross the Atlantic, to make, with her, what he
could of a new life, without the little D.'s and the house at Saltinge; and what could have been better, in the circumstances, on

this of all evenings, than to take this complete stranger to dinner, whose very profession was kindness? — and afterwards, back to his high-ceilinged and beautiful diggings in Brunswick Square, and the tray of handsome bottles, and the new treasures which he had found, the day before, at Kato's little shop in Holborn: the slight porcelain figurine, the burial figure of the Chinese handmaiden, standing under the tall oval mirror on the mantel, all meekness, all humility, her arms folded on her breast, the gentle face downturned as softly as a flower that is about to open, the whole attitude and expression that of silent expectancy, of one who waits to serve; and opposite this, but also, like this, reflected in the ghostly world of the mirror, the tremendous but silent pour of the great waterfall, the Chinese *kakemono* of the waterfall, pouring itself down as it seemed out of heaven itself, and past the vermilion pavilion (as the farouche John was to say) on the crag's edge, where the poet, or sage, leaned a little forward in meditation. How the little Kato, bending over to unfold its green-and-golden magnificence, had hissed for joy in the back room of the shop, when he had first displayed it, after bringing it up, long forgotten, from the cellar! How he had then, as if truly humiliated by its beauty, withdrawn his tiny hands from it, stepped softly back from it, even to averting his eyes, as if from something too bindingly in the nature of revelation to be looked upon without sacrilege! As with the figurine, too: he had shaken his head over it in genuine sorrow: for hadn't the greatness of human genius here shaped itself in the artifact of artifacts, the perfected, the crystal, symbol of its devotion to all that is best in man, and the becomingness of that best?

It was perhaps fitting that it was into these great presences he had brought Chapman, a few days after, in order to bid him farewell, their interests at last dividing and conflicting: to what is impermanent in humanity, or untrue in it, or superficial, or selfish, these could speak, as they infinitely did, of what is everlasting because it is beautiful; the waterfall spoke of eternity, was the voice of eternity, rushing past the small figure of the sage in his precariously perched little pavilion of thought; the handmaiden, meek before the tall mirror as once she had lain meek in the grave of her lord and master, stood ready, as always, to serve what was true. Fitting, too, that it was to these still presences he had again come, and again only a few days later, and just before his return to Boston and Cambridge, after the evening at the Victoria Palace with Jed, when he had taken Jed to his first music-hall. They had dined and wined at the Brice, of course, and enjoyed the vulgarity of the music-hall hugely; Jed had had the time of his life; it was the first spree they had had together, for Jed was growing up; he was now in school at Hampstead; and it was after seeing him off to Hampstead, on the 24 bus, that D., now beginning to feel his half-quarterns of gin, encountered the girl from the Gem Shop. What a scandal that had been — and what a narrow escape! And with what a wonderful and secret contrapuntal joy he had embarked on the adventure. For so immediately after leaving Jed had he met the girl that it was as if Jed were still physically present, still there as an accompanying and astonished witness to all that followed — the moonlight walk with her through Bloomsbury Square to Holborn and up the gaslit stairs to the grubby bedroom which was just above the famous Gem Shop, in the triangular corner opposite the post office; and then that fantastic fight — for it had been a genuine fight — over the change from the one-pound note. For she had refused him his change; and now drunk enough to be reckless and angry, for he felt cheated, he had begun breaking the flimsy toilet articles on the chest of drawers, and threatening to break yet others, if she didn't give him his change: and as she still refused, he smashed one gramophone record, and then another, and then a third: but at this point she began to scream, and to strike at him; she threatened to call the police, and suddenly she rushed down the stairs to the street, D. somewhat unsteadily following the belligerent figure, and now beginning to be a little alarmed. And with reason, too. For when he arrived in the street, it was to find that she was running towards the corner, and was crying, "Police —! Police —!" at the top of her lungs. And it was with delight and an extraordinary feeling of low cunning, and of *deus ex machina*, that he saw the taxi swing quietly up to the curb beside him, — the driver already sympathetically perceiving his plight, and reaching back a conspiratorial hand to open the cab door — so that in three seconds he had sprung in, and the cab, followed by screams of rage, had shot round the corner and away to safety, away to the waterfall and the waiting handmaiden.

One of the minor comic interludes, in the *éducation sentimentale* — a diversion, in its tone not unlike some of the early episodes with Helen Shafter, who had displayed, to his chagrin, a veritable genius for taking the nonsense out of love, for farcing it, and for making it ridiculous; and, like those hilarious and undignified adventures with Helen, in New York and Boston, it was a useful reminder of the fact that in love there are many mansions. Nor should one forget that even in the comic interludes, or ludicrous mishaps, there was not only a restorative draught of that low-level self-esteem, but also a brilliant reminder, from nature, that in life too there are many mansions, and as many levels of reality or meaning. Without these, one's life and one's truth would not have been complete; any more than the Beloved Uncle's would have been complete, for example, without that absurd adventure of his in Paris, when, strolling along the boulevard, he had suddenly made the shocking discovery that he had somehow forgotten, that evening, to put on a tie: a dinner-jacket, but no tie; and with the quite unforseeable consequence that, taking refuge in a bistro, and a drink, he found himself in conversation with a very charming young woman, who, discovering his unhappy plight, volunteered that if he would be so good as to come up to her room, which was just across the street, she would be only too happy to repair his omission — she had a tie which she would be glad to give him. It was too good to be true. And sure enough, on their arrival in the attic bedroom, with its very inviting-looking bed, she pulled out a drawer, and lo, such a glittering splendor of ties as he had never in his life beheld, much less ever dreamed of possessing. She thrust her arm among them, as one would thrust an arm into a net full of living fish, flashing and turning them, and then brought out the black satin tie of which he was in need. *Voilà!* The very thing! She held it up to him, laughing at his astonishment; and he was about to accept it from her, when he thought — of course: I must pay her for it. He fished out the notes, and saw with dismay that he had made a terrible mistake: white with fury, she thrust the tie into his hand, threw open the door, and ordered him out: to his attempts at explanation and apology she paid not the slightest attention: the door banged shut behind him, and the inexplicable adventure was over.

From base and basic need to low-level self-esteem, and thus to the energy for the artifact, and the mercurial substance out of which it must be wrought: mercurial, yes, because it was so seldom the merely factual elements — in the loves, the loves, the loves! — that would be of any use to the artificer, but rather the by-products of these, in animal drive, or psychosomatic; the renewal of the sense of wholeness and unity; and that extraordinary residual and nostalgic ache, the haunting overtone of something like an inexpressible sorrow, which, although unhappy itself, seemed invariably to accompany even the serenest and sunniest of loves, and to give it its true character. Was it the element of *moritura* in it, the feeling of impermanence, on the one hand, and of incompleteness on the other — the dazzle that was so perishable, the haloed sun-angel that was so momentary, the outline of magic that one instinctively knew was too beautiful to approach, and would vanish indeed, if one did? That nymph-cry in the forest, or in the forest of the bloodstream, the forest of the mind; calling one out of oneself, and into something else, daring the soul to run forward into the treacherous shadows, in the forever renewed hope of finding the forever unknown and new, the something beyond, the something true, the something that would at last make speech truly speech, life truly life, as if at last the whole mystery might be reduced to a simple but multiple radiance that one could — for one instant — hold in the hollow of one's hand: its compelling elusiveness, one knew all along, was of course in oneself: and in this, the love was perhaps interchangeably identifiable with one's own consciousness, one's own being and becomingness: it was simply another disguise for the poetic and poietic psyche which is the very center of existence. The onomastic making his onomasticon out of words and worlds, adding up the bright syllables and the dark to ever more hermetic meanings and combinations of meaning, even to cancellations, and negations, or contradictions deployed in a fixed counterpoint, or meaning dislimning into meaninglessness; wasn't this precisely the same action as that of love, love finding and making itself in love? They were the two voices of the one flute, the two-voiced ambiguous lyric statement which one overheard always in the garden at daybreak, where the invisible god played up the sun; but before the meaning could be made out, the song had come to its unfinished end, the sun was up, and the god was gone.

And the pursuit of that teasing echo, wherever it might lead, as in the pursuit of love, was the artificer's joy, as if the two pursuits were one and the same. Nor did it wholly matter whether the actual details of a particular experience were available, or usable, or ever actually used. Faubion, heaven help us, in *Purple Passage*, with the angry eyes, and the "cheap lace blouse, well-filled," feeling fiercely for his foot under the dining-saloon table, or knocking imperiously at his stateroom door, was real enough in all conscience, or out of it; so was the ineffable Cynthia, if a little too consciously in the tradition of Burne-Jones's Pre-Raphaelite beggar-maid: so was Helen Shafter, and long-legged Anita, and poor Amabel; so was Marian. And Sara, too, lying beneath him in the woods at Epsom Downs, while the mowing-machine clattered among the poppies in the field beyond; or bright-haired hot-tempered little Ee, all but seduced, all but willing to be seduced, in the flat in St. John's Wood, while the underground rumbled under the walls of that friendly house, in which — said the blue plaque — Thomas Hood had been born. All of these had been used in one way or another by the onomastic builder of meanings; as Lorelei One and Lorelei Two had been used, also; and others of the Loreliebchens, in one way or another, with or without whatever degree of translation or disguise. And yet, the latter didn't really matter. The echo, the shadow, the influence, the sound of the vanishing nymph-cry, could be heard in the work, or *for* it, even if the creature herself was gone. In *The Quarrel,* for instance, amongst so much else that was so obviously transposed directly from the life at South Yarmouth, with Lorelei One and Jean stepping out of the cottage in the blank Cape sunlight, as large as life and twice as natural, and the Robin Hood fur-thief bringing, from that extraordinary household of his, the painted pink cart, with gilded wheels, for Jean: amongst these and other so recognizable characters, speaking their own lines, it was Marian alone who was absent; or present only in the form of a letter which in fact she had never written, and never *could* have written; and nevertheless it was Marian who had been the germinating force for the entire action, just as, in delicious recollection, and with recollected love, she had so generously given him the love with which to write it. And hadn't little Ee similarly endowed him, over and over again, by looking over his shoulder, as it were, from that so inaccessible world of hers, at Ashford, or in

Barclay's Bank, or from the green slope of the dike, between Inglesee and Saltinge, where they had arranged the clandestine meeting — he from the Angchurch train, dismounting at Inglesee, she
walking across the fields from little Saltinge, which lay behind her
burnished by the sunset; hadn't she provided her own golden syllables for that ever-growing onomasticon? Like so many, in England, imprisoned in the cage of class — as in the Old Master's
novella, *In the Cage* — the poor child had been overcome with
glee at thus accidentally being let out, thus freed to move into another world; and if the odd literary couple in Watchtower Street,
the Cravens, had begun it, by inviting her to join Saltinge's rather
pathetic little Literary Society, with its solemn little meetings and
readings, and its occasional dramatics, which were more pathetic
still, it was D. who had really accomplished her release, from the
accountant's stool in the real-estate office, or at any rate had given
her the sense as of release, first by making her his confidante, and
then, during Lorelei Two's absence in Normandy, by making love
to her. Not that he had ever got much of anywhere with it, nor, for
that matter, that this was of much importance. Here, as so often, the
charm was in the fugitiveness, the very slightness of it, the hover;
they liked each other immensely; he had liked her the minute he
saw her, she had an extraordinary grace and lightness, the classic
sickle curve of thigh, the forward thrust of thigh, as she walked
swiftly down the cobbled street of Strand Hill, scarcely touching the
ground; and from the moment that she had come in to do that job
of typing for him, late in the evening, they had both known that
the whole arrangement, on both sides, was a ruse, a subterfuge,
and had accepted it as such — it was simply the ingenious means
by which they might encompass a meeting in private. They had
sat by the fire, under the blue Hiroshige, to discuss the typing; to
emphasize a point — and in order to do so, when the right moment
should arise, he had drawn his footstool a little closer to her chair —

he had touched her knee very lightly and casually with one finger; she had flinched, just for a second, drawing back; but then she had leaned tentatively forward again; and when, a little later, he repeated the gesture, and this time allowed his hand to come to rest, there was no more flinching, and the two bodies knew each other.

And if only briefly — for other events had unhappily intervened — and if always thus clandestinely, at Angchurch or in London, nevertheless with that particular kind of delight and rapture, that rapture wholly of the eyes, and which renders the mere physical rapture wholly unnecessary, when for one or the other of the lovers it is a first love. But also, for Ee, it was more than that. It was an escape: it was contact with a new and exciting world — a world of books, painting, theatre, ballet, music — and of the people who did these things — of which she had dreamed long and passionately, but into which she had never dared to dream that she might enter. How she had loved it! She couldn't possibly have enough of it. In this, she had been a little like Marian, she had perhaps loved him quite as much for the world he lived in, and for the treasure of news he could bring to her from it, as for himself. She couldn't hear enough of Paul, or Nicholas, or the so super-poetic Edward: as she devoured their work, so she devoured, too, all the details about them that he could supply her with: she was insatiable. She learned, too, with astonishing rapidity, for she had a natural taste, she was instinctively discriminating. And if, through those unfortunate events, their love was never to be quite complete, in retrospect that seemed hardly to have mattered. With what she had in fact given of herself, she had more than generously rewarded him. She had rewarded him, above all — and this still remained precious to him — by confiding in him, by letting him into that pitifully limited, and somewhat apprehensive, life of hers: she had worn her heart on her sleeve for him. And this, as he had been lucky enough to perceive even at the time, had taken immense

318

courage. For how could she be sure that he wouldn't be secretly condescending about it, or even think her ridiculous — ? She had risked it, anyway, and it was in this act of trust that she had most tenderly and poignantly rewarded him: this had been more intimate than any embrace. And her confession to him, when at last it came, as she wept with her face against his knee, weeping only a little, and silently, but out of such depths of self-control, and years of restraint, that it all but tore the small body in two — her confession of the attempted suicide, and of the years and years of misery and humiliation that had brought her to it — this too, like the farouche John's, as reported in that dreadful letter from Bedlam, was to add its brave dignity to the house. In the cage, indeed — say, rather, in the jail. Unhappy in her family at Ashford, unhappy in the class into which she had been born, exiled in Saltinge, and again exiled from Saltinge itself — seated, as she was, on that stigmatizing stool behind the counter, in the company of the other junior clerks; exiled, too, and finally — she had felt increasingly and desolatingly sure — by that dreadful trouble with her face, the periodically disfiguring attacks of acne, of which she was so ashamed, and which she knew, she knew, she *knew*, made her so hopelessly unattractive to everyone, but above all to men — and all this, too, in the very presence, the glow, the rich evidence on all sides, at Saltinge, of the life she wanted to live, and couldn't — well, it had become at last just too much to bear. After two years at Saltinge she knew nobody but an assistant postmistress, and the kindly butcher, and his wife, with whom she lodged, and the two black-coated and insufferable junior clerks, at the office, whose vulgar jokes and condescensions made her existence a daily torment. And therefore — she admitted it now with a queer kind of pride, even defiance — she had decided to die. She took the last night bus from Saltinge to Inglesee Beach, the bus by which the late cinema-goers could return home, and, dismounting at the White Hart, walked across the improvised golf-links, in their little grassy hollow among hillocks of gorse, to the deserted beach of shingle. The Channel was calm — across it, she could see, far away, the winking light of Gris Nez. And without hesitation, she walked straight towards it, straight into the sea, and towards that light, just as she was too, with all her clothes on, not even discarding her slippers. But my god, my god, my god! there she had stood — how long she didn't know; and somehow, she simply couldn't. The water was up to her chin; once or twice, or even three times, she submerged her head in it, or her face; but the sea wouldn't let her in, she simply couldn't. And at last, chilled to the marrow, and shivering as if with an ague, she had waded out again, crying in despair at this now added shame; and thus crying, and in her dripping clothes, had walked back the two long, dark miles to Saltinge. All she could now hope for was that the headlights of the late cars would not disclose her plight, that she would escape attention and get safely home to her bed, where she could cry her heart out. And, in this much, she had succeeded. She had got home, and cried her heart out all night long, as now she was crying it out again, for D.; but she had lived, she still lived; and perhaps it was as well. For — it was very strange — from that moment things had mysteriously begun to be better. And now — she rubbed her damp cheek against his knee — she was almost, yes almost, happy.

As, also, she had almost made *him* happy, in the small bright interval that had been allowed to them. For him, too, this had been the time when the shadows had begun menacingly to encroach, both without and within; the time when Lorelei Two and himself were more and more jarringly out of step; and when, in those serial essays of his, on attitude and definition, he seemed to himself to be disparting such unbearable *nuclei* of awareness and self-awareness as made it all but impossible for him to go on. And hadn't it been that clear face over his shoulder, and his knowledge

of that courage and that love, not to mention the love of life, which
had been able, in its moment of crucifixion, to accept even this —
hadn't it been Ee who had enabled him to carry that analysis of
his to its own crucial point, its own moment of crucifixion, in the,
at last, "willing loss of self" — ?

Yes, it was true; and had those unfortunate events not come
between them, and at last made all meetings any longer impossible, so that they had had to part, after that final and so beautiful
morning in St. John's Wood — parting by the Ritz, at the gate to
the Green Park, and on a note of interrogation, too, for at the
penultimate moment she had almost changed her mind, almost
decided not to go to Aldershot after all, but back to the flat with
him — if the unhappy events had not occurred, how could he be
sure that his own attempt at *felo-de-se* might never have been made?
In this, and so many years earlier, she might have performed for
him the office that Lorelei Three was later so all-givingly to per-
form: the renewal of the necessary courage, and the necessary love,
for a return to full consciousness and to the contingent problems
of insight and analysis and synthesis, a resumption of the translation of these into the artifact which was, for him, the only way he
knew of paying, or trying to pay, his debt to the ancestors, and thus
to mankind. Yes, with Ee, this might well have come to pass; her
courage might have become his courage; her order, his order. And
he need not have felt, in the pressure of other circumstances and
other problems, that the vision of "the indecipherable land, the
nameless land, the selfless land" was too much for the first be-
holder to bear: that wingless unhappy explorer — as D. had perhaps a shade sententiously put it — who had climbed to the verge,
and seen his own creation, stretched out below him, his own harsh
valley, his own unthinking stone. Nor (without that help) would
he perhaps have felt it necessary, after that vision — which was his
own self-shaping — to invoke a god thus now to remould *him,* as in

a dream — the instant agony creating the "splendid shape in which was the god's escape"; and all reduced, at last, to the primal cloud, in which the lightning was once again to dream a Name.

But no, all one could say of this was that it had been a possibility: it *could* have happened, but it hadn't. As dear Ee had had to go through with her own lonely debate with death, in the tawny Channel waters which had once drowned Old Inglesee, and could only by so doing become the resolved and resolute creature which she was, so D., as it had turned out, must inevitably go through with his own ironic colloquy, to its own ironic conclusion — not forgetting Ee's letter, either, upstairs in the handkerchief drawer — in order that he too might become sufficiently resolved and resolute to pick up that vision of his where he had dropped it; and, by now consorting it for the first time consciously and deliberately with his "consistent view," to make a first attempt at a statement of fundamental aim and purpose. And for this, at least, even if she could not have prevented that slightly theatrical reading of Wyndham Lewis in the gas-filled kitchen, while the flies sagged to the floor, Ee's gift had been priceless. He had been able to sail away to Gibraltar, with Hambo and Lorelei Two, and to meet Nicholas at Granada, with that vision of his now acceptable — and ready, when he returned, to be used. He had been prepared, with Ee's assistance, for that further vision, too, on the return voyage, the dream of the book which was to be called *Ushant*, the ambiguous book with the punning title: that still unwritten book, for which the notes still waited in their faded folder, themselves in faded pencillings on P. & O. notepaper. For, in its way, hadn't this dream-vision been really an extension of the other? That unattempted project, as of a breaking-down of reality into its so many and so deceptive levels, one under another, one behind another, as if one were peeling off the seven or eight layers of time, and language, and meaning, in a thousand-year-old palimpsest — the personalities and the situations

322

alike altering as the light upon them altered — that project, outlined in the dream, and then on the P. & O. notepaper, and then
(on the P. & O. boat) discussed and elaborated with Hambo, even
as the ship itself turned the blue corner of Cape St. Vincent, and
headed north to the Bay of Biscay and the Raz de Sein and Ushant
— that project, on which he could even now consider himself still
embarked, had been, as D. could at last realize, an integral part of
the very vision — of the indecipherable land — from which, for a
vital moment, he had been cowardly enough to flinch. It would
have been a projection, on a larger scale, of all that had been implied, in that view of the human psyche as an indecipherable, or
nameless land, a land of which one could make oneself the possessor
by a mere strictness of awareness: but what had been thus glimpsed,
and accepted, for a moment, was to have been deployed not thus
serially, as in a loosely outspread radial fan of aspects and angles,
but architected, with its own intrinsic and natural spiral of form,
as a whole drama of the human soul, from the beginningless beginning to the endless end. Too difficult altogether: Hambo had
agreed about that: so had Jed: and, to both, D. had more than
once said that for his own part he only wished to god that either
of them, or anyone else, for that matter, would take over the notes,
with his blessing, and get down to it. A drama, yes — but let us
admit it, a drama without drama, a story without story, in any sense
that the books would admit it to be; unless, as perhaps one should,
one could agree that the pursuit of this particular sort of Moby
Dick (or should one rather call it a Snark), this subliminal of sub-
liminals in consciousness, the slipperiest of elementals shaping itself
again and again for a split second, and then lost, and never, when
it thus reappeared (only to vanish) looking quite the same — unless one agreed that this pursuit was possibly the most essential of
dramas, the very stuff itself of drama, since that pursuit is the central undeviating concern of every living individual human being;

and thus, in aggregate, on the grand evolutionary scale, of all mankind. How shall the non-knower, who is in process of becoming the knower, convert himself into a language by which, first, to unravel his own beginnings and outlines against the matrix in which, like a trilobite (or an embroy! to quote Blimp), he found himself embedded, and then, with this basic knowledge, and out of its now co-ordinated constituents, begin a parallel "arrangement" of the world itself, the world outside and beyond (but within oneself too) — the microcosm, with full awareness of the laws and limitations of microcosm (but in love with it, just the same, and proud of its prismatic importance) receiving into itself the macrocosm, a world within a world — ? How indeed! — And nevertheless it was in this really staggering drama that every living human being was involved, to greater or less degree, every day of his life. That inherent necessity, that obligation, was the common inheritance of all. And in this sense, at least, wouldn't that unwritten book have been dramatic? Or *couldn't* it have been — ?

Dubious enough, as to this, and as to *Ushant,* all three of them had been — Jed, over a chess-game; and Hambo, over the ping-pong table, or the pub table at the Ship; and himself, walking up the terraced hillside above Saltinge, through the path called "New England," in the heavy fragrance of winter heliotrope, to drink orange gin on the garden steps with Nicholas, looking down past the bust of Alexander Pope, on the balustrade, to the baroque and somewhat battered Temple of Minerva. Dubious enough. It was obviously something that was far more entertaining to think about, to speculate upon, than to undertake. And their speculations had been frequent, and had been fun: it had become, for Jed and Hambo, a kind of thematic statement, anonymous and at large, on which anyone at all might play variations; or an inherited mythos, in the public domain, which could be adapted (it was a literary stratagem then popular) to ulterior purposes of one's own. Hadn't

Jed, as a matter of fact, actually once made a start with it? After one of these many discussions? They had hauled out D.'s notes and diagrams once again, and the faded P. & O. paper: examining anew the variants of design. At one time, the notion had been of a six-part affair, with a form which D. had expressed algebraically as:

In this, *a* was to have represented the zone of the actual — D., for example, lying in his bunk in the stateroom of a ship, taking account of his roommates, as he prepared himself for sleep; reconsidering, as at the beginning of a voyage, something of his past life, and the events which had led to his now being present, and sailing, say, to England; and from this, in turn, to a consideration of his plans, his purpose. Next, and as it were enclosed in *a* came *b*, the second zone of the actual, but this time concerned with D., for example, as a writer — a writer with a specific notion for a novel, perhaps: but the novel here viewed only as it existed *in relation* to the life-material — D.'s life, in all its aspects — out of which the novel would arise or was arising. Then came *c*, a new realm of reality, or the actual, and this was the novel as it was to exist in itself. But this too was in its turn divisible into three levels, had its own *a* and *b* and *c*. First, the dreamer, whose dream was to form the substance of the book: the dreamer, either lying awake just before falling asleep and into the dream, or waking from it, but only for a moment, to review it, and then to reimmerse in it. And second, the dream, in all its iridescent ramifications of landscape and figures, and the dream-atmosphere that held it all, as it were, lucidly in solution: the four people, and the house on the hill, in which they were gathered together, as usual, for their amiably disputatious task of translation. And thus, finally, to the third and central level, the core, the kernel — the little dream-like *novella*, in all its shimmering ambiguity, which the four people were engaged in translating, and about which they were so habitually in disagreement: the little *novella*, which so constantly changed in color and shape, and even in language, now seeming to be in archaic German, now in Provençal French, now in Spanish; just, too, as the *mise-en-scène* altered continually, so that one was not quite certain whether it was to a hill-town in northern Italy — perhaps San Gimignano — or to one in Spain, or even to one in England (like Saltinge) that the four characters in it were forever taking their way; and always with the sense of an obscure tragedy that impended for them, a timeless wave which hung over them, forever about to fall, but perhaps never falling; and themselves, in its shadow, timelessly approaching it, but perhaps never quite to arrive.

One of the many of its shifting outlines, in which all three of them — Jed and Hambo and himself — had had a hand — : for it never, when they returned to contemplate it, seemed itself to have stood still: while they had been looking away, both theme and design had obscurely moved. Nor had D. himself ever found a satisfactory point of entry into it, though many had been attempted. And Ushant — there was *that* element, and in its way the most important, to be got in, too: that name had dominated the germinal dream, and therefore the theme of the imagined book: for, like that timelessly unfalling wave, in the shadow of which the four people seemed to be waiting, so the vaster shadow of Ushant, the

Île d'Ouessant, and its rocks and reefs and shoals, towards which
the ship bore the voyager and his dream, overhung, with promise
of landfall or menace of shipwreck, both voyager and ship. *Enez
Eussa:* so the Bretons called it: to the ancients, and as early as
Pythias of Marseilles, it had been known as the end of the world,
and as the last resting-place of the souls of the departed — on their
way whither? On their way to the West? — *"Qui voit Ouessant,
voit son sang";* and again and again that had been true; its dolmens
and cromlechs had been dedicated to blood and death, like the
mighty bastions of granite cliff beneath them. On the chart from the
"Pilote Français," which the shipbuilder at Saltinge had given
him — his own voyage to Spain carefully traced in red ink round
those perilous coasts — he had studied out its names, and revolving lights, and soundings; as, on the aerial photograph, which Jean
had obligingly filched from the files of the Royal Air Force, he had
scrutinized also the saurian and sinister shape of the great rock
itself, which seemed to be in the very act of letting down its monstrous flanks and claws to plunge westward into the sea, wearing
the white scars across its back which were the goat-tracks of the
little beings who dwelt upon it — until it shook them off — and
the lighthouse buildings, like a cluster of barnacles. Here, when
the Atlantic fog rolled in, over the ground-swell which had swung
under gull-scream for four thousand miles, one could hear the
voices of the three fates, the three invisible sirens — Créach and
Jument and Stiff — alternating their melancholy cries to such
mariners as might be approaching. Here — the chart gave warning — to approach at all, in thick weather, was of extreme danger:
the currents frequently set right on shore: the tides were strong:
and the bottom so level, but "with local irregularities," that soundings were of little assistance, the lead all but useless: to judge the
"distance westward of the meridian of outward dangers," of those
savage claws, was all but impossible. Was it any wonder that

Chateaubriand had been wrecked there — on his way home from the "mystic" forests of America? And for him too had it not been a warning, lest he take too great liberties with that singular dream of his, that singular vision of the land towards which Ushant looked? —

"He opened the notebook under the green sea-light of the faintly sibilant porthole: he opened the typewriter-case on the green baize table in the corner of the deserted ball-room, or concert-room, of the ship: saw, in his mind's eye, over notebook and machine, beyond the empty platform and its silent yellow-toothed piano, the beginning shapes, the shadowy figures, the emerging landscape: and, listening intently, heard now the voices, coming closer, coming clearer, in that nursery schoolroom, hung with maps, as the four translators bent once more to their daily task."

Something like that was to have been one of the many rejected openings: but it was not satisfactory, did not begin at the right level, and obviously much too far "inside": so that, from that point, the inward progression (already too far advanced, or too much "given") would have had to be suspended, and somewhat awkwardly, too, until the "outer" rings could be first established. But how, then? If the form was to be thus annular, or spiral, then perhaps end and beginning must be identical? — To be sure, he had once attempted a formulation of this very problem in design, obliquely in reference to *Purple Passage* and *Dead Reckoning* — and, of course, to the project for *Ushant* — but it had remained fragmentary, at best. Everything was to be presented — in this view of the work of art — as on one time-level. As if — for instance — one were to focus, on a given star, an infinite series of telescopes, each of them one light-moment farther off, and, by co-ordinating this infinite series of visions, obtain a simultaneous view of all possible actions and at all possible times. As if the past, the present, and the future, were all presented at once, the single and the multiple, the important and the unimportant, the trivial and the tremendous, the whole of that infinite mechanism, or cosmogony, simultaneously in motion and at rest. Could something like this not be the pattern for a work of art? which would thus be intrinsically, and in its very nature, truer to the *natura rerum,* and, as in little Kato's waterfall, to its characteristic pour-in-stillness? In this sense, therefore, there would be no "progress," or of the ordinary sort, in a work of art: everything past would be hypothecated, everything future would be implied: the movement of these together would constitute a kind of static-dynamic, a stillness of motion round an invisible center. As action would have preceded any given moment in it, so action would follow: but the moment itself, *every* moment, was comprehension. And in this view of art one could say that the artist, the artificer, was like the general who is co-ordinating the multitude of conflicting or divergent reports from the fluctuating fortunes of a battlefront, and marks them down on his outspread map. X had advanced, y perhaps withdrawn; z is stationary, in a mammering and at a stay; c is without support on his right flank, d has not been heard from since early morning; e asks for reinforcements, f for artillery-cover. And his living map at last completed, with all available intelligence thus graphically deployed upon it and under his hand, the general is ready to issue the order of the day, which will set everything in motion. But no, the order of the day is already implicit in the very facts thus displayed: the necessary nature of the battle, and even its outcome, are already there, and the mere naming of it is already in a profound sense superfluous: for, with the completion of that co-ordination, and before the issuing of the order of the day, the work of art has been finished. It lies there, intensely still, as the all-embracing moment of comprehension, the invisible center of the circle.

Which was all very fine, in theory, but didn't in the least solve the primary question as to where, in god's name, in all that welter of material — that great "blooming, buzzing confusion," as William James had called it — one was to make one's first entry; or at exactly what point of the nebular spiral — as with a roundabout — dare to step on. All very fine, too, to have noted that once begun, the movement should be roughly from poetic to realistic and back again, through analysis of the given *natura rerum,* and constantly, if slowly, towards the final note — which was to be also the first — of spiritual, or mystic, affirmation. Or that it should concern itself with the examination of a whole human life in terms of its component parts, whether external — the outer experience; or interior — the changing psyche: the events, the mere happenings, but also the developing shapes and shades of desire, ambition, aim; and again, the preoccupations, the obsessions, the animal drive, as co-operating with, or opposing, the central concern with the Great Why, and thus, with any luck, the momentary or partial discovery of the Great How. Ah, yes, that Great How — ! Could one possibly, in this, have improved on grandfather's pretty explicit solution on the "little acceptance" of his fideism? And if one must thus move forever towards — or around — some sort of mystic affirmation, or acceptance, could there be any that was better "reasoned" than his — if to this one were to add the precious new element of evolutionary consciousness, as the final creative step in nature's evolutionary process, its forever unfolding finial of light — ?

Which should have been, to be sure, the very mainspring of light in the work itself; both in content and form; the unfolding finial, the knot of fire-leaves, which is both base and apex, and which, though it appears always to remain in the same place, is nevertheless always new. And to a considerable degree something of the kind had indeed been the concern of the work: but alas, it was very much easier said than done. That perpetually changing psyche, itself the changing coefficient of changing appetites and satisfactions, one had never been able to know in advance to what it might not next respond, like Coleridge's Aeolian harp, or to what purpose, of the universals out of which it was, fountain-like, forever recreating itself. Who could have guessed, for instance, that the brief encounter with William Blackstone, in the winter of work for the WPA, and the Massachusetts Guide — when, like Lorelei Three, he had been duly certified as "destitute" — would have lodged in him so powerful a seed of conversion? Or that it must wait so many years, and through so many vicissitudes and landscapes — from Charlestown to Mexico City and Cuernavaca, with Lorelei Three and Nicholas, and the fantastic visit to Hambo, beside his cloacal barranca; and thus to Saltinge (once again with a new wife) and into the war, and out of it; and so, at last, to the new house on Cape Cod, the 'new old' house, and the new life? The 'new old' life, too — for the Bass River still flowed there, past the house of Cousin Abiel, the Quaker; still flowed against the granite walls where little Jed had so characteristically, with that minuteness of observation which was inevitably to make him a scientist, first noticed the barnacles feeding themselves with their quick little threads of hands. And his own lilacs, planted round the house two decades before, still bloomed there; and, in the Cove, the scallops were still waiting for the gathering (Lorelei Three tucking up her skirts and wading in for them) and for the week-end feasts when the Bassett came down to smell his native air and stamp again on his native heath. But who, out of these simple and obvious elements, or repetitions, would have predicted that so deep a conversion was to arise?

For it had arrived, at the 'new old' house, hidden between its tender terraces of locust and spruce and cedar, in the bland Cape moonlight, with that capricious and miraculous suddenness of all conversions: all at once, it was there, it had spoken itself in the odd little poem, and just as compulsorily as in that first of all poems at Savannah. The same sort of experience, exactly; and if one looked for explanations and causes and sources, and found them all too

331

copiously everywhere, and in every direction, what nevertheless became unavoidably conspicuous in it was the basic importance in it of love. Love! Good heavens, how blind he had been. How blind, and how forgetful, too; for hadn't he again and again tried, in whatever sort of statement, to bring this in like a *leit-motif*? One loves everywhere, and all the time — so he had declared in *Purple Passage*. Ah, yes but there with a difference. For there he had expressly been speaking of sexual love, of that unsleeping alertness of the body that must automatically and swiftly appraise every newcomer, appraise the beauty and the grace and the promise of passion and delight, appraise the nimbleness of the imagination that would be brought to love, the delicacy or fierceness of sensuousness or sensuality, the potentialities — so terribly important — of that final possessiveness, as with claws and fangs, in the locking of the two golden and leonine spirits for the spirit's ultimate surrender and absolution. That mutual appraisal was as universal as it was instantaneous, and in a sense, too, it could transcend sex: it was equivocal, could measure the capacity for love, alike in man or woman, with a single eye-glance; and wholly, too, for the most part, without ulterior intent, and as if merely for reference, for one's secret files of value. And in the latter respect, insofar as it transcended sex, merely measuring the "love" in the newcomer, the outgoingness of his beauty, or brilliance, or warmth, or power, one was beginning to approach that other domain of love which had had its way with him, and so surreptitiously, so quite without his connivance, in the sudden conversion; and the writing of the ritual poem which was his unforeseeable celebration of it. One could ridicule this, or try to dismiss it (though one really didn't, or if one did, was ashamed) by relegating it to the "birds, bees, and flowers" department; for it was thus that Hambo and himself had habitually referred to it — or himself, at any rate; but the fact remained that it was by no means as simple as that, nor had it, except for a moment, and in a chain of other preoccupations — the war, the new house, the economic pressures that perpetually drove Lorelei Three and himself to ever new stratagems and low cunnings aimed at boiling the pot — been more than superficially forgotten. It had been there all the time. Even in the departure from the cottage at South Yarmouth to London, for the joint project of educating the little D.'s, and overtaking Cynthia — unless one were to add, too, the literary project, of amalgamating oneself with that new milieu, which had become so engrossingly necessary — even in this departure there must have been, and from the very outset, an unadmitted and secret sense of betrayal, a bleeding, of which it was going to take him a very long time to become wholly aware. The English landscape — ah, yes, it had been a love at first sight, there was no doubt about that. And perhaps even now it had a power to satisfy him which nothing in America could offer. And he had submitted, and gladly, to that enforced habitation. But just the same, how revelatory it was to remember the revulsion he had experienced, first at Inglesee, and then at Saltinge, and in his very own garden — the garden which he had himself re-shaped and re-planted — the singular repugnance he had felt about touching that dark, rich, and let us admit it, that alien earth! He had literally been unable to bring himself to touch it with his hands: even to use a trowel or spade in it had been offensive to him: the digging and planting he had had to leave to others. At the time, he had been able to dismiss this as a mere neurotic wantonness — a whim, a distaste for those gigantic English earthworms, which, at night, if one turned an electric torch upon them, as once he had done for the astonished Paul, could be seen outstretched obscenely on the black loam, or snapping back into their holes like glistening rubber-bands. But the real truth was that to touch that earth was treason. And the hands which had dug the sandy holes for the lilacs at South Yarmouth, on that night of frost and moonlight — hurrying, too, with Clarence, to get them safely

333

bedded in before the frost should strike the naked roots — could not bring themselves ever again to dig any other.

It had been, if he had only known it, as simple as that. From that sandy soil — that 'sandy loom' as they called it on the Cape — as from the heaped leaves of autumn at New Bedford, where the glossy eyes of the horsechestnuts looked up through spiked eyelids, or from the delicately branched clusters of the darkening china-berries in the baked back yard at Savannah, something ineradicable had passed from the fiery American landscape into the young American body, which, try as he would, in that perverse quest of his, he would never be quite able to exorcise. "Do you really feel at home here?" So Ted or Avvy or the Old Bird had asked him once, unexpectedly, on the Salts between Saltinge and the Castle, after an impromptu foot-race, as they pulled up to look towards the Channel, and then back to the little red-roofed town on its hill; and he still remembered with what a shock of surprise and recognition he had received the question, and the conscious duplicity with which he had answered it. He had answered, to be sure, in the affirmative; but the sudden question had revealed the truth to him: he did not — in the sense that the question implied — truly feel at home there, and he never would. Nor, for that matter, was it at all certain that he had ever really expected to. For had that actually ever been part of the bargain? And hadn't its value, for him, lain precisely in the fact that he *wouldn't* feel at home in it, and must remain constantly on guard *vis-à-vis* that ever-challenging presence? Once one felt at home, one would have no more to learn, or would have become so relaxed as to be no longer capable of learning; and one's very purpose for having come there at all, or a very important part of it, would be no longer valid. No, the truth was, as he had fleetingly realized there on the Salts by the Castle, that those other loves, those "little" loves, of the American scene, and one's roots in it, even if for so long he had obstinately put them out of mind, remained steadfast, remained vitally there, and had even, in fact, been growing. There might never have been anything in America — at Savannah, or Concord, or Duxbury — as classically beautiful as the long mountain-top walk round Fairfield, or across the great Marsh, and its cat's-cradle of dikes, to the sea-wall, so beloved of Paul, at Dymchurch, or along the gorse-honeyed cliffs of Fairlight to the broken-toothed castle on the hill at Angchurch; one could extend the list of such unforgettable treasures indefinitely, too, whether in town or country; but beautiful as these might be, they could never become part of one's own language, in the way that Tybee Beach would always mysteriously be, or Tuckerman's Ravine, or the swampy birchwoods in the spring at Concord, bright green with skunk cabbage and jack-in-the-pulpit, or the sandy wood-roads of Cape Cod which led, under scrub pine and oak, and through the hot fragrance of sweet-fern and wild indigo, from one secret pond or cranberry bog to another. It was to these that young Blackstone had come, but to make them his own; these had become his language of freedom, and the language in which all those spiritual descendants of his would speak; and from this spiritual language, in which even now the sound of the virgin forest could be heard, there could never be any escape. In effect, he had gone to England merely that he might, in the end, hear this the more clearly, understand it the more profoundly. And now, at last, in the new old house at Brewster, those syllables, freighted with the voices of the ancestors, had spoken down to him, in the queer little poem, as if from the very hillside: the very sidehill.

Not that the little poem had been of any particular importance or value in itself, for it hadn't; the somewhat precipitate statement, and in a medium which he had never mastered, was all too manifestly, as he had admitted himself, after reading it aloud to Lorelei Three and the Bassett, in candlelight, inadequate to the theme. No, what was important about it was that it represented the completion of a psychological circuit: it was D.'s confession, as abrupt as one made in a dream, of his discovery and acceptance of America, and specifically of New England, and his own ghosts in it. And could there possibly have been a truer symbol of this than the little clump of mayflower, which he had transplanted from Dry Hill to their own terrace, that little love to which, he had always liked to believe, the Plymouth fathers had given its name? That little love: the truth was, that the poem had been D.'s unexpected confession of love, and love, moreover, of a force so completely unparalleled, in his experience, that at one point he had broken down, and been for a moment unable to go on with his reading. To have had to wait all that time, and through so many disguises and infidelities, to find only this! Or that it was only this that any longer mattered, or had ever mattered! Like the dream, this little artifact had been his way of finding solution and resolution: and couldn't one say that this was invariably true of the work of art? One's way, as Coleridge had said, of esemplastically realizing what one was up to, where one was, and, to be exact, *who* one was? In its way, too, a quite perfect example of the nicety with which the mechanism worked: for if the predicament out of which the poem arose was perhaps too personal, too close, to become the basis for a construct of anything even remotely resembling universals, involving, as it did, that extraordinary childhood fixation on Ariel's Island, and the poet of White Horse Vale, nevertheless it was an excellent specimen of low-level close-to-consciousness resolution of conflict, whether by Coleridge's esemplastic or Freud's sublimation in synthesis. It was a shotgun marriage — a subjection to "form" — of apparently irreconcilable opposites: in this instance, of England and New England (with Savannah somewhere below). The Mayflower, in which the Pilgrims had come to Provincetown, was still here, in the little blossoms from Dry Hill; and in the language of these country roads, and the white villages, and in the names — elecampane, purslane, tansy, and Johnny-jump-up pansy, and all the rest — one could still, even now, hear the ancestral voices of Will and Ben. One could have these even here, even now. They were his own. The country clock was wound up again.

But if this happy discovery was the moment of itself of resolution, and the moment of discovered freedom — freedom to go or stay, the freedom one discovers in the delighted acknowledgment of one's debts, one's ties, one's roots, one's belongingness — one must not forget that it was itself only a link in the unfolding chain, and that William Blackstone, the prototypical Hambo, had already anticipated it, as, in all probability, he was also, in a sense, to inherit it. Even now, as the ship's forefoot sliced through the dark Atlantic towards the Devil's Hole and Daunt's Rock, far to the northwest of lonely Ushant, those notes for a book on the Blackstone theme were stealthily assembling themselves; as if already released from inhibitory checkings by the little mayflower poem, and by the feeling (which was new and astonishing) that the house at Saltinge really — after all — looked westward, like Ushant itself: and had been looking westward all the while. As the Bassett had truly said, the westward vision could be all the more persuasively and poignantly westward from that vantage-point in the past; it could, from there, be indeed Blackstone's own vision; just as it could still, for that matter, look even further westward, and into the Pacific, from Hambo's barranca, where Hambo had in fact been busily engaged in so extending it. Now that one was free, the symbol was good enough for them all; it could be used anywhere.

And exactly, now that one thought of it, as the three of them — Lorelei Three and Nicholas and himself, farewelled in Boston by the Bassett, and taking with them their pathetic little all, in the shape of Lorelei's sacrificial savings — exactly as they had themselves headed west and away from the Lords Lawyers, with their own vision of freedom, their own spiritual necessity. Their own legal necessities as well: for it was owing, at last, to these, that they had been forced to break up the enchanted life in the Elwood Street house in Charlestown, from the back windows of which — and how fantastic this had been — one could see, only a few blocks away, the red-banded funnels of the Savannah Line steamers, and hear the blasts of their sirens, under the steeple of the Old North Church, as they began the long voyage to Tybee Beach, and Tybee Light, and Fort Pulaski. Enchanted; and those ships, remembered from childhood — the City of Savannah, the City of Macon, the Chattahoochee — (from the latter they had taken home a kitten, and given it the ship's name) — those ships had from the beginning, from D.'s first visit to the little red-brick house, contributed a quite extraordinary part of this enchantment: just as, for that matter, Uncle John's Constitution, moored at the Navy Yard wharf only a little way off from them, had contributed also. Had the presence of these ships — these of all the ships in the world — been a sign — ? Hambo would certainly have said so: the coincidence, the reference, was Hamboish to a degree. For how was D. to know, when he and Lorelei Three, after their first meeting, took the taxi from Boston to Charlestown, pausing only to acquire a bottle of Jameson's Irish Whisky, that in order to reach the Elwood Street house they must pass the Savannah Line wharves? And how was he to know, either, that after this evening this was to be his home; and that it would be from this, and to return to this, that he would make the first visit he had made to Savannah since the day that he had left it: the day of the long drive behind the two black-plumed hearses, through streets crowded with the curious, to the cemetery at Bonaventure: where — as if in deliberate prophecy — his father had photographed him, beside the river, only a few weeks before — ?

For so it was to be, so it had been; from Elwood Street he had set forth for the first revisitation of the incredible city; the city lifting out of the southern sky its landmarks, of one spire or steeple after

another, which, after thirty-five years, were still as familiar to him
as his own blood in his own hands; as familiar to him as his own
heart; so that he had been able to drive into it from the country,
through the long aisles of palmettos, without the least hesitation,
and straight to the ancient and ornate hotel, from the roof of which,
as a boy, during the school recess, he had watched the ships sailing
down the river to the sea; straight to this, through the unchanged
streets, the unchanged houses; and straight then, on foot, past James
J. Joyce, the butcher's, still at the corner — ah, and it was from
this that he had fetched home from time to time the pail of oysters,
not forgetting, either, to dip into them — and straight, thus, across
the cemetery-turned-park, and to the House, and to ring once more
its bell, having climbed the brownstone steps of the crumbling stoop.
Yes — it had been like moving, by some extraordinary sort of magic,
rightly and profoundly into one's own heart, this homecoming.
Everything had waited for him, everything had stood still. The very
bricks in the sidewalks were the same, felt the same beneath his
feet: the sad, worn houses, with shabby shutters, more than ever
gave off that ineffable sense of genteel decay; the trees, the holm-
oaks, were dark and unaltered before them; only the peach-tree and
the chinaberry-tree, in the back yard, were gone. Only these, and
Dr. Duncan's nameplate, next door — Dr. Duncan, whose own
back yard had been filled with bins of terrapins, and the immense
green sea-turtles floundering in their immense tubs. But everything
else was there: the picture-book still lay open at the very page, the
sunlit page, at which he had left off reading. And in the midst of
this miraculous resumption, this heady reincarnation, the mockingbird picking up his meditative soliloquy just where he had let it
fall, among the purple blossoms of the crape myrtle; in the midst of
this all-healing recapitulation, this triumph of repossession, flooding
his veins and arteries with recollected beauty and power, what
could have been more summarily and pointedly appropriate than

that the final moment of decision should have been precipitated between Lorelei Two and himself — ? and that here, at the very moment when he had, after so long a separation in distance and time, once again joined self with self, he had at last had the wisdom and courage to see that for Lorelei Two and himself the moment of separation had come. The timing, the arrangement, were of an almost musical perfection. And that the cable of his decision should go from that ancient hotel, where Cousin Maud had stayed during the days that followed the tragedy, and where he had so often illicitly made entry — with Harry, or Butch, or Frank, or the other riffraff of those scapegrace days — that the decisive cable should be sent from this hotel to the house at Saltinge — and from Savannah — was the ultimate syllable of poetic justice. The wheel had come full circle: but without a vengeance. And if Saltinge might once more be lost, there was now a new and astonishing virtue to turn to: the house in Charlestown.

A vision, like so many others of that joyous winter, while Nicholas painted in the dining-room, and Lorelei Three in the upstairs bedroom, and D. (in the salon-cellar) worked on the Massachusetts Guide, which was to become the more refreshing and sustaining the farther they sped from it, in that abrupt hegira to Mexico. "Cuernavaca, Cuernavaca" — so they had sung, to the tune of "Cucuracha," in the days of feverish packing and arranging, and then the days and nights of sleepless travel — for sleep was a luxury they could not possibly afford — through unknown America to unknown Mexico City. There, if it should prove feasible, they would stay with Hambo on his barranca, until the divorce could be obtained, and the marriage performed under the same jurisdiction (as Alex had advised, so wisely); and thus back to Boston to take ship to Liverpool. And could there ever possibly have been an adventure so vivid, so unique, which had been put, by a would-be author, to so poor a purpose — ? For, of all D.'s many failures, this had been the most lamentable. Nor was it altogether easy, either, to uncover the reasons for it. The profound dislocation of his personal life might perhaps have contributed something: but then, there had been plenty of profound dislocations, and some of them worse, before. Yet this had entered into it, no doubt, among other things; as also had the unfamiliar and demanding work for the WPA — not to mention the somewhat raucous winter, and (yet once again) the somewhat impoverished return to Saltinge, there once again to introduce a strange wife. No, the failure had been a failure of vision. It was now possible to see that, before the encounter in Boston with Lorelei Three, his whole attitude to writing had become negative, sterile, valedictory: he had felt that he had come to the end of his rope, that he had nothing more to say, that he must give it up. With the serial notations on attitude and definition, hadn't he really come to an end? At any rate, so he thought; he had even said to Lorelei Three that as his own career might to all intents be regarded as finished, he could all the more usefully and gladly dedicate the rest of his life to the facilitation and encouragement of hers. All very nice, and a very pretty gesture, and he had meant it, too; but then, there was money, somehow, to be made, if they were to be able to stay at Saltinge; the dead donkey must be flogged into action again. And dead, there was no doubt about it, it had certainly seemed irrevocably to be. The failure of vision — when he had again sat himself down at the refractory table in the house at Saltinge — was at once apparent. It was as refractory as the table. It simply wouldn't function, wasn't there. And yet, that wasn't it, either. Wasn't it perhaps more exactly that, in the pressure for money, he had deliberately aimed at a potboiler, a short cut, a compromise, instead of going back (as he knew he should) to the severer task of tying off those bleeding arteries which the "serial notes" had left behind them — ?

Possibly. But there was yet another element in it, too. As he had more than once before discovered, after those interregnums in one's ability to write, whether of a month or six months or a year or more, the renewal of the attempt begins rustily and awkwardly, the tools are dulled with disuse, the hand has lost something of its cunning, the imagination its agility. The pump — like that at South Yarmouth, when returned to after long absence — must be primed. And so it had been with that melancholy and half-finished project, *A Heart for the Barranca*. Nothing whatever had worked right for it. And perhaps, as the design itself, both formal and psychological, had been shoddy, to have done any better by it was implicitly impossible to begin with. Six months later, for example, and no doubt as a result of this very piece of desperate unsuccess, he had found himself, for *The Quarrel*, in a complete state of readiness. One could complain of it that it was slight, certainly, but compared with *A Heart for the Barranca* it was at least alive, and if it falsified much of the life at South Yarmouth (for the two attempts were parallel in thus being a direct "raid" on the private life) it had nevertheless justified itself by an at least partial achievement of projection, and an at least partial fidelity to the truth. Thanks to the *Barranca*, the machine was working again. But if one could put down the *Barranca* to profit and loss — and so shamefully late in the career, too, when one ought to have known a little better — just the same it was interesting in retrospect to try to make out the joints in the failure, whether of statement or vision. Of course he had been too close to it: he had tried to rush it. The sheer violence of the little adventure — its outrageousness of color, and in this its contrapuntal comment on their journeys to Spain, the likeness in unlikeness — this violence of the scene itself, and its effect in turn on the emotions, already disturbed, of the three travellers, who found themselves thus so abruptly, by the uncontrollable force of events, flung into a new world, and into a venture of which they couldn't guess the outcome: all this, as D. had already begun to see on the Scythia, halfway back to England, offered a singularly tempting *donnée,* as the Old Master would himself have agreed. It looked almost disconcertingly easy: it looked like the ripe fruit ready to drop into one's receptive hand. It looked as if one would scarcely need to touch it. Wouldn't that scene — the long hypnotic train-ride through unknown America, and across the unknown Mississippi, and among such people as one had never seen in one's life, and then through Texas, past its ghostly oil-flares, like blond beacons in the night, and so into the raw, ancient, and almost reptilian, primitivism of Mexico — wouldn't that progress simply write itself — ? No such thing. It had proved to be no more than a fatal temptation to fine writing. The prolonged soliloquy on the train-ride, with its forced attempt to evoke past and present simultaneously, was worse than anything in Thomas Wolfe — which was saying a great deal. Yes, that train, "hollowing a golden and evanescent tunnel through the darkness, fleeting and impermanent as a falling star"; "denying all things but itself," as it dismissed the Indians of Deerfield, and the Puritans who had dismissed the Indians, and the wilderness which had dismissed the Puritans; that train, and its passenger, the incredible Blomberg — Blomberg, the Jew, gliding evenly among the haunted junipers of the Berkshires — "and weren't the Jews, after all, the protypical Puritans?" — the incredible father-wolf Blomberg, defending the stockade at Deerfield in deep snow, or bowling at ninepins with the Dutch trolls in the Catskills, or gazing sadly down, from the railway bridge, at Hendrik Hudson's brown-sailed Half-Moon, just at the moment when Hudson, at last despairing, came about, and turned again south, to vanish away down the river "like a cluster of rose-petals into the sunset"; that train, and its three utterly improbable passengers, its three ghosts, bore, alas, only the most coincidental of resemblances to the other, and its three all-too-human people — Lorelei Three and Nicholas and D., — who had actually, with few such emotions and sensations as these, made the

343

difficult and tedious journey. The basic trouble, of course, lay in that too-long held-over notion of somehow, somewhen, making use of the tragic story of Louisa; and the unhappy inspiration — if it could be called such — of now employing it as the "binder" for a pseudo-lyric descant on Mexico: with a dash of D. H. Lawrence's blood-madness, blood-worship, and blood-sickness, thrown in. A forlorn hope, and one that was to do justice to nothing and no one. Least of all to poor heroic Louisa — it had certainly, whatever else one might conclude about the outcome, been a disservice to her, and one that she, least of all, deserved. For what a gallant gal she had been, and how profoundly this saccharine and melodramatic "do-ing-up" of her life and death would have sickened her! Of this, D. would forever feel deeply ashamed. The most honest of women, the most loyal of friends, if also the most alarmingly and amusingly outspoken — as when, after one of their almost daily tennis matches, in the year of the Craigie Street apartment at Cambridge, and after saying (as little Jean, whom she was holding in her arms, had so calmly and publicly misbehaved), "Now, I call that *rude!*" — she had gone on to remark gaily to Lorelei One, "Now then, if you would only get *yourself* a partner, my dear, we could have a four-some!" — a remark which Lorelei One, of course, had never quite forgotten. A remarkable gal, and he had neglected her: the strong one of a weak family, she had made her way unassisted, and had maintained, in the prim Boston of those days, a singular and impres-sive freedom, both of action and thought. Had she had lovers — ? To tell the truth, D. had never known. Any more than he had ever known whether — as it now first occurred to him to consider — those tennis matches, which had been of her seeking, might have been intended as the overture to something more. Hadn't she told D., a little offhand, and a little with the air of one making a 'sound-ing,' of her conversation with the renegade and nymphomaniac min-ister, on a bench in Commonwealth Avenue, and his lisping suggestion that they might, didn't she think, walk down life's primrose path together — ? An offer which she had laughingly declined, with the answer that she already had quite enough trouble supporting herself. And hadn't her brother, D.'s classmate at Middleclass School, more than once, during her long and fatal illness — of cancer — when they had encountered at the Club, murmured shyly, with that soft stammer of his, that Louisa would be so happy if he would go out to Brookline and see her — ? And he hadn't gone: in the press of frivolity, that summer, on one of the many returns from Saltinge, he hadn't gone. And two years later, when he came back, she was dead.

A betrayal, one of the worst of which D. had ever been guilty. In her steady honesty, she had in effect become another conscience to him — she was one of those rare people, like Marriott's "Catfish" (but not in all particulars) who purify the stream in which they live, and all those with whom they come in contact. Hadn't she once, on Boston Common, where they met by chance, on one of those returns, very nicely pulled his leg about that trace of Anglicism in turn of phrase which had briefly afflicted him, and which, thanks largely to her, he had got rid of — ? "Seventy miles and a bit — ! — Seventy miles and a bit, from London — ! Now aren't you ashamed? You mean, dear D., a little over seventy miles, don't you?" But if she had been a conscience to D., D. had most emphatically not repaid her in kind, or at any rate not in anything more than intention, and for his own selfish use. For of course, in *The Barranca,* there was that one element of truth about her. Just one. For when he had learned of her death, it was to learn also, for the first time — as so many others had done — of the manner of her meeting it, and of the quite glorious *finis coronat opus* with which she had crowned her life. Apparently, when an honest doctor had told her the truth (which no doubt she would characteristically have insisted upon having) — and had, in fact, pronounced sentence

345

upon her, her decision had been instant and unhesitating. She was not rich, as such things go: her secretarial work had provided for her own needs, and for the occasional assistance to the family which was necessary: but she had saved something against a rainy day, and now, to the question of what to do with this, she had an immediate answer. She would, for one thing, indulge herself in something she had always passionately desired, and never been able to afford: she would all blatantly and vulgarly and plutocratically, and in utter disregard of all her socialist affections and affiliations, go on one of those do-or-die world cruises, in a fancy ship, and with all the trimmings, and hie herself magnificently round the world. But not alone: no, not alone. Not at all. For that would be too selfish altogether, there could be no fun in that, it would be meaningless. And so, she had selected two young people whom she admired, and in whose beginning careers she had taken an interest — a young musician and a young journalist, both of them poor, both of them underprivileged, both of them ideally likely to benefit most from the opportunity — and she had taken them away with her, on that wonderful journey, as breathlessly, and without warning, as ever a Jove took a Ganymede.

But without knowledge, too. They were neither of them to know anything whatever of the reasons for this sudden bounty. It was to be a lark; she allowed them to understand that from some unknown and miraculous quarter good fortune had befallen her, it was something she had wanted to do ever since she could remember, and she didn't, naturally, want to do it alone. And that was all. Off they had gone, for the better part of a year — the doctors had given her that much time, and a little more — and they had had themselves the most wonderful spree ever. They went everywhere, did everything, saw everything. And never for a single moment did Louisa's two *protégées* guess what it was all about. Back from Calcutta and Hong Kong and Tokyo, back across the Pacific, and to Boston; and then, without a word to anyone, she went uncomplaining into her retreat to die. And it would make her happy — her brother had murmured — if D. would go out to Brookline to visit her, for she was fond of him. Fond of him — ? And D., had he been fond of Louisa? Say rather that he had loved her, and indeed he had. She had become, and had remained, a veritable part of himself: he would never in his life be able to think of her, no matter how fleetingly, without feeling himself momentarily purified and integrated. But he hadn't gone to see her. There had been the Uncle to visit, and the Bassett to dine with; and the house at South Yarmouth to be remodelled and re-shingled, or to have electricity installed; and the Aunt to go motor-ing with, for she had bought a new piece of land on the North Shore, and wanted to show it to him; and there were the endless hilarious parties on Belmont Hill, those all-night starlit parties, with the gay voices under the trees, the shadows joining and separating to join again, in the capricious dance of Chaos and Eros; and so, although Louisa was dying — but had he ever really known it? — he never saw her again.

And it was this betrayal, and this love, that he had endeavored to use as a mere amalgamating device in the *Barranca;* and of the magnificent and unique creature that was Louisa, who had dealt so intrepidly and singly with her own precious span of life, he had chosen to make the altogether silly and insipid Noni — Noni, play-ing Bach very badly by candlelight, Noni, confiding all-too-hero-ically, and as it were with a catch in her voice, in Blomberg, while the fake train made its way through a fake America to an even falser — if that were possible — Mexico. For, of course, the falsi-fication of Louisa had inevitably falsified the whole thing. After that grievous initial error, there was never a chance that it could be anything but what it was — a piece of work of which not even the surface, the writing, could achieve any excellence, because the theme itself was entirely spurious: it was a fraud. The absolute

347

neutrality of the artist? serving mankind by translating himself, all anonymously, into the pure form of the artifact? No such thing. He had turned his back on the truth, and had been deservedly punished for it. Could one say that possibly, in the momentary glimpse of Hambo, and his barranca, the slightly absurd, but always altogether delightful, figure, advancing towards them with that stick of his — the tall sapling which he carried, because, he said, it helped him with his lumbago — advancing towards the *camión,* which had brought them over the mountains from Mexico City, his trousers knotted round the waist with a necktie, and looking as if they might fall off any minute; and grinning at them shyly, and affectionately, and a little drunkenly — could one say that here for a redeeming moment there had been a gleam of reality — ? A carelessly powerful and ingratiating figure, to which the curiously short arms, which he habitually thrust a little before him, lent an appealing appearance of helplessness. But no, not even Hambo had been given anything like his due: he too had been oversimplified and romanticized. Of the marital and alcoholic misery and despair into which he daily sank deeper — while he grappled stubbornly and unremittingly with his unappeasable vision, in that nest of old rags and blankets in which for the most part he lived, on the veranda of the villa — of all this, not a trace. Nor of the perpetual clack of the merciless high heels, the pitiless and faithless heels, along that tiled veranda, and over and into his heart. Nor of the look of longing and shame-faced devotion that he would lift from that slightly obscene nest as the beautiful little creature perpetually and indifferently passed and repassed. Nothing of this, and of course no attempt whatever to suggest reasons for the shape of tragedy which they could see obscurely rising before them, and which they were so powerless to prevent. No mention, again, of the extremely unhappy effect of all this on Lorelei Three and Nicholas and D., who, to their own predicament, now had this

348

too to add, the daily death of Hambo, the daily triumph of the faithless and pitiless heels, while the thunderheads punctually amassed themselves over the volcano for the tremendous assault of lightning and downpour at evening. What had brought it about — and how long had it been going on? And was it really as bad as it looked? They could speculate endlessly about this, and they did, but of course any sort of intervention was unthinkable. That it was actually just as bad as it looked they had finally been compelled to believe after the episode of the earrings, the pathetic episode of the earrings. For the faithless little heels were all too faithlessly and obviously going away: they had announced it as if it were a challenge, which it was: they were going to the north, to the silver-mines, and, quite frankly, to stay with those two friends of hers, the engineers: alone, too, and for a week, and no question of any chaperonage, either: it was, and publicly, too, a flat declaration that the heels were damned well going to be unfaithful. From the parting at the bus station, where they had all gone to see her off, they had done their best to avert their eyes. The stonily beautiful little profile avoided the anguished and hangdog gaze of poor Hambo, she was already looking ahead, over those propitious mountains, to the wealth of those silver-mines, and the promise of gay nights, and, as always on such occasions, the lavish and expensive gifts which awaited her there. And with this enthralling prospect before her, how could she possibly pay the slightest heed to the little gift which Hambo had brought, the little gift of silver earrings? They were for her birthday — he murmured — handing them awkwardly and shyly through the *camión* window: they were for her birthday, day after tomorrow — did she remember? But, if she did, she expressed no surprise. She accepted them with a glance of repressed annoyance, thrust them almost angrily into her handbag — as if they were a sort of rebuke, and perhaps they were — and then the bus shot away, the usual cloud of dust whirling up

349

from it, over the square and its baroque bandstand, and she was gone.

None of this had been considered useful for the *Barranca:* nor the repeated and frustrating interviews with the not-too-trustworthy Mexican lawyer: and the endless waiting, the perpetual postponements, which meant a steadily mounting anxiety over their dwindling supply of money. To be sure, Lorelei Three could do some water-colors, and she did; and so did Nicholas; and beautiful, too, they were, and it helped to pass the time during the long wait; and D. was himself lucky in having an article to do on Faulkner. But the delay, and in that so tragic little house, with its discomforts, too, and the dreadful stench from the little sewage canal which ran directly beneath their bedroom windows, all this ended by depressing them to such a pitch — and with the bad food which the Indian cook provided for them, on her feeble charcoal fire — that all three of them became ill, and Nicholas seriously. It was recognized that he could no longer safely stay, he would have to struggle back to Charlestown, and alone, there to await them. Scarcely able to walk, he had been got into the taxi, which would take him to Mexico City; and the Bassett was wired to, with instructions to meet him on his arrival in Boston; and that was that. And, to be sure, bad enough. And to their already quite sufficient burden of difficulties now was added yet another. For the wretched Hambo, now almost unable, in his despair, to work, and in great pain, too, from his lumbago, began a series of alcoholic fugues from which they were often afraid he might never return. He would vanish for a night: he would vanish for two. His appearance became more and more disheveled, and if he kept his sense of humor, and his wonderful visionary gift of the gab, nevertheless it was with an increasing irritability, on the one hand, and an increasing indulgence in that fantastic mysticism of his, on the other, in which, of course, as in the years before, but now with an almost insane obsessedness, he

350

must cast D. in the role of father. Extraordinary, those midnight conversations had been, and sometimes angry. Hambo had drifted pretty far, politically, towards something like communism: he had been through something like a social conversion, and clearly felt a need for some sort of fraternal joining and belonging: and D.'s and Lorelei's more abstract political views were not calculated to make him happy. It was true that D. had once voted for Debs, and that he had twice, too, voted for his great liberal cousin; but he had never found it possible to take more than a casual and superficial interest in practical politics, viewing it, as he did, as inevitably a passing phase, and probably a pretty primitive one, and something, again, that the evolution of consciousness would in its own good season take care of. Revolutions were a waste both of time and human material; — you lost a hundred or more years only to find yourself just where you'd begun. A revolution was an attempt to freeze society on a particular level, and this was itself stultifying, no matter what that level might be. If the Nazis had frozen theirs on a slightly higher level than the Russians, with a shade less destruction of its living inheritance of culture, well, that made it a trifle less wasteful, but that was the best that could be said for it, and no excuse.

A slightly Olympian attitude, and it had led to some pretty acrimonious scenes, while they sat in candlelight, the thunderstorm intermittently dousing the electric lights, and drank the impossible tequila or the still more impossible *habanero,* endeavoring to disguise the taste with limes from the jungle garden. The scorpions could be heard rustling under the tiles of the roof, the rain once again lifting away, and the sewage canal, the Bilbo Canal, splashing past the window under the banana trees. Ah, that Bilbo Canal, and the night Hambo, staggering through the lightning, fell into it headlong, stick and all, and had had to be hauled out, and cleansed of the filth, and dried, and put to bed! They had heard his cry from the far end of the garden, in the pitch darkness, where the taxi had

351

dropped him; and before they could find the flashlight, and go to his assistance, he had somehow missed the path to the little foot-bridge, and plunged in. And ah, yes, that climactic talk between them, too, at Charlie's Place, a day or two after, over the café table, when they had finished with Hambo's exercise in sonnet-form — "Airplane, or aeroplane, or just plain plane" — and gone on, taking full advantage of Hambo's noontime lucidity, to final disposition of the extraordinary psychological situation between them — the final exchange of views, between the father who had taken the father's place, and the son who had taken the son's. For hadn't D. become a substitute for the cotton broker of Calder and Liverpool? Just as Hambo had usurped the succession of Jed — ? And hadn't all this been caught up into the ambiguous theme for *Ushant*? And couldn't one, even now, so many years later, still hear the drunken words, competing with the uproar of the Square, the barking of maimed dogs, the mad bicyclists, the buses roaring in and out, and that demonic bird in the café next door? —

"Well, it was then, you remember, D., three years ago — or when? — understood between us. At Saltinge. You had eaten your father's skeleton — why then shouldn't I eat yours? Not symbolically only, either, my dear old fellow. No, by no means. Not in the least. You as much as admitted that now it was my turn — my turn to kill you. First, by taking Nita. Yes. For of course we both knew that both of us were powerfully drawn to that open wound — you first, but with your own obligations to Lorelei Two, and therefore guiltily offering her up to me, but in effect proposing to share her. Not so? Yes — in the shadow of the Hundred Fountains, at the Alhambra, you proposed to share her, as foul a sort of voyeur's incest as any second-rate god could imagine."

"True. Admitted. All my own visceral and feculent scheme. Projected in a flash, too — she was no sooner seen, clipping over the marble tiles with those absurd high heels of hers, and those fierce all-excluding eyes, under the ridiculous expanse of American hat — "

"Christ yes, that hat — "

"I had already embraced her all over. Known everything. By the time she had signed the hotel register and flashed up the dirty marble stairs. But to hand her on to you, I could thus keep her — at least, at one remove, and with your imagination to magnify it for me. Very simple. And twofold in function, too — for this might stop your drinking. Pull you together. Take you out of the endless chain of aguardientes, the daily round of cantinas, and the ultimate slobber of drunkenness in which you daily threatened to kill me. It was a good scheme, Hambo."

"Very good. As we both saw instantly. I had her, the first night. Upstairs. And you looking over my shoulder."

"My chin was on it."

"I could hear you breathing."

"Yes, it worked. And this, as you say, was the first murder, my first death at your hands, the first blood transfusion by which you began, shall we say, to stand upright and achieve stature?"

"We could put it so. My devoted blood donor! Yes. A kind of voluntary suicide. But as you say, this was only the first death. Only your first; and only, as a matter of fact, a faint foretaste, an appetizer."

"And now, we come to the real thing."

"Have another tequila?"

"Yes, how I hate the bloody stuff. — Charlie! — And these bloody little limes. And good jumping Christ, there's that bitch again, and that bloody bird, what do they call it — "

" — some musical instrument — a pipitin — a cornetin — "

" — tamborin — it's outdoing itself this afternoon — must be the thunder coming. Well, here's to death and betrayal. Mine first. Yours afterward."

"Oh, yes, mine will come too."

"At whose hands, I wonder."

"The betrayal — ? At Nita's, of course. You know, the same pattern as yours with — no matter. And just as it had to be. Oh, I'm faithful, I mould myself to your pattern; only give me a rainbow and like a chameleon I'll lie into every last shade and radiance of it. If you were a tweed rainbow, I'd be a tweed rainbow. In a twinkling. Yes — if you had to play Merlin to some phosphorescent horror of an anonymous-souled Vivien — the eternal, shall I say, Agnes Fatuous of womankind — and get your little heart torn out of you by gilt-enamelled fingernails, and love ripped out of your mind, constellation by constellation — "

"Yes, we all love that woman. What a through-shine face she has: and a magical soft glory shining out of it, pulling your soul right out of your eyes — and every glimmer of it as false as a foxfire!"

"We have been warned, we have been warned."

"Does every man have to do it once? make that mistake just once? Down, down, you go, deeper every day and night, deeper into love, deeper into despair, deeper into the shame and terror of loving a sham, a lie, a veritable piece of original dirt. Or is such primal dirt really innocent? flawless and the only real right thing? And do we make a profound mistake if we abandon her? My god, how we suffer, how we make *her* suffer. Or, I wonder. *Does* she suffer? *can* she suffer?"

"Clarin — that's what it's called — "

" — and fits her, too. The same brilliance, exactly, the finest nuances of apparently ingenuous charm, of gentleness, tenderness, and every note of it deceptive. Her eyes flying like birds after every male on the horizon — all of them. Cities of them — nations of them. Her infidelities — "

"More numerous even than yours?"

354

"Call it a dead heat. And now, of course, you must emulate me even in that, have in fact done so. Those bracelets she wears — "

" — given to her by the engineer at the silver-mine."

" — and the ring and necklace, the plumed serpent — "

" — by the pelota player and the taxi driver."

"The laying-on of hands."

"My god, how I hate you at moments like this — I could *kill* you now."

"My dear Hambo, you *are* killing me."

"Yes. I am. But I could kill you physically, you know."

"Quite easily. Perhaps you will. You are very powerful."

"It would be satisfactory. But perhaps not as satisfactory as murder number two, when I shall at last, slowly and lasciviously, play conscious starfish, shall I say, to your unconscious oyster — ?"

"The oyster, my dear fellow, is reputed to be endowed with an extraordinarily acute sense of taste — don't forget that he savors you — tequila, soul, and all — quite as discerningly as you savor him."

"Ah, but doesn't digest me. But you — I shall wholly absorb you. I *am* absorbing you; now. And it's your own wish, moreover — you said so. Am I not your son, in whom you are destined to be well pleased? All modern improvements, too. What possible escape is there for you from the logical and temporal sequence, as members of a series, by which it is your fate simply to become a better 'you' in me — ? I shall become a better 'you,' and you will be dead."

"How wonderfully tempting it is. Wonderfully tempting. You are very plausible, Hambo. Or is it I who make it plausible? Yes, I began by imagining, which is to say, *willing*, the thing, and here now it gigantically looms for us. Could I backtrack now? — Charlie! — "

"Too late now. Your virtue has already passed over. You've been bled too badly, you no longer feel too surely just where your boundaries are. You admitted as much. Remember? Night before last. When I fell in the Bilbo Canal, and you played gentle Jesus to my dirty Judas. With lightning making a halo for you, and my muddy shoe flattened against your paternal and pious breast. I was drunk, but not too drunk to know what was happening. I had gotten possession of your mind, your soul, your power — listen to me, it's your own voice now speaking — so how can you resume? You no longer know your own boundaries. You are a nation invaded. And as I'm younger, and as I'm stronger, in appetite, in will, in recklessness, in sense of direction, it will be no use your trying to compete with me, you will only appear to be echoing *me,* imitating *me,* parodying *me* — you will no longer have a personality of your own."

"If I ever had one. Here's to betrayal and death."

"Betrayal and death."

"But you know, I wonder . . . Could it be more complex still? — I begin to see — "

"You begin to see — ?"

"Perhaps, my dear Hambo, just at this marvelous point of intersection, our involved intersection, I can imagine a starfish turn of my own."

" — yes — ?"

" — but secret, mind you, secret."

Yes, it had been an astonishing conspiracy, in its way a conspiracy in lunacy, full of its own intentional ambiguities and low cunnings: an *agon,* to be played again and again between them, all the way from that first idyllic summer in Cambridge to Saltinge and Granada and Mexico: and now, reaching its logical end in this delicious absurdity. Every angle of it had been studied in mirrors, each of them with an eye to its use; each of them with an eye to making use of it first. And after all, in that so-long-elaborated symbiosis, who was to say just what was whose, and just which prop-

356

erties, of perception or invention, belonged to either? "He thinks
I'm a bird in a tree" — so D. had observed of the little cat, at his
feet, in the garden, who, hearing D.'s low whistle, had looked up
at him with startled inquiry; and Hambo, chuckling at the empathy,
and empathizing with it himself (at one remove), could already
be seen in the very act of entering that note, that bird-note, amongst
the pile of other notes, in that creative nest of his on the verandah,
where the new book was taking shape.

"*Tout passe, l'amitié reste.*"

Thus had gone the little French quotation, which was forever
at intervals reappearing at the top of the agony column in the London Times; a lost signal, which, as it *did* so often reappear, presumably never found the eyes for which it was intended. *Tout
passe, l'amitié reste!* And so it had been, and so it was; D. had been
driven to Jojutla, the legal capital of the state, for the divorce hearing; in a combination of jail and court, in a dejected town square,
to which they had had to approach through a sea of what appeared
to be urine; where, while the prisoners played guitars, and chatted
with their wives and children in the patio, D.'s lawyer and the judge
discussed the old times when they had been classmates together at
the law school in Mexico City. And so, the last colored page was
turned, disclosing Hambo and Nita, seated, like Sacred and Profane Love, on either side of the civic fountain, in Cuernavaca, while
the boy-scout band made hideous practice, and in the Mayor's office,
just inside, the interminable marriage certificate was copied out,
calligraphically, in longhand, and bound up with scarlet ribbons,
and stamped and sealed. For a last time, Hambo was pursued into
one cantina after another, in order that he might bear witness.
And then, that page, too, was turned.

But not to be forgotten, not forgotten. And was it too late to make
another attempt at the *Barranca* — if only to see what a little cold
dexterity — and a little more love — might salvage from the mis-

shapen and uncompleted sketch? Conation, conation — all was conation, everything was in the ever-renewed attempt, the ever-repeated and undiscouraged endeavor: here, too, loomed the shadowy outline of Ushant, with its formidable invitation to approach and make landing, or to approach and die. One could begin, perhaps, by reversing the whole affair in time, begin in fact with the ending, and then reach backward: one could begin with the death of Louisa; and if one proposed to retain the Mexican setting at all, merely use this, and of course the plight of Hambo, as also that of D. and Lorelei Three, for contrast: their somewhat mean and graceless problems contrasted with the tragic disinterestedness of hers. The train journey, if kept at all, to be greatly condensed, and given only in retrospect; and analytically, not lineally. But would one need it at all? Better, probably, to get into the thing, periodically and casually, the more ordinary, and disjunct, and merely quotidian aspects, and not only those of Mexico, but of Spain as well. The bull-fights, for instance: the death of the small boy *aficionado*, carrying his little brown flag out into the bull-ring at Mexico City, to make his one perfect pass, and then to be so suddenly sacrificed to his own *hubris* — wouldn't this automatically suggest the similar scene, of the drunk at Granada, falling into the ring, and with such difficulty extracted from it, after that one paralyzing moment when the bull's glorious target was no such thing as a single horse, or human, but a living, Laocoön-like tangle of arms and legs, with the struggling drunk at its center? That bull-fight to which, of course, they had gone with the *Principles of Literary Criticism*. And the bull-fight which had initiated, for D., that classic sequence of bull-fight nightmares — itself a perfect example of series — with which he had dumfounded, years later, the psychoanalytic tea-party in Cambridge. They had been incredulous, quite frankly so — implying, as if flatteringly, that he had made it all up, and with admirable skill, and that of course it was a great credit to his knowledge of

psychology. But although he had been too surprised by this reaction, and too shy, to make more than a token denial, the fact
was that it all was, if incredible, absolutely true. For the nightmares — which were at first genuine nightmares, from which he
woke barely in time to escape the horns of the bull, and in a screaming terror — these had continued for well over a year — but
gradually changing. After perhaps a half dozen which were more
or less alike, one night it was no longer a bull from which he was
trying to escape, but an elk — or something of about that size, at
any rate — perhaps a moose? — but still so menacing that he was
compelled to wake. And then, after an interval, in what was still
recognizable as the bull-fight dream, since it involved the charge
of an animal (and in a setting like that of the *corrida*) came the
night when it was somewhat smaller than an elk, but larger than a
goat; and then a goat; and later still (but now in dreams from which
he no longer needed to take flight by waking) a whole series of
animals of steadily diminishing size, and, if with a threat somewhere implicit, now no more than symbolically alarming. Had the
bull been finally vanquished? No, not quite. It needed one more
turn; and that old reliable, the unconscious, came up with it. This
time, the dream was of the *pensión*, at Granada, from which they
had descended the hill into the town for the bull-fight — (exactly
as in the little *novella* which the four translators were reading);
but they were not now so descending that hill: instead, it appeared
that a *ratoncito*, a mouse, had got into one of the downstairs rooms,
perhaps the dining-room, and the entire Carmona family — the two
young men, the father, the mother, one of the young women, and
the cook — all armed with brooms, or sticks, were mercilessly at-
tacking it. Wasn't this just a shade one-sided — ? D.'s sympathies
began to be aroused, although not yet to the point of his presum-
ing, among strangers, and in their own house, to intervene. But
when they had driven the poor creature out into the patio, under

the pomegranate tree, and there all began flailing at it, where it could no longer hide, or find cover, it was too much. At this point, D., leaning theatrically out of one of the dining-room windows, precisely as if he were participating in the opera itself (as once, as a super, he had — and as a picador, too), and now very angry, started singing, loudly and derisively, the Toreador Song from Carmen. The bull had not only become as powerless as a mouse: it was being, in contravention of all decency, attacked by a numerically superior force of animals larger than itself; it needed protection. And D., by ridiculing the scene with a suggestion that mouse-killing was hardly bull-fighting, had come gallantly to the rescue. He was now on the side of the bull, and there would be no more nightmares.

But no, even with "filler," or local color, of this sort, amusing as it might be, the enterprise was a dubious one; and as to a very considerable extent the whole Hambo saga had always been earmarked for subsumption into the *Ushant* theme (if one ever got around to it), the sensible decision must be to keep it for that, and perhaps there, if it proved workable, to "double" the *Barranca* and *Ushant* situations — as, of course, he had long since had it in mind to do. That fragment of lunatic, or not so lunatic, dialogue with Hambo — wouldn't this go over, practically intact, into the little *novella*? Wouldn't this translate itself perfectly into one of the passages for the Teacher from the West, and the Narrator, and Elspeth (the dark and closed Elspeth, for whom Hans and the Narrator were subliminally competing), through which the shape of the impending tragedy could first be obscurely imagined? And, if it came to that, wasn't the original dream — of *Ushant,* or *Reading a Book* — a first projection of D.'s situation *vis-à-vis* Hambo into artifact? the complex on the point of crystallization? and hadn't they both known this to be so when they discussed it that morning on the P. & O. boat, off Cádiz? For the Hans in the little story was quite transparently Hambo. Just as Elspeth was Nita, and D. the Narrator. And this lunatic passage of dialogue would fit in very neatly as the first signpost which pointed towards an approximate climax between the older and the younger man, the first shadow of that true or false insanity of Hans on which every-thing was to hinge. And D., in that sly threat of a starfish turn of his own, was dropping his own first murderous hint that in the so shadowy war between them he could himself exert pressure of a sort which Hans might foresee but could probably not endure: it might be that Hans would find himself somewhere, in that toy town, on his way to the assignation at the roundabout (of which he already appeared to be apprehensive), cut off, or fatally delayed.

Far away, and long ago. And so many ships between, so many ships between. Those bells, which were intended, in the book, to run — but with altering voice — from one level of reality to an-other — at each level with a different meaning; whether church bell, striking the hour, or fire-bell, or ship's bell — those bells had rung with him on many waters; were now ringing once again; rang forward and backward, in time, as if they were themselves, like Thompson's inked line on the chart from the *Pilote Française,* mark-ing out the course of a life. Backward, one could look again to Cynthia, to Faubion; to Hay-Lawrence, to Smith; to the psycho-analyst, on the Majestic, in midwinter, who had supported him in his conviction that to go to Vienna, and an analysis by Freud, would be a mistake. Or to that other ship, at midnight, on which, after the usual poker-game, the very rich porcelain manufacturer from Manchester, a little drunk, had begun kicking the nocturnal shoes, the paired shoes, away from the cabin doorways, to which the night-watchman had just returned them, polished: and D., a little drunk, had so effectually lectured him on brotherly love that he had burst into tears and spent half the night re-mating the scattered shoes — with the assistance of that pathetically grateful little man. Yes, Leyland, where was Leyland — ? And where the athletic young doctor, who, at the same poker-game, had so skillfully and good-naturedly saved the genial, but a little fatuous, young Englishman — whose gaitered father would wait for him on the dock at Liverpool — from the two card-sharps? Or the chess-playing bar-steward of the Celtic? And beyond these, backward further still, one could look to the Tallahassee, or the Chattahoochee, and so to Savannah. As again forward, then, to war-scarred and still bleeding England — and the dark house at dark Saltinge — forward with this ship, the Grey Empress, and her cargo of uprooted and frightened people.

With Blimp, now no longer tolerated by his cabin-mates, who fled from that monologue at the very sight of him — Blimp, with his "Now take democracy, that's another misonomer — another misonomer." And the good Hardie, to whom he would say, god helping him, before he got off this ship, that he was the best and tenderest father he had ever known. And little genius Geordie, dancing round the pink-nosed little governess — that alcoholic pink nose, half-hidden by the fur neckpiece — and inventing for himself a whole new astonishing world. Where would they all get to? Would they arrive — now or ever — at anything in the least resembling what they had hoped for? Would anyone? Or did it matter, provided one had at least set out on that voyage, made the endeavor? Or did it matter if what one arrived at wasn't *quite* what one had envisioned? Well, they were all heroes, every one of them; they were all soldiers; as now, and always, all mankind were soldiers; all of them engaged in the endless and desperate war on the unconscious. And the two luminously beautiful Canadians, and the soft-faced young Jewess, setting forth on that superhuman task of hers, the search for the innumerable lost people of northern Europe — could one now see them deploying, as the lights of Ireland

362

fell behind, and the lights of Anglesey blinked ahead, and the sea-gulls circled at the stern, crying their *klio-klio*, like the Eumenides? Yes, one could see them go, one could see them go. The Blimp first, waddling down the gangway, after the steward whom he had bribed to sell him black-market pounds. And the tall Canadians, whisked away in the important car that had come for them all the way from Banbury. And the little Jewess, carrying her endless lists of names, human names. And Hardie, shepherding the two boys, with par-ticular tenderness for the elder, little Hanky, whose head, "owing to an accident in delivery," was too small in circumference by many inches — "that's a lot of inches, yes, a lot of inches" — so that his brain would never grow. The mad Swiss, too, after his final dinner of "Soup — one boons — ice cream!" And little Geor-die, and the governess — ? "We live like lords," she had started to say, and checked herself with amusement: and the "Lord" would come, and sit at the bar-table with the governess, eager for a report on all that had been done, for his extraordinary little hare-lipped son, during the war years at Vancouver.

But what of England, and Saltinge, and Lorelei Three — what for D.? and Lorelei Three? Already Lorelei Three was on her way to Saltinge, on her way to the dark house, bearing, like an altar-boy, the lights that would once more make it shine. Might she not be there at this very minute, as he composed himself for his last sleep, on the weary ship, might she not already be surveying the poor damaged walls, the torn panels? And what would they make of it now, that dear house, in the light of their new love, the new old house at Brewster? Would the ancestors now, at last, have their say? And would they find, after a little, that a return to Cape Cod was now to be as compulsory for them, as once, for D., the first of all his voyages to Ariel's Island had been? Would it any longer be enough that Paul was at Oxford, making magnificent sunsets of his own magnificent sunset; or Nicholas at Saltinge; and the little D.'s, at Hampstead, or Manchester, or Lewes; and the Tsetse in Cheyne Row — a stone's throw from the house to which D. had once gone to see his Cynthia? Would it be enough? —

Sleep, and the approach of sleep. The pouring texture, beginningless and endless, that fulfills a dream. The dream-song at the end of little Jean's famous poem, "The Playlanders," which she had written, all magnificently, at Inglesee, when she was five — that masterpiece of alternative spellings, with its wonderful, and somehow so world's-end, mountain, Juhoohooa.

> One day some Playlander warships
> Were sailing along the sea
> And they saw a lovly lovely island
> In the Mediterranean Sea
> With blew blewe rivers in it
> And buttfull pine foristes in it
> And they sailed to its shores
> And when they got there
> They saw a buttful lake lak among the montens
> And there was one montenn witch they called Juhoohooa
> Witch was larger than all the others
> With lovly beards berds beairds in it
> And buttful beests that would come
> When you called them
> And buttful cats that would come in your window
> And lovly froats and flowres flowrs
> Witch would flowr all the year round.

World's-end — for wasn't Juhoohooa another Ushant —? The child had been father to the man. And wasn't it all too ridiculously like the vision, somewhere described in the notes for that book, the final vision for its beginningless and endless end? — "But of course, although they go far, they never really get to the center of the town — in the end have not arrived there." And this is all on a ship? Is part of the dream of someone on a ship, a ship that is perhaps in difficulties off the shores of Ushant? Where the roar of the surf mingles with the alternating cries of Jument, and Créach, and Stiff? — Yes, now we are drowning — all of us are drowning; but as we drown, we seem somehow to be floating upward, we are all floating upward and singing. Floating upward towards that vast, that outspread, sheet of illuminated music, which is the world; and above which, as we now dimly make out, is — what exactly? the face of the Teacher from the West? — But first, no, it is only a hand that we see; and then, above the hand, a face that is turned away from us, as if it were turned away to sing to someone else, someone behind, and farther off; and towards this as yet unseen face we rise, we rise, ourselves now like notes of music arranging themselves in a divine harmony, a divine unison, which, as it had no beginning, can have no end ——